MEDIATING CHILD CUSTODY DISPUTES

MEDIATING CHILD CUSTODY DISPUTES

A Strategic Approach
A New and Revised Edition

Donald T. Saposnek

Jossey-Bass Publishers
San Francisco

BOWLING GREEN STATE
UNIVERSITY LIBRARY

Copyright © 1998 by Jossey-Bass Inc., Publishers, 350 Sansome Street, San Francisco, California 94104.

All rights reserved. No part of this publication may be reproduced, stored in a retrieval system, or transmitted, in any form or by any means, electronic, mechanical, photocopying, recording, or otherwise, without the prior written permission of the publisher.

Substantial discounts on bulk quantities of Jossey-Bass books are available to corporations, professional associations, and other organizations. For details and discount information, contact the special sales department at Jossey-Bass Inc., Publishers (415) 433–1740; Fax (800) 605–2665.

For sales outside the United States, please contact your local Simon & Schuster International Office.

www.josseybass.com

 Manufactured in the United States of America on Lyons Falls Turin Book. This paper is acid-free and 100 percent totally chlorine-free.

Excerpt in Chapter One from *The Resolution of Conflict* by M. Deutsch. Copyright ©1973 Yale University Press. Reprinted by permission of Yale University Press.

Excerpt in Chapter Two from *Interventions for Children of Divorce: Custody, Access, and Psychotherapy* by W. F. Hodges. Copyright ©1986 John Wiley & Sons, Inc. Reprinted by permission of John Wiley & Sons, Inc.

Library of Congress Cataloging-in-Publication Data

Saposnek, Donald T.
    Mediating child custody disputes : a strategic approach / Donald T. Saposnek. — A new and rev. ed.
        p.   cm.
    Includes bibliographical references and index.
    ISBN 0-7879-4051-8
    1. Custody of children—United States.   2. Family mediation—United States.   I. Title.
    KF547.S26   1998
    346.7301'73—dc21   97-45299

REVISED EDITION

PB Printing   10 9 8 7 6 5 4 3 2 1

CONTENTS

PART FIVE
Challenges and Professional Issues

PREFACE

IN THE DECADE AND A HALF since the original version of this book was published, a veritable divorce industry has developed and flourished. Although accurate demographic data on divorce are difficult to obtain,* especially since remarriages result in higher rates of divorce (Glick, 1988) that also occur more quickly (Furstenberg, 1994), estimates of the probability that an adult will divorce at some point in his or her life are between 49 percent (Furstenberg, 1990) and 65 percent (Martin & Bumpass, 1989). Taking into account the individuals directly and indirectly affected by these divorces, including grandparents, other relatives, friends, and even neighbors, some ten million people are directly or indirectly affected by divorce each year! (Irving & Benjamin, 1995).

The bottom line of all this is that every year since the mid-1970s, more than one million children living in the United States experience the divorce of their parents (Shiono & Quinn, 1994). To service this enormous population of children and families, a sizable cadre of divorce professionals, in both the public and private sectors, has emerged. Over the past ten to

---

*The divorce rate in the United States increased steadily after the Civil War, with an estimated 5 percent of marriages ending in divorce in 1867 rising to about 36 percent in 1964 (Preston & McDonald, 1979). As Furstenberg (1994) noted, this prevalence of divorce was solidly in place in this country even before the divorce revolution of the 1960s. Over the next two decades, the divorce rate rose dramatically then leveled off and actually declined by about 10 percent during the mid-1980s (Norton & Miller, 1992). The crude divorce rate (that is, the number of divorces in a given year expressed as a rate per 1,000 total population) reported in 1995 of 4.5 per 1,000 was the lowest rate since 1974 (National Center for Health Statistics, 1996). However, as Furstenberg (1994) notes, the slight decline in the legal divorce rate does not necessarily suggest that marriages are becoming any more stable. He points out that factors such as postponed marriages, increased rates of cohabitation instead of marriage, and fewer marriages as a result of premarital pregnancy artificially reduced divorce rates, but this does not necessarily indicate increased family stability.

twenty years, family courts throughout this country and others have developed a multitude of programs in the public sector to help families resolve their parenting disputes, and mental health professionals and attorneys in the private sector have become increasingly interested in learning skills to become family mediators in order to help divorcing families resolve their disputes outside the doors of the court.

This book was written to serve as a practical guide for professionals who want to learn to resolve custody disputes efficiently and effectively. The perspectives and techniques described here are useful to a wide range of practitioners who work with custody or visitation matters, including psychologists; social workers; marriage, family, and child counselors; child and family psychiatrists; family therapists and divorce counselors of every discipline; attorneys who practice family law and/or mediation; family and conciliation court counselors; and judges who deal with family law matters.

This book will be of benefit to mediators specializing in financial aspects of divorce settlements as well as to those who deal only with custody and visitation matters. It will also serve students in law schools studying family law and trainees in the emerging graduate degree programs in alternative dispute resolution.

Much of the focus of this book is on the more difficult challenges encountered in mediation. It is my contention that when mediators are fully knowledgeable about, and have grappled with, the more difficult cases first, then they will be more comfortably prepared to undertake the easier ones.

Testifying in court as an expert witness in many custody battles during the earlier years of my practice as a clinical child psychologist contributed to my disenchantment with the adversarial approach to custody and visitation disputes. From the family systems point of view, which I espouse, it made little sense to justify to the court why, in most circumstances of separation and divorce, one parent was better for the children than the other parent. The task seemed similar to arguing that the length of a rectangle was more important than the width in determining its area. Clearly, whenever possible, children need to experience both their parents as adequate rather than be confronted with critical evaluations of their parents' worthiness. Moreover, the inevitably bitter and stressful interactions among spouses, their attorneys, and their expert witnesses in the courtroom left me feeling frustrated and dissatisfied.

Indeed, from the earliest to more recent longitudinal studies of children of divorce, there have been consistent findings that the best predictors of improved outcomes for these children are reduced interparental acrimony and regular and continuing contact with both parents, whenever possible. While later research revealed much more complexity to the formula than we initially believed (we review this research in Chapter Two), these findings have generally been confirmed.

Largely as a result of such findings, there has been a significant increase in the use of mediation as a valuable method for resolving parenting disputes through and after divorce. Mediation allows the parents, in a safe and nonadversarial setting, to sort out the multitude of relevant variables that need to be explored in order to develop a sound coparenting plan for their children. Through this process, the parents are encouraged and supported in maintaining the cooperative coparenting relationship that is necessary for the children to emotionally survive their parents' divorce in the long run.

Family mediators typically are therapists or lawyers who work to help separating or divorcing couples amicably resolve some or all the issues in dispute, including custody issues, spousal and child support issues, property settlement, and related tax issues. Certainly, given the complexities of financial issues in many divorce settlements, mediators need competent training to achieve expertise in legal and financial matters if they are to do justice to any couples they advise. Because even lawyers who are not specifically trained or experienced in family law may have difficulty dealing with the increasingly complex legal and financial aspects of divorce settlements, formal training for mediators is strongly encouraged.

In the past two decades, a number of excellent books on divorce mediation have been published (see especially Coogler, 1978; Erickson & McKnight Erickson, 1988; Folberg & Milne, 1988; Folberg & Taylor, 1984; Grebe, 1985; Haynes, 1981, 1994; Haynes & Haynes, 1989; Irving, 1980; Irving & Benjamin, 1987, 1995; Johnston & Campbell, 1988; Landau, Bartoletti, & Mesbur, 1997; Lemmon, 1985; Marlow & Sauber, 1990; and Moore, 1986). These books focus on the broad aspects of divorce mediation, including the financial aspects and the legal aspects of divorce settlement, as well as on the custody and visitation issues.

This book, however, focuses exclusively on the mediation of custody and visitation disputes, for which it presents a comprehensive and detailed model. Because of the complexities of these issues, which have increased significantly over the years, at least as much specific expertise and skill are required in mediating custody and visitation matters as in mediating financial issues. Hence the in-depth approach, perspectives, and techniques for successful custody mediation provided here will be of significant value to therapists, lawyers, and judges involved in this extremely sensitive, difficult process.

As suggested by the new subtitle *A Strategic Approach,* this new and revised edition of the book showcases the process of mediation within a more sophisticated paradigm: the metaphor of the martial art of *aikido.* This graphic metaphor was included at the urging of participants in my training workshops over the years, who found it very useful for understanding the strategic approach to mediation.

Part One provides a range of perspectives on child custody mediation. Chapter One presents an historical overview of the ways in which child custody and custody disputes have been conceptualized and dealt with in Western society and then traces the recent changes in divorce and custody laws that have had an impact on the work of professionals in the field. New insights are offered into the problems of the adversarial system for dealing with these issues, and a comparison of the adversarial and mediational approaches is made. The prevalence of new mediation programs is then discussed, along with sobering research findings on the limitations of mediation, in light of the increase in difficult, multiproblem cases contemporary mediators are encountering.

Chapter Two, new to this edition, presents a review of the expanded literature on the effects of divorce on children and on their needs through the divorce process. The accumulated research to date, including longitudinal studies not available at the time the book was first published, is quite daunting. The insights gleaned have changed our views on the variables that appear to predict the best interests of the child.

The difficulties and challenges of mediation work are examined in Chapter Three. Beginning and experienced mediators alike will no doubt recognize many of the dilemmas presented in this chapter. In addition to identifying the elements of mediation that are stressful for the mediator, Chapter Three describes attitudes and approaches that mediators can employ to cope effectively with the pressures inherent in this kind of work.

Chapter Four, another new chapter, is entirely devoted to presenting the strategic approach to mediation using a comprehensive elaboration on the metaphor of aikido. The conceptual framework drawn in the comparisons between this martial art and mediation will be very useful to the reader in grasping the basis of strategic mediation.

The three chapters in Part Two explain how the mediation process is structured. Because setting the context is of primary importance, all of Chapter Five is devoted to detailing how to prepare the spouses for the mediation process. After discussing how many, how long, and how frequently sessions are scheduled, how fees are set, and how relationships with attorneys are handled, this chapter tells how to explain the mediator's role and then presents a prescriptive, verbatim monologue for ex-

plaining the benefits of mediation to the spouses. A prescriptive monologue with commentary is then presented, detailing the explicit assumptions and ground rules that the mediator tells the spouses in beginning the
mediation process. These explicit assumptions serve to preempt much of
the spouses' resistance to the mediation process.

Chapter Six presents the three phases of mediation in detail. Specific
guidance is given for gathering essential information both on the phone
and in the first session, in the beginning phase of mediation. Then details
of the various coparenting options available are presented for consideration in the middle phase of mediation. Included with this information are
cautions for the mediator in developing coparenting plans, suggestions for
utilizing new language in discussing coparenting proposals, and an extensive section on when and how to interview children within the mediation process. Specific techniques are offered for structuring these
interviews, building rapport, and utilizing the children's input. Finally,
strategic ways for requesting proposals from the spouses are presented.
For the ending phase of mediation, specific guidance is offered for strategically shaping the proposal, maintaining balance, and eliciting agreements. An examination is made of the "last issue"—a typically trivial but
symbolically important issue that occasionally deadlocks the negotiation
process and frustrates the mediator.

Chapter Seven concerns the construction of the final mediation agreement. The various sources of referral and the ways in which they determine the specific structure and formats of the agreement are detailed in
this chapter. The specific content of the agreement includes the designation of legal custody, the regular time-sharing plan, the plan for sharing
holidays and special days, the adjunct clauses for facilitating cooperative
time sharing, and the plans for future modifications of the agreement. Finally, a discussion is presented of how financial issues may be linked with
time-sharing plans.

The chapters in Part Three elaborate the various strategies that participants use to maneuver each other through the custody dispute and mediation process. My basic premise is that people's attempts to influence
each other are rooted in certain needs. Rather than try to determine *why*
people have these needs (as the traditional psychotherapist is likely to do),
the mediator observes *how* participants attempt to meet their needs and
then initiates interventions designed to address those needs without obstructing mediation. The mediator may be able to help participants satisfy their needs in whole or in part; redirect them into therapy, where
resolution may more appropriately take place; or encapsulate them
enough to allow parenting negotiations to proceed to agreement without

disruption. Very often obstructive needs can be set aside, if not satisfied, once a structured parenting agreement is developed.

The concept of strategies, as it is used here, derives from family systems theory, which has been developing in the field of family therapy for several decades. According to this view, the family is conceptualized as a cybernetic system in which the actions of each member influence the actions of each other member reciprocally. This view has gradually replaced the traditional linear view of causality, and it is the conceptual basis for the mediation approach presented in this book.

Chapter Eight elucidates nine strategies that children employ in their attempts to cope with their parents' divorce. One example is their use of *reuniting strategies,* which are innocent attempts to appeal to each parent to be drawn by need or attraction to the other and to reunite. Through such efforts, the child often becomes what I have called an *innocent but functional contributor* to the spousal conflict, since parents' frequent misinterpretations of their child's strategies regularly result in needless escalations of their custody battle. Among the factors motivating children's strategies are the need to reduce the distress of separation, to reduce tension in the family unit, and to protect their own and their parents' self-esteem.

Chapter Nine provides insights into thirty-one specific strategies that spouses use before, during, and sometimes even after mediation. These interactional maneuvers, regularly seen in mediation, usually take the form of indirect resistance, undertaken to satisfy a hidden personal agenda, often under the guise of "seeking what is in the best interests of the children." Among the many reasons spouses may employ maneuvering tactics are the needs or desires to reunite the family, to disengage emotionally, to ease feelings of distress over the family's breakup, to protect their financial status, and to assert power or seek revenge or retaliation. On occasion, strategies employed by one spouse may be complementary to strategies utilized by the other—all of which leads to very difficult challenges for the mediator and requires effective tools to facilitate the difficult negotiations that result.

Chapters Ten and Eleven present twenty-one specific mediator interventions for facilitating the mediation process to a successful conclusion. Chapter Ten is devoted entirely to showing the mediator how to elicit cooperation between the spouses and how to reduce resistance to compromising and reaching agreements. The specific strategies presented are grounded solidly in the techniques of brief strategic therapy, which have proved extremely effective in reducing therapy clients' resistance to change. In Chapter Eleven, a wide array of specific interventions for deal-

ing with conflict are examined. After a discussion of general aspects of conflict management, strategies to reduce or divert conflict and to break impasses are presented. These interventions are arranged sequentially, from
the less potent to the maximally potent techniques. They derive both
from brief strategic therapy methods and from insights I have gained over
two decades of guiding couples through the minefields of hostility toward
compromise and agreement.

Part Four contains two chapters, each presenting a new case that
demonstrates the process of mediation from a strategic point of view. The
full dialogue of each case is presented, with commentary after each significant interaction and then an aikido recasting of the interaction. The
aikido metaphor has at its core that the mediation process operates as a
field of energy that the mediator must learn to maneuver to a successful
outcome, and these images provide a graphic picture of how the intervention accomplishes its goal. The layout in these chapters will give the
reader a multilevel ringside view into the analysis of each case and the
thinking behind each intervention.

Part Five explores the various challenges and professional issues that can
arise in mediation. Chapter Fourteen provides an extensive discussion of
the changing views and laws regarding move-away cases; the roles of
stepparents and grandparents in the mediation; the changing attitudes toward parents' sexual mores and behavior, including homosexuality; substance abuse; and domestic violence. The very volatile issues of child
sexual abuse and parental alienation are newly presented in this edition.
Helpful perspectives and specific guidance are offered for appropriate mediator response to these diverse issues.

Chapter Fifteen presents various ethical and moral issues and values
conflicts that regularly confront mediators: the problem of mediator bias,
issues of quality of parenting that arise when one or both parents manifest inadequate parenting abilities, the dilemmas of balancing fairness
against feasibility in agreements, parents' rights versus children's rights
and needs, individual parental "freedom" versus maintenance of family
integrity, and other challenging family and social values conflicts. This
chapter poses more questions than answers and, it is hoped, will help provoke critical thinking so necessary in new areas of social intervention.

Chapter Sixteen summarizes the challenges covered throughout the
book. It highlights the ideal spirit of custody mediation and offers specific
recommendations to mediators, attorneys, and judges for continued development of mediation work as a positive and effective alternative to adversarial approaches.

Specific details relevant to various aspects of mediation are presented in six appendixes. Appendixes A and B reproduce current versions of the standards of practice developed recently by the Statewide Office of Family Court Services in California, a national leader in mandatory mediation services for court-annexed cases, and by the Academy of Family Mediators, the most prominent national organization of private family mediators.

Appendix C contains sample confidentiality forms for private and court-related mediation. Appendix D provides a comprehensive list of the preempting statement categories for commencing child custody mediation (from Chapter Five), and Appendix E provides a comprehensive list of the parent, child, and mediator strategies that are presented in Part Three of this book, for the convenience of the reader. These two lists have been frequently requested by training workshop participants, to serve as an easily accessible reference guide for designing preempts in particular cases.

Finally, Appendix F offers four sample mediation agreements, a representative sampling of the detail and content typically developed in mediation.

Please note that the pronouns *he* and *she* are used judiciously throughout the book. If one pronoun or the other is used in a given discussion, it should be understood that the other pronoun could just as easily have been substituted, and no assumption of gender is intended. Similarly, for convenience' sake, the term *spouses* has been used to designate the clients of a mediator. In light of the increasing number of never-married parents seen in mediation, the term *spouses* should be understood to refer to the parents, whether married or not.

Acknowledgments

I am indebted to numerous colleagues, friends, and family whose insights and understandings I incorporated in preparing the new and revised edition of this book. I would like to express my deepest appreciation to my colleagues in Family Mediation Service—Michael Scott, Michelle Samis, and Janeen Carlo—who for years have stimulated my thinking about the many critical and emerging issues in this field, and to Bruce Ross, whose poignant questions in his learning of strategic mediation has regularly forced me to come up with poignant answers for him.

I would also like to extend my respectful appreciation to Santa Cruz County Superior Court Judges Bill Kelsay and Rich McAdams and to the many fine family law attorneys of Santa Cruz County for their continued support of our family mediation programs and the challenging service that we all endure. Many thanks to Tomasz Poplonski, for his artistic rendering of the aikido illustration, and to Monica Harder, for her helpful computer assistance in the preparation of this manuscript.

From my daughter, Sativa, who has taught me so much about children, about love, and about quality, I am continually learning. Finally, I am forever grateful to my wife, Donna, for her amazing intuition, which unfailingly generates accurate and insightful advice, and for her kind, loving, and loyal support in spite of my regular mysterious disappearances during the preparation of the new and revised edition of this book.

Aptos, California   DONALD T. SAPOSNEK
January 1998

For Donna and Sativa—again

MEDIATING CHILD CUSTODY DISPUTES

PART ONE

PERSPECTIVES ON CHILD CUSTODY MEDIATION

MEDIATION AS A COOPERATIVE PROBLEM-SOLVING APPROACH

And the king said, Bring me a sword. And they brought a sword before the king. And the king said, Divide the living child in two, and give half to the one, and half to the other. Then spake the woman whose the living child was unto the king, for her bowels yearned upon her son, and she said, O my lord, give her the living child, and in no wise slay it. But the other said, Let it be neither mine nor thine, but divide it. Then the king answered and said, Give her the living child, and in no wise slay it: she is the mother thereof.

—I Kings 3:24–27 (King James Version)

ALL TOO OFTEN, modern arbiters of child custody do not encounter parents of such self-sacrificing conscience and must resort to and rely on the procedures of legal justice. However, our procedures of *legal* justice have, for the most part, not blended well with our contemporary understanding of *psychological* justice in child custody disputes. We all too frequently summon the sword and sacrifice the child in the name of legal justice for the parents, rather than support and encourage conciliatory efforts between the parents in the name of psychological justice for the child.

Child custody mediation is an alternative approach for resolving custody disputes in a way that is most congruent with our current knowledge of the needs and development of children of divorce. When applied skillfully and supported by a network of legal and mental health professionals, the methods of mediation can provide a truly sensible and psychologically sound alternative to adversarial methods. To gain a perspective on the issue of child custody disputes and resolution by mediation, let us first briefly explore the historical roots, the contemporary research on children of divorce, and the different approaches to dealing with custody disputes.

Historical Perspectives

In the Roman Empire of two thousand years ago, fathers had complete and absolute control over their children and over their wives and property as well. Under Roman law, fathers could sell their children or condemn them to death with impunity. In those times, children were viewed as unimportant creatures that needed only physical care until the age of seven, at which time they were treated, and expected to act, as servants to their masters (Aries, 1962).

English common law condoned fathers' absolute rights over their children, a condition that extended into the nineteenth century. As their fathers' property, children were considered valuable as income-producing workers in factories and mines during the Industrial Revolution. The exploitation and abuse of children was extraordinary during this period. Children as young as four or five were put to work in the mines, and seven-year-olds would not infrequently be worked fourteen to sixteen hours a day (Leve, 1980).

During the first part of the nineteenth century, the courts of England began to recognize that parenthood involved not only rights and privileges but also responsibilities for the welfare of children. The development of the doctrine of *parens patriae* gave courts jurisdiction over the welfare of children. This doctrine was formally enacted in 1839 in what was known as Talfourd's Act, which empowered the court to determine custody of children under the age of seven. Soon thereafter, English mothers' rights to custody gradually increased until in 1925, the Guardianship of Infants Act was passed. This gave mothers and fathers equal chances of receiving custody (Derdeyn, 1977).

In the United States, custody decisions reflected English law. In various court decisions, fathers' superior rights to custody were justified by their control over family money and resources. An 1826 text contains the observation that "in consequence of the obligation of the father to provide for the maintenance of his infant children . . . he is entitled to the custody of their persons, and to the value of their labor and services" (Kent, 1826, quoted in Derdeyn, 1977, pp. 162–163).

Toward the middle of the nineteenth century, the status of women began to change. Women entered the workforce and obtained the vote and the right to own property of their own. Child welfare took on a new light as reformers urging child labor laws influenced public opinion. As interest in child development increased, the importance of maternal care was emphasized. King (1979, p. 156) notes that "after centuries of legal bias in favor of the father, a number of states enacted statutes creating a legal presumption that the mother should be given the custody of a child of tender years." Moreover, at the turn of the twentieth century, even when custody was awarded to the mothers, fathers still were considered to be financially responsible for their children. This made awards of custody to mothers easier, since the previous linkage between fathers' custody and financial support was broken.

The "tender years" presumption grew in strength quite rapidly as numerous awards of custody were made to mothers. This was soon followed by court decisions based upon a "best interests of the child" standard. Derdeyn (1977) points out that it was the frequent use of the "tender years" and the "best interests of the child" standards that eventually resulted in the mothers' superior right to custody. Moreover, where fathers' rights to custody had been based upon financial advantage and the tradition of English law, mothers' rights to custody were based upon a moral assumption that mothers were better caregivers for children (Oster, 1965).

The moral presumption that mothers should be favored in custody disputes made functional sense in American society in the early 1900s. As Roman and Haddad (1978, pp. 36–37) noted:

> Industrialization, which divides the wage labor of men from the private labor of women, is behind the exaltation of motherhood and the invention of maternal instinct. That is, maternal instinct came along precisely when it was required, making a virtue out of what seemed to be a necessity. Its enshrinement parallels the development of a new, not god-given, family form which we have come to call the nuclear family, a refuge from the world and the social—but not economic— center of personal life. As our culture became both urban and industrialized, the father worked away from the house and left the raising of children, for all practical purposes, in the hands of the mother.

However, these authors add that even today in agrarian communities, farm labor is still divided between husband and wife, and there is no inequality of importance in parenting. Mother and father work in the fields together and take care of the children together.

Reflecting the transformation from the Industrial Revolution to the Information Age, and the changes in organization and function of the nuclear family (Ahrons, 1994; Ahrons & Rodgers, 1987; Carter & McGoldrick, 1988; Schwartz & Kaslow, 1997; Toffler, 1980), our conceptualizations regarding the custody of children have continued to change. Under California's 1970 Family Law Act, the "tender years" presumption within the civil code was amended "so that the mother no longer automatically receives legal preference over the father as to the custody of a child of tender years" (King, 1979, p. 156), thus giving way to the use of the more gender-neutral "best interests" test. This new approach to custody decisions has since become the standard of most custody statutes (Folberg, 1991).

Part of the intent of the "best interests of the child" standard was to counter the historical trend of deciding custody issues on the basis of parental culpability. With widespread acceptance and/or availability of no-fault divorce in every state of the United States and all jurisdictions of Canada (Irving & Benjamin, 1995; Kay, 1990; Schwartz & Kaslow, 1997), the courts have been trying to separate out issues of moral unfitness—which may include adultery, other sexual misconduct, alcohol and substance abuse, and unpopular religious, political, or social beliefs—from behaviors that clearly would interfere with the parents' ability to give adequate care to a child. Moreover, courts have tried not to punish parents for what may be considered immoral behavior by depriving them of or restricting contact with their children. Apparently, however, this tendency is difficult to abandon, as the practice still continues. Under the guise that it is in the best interests of the child to deny custody to a parent who may be viewed as immoral or at fault, many courts still today perpetuate the practice, especially in judgments regarding property and child support issues (Irving & Benjamin, 1995). As Derdeyn (1977) aptly noted, "The human penchant for obscuring difficult decisions with a moralistic overlay of right and wrong or reward and punishment can be relied on to maintain culpability as an externally important issue" (p. 724).

The trend toward equality of rights for both parents was given a large boost when in 1980 the California Legislature enacted its joint custody statute. Although four states had preceded California in legislating a joint custody option (McIsaac, 1991), California's particular version inspired many other states to follow suit (Jacob, 1988). California has amended its statute over the years, while some states have gone beyond California's and others have fallen short of it (Folberg, 1991). Currently, only three states have no statutes relating to joint custody, but even those states allow it by court decision. Depending upon the particular jurisdiction, every state currently has a mandate, presumption, preference, or option for joint custody (Lyster, 1996).

With the designation of equal parental rights, the decreasing use of parent-oriented fault-finding presumptions, and the increased awareness of the importance of determining the child's emotional and developmental needs, judges must exercise ever-increasing discretion in each custody decision. This points the courts in a more humanistic direction but leaves the judges with the task of deciding, at any given time, what is indeed in the best interests of a child. This task is particularly difficult given that the concept of "best interests of the child" is ill-defined, broadly encompassing, highly reactive to social trends and fads, and systematically changing in response to the continually emerging research findings on children of divorce (see Chapter Two).

The Adversarial Approach

In 1980, only 10 percent of divorcing parents were in dispute about custody decisions (Foster & Freed, 1980). Over the next decade, this number increased to 20 percent in California (Maccoby & Mnookin, 1992; McIsaac, 1991). Indications are that this number is rising still and that these cases are increasingly complicated by serious allegations and serious social problems. As Depner, Cannata, and Simon (1992) stated in their report of the snapshot study of California Family Court Services, "We found that serious family issues were pervasive and that families usually faced multiple problems. Only one case in five was free of all the problems listed [including child stealing, child sexual and physical abuse, neglect, substance abuse, domestic violence, and criminal activity]" (p. 193). As such, these cases present formidable challenges to divorce professionals. Increasing numbers of these cases present some of the most volatile, hostile, and destructive transactions seen between two humans in a court of law.

Until the relatively recent trend toward the use of mediation, these contested cases had been dealt with exclusively by an adversarial process. For the most part, the adversarial process has proved itself a just and effective approach for discovering the facts and critical issues in criminal and other matters, so that decisions could be made to attribute blame and responsibility or to resolve disputes. However, this same adversarial process, when applied to domestic conflicts, tends to do more harm than good. As Coogler (1978, p. 8) noted, "Whatever may be said in support of the adversarial process for resolving other kinds of controversies, in marital disputes this competitive struggle is frequently more damaging for the marriage partners and their children than everything else that preceded it."

Because divorces and custody decisions were, in the recent past, made on the basis of finding one person at fault and/or unfit, the adversarial process seemed appropriate as the most efficient method for arriving at such decisions. Each contest had a winner and a loser, and the courts assumed that once the decisions were made, the matter was settled. While the matters of property and the legal dissolution of the marriage were indeed settled, the matters of custody and visitation were very often far from settled. Frequently, in reaction to the humiliation of defeat, the losing spouse would try to get back at the winning spouse by gathering damaging evidence regarding that spouse's fitness, the quality of care given the children, or the spouse's morality and by filing an order to show cause (OSC) petition to reverse the custody decision. Relitigation frequently continued for years beyond the initial decision. As Wright (1981, p. 5) observed, "When the triumph of victory and the humiliation of defeat were the only outcomes likely in the traditional custody battle, many couples would throw their energies into this very dramatic, win-or-lose conflict."

The recent trends toward no-fault divorces and custody decisions based on the best interests of the child rather than on the fitness of the parent have been attempts to reduce the acrimonious nature of such domestic conflicts. Yet the adversarial process by which these new standards are applied inherently breeds acrimony. Moreover, when children are involved in the process, they typically become repeat victims. This victimization can be obvious and publicly painful, as when a child must betray one parent by testifying in court on behalf of the other. Or it can be more subtle and insidious, as when a parent or lawyer solicits an "evaluation" of, or "treatment" for, the youngster by a child psychologist or psychiatrist as a tactic to help achieve the goal of obtaining custody.

Without doubt, many parents (and attorneys) who seek a therapist for help with the child's distress do so out of a genuine concern for the emotional well-being of the child, in spite of the fact that the parents are in the midst of a custody or visitation dispute. Indeed, when the child's distress is evident, such professional support may be quite advisable. However, when such an action has a primarily tactical intent, it can be problematic for the child. Typically, in such cases, the parent who is about to launch a bid for custody of a child seeks a therapist to help the child deal with the emotional upset manifested in the aftermath of the divorce. However, what that parent often does not tell the therapist until later is

that the parent was sent there by the attorney in the hope of documenting some harm that has occurred or will occur to the child as a result of
being in the custody of the other parent. If there is no chance of finding
harm, the attorney may hope that the therapist, by seeing the one parent
and child together, can be enticed into writing a report and perhaps even
testifying to the effect that a "strong bond of attachment clearly exists between this parent and the child." Frequently, if the therapist calls the attorney on being informed of the referral, he or she will be told that the
attorney simply wanted a skilled professional to help the child work
through some emotional problems. However, on completion of the assessment sessions, the therapist is not infrequently requested, or subpoenaed, by the attorney to testify on behalf of his or her client.

Regardless of whether the request to evaluate the child or child-parent
relationship is presented in a straightforward or in an indirect manner, the
experience of the child will be nearly the same. The child will be led to
consider and/or express a preference for a custodial parent and will be coerced in various ways to participate in discussions that will likely result
in the betrayal of one parent. Moreover, when evidence of harm to the
child is sought or suspected, the child will feel the intensity of focused
probing for pathology. This can cause considerable discomfort in the child
and lead to the development of a self-fulfilling prophecy, in that the
child will begin to manifest what is being looked for in hopes of pleasing
the probing adults.

Evaluations and therapy are never neutral events for children, who frequently feel scared, guilty, and/or resentful at having to participate. They
may be well aware of the intent of the sessions, or even worse, they may
have their own distorted understanding of that intent. As we well know,
children's personal, uninformed explanations of events are often far more
frightening than any reality could be. Moreover, any evaluative data that
come out of such a one-sided, restricted context are guaranteed to be biased. For one thing, there is a tendency for individually oriented therapists
(in contrast to family systems–oriented therapists) to attribute children's
problems either to internalized conflicts or, in the broadest perspective, to
a dyadic parent-child interaction rather than to the triadic parent-parent-
child interactions inherent in custody disputes. For another, the demand
characteristics of the soliciting parent's reports and the attorney's implicit
or explicit appeal can strongly bias the therapist into attributing cause and
blame to the other parent. This is particularly easy to do when the therapist conceptualizes from an individual or dyadic model of problem formation and when the therapist receives no contrary data from the other
parent, by virtue of having no contact with that parent.

It is also noteworthy that children who participate in such evaluations occasionally feel betrayed when they later find out that a judge made the custody decision based upon what they told the therapist. For in spite of what they may be told to the contrary, they often believe that their conversations will be confidential. Moreover, they not infrequently say what they think the therapist wants to hear, rather than what they really feel, especially if the therapist subtly pressures the children to support the soliciting parent's position. (This has striking similarities to the well-documented research findings of young children's suggestibility and how easily they can be led by a biased interviewer to report events, like sexual abuse, that in fact did not occur. For an excellent review of this research on children's suggestibility, see Ceci and Bruck, 1995.) The children may also feel betrayed if they find that the therapist's promise to help them obtain what would be best for them is not fulfilled. For example, although the therapist may believe that placement away from the less adequate parent would be best, what the children may actually need is for their parents to stop fighting and share parenting. However, because acrimony often increases rather than decreases after a sole custody win, the therapist's one-sided participation in the adversarial struggle does, functionally, betray the children. Such experiences can cause children to lose trust in any help that mental health professionals might offer in the future.

While the adjustment problems that children have following a divorce are commonly attributed by each parent to the quality of caregiving by the other parent, it is much more often the case that they are due to the many stressful changes that children must endure in a parental separation and to the interparental conflict that either begins at separation or continues from the marriage to play out after separation. It has also been found that the adversarial approach exacerbates the effects of these factors. In their study on the outcome of relitigation, Ilfeld, Ilfeld, and Alexander (1982, p. 65) concluded "that relitigation over a custody issue represents moderate to severe parental conflict that adversely affects the children."

One salient postseparation dynamic that occurs was described by Johnston and Campbell (1988) as the "negative reconstruction of spousal identity." It is the tendency of one spouse to cast the other in as negative a light as possible by selectively perceiving and remembering only those events, behaviors, and characteristics of the spouse over the years that fit with the present negative view. These intensely negative ways that divorcing couples in conflict characterize each other become real to them and are frequently unchangeable. The spouse, in essence, rewrites marital history in light of the present negative view, which is often supported and enhanced further by well-intentioned therapists, attorneys, family, and friends, who, in their efforts to help, simply exacerbate the conflict and thereby unwittingly hurt the children.

The Committee on the Family of the Group for the Advancement of Psychiatry (1980) points out that the major defect of the adversarial process is that it "accentuates differences rather than diminishes them" (p. 122). The committee cites one of the most eloquent critics of this process, Judge Byron F. Lindsley:

> The adversary process, historically effective in resolving disputes between litigants where evidentiary facts have probative significance, is not properly suited to the resolution of most family relations problems. . . . [Where] there are children and the parties cannot or will not recognize the impact of the disintegration of the marriage upon the children, where they fail to perceive their primary responsibilities as parents—that is, custody and visitation—we make it possible for parents to carry out that struggle by the old, adversary, fault-finding, condemnation approach. . . . This kind of battle is destructive to the welfare, best interests, and emotional health of their children [Committee on the Family, 1980, p. 122].

Indeed, the adversarial process trains parents, through discussions and modeling, to fight even more effectively, using slander, accusation, defamation, and any other weapons available. Yet such contests are construed as a proper means of achieving the best interests of the child. By any standard of common sense, as well as the accumulated research data showing that children need coparenting and a cessation of interparental conflict, the adversarial process must rank very low as a method of making satisfactory and lasting postdivorce parenting arrangements.

The Mediation Alternative

Short of parents amicably agreeing between themselves, mediation is the next best approach for making postdivorce coparenting arrangements. There are a number of reasons for this. In contrast to the adversarial approach, mediation is a cooperative problem-solving method. Instead of pitting one parent against the other, both parents are encouraged to solve their mutual problem, which is how to optimize the time their children share with each of them. The essential differences between a cooperative and a competitive or adversarial process were eloquently outlined by Deutsch (1973, pp. 29–30):

1. Communication
    (a) A cooperative process is characterized by open and honest communication of relevant information between the participants. Each is interested in informing, and being informed by, the other.
    (b) A competitive process is characterized by either lack of communication or misleading communication. It also gives rise to espionage or other techniques of obtaining information about the other that the other is unwilling to communicate. In addition to obtaining such information, each party is interested in providing discouraging or misleading information to the other.
2. Perception
    (a) A cooperative process tends to increase sensitivity to similarities and common interests while minimizing the salience of differences. It stimulates a convergence and conformity of beliefs and values.
    (b) A competitive process tends to increase sensitivity to differences and threats while minimizing the awareness of similarities. It stimulates the sense of complete oppositeness: "You are bad; I am good." It seems likely that competition produces a stronger bias toward misperceiving the other's neutral or conciliatory actions as malevolently motivated than the bias induced by cooperation to see the other's actions as benevolently intended.
3. Attitudes toward one another
    (a) A cooperative process leads to a trusting, friendly attitude, and it increases the willingness to respond helpfully to the other's needs and requests.
    (b) A competitive process leads to a suspicious, hostile attitude, and it increases the readiness to exploit the other's needs and respond negatively to the other's requests.
4. Task orientation
    (a) A cooperative process enables the participants to approach the mutually acknowledged problem in a way that utilizes their special talents and enables them to substitute for one another in their joint work, so that duplication of effort is reduced. The enhancement of mutual power and resources becomes an objective. It leads to the defining of conflicting interests as a mutual problem to be solved by collaborative effort. It facilitates the recognition of the legitimacy of each other's interests and of the necessity of searching for a solution that is responsive to the needs of all. It tends to limit rather than expand the scope of conflicting interests. Attempts to influence the other tend to be limited to processes of persuasion.

(b) A competitive process stimulates the view that the solution of a conflict can only be one that is imposed by one side on the other. The enhancement of one's own power and the minimization of the legitimacy of the other side's interests in the situation become objectives. It fosters the expansion of the scope of the issues in conflict so that the conflict becomes a matter of general principle and is no longer confined to a particular issue at a given time and place. The escalation of the conflict increases its motivational significance to the participants and intensifies their emotional involvement in it; these factors, in turn, may make a limited defeat less acceptable or more humiliating than mutual disaster might be. Duplication of effort, so that the competitors become mirror-images of one another, is more likely than division of effort. Coercive processes tend to be employed in the attempt to influence the other.

Although Deutsch was writing about the general nature of interpersonal conflicts, the relevance to custody disputes is striking. Resolving custody disputes by a cooperative approach has qualitative benefits for children that cannot be achieved through competitive procedures. Such benefits include increased chances for continued cooperation and communication between the parents, reduction of ongoing conflict as a result of both parents perceiving themselves to be on the same side, and an attitude of mutual flexibility in problem solving. While mediation does not always elicit all these benefits (see Kressel, Pruitt, & Associates, 1989; Pearson, 1991), it does achieve a level of cooperation that is basically unattainable in an adversarial context.

In addition to providing a constructive context within which specific negotiations can take place, mediation greatly expands the variety of possible resolutions to the custody dispute. While it is rare for judges to award physical custody using any formula other than the traditional one—primary residence with one parent and alternate weekend visitation with the other—mediation offers broader possibilities. The importance of having more choices available increases the chances that the children's needs will be met in the postdivorce parenting plan that is developed. This flexibility of mediation allows parents to arrange a coparenting situation that, if feasible, can provide a child with significantly greater access to both parents than that typically attainable by a court-rendered decision. Moreover, it helps children feel safer and more loved when they know that the decisions about postdivorce parenting arrangements were made by their parents rather than by a judge who is a total stranger to the children.

Mediation can be voluntary or court ordered. While, as of this writing, a majority of the states (thirty-nine, according to Lyster, 1996) have provisions that allow the court to order parents to participate in mediation before bringing a custody or visitation dispute to court, most mediation is voluntarily chosen by couples who seek it on their own or at the urging of their attorneys. It has appeared to many mediators that couples who choose a mediation approach tend to be less adversarial and irrational and more willing to compromise than couples ordered by a court to mediation. The voluntary couples also tend to be of higher socioeconomic levels and to have better spousal communication patterns (Pearson & Thoennes, 1988), and they hold a more positive view of their spouses as individuals who are honest and fair minded (Kelly, 1988).

In contrast, there is strong evidence that court-ordered cases have very serious and complex problems and therefore are more challenging (California Statewide Office of Family Court Services,* 1997; Pearson, 1991; Pearson & Thoennes, 1985). Depner et al. (1992), for example, found in their comprehensive "snapshot" study of mediations in California family courts that 79 percent of the sessions dealt with "difficult" issues and that 71 percent of the sessions were rated as having "high tension." Nonetheless, mediators rated 76 percent of the sessions on the productive end of the rating scale. Donohue, Drake, and Roberto (1994) point out that court-ordered mediators, often working under time restraints and with limited resources, tend not to focus on relational issues, which are so often at the core of difficult custody disputes (see Chapter Nine). Hence there is an implication that, given more time to work in mediation at relational levels with these difficult cases, even more productive outcomes could result.

Recent research has presented a number of clear and consistent benefits of mediation over litigation. These include greater client satisfaction,

---

*The California Statewide Office of Family Court Services surveyed all family court direct service providers across the state in September 1996 and found an almost 59 percent increase in the child custody mediation caseload over the preceding decade. Moreover, in 54 percent of all mediation cases, parents presented very serious allegations of child physical, sexual, and emotional abuse, neglect or abduction, substance and alcohol abuse, domestic violence, and/or other criminal activities. Nearly half (47 percent) of all mediation clients are either unemployed or below the poverty level; well over half of the cases have at least one client *in pro per*; increasing numbers of never-married parents; custody and visitation disputes involving grandparents, stepparents, and other relatives; and more parents in disputes involving a move-away circumstance.

modest to significant cost savings (even if mediation is unsuccessful), parents rating the process as fairer and more responsive to their needs, and modest to significantly lower relitigation rate and compliance (Depner et al., 1992; Irving & Benjamin, 1995; Kelly, 1988; Pearson & Thoennes, 1988; Saposnek, Hamburg, Delano, & Michaelsen, 1983, 1984; Slater, Shaw, & Duquesnel, 1992). Less clear but suggestive are data that point to fewer ratings of symptomatic behaviors of children whose parents successfully mediated (with the exception of somatic complaints) (Pearson & Thoennes, 1988), better ability to continue to resolve disputes informally after mediation (Irving & Benjamin, 1995), better mutual understanding of each other's anger, increased quality and clearer future direction of the spousal relationship, and greater cooperation between the parents (Kelly, 1988).

The ability of mediation to increase ongoing cooperation between the parents has not consistently been found in the research. Early expectations for this ability were implicit, for example, in the statutory language of California's mandatory mediation law (Civil Code, sec. 4607): "The purpose of such mediation proceeding shall be to reduce acrimony which may exist between the parties and to develop an agreement assuring the child or children's close and continuing contact with both parents after the marriage is dissolved." While successful mediation can reduce acrimony during the session and facilitate reaching agreement, the more amicable atmosphere does not necessarily persist once the parties leave the room.

Attempting to account for this, Pearson and Thoennes (1988) point out that mediation, especially in the court setting, is a very brief intervention, with parties who typically have "lengthy, intimate, and problem-ridden histories and deeply established behavioral patterns including spousal abuse and noncommunication" (p. 444). Irving and Benjamin (1995) add that "family patterns in divorce tend to be extraordinarily stable and thus difficult to disrupt." Acknowledging the insight of Thoennes and Pearson (1992) regarding the double standard that exists between litigation and mediation, Irving and Benjamin (1995) further ponder how such a double standard arose, "with litigation only expected to produce settlement, although mediation—in some cases, only 2 hours long—is also expected to transform intense marital conflict into affectionate cooperation, and intense distress into positive postdivorce family adjustment" (p. 423).

Mediation is no panacea, but its benefits are quite significant. Over and above the savings in time, effort, money, and emotional stress, participants not uncommonly will experience a shift in consciousness about the nature of conflict resolution. The conceptual framework of mediation requires the participants, who are generally used to adversarial thinking, to shift attitudes, beliefs, feelings, and behavior. This shift in consciousness can snowball and diffuse its effects throughout a community (see Bush and Folger, 1994, and Saposnek, 1993b regarding the aspirational goals for mediation). It may well be too idealistic to hope that a society as complex as ours could resolve most of its conflicts through cooperative rather than competitive approaches. However, it clearly makes much sense to eliminate or reduce competition in the areas of dispute resolution where competition is more destructive than constructive. In particular, it does not seem too much to ask that we at least spare children the wrath of their competing parents after a divorce. Through the cooperative process of mediation, parents can retain control over decisions affecting their children and work together to make the most appropriate plans for them.

2

THE NEEDS OF CHILDREN
THROUGH DIVORCE

EFFORTS TO ASSIST AND INFORM judges in making custody decisions in the early days of divorce research were based largely on theory and very minimally on empirical data on the needs of children in divorce. One of the first and quite influential books, *Beyond the Best Interests of the Child,* by Goldstein, Freud, and Solnit (1973), took the position that maintaining the child's need for stability and continuity of relationships and environment was key to minimizing the detrimental effects of divorce. For courts to accomplish this, the authors proposed, custody should be awarded to a single "psychological parent," with whom the child will maintain a continuous, day-to-day relationship and emotional bond, and that the noncustodial parent should be stripped of his or her legal rights to parent the child: "Once it is determined who will be the custodial parent, it is that parent, not the court, who must decide under what conditions he or she wishes to raise the child. Thus, the noncustodial parent should have no legally enforceable right to visit the child, and the custodial parent should have the right to decide whether it is desirable for the child to have such visits" (p. 38).

Unfortunately, as Roman and Haddad (1978) noted, these conclusions were based almost exclusively on psychoanalytical speculations and ignored the more empirically based literature of developmental psychology regarding the needs of children. They further pointed out: "The authors do not cite, nor does there exist, any social science data to support the proposition that a single official parent is preferable to two" (p. 109).

In later defense and response to the many years of such criticism of their position, Goldstein (1991), writing on behalf of his coauthors, noted that their position had been based upon their profound distrust of the court's abilities to ensure that the best interests of the child could ever really be considered. Moreover, they later proposed in their follow-up book, *Before the Best Interests of the Child* (Goldstein, Freud, & Solnit, 1979), that they preferred to call the "best interests standard" the "least detrimental available alternative standard." They believed that shared parenting, when legislated or foisted by the court upon unwilling parents or on parents whose motives for joint custody was questionably in the best interests of their child, was not a concept that could work to the benefit of children. Goldstein (1991) writes, "The word 'agreement' in the context of the child's best interest does not mean a legally enforceable agreement or a token agreement camouflaging the coercive force of the state. It means real, *and probably rare* [emphasis added], agreement on the part of both parents to share in the care and custody of their child and to cooperate with one another in fulfilling their parental roles despite their inability to find a satisfactory basis for living together" (p. 17).

Some years later, Wallerstein and Kelly's seminal book *Surviving the Breakup* (1980) presented empirical research that pointed to conclusions that were diametrically opposed to those recommended by Goldstein, Freud, and Solnit. Wallerstein and Kelly demonstrated that children need continuous and regular contact with *both* parents, as well as a reduction or cessation of interparental conflict following a divorce. Their research was highly influential in beginning the trend toward joint custody.

In attempts to blend these two "diametrically opposed" views, Samis and Saposnek (1986) presented the perspective that in contemporary families there are often two psychological parents in a child's life who both work, share in the parenting responsibilities, and have strong attachments with their children. There are also families, both intact and divorced, in which the children have formed an attachment to only one of the parents, while the other parent is peripheral or even absent. And there are families in which children are strongly and meaningfully attached to more than two adults. As Huntington (1985) noted, children can be attached to one parent for the nurturing, soothing, and relaxing interactions offered, to a second parent for the excitement, humor, and high level of activity offered, to a stepparent for the intellectual stimulation provided, to an uncle for the shared interest in music, to a day-care provider for the comforting rituals of cooking wonderful foods together, and so forth.

Finally, Samis and Saposnek (1986) point out, there are also situations in which, sadly, a child has no bond with either parent—for example, when one parent is immersed in chronic depression when the child is born and the other is an active alcoholic, drug abuser, or psychotic, or when neither parent really wanted the child and both remain disengaged from the infant, turning the infant over to a succession of caregivers and day-care centers. Hence it is important that we not lock into the theoretical position that only one custody arrangement fits all children. Truly considering the child's best interests requires that we utilize the best of each theoretical option available, as well as a host of other pragmatic factors, to help parents and the courts tailor custody arrangements on a case-by-case basis. The dichotomy of stability and continuity versus equality of parenting is both erroneous and political, a construct that has slowed the development of more creative and fitting resolutions to parenting disputes.

Early Research Findings

With the precipitous increase in the incidence of divorce two decades ago, researchers began earnest efforts to document the needs of children through the divorce process. Because the early studies were so influential in setting legal precedents, they are reviewed here and then followed by a review of the more current research.

Initial Reactions to Separation

Much emphasis in the early literature on children's needs in divorce focused on the significance of the loss of a parent and on the importance of both parents continuing to be significantly involved in the child's life. From the qualitative reports published, the findings about children and parents going through divorce were filled with expressions of traumatic, confusing, and painful feelings and responses.

Wallerstein and Kelly (1980) found that even when children (of all ages) acknowledged the destructive, neglectful, and unhappy quality of their parents' marriage, very few wanted their parents to divorce. The overwhelming majority seemed to prefer the unhappy marriage to the divorce. "Many of the children, despite the unhappiness of their parents, were in fact relatively happy and considered their situation neither better nor worse than that of other families around them. They would, in fact, have been content to hobble along. The divorce was a bolt of lightning that struck them when they had not even been aware of the existence of a storm" (p. 11).

These initial reactions are understandable, considering the major impact that divorce typically has on children's lives. The basic security provided by the nuclear family unit is shattered, the children's trust in their parents' love for them comes into question, and the children may develop deep worries about whether they will continue to be cared for or even wanted. Moreover, they experience the immediate loss of one of their parents, and regardless of later time-sharing arrangements, from the day of separation on they miss one of their parents virtually 100 percent of the time. In addition, they frequently experience the personal decompensation, deterioration of parental functioning, and reduced availability of the other.

Effects of Stress and Change

While most children generally can handle a single divorce crisis with minimal psychological risk, children who have been exposed to chronic stress or several concurrent stresses and then have to deal with major family disruptions suffer adverse effects that are compounded exponentially (Benjamin, 1980; Rutter, 1978). Therefore, children who have already experienced earlier stressors in their lives are at high psychological risk when facing the consequences of a divorce. Such consequences may include geographical uprooting, economic deprivation, increased use of child care, changes in intrafamilial relationships, and changes in support systems outside the nuclear family (Kurdek, 1981; Hetherington, 1981). Moreover, to this list we must add the effects of the child experiencing multiple parental divorces, an occurrence that increases in frequency with each successive marriage.

For children, one of the most frightening aspects of such changes is their own sense of a loss of control over what is happening. At each stage in a child's (as in an adult's) development, it is the sense of being in control of one's world that gives the confidence to attempt mastery of each new developmental task. Without this sense of control, children and adults are prone to feelings of helplessness and depression. And indeed, Wallerstein and Kelly (1980) found that a full 37 percent of the children were psychologically troubled and manifested moderate to severe clinical depression five years after the divorce. The children experienced rejection and neglect by one or the other parent and repeated disappointment in the unreliability of the "visiting" parent. While older adolescent children were able to turn to others for support, younger children were literally at the mercy of their poorly functioning parents, with no sense of being able to do anything about their circumstances. Moreover, it was found that children who did turn to others for support could also turn to their parents, while the ones who could not count on their parents for support also could not turn to others. Over time, this tendency resulted in the better-adjusted youngsters getting better and the more poorly adjusted ones getting worse.

Loss of a Parent

Probably the most salient aspect of the divorce experience for children is the sudden loss of a parent from the home and the concomitant morbid fear of abandonment. Wallerstein and Kelly (1980) point out that contrary to the belief of many clinicians, children tend not to have foreknowledge of their parents' imminent divorce. It is very common for parents to tell their children nothing of the impending separation and divorce (Irving & Benjamin, 1995). In Wallerstein and Kelly's study (1980), a full 80 percent of the preschool children were not given an adequate explanation of the divorce or assurance of continued care. "In effect, they awoke one morning to find one parent gone. Among this relatively educated and concerned group of parents, the hesitancy in explaining their divorce reflected a high level of anxiety and discomfort about discussing the family breakup with their young children" (p. 39). Moreover, even when divorce plans are discussed ahead of time, this knowledge does not help the children accept or deal with the divorce any more skillfully.

Particular responses to the sudden disappearance of one parent are closely linked to the child's developmental stage. Because younger children are less able to understand the meaning of the separation and are cognitively egocentric, they blame themselves, expect reconciliation, and fear abandonment. Neal (1982) points out that preschool children tend to explain such situations in terms of their personal subsystem; that is, although they often accurately perceive an event, they interpret it in a way that causes excessive personal distress. He writes, "Children at this level understand parental divorce as one parent moving away from the child—an accurate perception—and assume that they must have done something bad in order to cause this distance to occur. The syllogistic quality of this inference is that: A person who does not like someone else moves physically farther away from them; Daddy moved physically away from me; Daddy does not like me" (p. 13).

Older children tend to respond to the absence of a parent less egocentrically, but still in a cognitively restricted manner. Five- to eight-year-olds can attend to triadic behavioral sequences and often believe that they caused a fight between their mother and father that led to the divorce. Nine- to twelve-year-olds, by contrast, can understand that one parent may feel upset at the other parent, irrespective of the child's behavior. But these children are still restricted to believing that one parent can feel negatively toward the other parent only in response to that other parent's behavior. They cannot yet appreciate parental feelings changing independently of the people or situations that evoke them. Adolescents can view adult feelings as independent of the social context, but they cannot make sense of why good intentions on the part of adults do not guarantee positive responses from others. Hence adolescents believe that if parents really wanted to try, they could make their marriage work. Consequently, teenagers frequently blame their parents for the divorce (Neal, 1982).

The impact of father absence after a divorce has received much attention in both the earlier and later research. Contrary to the belief that other people (relatives, siblings, friends, neighbors, day-care centers) can replace the functions of a father, many researchers assert that fathers make a unique contribution to the functioning of the family and the development of the child (Hetherington, 1981; Irving & Benjamin, 1987; Pederson, Rubenstein, & Yarrow, 1979; Wallerstein & Blakeslee, 1989). This contribution is both direct and indirect. The father may play an active, direct role in shaping the child's behavior by providing discipline, offering guidance, and acting as a model. When the father is absent, there is only one parent to carry out the functions of both parents. The single parent, or even two adults of the same sex, offers the child a more restricted assortment of positive characteristics to model than a mother and a father do (Hetherington, 1981).

Indirectly, the father can support the mother in her parenting role in three ways: with monetary aid, with assistance with child care and childrearing tasks, and with emotional support, encouragement, and validation of her functions as a mother. Moreover, as Hetherington, Cox, and Cox (1978) point out, when the mother feels valued and cherished in her role, her self-esteem, happiness, and competence are increased, which in turn improves her relationship with her children. A father can also serve as a buffer between the children and an emotionally unstable mother. In this way he can help counteract any deleterious effects the custodial parent's behavior might have on the children. His complete absence, of course, would prevent this buffering function (Hetherington, Cox, & Cox, 1979). One can speculate that the same findings would also hold true in reverse when the father is the primary custodial parent.

Children deprived of frequent access to their fathers show diminished self-esteem lasting many years after the divorce (Wallerstein & Kelly, 1980; Wallerstein & Blakeslee, 1989). Moreover, when left in the exclusive care of a distressed and inconsistent mother, they show a disruption of cognitive skills, social behavior, and self-control (Hetherington, 1979a). The children who were most stressed were those who had close and affectionate relationships with their father during the marriage and who experienced a disruption in this relationship after the divorce. Hetherington (1981) notes that with the exception of a poorly adjusted or immature father, frequent availability of the father is associated with positive adjustment and positive social relationships, especially in boys. Moreover, a continued and mutually supportive relationship between father and child is also the most effective support system for divorced women in their parenting role.

Parental Conflict

Research has consistently pointed to the destructive consequences to children of continued bitterness and conflict between the parents. While varying degrees of parental discord are expected during the first year following the separation, discord that continues longer than one year has serious negative effects on children. One distressed twelve-year-old boy, whose divorced parents had been arguing and battling in court over custody for the previous ten years, told a mediator that he wanted to teach first or sixth graders when he grew up. When asked why he wanted to teach those particular grades, he replied, eloquently, "'Cause they don't argue so much in those grades, . . . but in all the other grades they argue a lot; . . . I hate arguing!"

Wallerstein and Kelly (1980) found that a central cause of children's poor adjustment at five years after the divorce was the failure of the divorce to provide its intended relief. When parents continued fighting after the divorce, and especially when the postdivorce conflict exceeded the marital conflict, the children had a great deal of difficulty accepting and integrating the divorce. Moreover, children are frequently coerced or cajoled into taking sides in parental battles, which creates a terrible conflict in them over divided loyalties. Such a tug-of-war greatly compounds the children's difficulties. When the mother is hostile to and critical of the father, the child begins to denounce the father as an acceptable role model. For young boys, this results in a disruption of sex typing (Hetherington et al., 1979), and for girls, it can be associated with disruptions in heterosexual relations at adolescence (Hetherington, 1972).

Current Perspectives and Research Findings

While earlier influential research on children of divorce was often based on anecdotal evidence from small samples, lacked appropriate matched control groups, and drew conclusions that inappropriately generalized to all children of divorce, many of the early insights have held up through the test of time. However, many have not. More recent research has shown that divorce is difficult for children, but it is not always as devastating as earlier reports assumed. Children actually appear to show a wide range of short-term responses to their parents' divorce. This range extends from the minority who show positive responses—for example, when an older child develops independence, self-reliance, and greater maturity from handling extra responsibilities in the home following a divorce when parents cooperate supportively (Gately & Schwebel, 1991, 1992); when a child's daily contact with a parent who is immature, abusive, violent, or destructive ceases (Guidubaldi & Cleminshaw, 1985; Kaslow & Schwartz, 1987; Wallerstein & Blakeslee, 1989; Warshak & Santrock, 1983); or who show little or no apparent upset (Kurdek & Siesky, 1980; Rosen, 1977)*—to the responses of the majority of children (especially boys), who show clear signs of emotional, psychological, behavioral, and social distress; have significantly more adjustment problems; and show lower academic achievement when compared to children from never-divorced parents (Amato, 1994; Camara & Resnick, 1988; Emery, 1988; Hetherington, 1987, 1989; Kelly, 1993a; Wallerstein & Blakeslee, 1989).

Recent researchers documenting the longer-term consequences of divorce on children no longer believe that the factors predicting long-term adjustment of children are simple or few (Berner, 1992; Emery, 1988; Irving & Benjamin, 1995; Kelly, 1988, 1993a, 1997; Schwartz & Kaslow, 1997; Wallerstein, 1991, 1997; Wallerstein & Blakeslee, 1989; Zill, Morrison, & Coiro, 1993). No longer is adjustment considered assured by a child simply having consistent psychological attachments (one or several) and regular contact with both parents who are cooperative with each other. The singular importance of joint custody for positive child adjustment, widely highlighted through the 1980s (Folberg, 1991), appears to have receded into perspective when compared to the powerful impact made by the interaction of numerous other factors that more current research has brought to the surface. This multivariate mixture is now known to be quite complex.

Let us examine more closely some of the most important variables related to child adjustment.

---

*Guidubaldi (1988) suggests, however, that these neutral to positive findings are flawed by a lack of control groups and inclusion of only child questionnaires and interview data, which can result in failure of reporting negative perceptions due to defensive responding, as described by Warshak and Santrock (1983).

Child's Age at the Time of Separation

The research has suggested that younger children are more affected by their parents' divorce than older children are (Irving & Benjamin, 1995; Kalter, Kloner, Schreiser, & Okla, 1989; Wallerstein & Blakeslee, 1989). Explanations for this inverse relationship between age and adjustment have included the fact that younger children explain their parents' divorce in egocentric, self-blaming ways, whereas older children project blame onto others, thereby protecting their own self-concepts from contamination (Grych & Fincham, 1990). However, Allison and Furstenberg (1989) demonstrated that these age differences were significant only following the separation and diminished over time. Also, Amato (1994) notes that age at divorce and time since divorce have been confounded in much of the research on this variable, making findings inconsistent. He points out, though, that "it is safe to say that divorce has the potential to impact negatively on children of all ages (p. 149).

Gender

Early studies found that boys from divorced families had more adjustment problems than girls from divorced families did (Guidubaldi, Cleminshaw, Perry, & McLaughlin, 1983). However, these gender differences were later shown to be a function of the child's age at divorce. For example, Frost and Pakiz (1990) found that adolescent girls whose parents divorce initially experience more difficulties than adolescent boys, while younger school-aged boys have more problems than school-aged girls. Finally, a more recent meta-analysis by Amato and Keith (1991), which statistically leveled and combined the results of all the studies on gender differences, found that the only gender difference that was salient was a negative effect by divorce on the social adjustment of boys but not of girls.

Predivorce Adjustment of the Child

Personality and temperament characteristics of a child are influenced by (and in turn influence) indirect family processes that exist during a marriage. As such, patterns of marital discord and high conflict can exacerbate unadaptable and inflexible child personality styles, generating poor adjustment of a child during the marriage. The added chaos, forced changes, and resulting stress of a divorce can further magnify the child's poor predivorce adjustment. Indeed, serious problems in young boys were noted several years before the parents' divorce, in a study by Block, Block, and Gjerde (1986). Moreover, Peterson and Zill (1986) found that children in high-conflict marriages had three times more psychological distress than children in families with low or moderate conflict during the marriage. And Tschann, Johnston, Kline, and Wallerstein (1990) found that a predivorce history of psychological difficulties in a child was one of the best predictors of postdivorce adjustment.

Custodial Parent's Psychological Adjustment

Wallerstein and Kelly (1980) pointed out that for the year or two following the separation, parents showed a "diminished capacity to parent." Hetherington, Cox, and Cox (1982) added the observation that during the first year after separation, custodial parents were less affectionate toward their children, made fewer maturity demands, supervised them less, were more punitive, and were less consistent in disciplining. More recent research is suggesting just how critical the custodial parent's adjustment is for the children's adjustment (see Amato, 1994; Furstenberg & Cherlin, 1991; Irving & Benjamin, 1995; Kelly, 1993a, 1997).

Maternal depression and anxiety at the beginning of the divorce process predicts children's emotional and social adjustment two years later (Kline, Tschann, Johnston, & Wallerstein, 1989) and predicts psychological adjustment of the custodial parent several years postdivorce (Coysh, Johnston, Tschann, Wallerstein, & Kline, 1989). Moreover, the better the mother's adjustment to the divorcing process, the better the children's adjustment (Copeland, 1985). The mechanism behind this relationship is based partly upon the reciprocal influences between parent and child (Ambert, 1992; Lerner & Spanier, 1978). Thus, just as maternal adjustment enhances positive child adjustment, child adjustment enhances positive maternal adjustment (Hetherington et al., 1978). It is no wonder, then, that when custodial parents are offered adequate social support, their children have fewer difficulties (Amato, 1994). Finally, it should be noted that almost no research has been done on the impact of paternal adjustment on children. However, Kelly (1993a) notes some research that suggests that the father's depressive mood was not a predictor of adjustment of children in maternal custody.

Access Frequency and Quality of the Noncustodial Parent-Child Relationship

Much of the early research consistently attested to the profound sense of loss reported by children whose postdivorce contact with their noncustodial parent (most often their father) was diminished or absent. And these studies showed that child adjustment was directly related to visitation frequency, with more frequent contact associated with improved child adjustment (Bisnaire, Firestone, & Rynard, 1990; Hetherington, 1979b; Hetherington et al., 1982; Kurdek & Berg, 1983; Wallerstein & Kelly, 1980). However, more recent research suggests that this effect is more complex and that the child's sense of loss may not directly affect the child's adjustment. Some investigators report a positive association but qualified by the age and gender of the child, the degree of closeness between father and child, and the level of coparental conflict (Healy, Malley, & Stewart, 1990; Thomas & Forehand, 1993). Others report either very weak or absent association between frequency of visitation and child adjustment (Furstenberg & Cherlin, 1991; Furstenberg, Morgan, & Allison, 1987; Kalter et al., 1989; Kline et al., 1989).

However, Irving and Benjamin (1995) note that these results appear to be a function of other variables. Specifically, if the preseparation relationship between father and child was positive, the loss results in distress. If it was poor, the loss of contact will be met with relief. Kelly (1993a) adds that child adjustment is not improved with increased frequency if the father is poorly adjusted or extremely immature; this is especially true for boys.

Other researchers have noted that custodial mothers have a good deal of influence on the father-child relationship after divorce. For example, Braver, Wolchik, Sandler, Fogas, and Zvetina (1991) found that custodial mothers interfere with fathers' visits with the children 20 to 40 percent of the time and that mothers' hostility at the beginning of divorce is significantly associated with fewer overnight visitations three years after the divorce.

At year twenty-five of her longitudinal study, Wallerstein (1997) concluded that regardless of the reasons, if the father-child relationship was not good from the start, no court-ordered or mediated visitation arrangements generated a positive relationship between them. Many subjects reported that as children, they and their fathers "tolerated" each other but later, as adults, they rejected their fathers. This was especially true for children whose fathers rigidly enforced a court-ordered schedule that went against the child's desires.

In summarizing the research, Kelly (1993a, p. 41) writes, "It is evident from the research literature that when mothers allow and/or encourage visitation without excessive hostility and when children have had positive relationships with their fathers prior to divorce, then frequent and predictable contact with fathers can be demonstrated to be beneficial for children."

Residential and Time-Sharing Arrangements

For many years, the question that researchers asked was whether joint custody works for children of divorce. Saposnek (1987, 1991a) notes that current research suggests that the complexity of this issue more appropriately warrants the multilevel question "Which divorcing families, with what kinds of marital histories, with what specific kinds of pre-and post-separation disputes, with what age children, with what coping styles, temperament styles, and qualities of parent-child relationships, presented at which times in the divorcing process, can handle what specific kinds of decision-making patterns and time-sharing schedules within a joint custody arrangement?" (1991a, p. 31).

Despite our early hopes, joint custody (or shared parenting) does not appear to increase a child's adjustment to divorce. In fact, most studies demonstrate that custody type alone does not predict adjustment (Camara & Resnick, 1988; Warshak & Santrock, 1983). Moreover, McKinnon and Wallerstein (1986) and Wallerstein (1991) conclude that there is no evidence to suggest that joint custody protects children from the effects of divorce, nor is there evidence that sole custody is any better. While shared parenting can offer certain benefits to both children and parents, these apparently only can be achieved when variables other than the schedule per se are operative. These include continuity and closeness of parent-child interaction; regularity and predictability of child movement between households; coparental cooperation (Irving & Benjamin, 1995); parental capacity for objectivity and empathy with the child and other parent, for shifting from spousal to coparental role, and for maintaining high self-esteem, flexibility, and openness to help (Steinman, Zemmelman, & Knoblauch, 1985); low interparental conflict (Luepnitz, 1986); and positive motives for sharing the children (McKinnon & Wallerstein, 1986; Saposnek, 1983).

Characteristics of children that facilitate positive shared parenting include being under three years of age and not yet experiencing the disruption of friends and activities characteristic of older children in joint custody situations, having solid cognitive organizational skills that prevents the child from becoming disoriented and distressed by change, being free of disorganizing levels of anxiety (Steinman, 1984), and being temperamentally adaptable to change and more quickly able to warm up to new situations (Saposnek, 1983; Thomas & Chess, 1977). For excellent reviews of the issues involved in joint custody and shared parenting, see Folberg (1991), Irving and Benjamin (1995), and Kelly (1993a).

Conflict Between Parents

Rheinstein (1972) noted long ago that it is not divorce per se that causes the social and emotional problems of children of divorce but rather the actual emotional breakdown of the marriage. This early and insightful point was further supported by the findings of a large longitudinal study by Cherlin and colleagues (1991) conducted on more than fifteen thousand children from Great Britain and the United States. These researchers found that it was family dysfunction and parental conflict that existed *prior to* the divorce, rather than the divorce itself, that substantially predicted the negative effects of divorce on children.

This finding, of the deleterious effects of interparental conflict on children—in intact two-parent families (Emery, 1988; Grych & Fincham, 1990), during the marital separation, and/or after the divorce (Cummings & Davies, 1994; Garrity & Baris, 1994; Johnston & Campbell, 1988; Johnston, Kline, & Tschann, 1989; Johnston & Roseby, 1997; Portes, Howell, Brown, Eichenberger, & Mas, 1992; Shaw & Emery, 1987)—has in the past decade been so amply documented that it has become common knowledge among contemporary divorce professionals. Fascinating corroboration regarding these conclusions came directly from children of divorce in a study by Sandler, Wolchik, and Braver (1988). These researchers had children of divorce rank the degree of stress experienced or imagined by each of sixty-two typical events that occur in divorce (using their research instrument, the Divorce Events Schedule for Children, or DESC). The children rated the three most stressful events as a parent blaming the child for the divorce, interparental conflict, and derogation of the parents.

Interparental conflict appears to interact with most of the variables detailed here and so can be viewed as the backdrop against which all the other effects of divorce on children operate. Although the relationship between parental conflict and adjustment of children has always been considered linear—the more conflict, the greater the degree of maladjustment—recent evidence suggests that it is more complex than this. The correlations between conflict per se and child adjustment are low, suggesting to Kelly (1993a) and Irving and Benjamin (1995) that conflict may have more indirect relationships with child adjustment.

Basically, two variables seem necessary for interparental conflict to exercise its full deleterious effect on a child. One is that the child must experience being "caught in the middle" (Buchanan, Maccoby, & Dornbusch, 1991; Johnston et al., 1989; Maccoby, Buchanan, Mnookin,

& Dornbusch, 1993)—for example, when the child is pumped for information about the other parent's private life, is used as a messenger between the parents, receives the wrath of both parents, is forced to keep secrets about one parent from the other, or hears one parent denigrate the other parent, all of which create terrible loyalty conflicts for the child (see Garrity & Baris, 1994). When parents refrain from expressing their conflict by triangulating their child in these ways, evidence suggests that the child may be spared the negative adjustment consequences. Children who are not used as pawns by parents who wish to "get back at" each other apparently show better adjustment to the divorce, even if their parents remain in conflict.

Second, Camara and Resnick (1989) found that the strategy of conflict resolution used by the parents, whether in a marriage or in a divorce, predicts the impact of their conflict on the child. A parental strategy of verbal attack appears to generate poorer adjustment in children than a parental strategy of compromise. Hence, as many family therapists have observed, conflict between parents is not in and of itself detrimental; it is harmful only if the child never experiences the parents resolving it. Without the resolution, children are left in a state of unrelieved chronic tension. Amato (1994) also notes that children raised in high-conflict households may not learn skills of effective negotiation and compromise for managing conflicts in their own friendships and other relationships.

Suggesting other mechanisms to account for the indirect effects of interparental conflict, Irving and Benjamin (1995) point out that high conflict may sabotage and disrupt a previously positive relationship between the noncustodial parent (typically the father) and the child, resulting indirectly in negative adjustment of the child. Further, Kelly (1993a) opines that "children respond to parental conflict in different ways. Some children try to placate an angry parent or attempt to mediate parental disputes. Others cope by withdrawing or form an alignment with one parent and reject the other" (p. 36).

Temperament Differences of Children

A major variable that affects adjustment of children within both intact and divorced families is the child's temperament and how interactions with caregivers influence the personality development of the child and shape the child's adjustment to various life stressors. Although this concept has been occasionally mentioned in the custody literature as a variable that contributes to adjustment, its implications have not been fully developed. A brief elaboration here will fill this gap.

The concept of "temperament," as it relates to normal and deviant development, has been most thoroughly described by Thomas and Chess (Chess & Thomas, 1984, 1986; Thomas & Chess, 1977; Thomas, Chess, & Birch, 1968; Thomas, Chess, Birch, Hertzig, & Korn, 1963). In their anterospective New York Longitudinal Study, they tracked and observed 133 subjects from early infancy to adulthood and emerged with nine dimensions of temperament that described styles of behavior of their developing subjects. The dimensions are activity level, rhythmicity (regularity of eating, sleeping, and elimination cycles), approach to new situations, adaptability, intensity of reaction, threshold of responsiveness (sensitivity to stimuli), quality of mood, distractibility, and attention span/persistence.

The significance of this work is not only that these temperament styles (for which there is promising evidence of genetic etiological contributions) remain relatively stable throughout development (with some fluctuation during certain phases, such as in adolescence) but that the interactions of these characteristic styles of behavior with reactions of significant people (parents, siblings, caregivers, teachers) in the child's life make for prospectively predictable outcomes in development. Behavior disorders are created when a parent wittingly or unwittingly tries to deal with a temperament characteristic of the child that the parent considers extreme or unacceptable by forcing the child to try to change it. Unfortunately, like other genetically loaded behavioral characteristics, temperament characteristics tend to exaggerate even further in the direction in which they are already leaning when the child is stressed or pressured. So, paradoxically, attempts to forcibly change the behavior style lead to magnification of it.

Ironically, a divorcing couple is in a unique position to utilize these research findings to their own benefit and that of their children. Being aware of various areas of better or poorer compatibility (referred to in the research as "goodness of fit") allows parents to develop ways for optimizing parent-child compatibility as they develop their parenting plan. For example, a boy with a high-activity-level temperament style would do better spending more time with a parent who viewed this behavioral tendency with joy and excitement and who enthusiastically channeled the boy's energy into activities such as sports. In contrast, problems would surely arise if the child spent much time with the parent who found the boy's energy level annoying and who constantly yelled at the boy to calm down and stop being so disruptive, which would merely activate the boy even further. (This is the conceptual model for the development of adjustment problems in children.)

Or consider a child who, by her temperament, is slow to warm up to new situations and is nonadaptable. Putting such a child on a joint custody schedule that involves switching households every three or four days, or alternate weeks, could keep the child and the parents in constant stress, as the child experiences each switch as a major challenge to her temperament. Such a child would optimally benefit from the fewest possible changes in households.

Or consider a girl with a high intensity of reactions, whose every behavior is loud, strong, and intense. When she speaks, it is with a big, booming voice; when she hugs, she gives a bear squeeze; when she closes a door, she slams it. These actions are not intentional and are very difficult for her to modulate voluntarily. A mother with a low threshold of responsiveness (heightened sensitivity to stimuli) would be chronically irritated by a daughter with such intensity. All else being equal, if the girl's father was more tolerant of the daughter's intensity, he would be the better choice as primary parent; a parenting plan that had this girl spending the majority of time with her mother might be a setup for the development of behavioral and interactional problems.

In addition to the obvious impact of each separate temperament characteristic, Thomas and Chess (1977) describe three constellations of functional significance that arose from a qualitative analysis of their data. The "easy child" (about 40 percent of the sample) had a profile that included regular rhythmicity, positive approach responses to new stimuli, high adaptability to change, and a mild or moderately intense mood that is preponderantly positive. These children quickly develop regular sleep and feeding schedules, accept new foods easily, smile at strangers, adapt easily to a new school, and accept most frustration in stride. Such children could probably handle most coparenting schedules with very few adjustments needed.

The opposite profile is characterized as the "difficult child" (about 10 percent of their sample). This child shows erratic patterns of biological functions (such as unpredictable sleep and eating cycles), negative or withdrawal responses to new stimuli, nonadaptability or slow adaptability to change, and intense mood expressions that are frequently negative. These children show irregular sleep and feeding schedules; slow acceptance of new foods; prolonged adjustment periods to new routines, people, or situations; and relatively frequent and loud periods of crying. Frustration typically produces intense temper tantrums. Such children present a real challenge to the most competent, calm parent and will cause stress in any parent. Temperamentally difficult children need to have their time maximized with the parent who can better tolerate them, and such children sometimes do better in shared custody arrangements, where the burden is distributed between households, if neither parent can tolerate the child particularly well.

The third profile is called the "slow-to-warm-up child" (about 15 percent of their sample). These children are characterized by a combination of negative responses of mild intensity to new stimuli and slow adaptability after repeated contact. In contrast to the difficult children, these children show mild intensity of reactions, whether positive or negative, and have less tendency to show irregularity of biological functions. The mild negative responses to new stimuli are seen when the child encounters any situation or thing that is new, such as a new food, a stranger, a new school, or a new coparenting schedule. Dealing with such a child requires patience, ample time and preparation to help the child adjust to changes, and regular acknowledgment of the child's feelings. Arranging for such a child to spend much time with an impatient parent can be disastrous for the slow-to-warm-up child.

Temperament characteristics do not function in a vacuum but interact with each child's learned behavior patterns, habits, preferences, tolerances, attitudes and beliefs, talents and skills (intellectual, social, and physical), and feelings. Because of a presumed polygenic pattern of inheritance, siblings within a family may have very different degrees of "goodness of fit" with a particular parent. Hence each child may require a separate coparenting schedule.

Concept of Time in Early Development

Most adults' comprehension of the concept of time is taken for granted. Few parents understand that young children (below the age of seven or so) do not have a real sense of time perspective. Such a perspective develops gradually over the preschool years. The child slowly understands that "seeing Daddy tomorrow" is different from "seeing Daddy next week." Before the preschool period, "tomorrow" and "in a year" are indistinguishable, since all that exists for the young child is "now." Young children truly live in the present. Hodges (1986, p. 159) explains:

> For the young child, "tomorrow" is an undefined, infinite time away, yet the child slowly learns the meaning of tomorrow. "The day after tomorrow" is a far more complex concept (thus making weekend visitations a potentially confusing pattern for the young child).
>
> The concept of tomorrow is seldom understood by 3 year olds, but 4 year olds understood the idea. By age 5, "the day after tomorrow"

is conceptually understood, but a "week" may be a vaguely conceived time period. By age 6 or 7, the child can count and can understand the concept of "a week" or "a month." By age 7 or 8 an infinite time sense develops so that the child understands the concept of "forever."

Since the time perspective of children is variable and changeable before the age of 7, these recommendations imply that visitation agreements of children under 7 should take into account the changing stages of the child. Longer and longer visitations could occur during the ages from birth to 7, from brief hour-long visits to full weekends to weeks. If the visitation pattern violates the short time perspective of the child, the child may have difficulty remembering the absent parent and will not be able to understand intuitively when he or she will return to the custodial parent. The results will be insecurity, anxiety, and difficulty in establishing a firm identification with either parent. Keep in mind, however, that basing the visitation patterns on chronological age could be a mistake, since each child has a unique age pattern for learning time concepts.

Understanding the developmental nature of the concept of time can help the mediator educate parents of young children about the limited cognitive and emotional capacities of their child, which might necessitate more frequent contact with each parent. A commonly used rule of thumb (with many exceptions, of course) is that a younger child can continuously be away from a primary residential parent for one day for each year of age. So a three–year-old can handle three days away, a seven–year-old can handle a week, and so forth.

Other Variables

Additional factors that appear related to children's adjustment in divorce include coping skills of the children, communication skills and degree of cooperation of each of the family members, effectiveness and consistency across households of parental child-rearing practices, the social support systems available for each parent, their social class, ethnicity, and the economic condition and viability of each parent. (For excellent reviews of the many variables related to children's adjustment, see Emery, 1988; Irving and Benjamin, 1995; and Kelly, 1993a).

○

Irving and Benjamin (1995) poignantly summarized the complex mix of variables that is essential for optimal short-term adjustment for a child of divorce. They conclude that the child's adjustment will be optimal *if* marital and parent-child relations before the separation were not manifestly dysfunctional; *if* the parent with whom [the children] live is not manifestly dysfunctional; *if* that parent adjusts well and *if* he or she continues to provide consistent supportive care; *if* material resources continue to be available adequately and *if* unavoidable lifestyle changes are not too drastic; *if* coparental relations are cordial or at least not unduly conflictual; *if* coparental conflict is not exacerbated by a court battle; *if* the noncustodial parent is not manifestly dysfunctional; *if* that parent is consistent in contributing to the children's financial support and maintains involvement with the children on a consistent and predictable basis, even *if* this means less frequent visits; and *if* the children have access to relations with supportive adults other than their parents [p. 72].

While most children show distress and disruption for the first two to three years following divorce, the majority eventually adjust successfully and move on with their lives (Irving & Benjamin, 1995). When assessed in the years following the divorce, the majority appear to be functioning within normal limits (Amato & Keith, 1991; Kelly, 1993a). However, a significant minority (from 26 to 40 percent, estimated by Irving and Benjamin, 1995) to almost half (estimated by Wallerstein and Blakeslee, 1989) continue to show negative consequences from having gone through the divorce experience.

Wallerstein (1997) sums it up well: "Divorce is a cumulative experience by the child. At each stage it gets reformulated, and it requires coping beyond normal development challenges."

3

ATTITUDES AND SKILLS NEEDED FOR EFFECTIVE MEDIATION

TYPICALLY, SPOUSES BEGIN mediation at their psychological worst, struggling for their very self-esteem and self-worth as human beings. As Felder (1971, pp. 227–228) noted quite early:

> People going to a divorce lawyer are mostly bitter and revengeful, . . . reduced to a basic level, filled with greed, vengeance, pettiness; . . . adults fighting over the most trivial things, women hurting men even when they can gain nothing by doing so, people ready to sacrifice their children as tools against the other spouse. . . . In matrimonial cases, everything goes, there is no limit to the hurt people will inflict on one another. . . . There are few conditions of stress so protracted and so personal and incapable of being shared with other people. It seems to get worse and worse as the litigation drags on. Friends are ripped apart, the whole fabric of life is torn. It is unlike any other stress situation.

Many couples find that mediation exacerbates the animosity in their relationship. In addition to the typical marital issues, with all the paradoxical and convoluted patterns of interaction, another problematic element is present: a survival threat. Each spouse's self-concept, lifestyle, moral values, competence as a parent, worth as a human being, and feelings of being lovable are threatened. Moreover, each spouse's capacity for flexible compromise, for empathy, and for dealing with often overwhelming feelings of anger, grief, jealousy, resentment, and revenge is also challenged.

Both spouses have much to protect. They must each protect their own relationship with their children, their finances (often from threat by the other spouse), their integrity, and their sense of personal worth. They may feel subject to explicit and implicit criticism by their former spouse, by their children, by the judge, and even by the mediator. Each may put up a childlike resistance, for each will feel that his or her own inner child's emotional survival and autonomy are at stake. It is ironic that in this struggle, each spouse perceives himself or herself as powerless and the other spouse as powerful. The result is like a tug-of-war, with each spouse feeling overpowered by the other although in fact neither has moved an inch. It is the task of the mediator to help the couple to develop an awareness of the futility of this struggle and to create some slack in the rope so as to be able to direct the couple's energies to more productive purposes.

Interactional Struggles

A primary task of the mediator is to get the spouses apart when they feel stuck together. The mediator has to get the couple to work together just enough to cooperate in sharing the children while keeping them enough apart that their conflictual patterns are not triggered off into self-perpetuating vicious circles. In carrying out this task, the mediator often finds himself or herself in what can only be called a double-bind situation (Bateson, Jackson, Haley, & Weakland, 1956), in that the mediator is expected to respond in one of two ways, for both of which he or she will be punished. Negotiations often reach such an impasse that they seem unsolvable. If the mediator expresses pessimism, one of the spouses may well pull out of mediation, saying things like "This is hopeless; he obviously has not changed, and this is a waste of time; I'd rather go to court." As soon as one spouse pulls out, the other defends by throwing an accusation back, and the hostility escalates once again. If, however, at some other point when the negotiations appear to be going very well, the mediator says, "The situation seems very hopeful; I know you can do it," one of the spouses may well resist such optimism by triggering off resistance in the other spouse, with accusations or innuendos. Or the spouse may suddenly throw out a radical, poorly timed proposal in an attempt to resolve the whole situation too soon, putting the other on the defensive. Then the one spouse quickly pounces on the other for being resistant.

Because the stakes are so high, the tactical struggles between spouses will be numerous. The mediator must be alert if he or she is to stave off the destructive effects of these struggles. There is no time for passive observation, since the couple's interactions rarely calm down. Moreover, at some point during the process, their interactions almost always reach a point of tension that threatens to terminate the mediation process abruptly and prematurely.

The mediator must constantly be thinking many moves ahead. The only possible resting spot is a mutually agreeable resolution to the custody issue, with built-in steps for preventing or settling future disputes. Hence the mediator must continuously assess each spouse's emotional state, perceptions of the other spouse, possible next moves (such as voicing proposals, accusations, criticisms, or support), feelings about the mediator, and understanding of the mediation process itself. In addition, the mediator must assess each spouse's needs regarding the children, what it means for the children to be with each spouse, and what "giving them up" might mean to each spouse. He or she must assess the ambivalent feelings each spouse has for the other, the degree of their remaining attachment, the degree to which their comments reflect genuine concern for the welfare of the children, and so forth.

Maintaining Neutrality and Balance

The mediator must pay exactly equal attention to the concerns of each spouse. From the mediator's point of view, the balance point between them is the only workable leverage spot. As in political campaigns, each spouse may persistently try to convince the mediator, lawyers, friends, relatives, personal therapist, and judge of the virtue of his or her side and the villainy of the other side. Often each will tell convincing and self-righteous stories that reveal the other spouse to be an uncooperative, immature, unjust fool. Moreover, the emotional impact of such an appeal within a context involving children is tremendous. Even therapists and lawyers who can remain impartial in other contexts will often get swallowed up in the perspective of only one side of the dispute. The mediator must make every effort to resist such tactics and remain neutral.

It is not uncommon for the mediator to receive calls from a therapist (or even a lawyer) who is aghast at hearing (from the mother) that the mediator is even considering helping a "bad" father continue contact with the "victimized" child. The mediator then has an even more complex problem: he or she must deal not only with the feuding couple but also with the other persons who are unbalancing the interactional system by giving too much support to one side (this has been characterized by Johnston and Campbell, 1988, as the "external" level of the impasse, the level of "helping" professionals, family, friends, coworkers, and others who join in and thereby enhance the dispute).

For the mediator, such persons from the external level of the impasse who assert one-sided positions merely hamper the mediation process. The mediator must deal understandingly with those persons and their concerns but must not be swayed. Since neither individual truth nor objective reality is easily attainable in custody disputes, the mediator can succeed in resolving the dispute only if he or she adheres to the systems point of view, in which the mediator deals with varying degrees of descriptive accuracy about the system itself. (Further discussion of the systems perspective can be found in Chapters Four and Eight.)

Haley (1976) observed that when one intervenes from a systems point of view—which assumes that all members reciprocally affect one another—every person who is significant within that system automatically becomes part of the "problem." In marital therapy, the therapist becomes part of the marital problem. So in mediation, the mediator becomes part of the mediation problem. He or she will often be disliked by at least one, if not both, of the spouses and at one point or another may be viewed as uncompassionate, naive, incompetent, unhelpful, or destructive. Whichever spouse loses the leverage typically will cast the mediator with these negative attributes. Often one spouse will express such negative feelings to another significant person, such as a lawyer or new spouse: "My mediator doesn't really understand my side, or he wouldn't have been taken in by those lies from my ex-spouse."

Because the mediator receives very little information ahead of time and must work within a time limitation, the task can feel quite difficult at the outset. The issues are obscured and the spouses typically very well defended. This situation can be characterized as the mediator stepping lightly across a minefield. If he or she accidentally steps in the wrong place, the entire process can blow up. Moreover, the wrong place may be one that appears neutral to the mediator (for example, talking about the benefits of joint legal custody), but to one of the spouses (who desires sole custody) it appears as if the mediator is siding with the other spouse. Often that spouse does not speak up about this perceived bias at the beginning of mediation but later suddenly challenges the mediator's position. In response, the mediator may well reflexively defend his or her position and before realizing it ends up backed into a corner of partiality. Such an event may abruptly terminate the mediation process or cause the affected spouse to cultivate insurmountable resistance to any compromises.

For the mediator, this is very similar to the courtroom experience of an expert witness who, as the court's representative, attempts to remain neutral. Through cross-examination, the witness is forced to state a position and, by defending it, loses the original position of neutrality. Hence it is essential that the mediator remain aware of potentially explosive issues.

Unpredictability

Perhaps the most challenging aspect of the entire mediation process is the unpredictability of the outcome until the very end. The mediator never knows from moment to moment in the negotiations whether a couple will suddenly escalate their hostilities to the point of stalemate or proceed to resolve the issues peacefully. This unpredictability is seen at various levels of the mediation process.

At one level, it is manifested in the unexpected behavior of a couple within a given session. Spouses will often enter the first mediation session in a very hostile mood. Throughout the mediator's introductory statements, they may sit and glare. As they are encouraged to speak, they may begin by blurting out accusations, prophecies of disaster, statements of hopelessness about the mediation process, and refusals to compromise. Then, just as the mediator proceeds in spite of the ominous discouragement, something unexpected may happen that gets the couple unstuck from these stances and ready to consider compromises. The unexpected may include the resolution of a particularly emotional issue, the couple's acceptance of a suggestion by the mediator, an emphatic comment made by one of the parties to the other, or any of a number of unforeseeable factors.

Other spouses enter mediation appearing friendly, lighthearted, and cooperative. Occasionally, spouses may even touch affectionately. (On a number of occasions, spouses I worked with even held hands.) This cooperative demeanor may persist for some time into the session. Experience has shown, however, that it is a dangerous mistake to assume that it will necessarily continue throughout the negotiations. Often the spouses will suddenly and unexpectedly turn on each other. Coming as it does out of the blue, this reaction will throw even experienced mediators off balance. Seasoned mediators learn to be cautious with couples who appear cooperative. If the spouses were really all that cooperative with each other, they would not need to seek mediation. Truly friendly couples work out custody and visitation issues before consulting lawyers, judges, and mediators (Ahrons and Rodgers, 1987, provide a good description of such "perfect pals" postdivorce couples). Although it can be very appealing to listen to a couple talk in a friendly, respectful, or even loving manner about their early marriage and about each other, a mediator working with such a couple should be prepared for the hostility that often erupts during the actual discussion of custody, or else it may come as a disheartening shock. The mediator must be prepared to remain skeptical or, at best, cautiously optimistic throughout the session and even to expect the worst while working toward the best outcome. This attitude is a necessary survival tool if the mediator is to cope with unpredictability within a session.

Unpredictability is also a problem between sessions. A couple may leave a session angry, resisting compromise, and pessimistic about the mediation process. Although the mediator may feel that the negotiations are guaranteed to fail, he or she schedules the next appointment anyway. At the next session, the spouses come in acting friendly and cooperative and inform the mediator that they have "worked everything out." The mediator may feel puzzled, though delighted with the surprise.

Another possibility is that spouses may leave a constructive session joking, talking affectionately, and even hugging and kissing in the parking lot. Then, an hour before the next session, one spouse calls the mediator to cancel the session because the couple has decided to go to court, having just had a major fight. Such sudden decisions occur for a variety of reasons, almost all of which are unpredictable. The mediator who expects a linear, logical process may be quite demoralized by such vagaries. Once again, expecting the unexpected is the safest policy.

Perhaps most frustrating of all for the mediator are the unpredictable moves that occur just before signing the final mediation agreement. At this final point, one of the spouses may suddenly refuse to go along with the agreement, even though he or she helped design it. That spouse may be taking the last opportunity to make a power play, to express fears about letting go, or to get back at the other spouse. Such a move is also a challenge to the mediator, who finds the proverbial rug suddenly pulled out from under him or her, after spending hours laying a groundwork of trust. Often, after further negotiations, the agreements can be revised and accepted. Some couples, however, are unable to reach agreement and must return to court for adjudication.

Occasionally, it happens that one spouse calls the mediator the day after signing the agreement and announces that the agreement is off. The spouse explains that after thinking it over, he or she is not satisfied with the agreement and will not abide by it. Such occurrences, fortunately, are rare, and because the spouse who reneged is usually unwilling to return to mediation, the case is best referred to the lawyers.

The context of mediation is a central factor contributing to the variety of unpredictable behaviors shown by couples undergoing this process. Mediation takes place in a time-limited and highly structured context, deals with emotionally charged content, and concerns itself with participants who frequently are both angry and mistrustful. Moreover, both spouses feel the pressure of the mediator's explicit expectation that they will cooperate and compromise with each other, even though they may feel very little mutual trust. Furthermore, small crises are often catalyzed in the mediator's efforts to restructure the marital system. The resulting potential for unpredictable behavior is clearly very large.

Mediation offers some spouses a controlled and efficient setting in which to vent anger and express hurt over specific issues, after which they often can cooperate with each other enough to reach resolutions within a session. Other spouses may remain angry with each other in the office and feel inhibited by the presence of the mediator but be able to reach agreement on their own after the session. In both cases, the mere opportunity to talk with each other away from the adversarial context can rapidly yield cooperation out of hostility. Interestingly, research on clients' views of mediation consistently reveal overall positive ratings of the process, even if they did not reach agreement. Pearson and Thoennes (1982) found that 93 percent of successful mediation clients and 81 percent of unsuccessful clients "would recommend the process to a friend." My own research (Saposnek, Hamburg, Delano, & Michaelsen, 1984) found that clients rated their own experience in mediation a mean rating of 6.0 out of 10 but gave mediation in general as a positive way of resolving parenting disputes a mean rating of 8.2 out of 10. Finally, Depner, Cannata, and Simon (1992) found that 90 percent of their client sample (both successful and unsuccessful) rated mediation "a good way to develop a parenting plan" (p. 199).

Another variable that contributes to unpredictable behavior is the natural emotional ambivalence that exists between two divorced spouses. An emotional divorce rarely occurs at the same time as a legal divorce. Moreover, there can be a discrepancy between the spouses in their respective time lines of the emotional process of divorce, resulting in a temporal discrepancy of up to several years in the acceptance of the divorce decision. Strong feelings that bind—love, dependence, fear—can alternate rapidly with strong feelings that divide—anger, hatred, resentment, revenge (Saposnek & Rose, 1990). One spouse, for example, called me before our first session demanding assurance that she would be permitted to enter the mediation office before her former husband arrived so that she would not have to be together with him in the parking lot, since, she said, he was "violent and assaultive" and she feared for her life. She declined the offer to have a support person or even separate sessions (it is required of California court mediators to offer these safeguards in cases with a history of domestic violence). Then she arrived for the first session in a car driven by her ex-husband, held hands with him in the parking lot before the session, and spent a good part of the session, as well as later on the phone with me, praising him for his kindness. They reached an amicable settlement in the next session.

Such ambivalence is not unheard of by marital therapists, who may spend six months supporting a woman's decision to leave a "cruel and inconsiderate" husband, only to have her cancel the next appointment because she has reunited with him. However, when such a move occurs within a week of hearing what might be considered life-threatening concerns, the contrast can be disorienting to the mediator. It should be noted that battered women often fear confronting their abuser, placing the mediator in an ethically awkward position. For if the client, after being fully informed about and offered safeguards for her protection, declines to accept them, does the mediator have a duty to reject her decision and refuse to mediate, or should the mediator proceed under the assumption that the client is responsible for her own consequences? As of this writing, this issue is in full and controversial debate within the mediation community, with one side saying never mediate in cases of domestic violence and the other side saying that such cases can be successfully and safely mediated as long as the safeguards have been offered and provided. (This issue is discussed further in Chapter Fourteen.)

The transactions that take place between each spouse and his or her children, new spouse, parents, and friends between mediation sessions may also contribute to unpredictable behavior. For example, one man who had filed for sole custody of both his children and insisted in the first mediation session that he would settle for nothing less then came into the second session offering sole custody to his ex-wife. Although he gave a variety of inconsistent reasons for this action, it turned out that during the interim week, one of his children had unexpectedly (and for equally inconsistent reasons) told him that he wanted to live with his mother. These words hurt the father deeply, so he reversed his position and tried to save face by offering pseudo-reasons for his action. In essence, he attempted to deal with his hurt feelings by depriving himself of his desired choice.

In another case, a father had agreed to a very reasonable and workable shared custody plan, only to arrive at the next session insisting on sole custody. During the interim week, his new wife had informed him that his ex-wife was taking advantage of him and that he had better go for sole custody to prove that he would not be pushed around. Such transactions are clearly beyond the control of the mediator but can result in puzzling sudden moves that hamper the mediation process.

Further contributing to unpredictability is the occasional poorly timed legal maneuver occurring right in the middle of the mediation process. For example, one man who had come to many constructive agreements with his ex-wife in the first mediation session refused to return for the next session. It turned out that during the interim week, he had received a subpoena for a court hearing on the custody issue. The secretary of his wife's lawyer, not knowing that mediation efforts were in progress, had mistakenly sent a subpoena to the husband as a matter of standard legal procedure. However, the husband interpreted this as power escalation by his wife, and he refused to cooperate any further in mediation. Even though he was given an adequate explanation, his trust had been irreparably damaged. Such mischances are not uncommon among courts and law offices during the mediation process. They often function as "disinformation" (Watzlawick, 1976), in that the perceived validity of certain information is determined by a particular context, making later evidence of its invalidity difficult to accept.

The unpredictability of a couple in mediation often leaves the mediator wishing that he or she could exert more control over the situation. A helpful axiom for mediators to follow is this: never expect a couple to be cooperative or uncooperative until the final agreement is fully signed. Or as Yogi Berra once said more eloquently, "It ain't over till it's over."

Even then, of course, there is no certainty of a predictable follow-through. The mediator really has no choice but to accept such unpredictability as the grandest challenge of the process. It has been my experience that when a mediator grapples with the most difficult cases first, the easier cases can be surprisingly enjoyable. It is with such a belief that this book is focused on the more difficult challenges presented in mediation, so that the reader may be comfortably prepared to deal with the easier ones.

Helpful Mediator Style

Because of the many special difficulties that arise in mediation work, it is necessary to bring certain attitudes and skills to the process. These contribute both to the effectiveness of mediation and to the survival of the mediator.

An effective child custody mediator's style might best be characterized as active, assertive, goal-oriented, and businesslike. The mediator must utilize the skills of brief behaviorally oriented family therapy, crisis intervention, negotiation, organizational development, and child development counseling, coupled with a sensitivity to the emotional and psychological aspects of the mediation process. The mediator must deal with the emotional aspects of the process without allowing them to disrupt the problem solving. Too tight control restricts the complexity of the emotional issues that need to be assessed, while too loose control allows the emotional charge to overwhelm the rational structure needed to reach resolution. There is a thin line between these extremes that the skilled mediator learns to walk.

The mediator must truly enjoy skilled, controlled problem solving. Because of the unpredictable and sudden moves often made by the couple in mediation, the mediator must be prepared at all times to respond appropriately and instantaneously to each crisis as it arises. Since there is so much at stake at each crisis point, there is little room for error on the part of the mediator. Each intervention must be at once well thought out, accurately timed, and rapidly implemented. These requirements necessitate that the mediator possess both the professional skills and the emotional stability demanded of a psychotherapist. The mediator must be capable of leading a hostile couple away from antagonism and into cooperative areas of negotiation. Mediators who cannot tolerate open and intense conflict will burn out quickly and, moreover, may cause irreparable damage to the couple's potential for future negotiation.

While potential negative effects of psychotherapy on clients have been documented (Strupp, Hadley, & Gomes-Schwarz, 1977), potential negative effects of mediation on couples are as yet unknown. However, we can speculate that if a psychotherapy client experiencing such effects can become discouraged or turned off to the possibility of obtaining future help (as most therapists have discovered to be the case), negative effects from a mediation experience may have an even greater impact, considering the intensity of emotions involved, the enormous personal significance of the issues at stake, and the extraordinary necessity—and difficulty—of the mediator's maintaining a balance between the couple at every point throughout the mediation process. Hence it is incumbent on the mediator to maximize the probability of a satisfying resolution to the mediated issues by being properly prepared. It should be kept in mind, however, that successful resolution is at times well out of the control of even the most skillful mediator.

Maintaining Functional Perspective

The mediator needs to maintain a functional perspective in dealing with the interactional dynamics that are the grist of the mediation process. A functional perspective deals with the effect that a particular behavioral sequence has on interpersonal interactions. For example, suppose that a father insists on having the children live with him exactly 50 percent of every week, is unwilling to compromise, and is willing to go to court to fight for this plan, even though such a schedule of time sharing would be inconvenient for all the parties involved, including himself. Regardless of his real motives (which might be based on power assertion and/or revenge and retaliation strategies; see Chapter Nine), his behavior has the effect of scaring the mother into protecting her own relationship with the children. She may then come back with an insistence on sole custody (which might be based on an emotional survival strategy; see Chapter Nine). Her behavior is likely to escalate the conflict, which could have the effect of scaring the children into defusing the tension between their parents through the use of a tension-detonating strategy (see Chapter Eight). The children's behavior might have the effect of further polarizing their parents' positions, since the parents might each interpret the children's behavior as evidence for the validity of their own respective positions.

Throughout, each member's behavior can be viewed simply in terms of its functional effect on the other members. Such a perspective circumvents the moot theoretical questions of whether a particular behavior is conscious or unconscious, intentional or impulsive, normal or psychopathological. When the tactics that children and spouses employ are described functionally, they can be used by the mediator to form specific intervention strategies of his or her own that serve to direct the course of mediation more sensitively. Such a functional perspective helps the mediator maintain objectivity, since particular strategies are intrinsically neither good nor bad, honest nor dishonest, right nor wrong, but merely serve to influence the thoughts, feelings, and/or behavior of other persons. Working from this perspective, the mediator does not feel so inclined to judge the participants, which would risk bias and the loss of neutrality. By understanding the participants' strategies, the mediator can plan counterstrategies to facilitate a constructive outcome.

Being Nonjudgmental

It is very important that the mediator maintain a nonjudgmental attitude. Each spouse frequently attempts to tell the mediator negative things about the other spouse, implicitly and explicitly trying to sway the mediator's sympathies. In order not to succumb, the mediator needs to understand fully the dynamics of marital and family interactions so that when empathy is elicited from the mediator, it can be put into a helpful systems perspective. If the mediator becomes overtly critical of one of the spouses, the impartiality necessary for a successful resolution will be lost. Clearly, no intervenor is devoid of personal reactions and values, yet the necessity for keeping them out of the mediation process is paramount.

The ability to remain nonjudgmental also requires that the mediator be aware of, and reasonably resolved about, his or her own familial issues and personal values, which might be aroused in the course of mediation.

Issues arise in custody disputes that touch every person on some level. The mediator is confronted with a broad range of emotional triggers—from the overt pain of children and parents going through divorce to the mediator's covert personal response to allegations of child neglect or molestation, alcoholism, or drug abuse. Moreover, it may be difficult for the mediator to deal fairly with spouses who have authoritarian child-rearing practices, religious beliefs that seem extreme or destructive to healthy child development, or vengeful motives for spending time with their child. These issues can elicit what psychoanalytical theory refers to as "countertransference reactions" and lead a mediator away from the task of fair management of the dispute. Keeping such reactions in check is especially important in mediation work because, unlike psychotherapy, there is little or no time to digest or even dissipate such reactions. They must be dealt with immediately and thoroughly by the mediator, since the expression of such reactions has no useful place in the mediation process. Allowing a personal reaction such as anger to intrude into the mediation process can unnecessarily prolong it, complicate it, or cause it to fail—ultimately, in most cases, at greater cost to the children involved. Hence although there are strategic ways to ensure greater degrees of physical and emotional protection for the children within the final settlement (see Chapter Six), the mediator must be able to accept a wide variety of lifestyles and child-rearing practices and not feel that the only good ones are the ones he or she values.

The mediator must function as a diplomat, allowing each family member equal protection for his or her vulnerability throughout the mediation process. Each member must be given the maximum opportunity to save face in the midst of the threats and accusations that are frequently thrown about. A successful resolution can best come about when both the spouses and the children feel reasonably secure and esteemed. The message "you are not lovable" often rings through the house of the divorcing family. Each spouse may offer proof of this statement, and the children may absorb it as an assumption about themselves that is a natural outcome of the divorce itself. Hence the mediator must work diplomatically to minimize any judgments and criticisms proffered about the spouse by the person who knows all of his or her faults better than anyone else, the ex-spouse.

Maintaining Scientific Objectivity

The most effective way to ensure objectivity in the mediation process is to adopt a sensitive scientific approach to the task. Each session of the mediation process can be viewed as a mini-experiment. Each case begins against a backdrop of previously known patterns to mediated settlements of custody disputes. And each case also begins with a set of new data unique to the particular family involved. The initial data collected before mediation begins generate hypotheses that are then tested in mediation, and the feedback that is obtained is used to generate new hypotheses about each family member's strategies, real needs, and likely acceptable outcomes. When the mediator has clear evidence that he or she has generated enough useful hypotheses, negotiations are begun for the creation of the final product—a balanced, workable settlement. This scientific, methodical attitude helps the mediator stay objective, calculate each next move carefully, and remain skeptical of the validity of any sudden changes in a family member's position until he or she is satisfied that the new data are indeed valid and not just artifacts of a temporary emotional state.

Although the scientific aspect of this attitude is essential, it must always be complemented by the aspect of *sensitivity*. Support for and understanding of the psychological and emotional state in which each spouse appears to be and sensitivity to the pace needed for the process to unfold properly may be key factors in the long-term stability of any final decisions made by the couple. Whereas a strictly mechanical, scientific approach might result in further alienation of the couple, a sensitive scientific approach will maximize efficient human contact throughout the mediation process. I took this notion further by noting that "mediation is both a science and an art" (Saposnek, 1993a, p. 5). Elaborating on the methods of the artistic or sensitive aspect, I included the necessity of facilitating communication and promoting empathy, reframing conflict, moving energy within the process (viewing the mediation session as a field of energy and regarding conflict and impasses as energy that has become stuck), and recognizing the importance of timing of interventions. All of these features are significant as the essential fine tuning to the mechanics of mediation (the scientific aspect). When both the science and the art are blended well, the benefits of mediation are optimized.

Uniqueness of Custody Mediation

It is also important for the mediator to acknowledge the uniqueness of the content of child custody mediation. Some generic mediators—working in such areas as tenant-landlord disputes, small-claims disputes, consumer-seller disputes, and collective bargaining disputes—believe that the skills they utilize in their work are sufficient for child custody mediation. While it may be true that such general mediation skills are necessary for child custody mediation work, they are not sufficient. Child custody mediation is a very special type of mediation. The mediator must be competent to give valid, current, and helpful information about child development, about children's typical and atypical responses to family conflicts, about family members' needs and feelings, about family dynamics, about the divorce process (emotionally, structurally, and legally), and about the likely future outcomes for children and parents of a variety of different postdivorce family structures. The mediator should be knowledgeable about individual psychodynamics, interactional dynamics, family systems, and behavior change and should have a broad general knowledge of psychological functioning of both adults and children of various ages. Child custody mediators who are not specifically trained in these areas may seriously compromise the benefits of child custody mediation.

Wallerstein and Kelly (1980) emphasized, early on, that the mediator must remain an advocate for the children. Although this point may seem obvious, it has actually been quite controversial in the development of the field of family mediation. Theoretical positions on this issue have had a wide range. At one end of the continuum are theorists who believe that the mediator should be a strictly neutral facilitator of the couple's negotiations, with no substantive content ever contributed by the mediator. In this model, if the couple ask the mediator whether a particular coparenting schedule is likely to damage their child, the mediator should refer the couple to a child psychologist for an answer (Haynes, 1988, 1994). At the other end of the continuum are theorists who believe that child custody mediators should be strong advocates for children and should provide the parents with whatever current knowledge and perspectives are available about the needs of children in divorce. In this model, the mediator is expected to defend the psychological and developmental needs of the children and actively educate the parents about these matters (Wallerstein, 1991; Wallerstein & Kelly, 1980; Saposnek, 1985, 1991b, 1992). Most mediators are somewhere between the two extremes of this continuum.

This theoretical debate appears, though, to pertain more to mediators in the private sector, since those in the public sector often have statutory guidelines that inform their role. For example, under California's mandatory mediation statute, Civil Code Sec. 4607.1 states: "The Legislature finds and declares that the mediation of cases involving custody and visitation concerning children should be governed by uniform standards of practice . . . [which] shall include . . . provision for the best interests of the child and the safeguarding of the rights of the child to frequent and continuing contact with both parents." It is clear that such a mandate is at the "advocacy for children" end of the theoretical continuum. This mandate for child advocacy was further bolstered by language in the legislatively mandated creation of the Uniform Standards of Practice for Court-Connected Child Custody Mediation for the State of California [see Appendix A, especially section (c)(2)], which took effect January 1, 1991, and now guides California court-connected child custody mediators' practice (Norton, Weiss, Ricci, & Fielding, 1992).

The traditional adversarial approach to child custody determination has failed to provide meaningful advocacy for the children of divorcing parents. Attempts have been made to provide legal counsel for children in custody proceedings (Shears, 1996, gives an excellent review of the complex issues regarding this practice), but the legal system so far has not been able to clarify an appropriate place for the needs and wishes of the child in the adversarial scheme. Moreover, the lawyers who typically are assigned the task of legal advocacy for the child usually have no special training for this task and therefore are not necessarily more knowledgeable about or sensitive to the needs and feelings of children than the judges or the parents' own attorneys. Hence the attorney for the child bears the risk of impeding the legal process and confusing rather than clarifying the issues.

If the mediator is to be a helpful advocate for the children, it is incumbent on him or her to be fully knowledgeable about how children think, feel, and act during and after a divorce, as well as in different stages of development. Using only intuitively gleaned assumptions about what the child is experiencing is not enough; indeed, often it is just such assumptions made by parents that lead to court battles (see Chapter Eight). Acting on incorrect assumptions can have devastating consequences. Hence both insight and information about children are essential. While this book can provide perspectives, information, and strategies, supervised training is necessary before one can competently carry out the tremendous responsibilities involved in child custody mediation.

Collaborative Professional Support

A final important attitude in mediation is the degree of positive conviction held by judges and attorneys about the potential effectiveness of child custody mediation. Even after several years of successful voluntary mediation (arranged by attorneys) and a year of successful involuntary mediation (legislatively mandated), numerous judges and lawyers in the state of California remained skeptical about mediation's potential for resolving custody and visitation disputes. This attitude was grounded in a persistent belief that spouses who are divorced or divorcing with a contestation about custody cannot even talk constructively with each other, let alone agree on issues as important as custody. At bottom, this myth assumes that if the spouses could talk constructively and civilly with each other, they would not have gotten divorced in the first place. One attorney who, along with the opposing counsel, sat in on his first mediation session involving a client (the mother), commented afterward, "I was astounded to see them actually talking nicely and constructively with each other after what I've heard about that s.o.b. from the mother." It is the adversarial approach to such disputes that has perpetuated these myths in the past. Since there was no opportunity for nonadversarial approaches, no cooperative solutions were forthcoming. It was therefore concluded that given the hostility surrounding custody battles, cooperative solutions were not possible. However, once the opportunity arises, new solutions are possible.

Without the support of judges and attorneys, the mediation process is extremely difficult. When the mediator is working against an upcoming court date and against attorneys who are discouraging their clients and expressing resistance to mediation, either spouse, encountering the slightest frustration in a session, may run back to his or her attorney and say, "Let's go to court. I don't like what she (he) said." Or knowing that the court date is coming up next week, the spouse might simply sit through the mediation sessions and passively resist all requests for a compromise. With the support of the legal representatives, the process becomes significantly easier. When a judge is willing, indefinitely, to continue the court date for custody determination and when both attorneys in the case are firmly and strongly supportive of the mediation efforts, the mediator's task is markedly easier, and mediation proceeds much more effectively.*

Differences Between Mediation, Therapy, and Adversarial Law

Part of the challenge of mediation is its attempt to stand between adversarial law practice and psychotherapy. Mediation work requires the precision and strategic thinking of legal work, coupled with the insightfulness,

---

*Justice Donald B. King, retired associate justice of the First Appellate Court, Fifth Division, of the state of California, exemplified the ideal degree of legal support offered for mediation, beginning several years before California's mandatory mediation. When he was a serving as a Superior Court judge in San Francisco, he required all couples with custody or visitation disputes to settle their disputes with their attorneys or a family court mediator before the judge would hear the rest of their dissolution proceedings. He reported a more than 99 percent success rate for such mediation efforts, with success defined as settling the present dispute and not returning to court with similar future disputes (King, 1979).

emotional sensitivity, and supportiveness of psychotherapy. In other ways, however, mediation differs from law and psychotherapy, and the dissimilarities are worth elaborating here, since failures in mediation are often due to the mediator unintentionally slipping into one of the other roles.

The task of lawyers functioning in an adversarial role is to protect their client's legal rights and to maximize the client's leverage within a dispute through various legal maneuvers. In his excellent article, Brown (1982) cites severe criticisms of the adversarial system by a wide variety of professionals who work in the domestic relations field. Among these are the perspectives of Felder (1971, pp. 1–2), a prominent divorce lawyer:

> I am in business to win. . . . Once I have been hired, my sole aim is to gain victory; and in doing so, I will do anything and everything I think necessary to serve the interests of my client, to achieve his purpose, to gain him a divorce in which he will come out financially, psychologically, in every way on top. That is what I have been hired to do and if in doing it, I appear cold and calculating, then that's the way it has to be. I am tough because I assume the lawyer who opposes me will also be tough [and] when I take a case, I am not concerned with whether my client is always right. As far as I am concerned, a client is always right.

Unfortunately, though Felder asserted this more than a quarter century ago, his perspective remains contemporary for all too many family law attorneys. From this perspective, the term *family law* comes across as an oxymoron.

This martial attitude is firmly trained into lawyers and gets reinforced ethically, through peer esteem, and financially, through winning clients. Moreover, if a lawyer does not advocate to the fullest extent possible for his client alone (typically one parent), he is failing to live up to the American Bar Association's canon of ethics, which specifically requires him to represent only one party in a dispute, with the understanding that the other party is entitled to full representation by separate counsel. Hence within the adversarial system, a lawyer who eases up on advocacy for his client in a custody dispute, because he understands the systemic nature of such disputes and empathizes with the pain and injustice experienced by the other spouse and the child, may be accused of questionable ethical practices. This clearly places the adversarial lawyer in a difficult position. While personally he may fully appreciate the destructive nature of adversarial efforts to resolve such domestic issues, professionally he is ethically bound to perpetuate such destructiveness.

The lawyer's dilemma is resolved when he assumes a mediator's role. In this role, he can step out of his advocacy position and can work with both spouses simultaneously, legally representing neither of them but letting them know that each has the right to seek separate attorneys if they feel the need for a legal advocate. However, when lawyers are functioning as mediators with divorcing parents, they must work against their professional reflexes to advocate, defend, argue, and win. Lawyers must view success not as their client winning but as the children winning. The errors made by lawyers doing mediation are typically in the direction of either subtly advocating for one of the parents and leaving the other parent feeling unsupported or excessively exploring the feelings of one or both of the clients to such a degree that more distress than constructive emotional venting is experienced. Often the lawyer attempts to deal with the emotions but may have inadequate training and skills to work through them sufficiently so that negotiation efforts can get on their way. The error in the first case is in behaving too much like a lawyer, and the error in the second is in behaving too much like a therapist. In both cases, the approach is inappropriate and may result in failure of the mediation effort.

A middle role between the adversarial lawyer and the mediating lawyer is what has been termed the "collaborative family law practitioner" (Rose, 1996). This new and emerging role is based upon the premise that lawyers who work collaboratively rather than competitively will more likely reach a settlement for their clients (see Kressel, 1985). Both attorneys stipulate in a written agreement not to litigate any aspect of the case and to remove themselves from the case if their client insists on litigating. Within such an explicitly safe structure, more successful settlements are reached that are beneficial to both parties and to the children. Collaborative negotiation provides client control of the process and outcome, generates the widest range of settlement possibilities before decision making, allows parties to speak and to be heard, creates a safe environment in which to communicate, and maximizes each party's satisfaction. Thus this approach has most of the benefits of mediation yet operates with two attorneys representing their respective clients.

From the bench, King (1993) presented a parallel experimental innovation in family law cases, "judicial hands-on case management," which, by simplifying family law procedures, eliminates the negative aspects of the adversarial system. He utilized telephone conference calls instead of court appearances and cut costs for the clients by eliminating expensive court hearings and reducing the need for court staffing, secretaries, bailiffs, court reporters, courtrooms, and so forth. His experiment was highly successful in supporting collaborative, settlement-oriented resolutions to family law disputes.

In contrast to the task of traditional lawyers, and in many important ways different from a mediator, the psychotherapist has the goal of helping her client understand and deal more effectively with emotional distress and behavioral problems. Usually the therapist offers a great deal of support to the client (who, typically, is defined as the person who makes the appointment and pays for the therapy), and this unilateral support may well continue even if another significant person in the client's life is brought into the therapy (for example, a spouse). Or if a couple begin therapy together and then, out of discontent, one of the spouses drops out of the therapy, it is not uncommon for a psychotherapist to give the remaining spouse her full support in continued individual therapy. Clearly, traditional psychotherapy practice is based upon an individual rather than a systems model of intervention, and thus, even when working with a couple, the therapist conceptually views the couple as two separate individuals with, perhaps, interdependent needs.

In most traditional forms of psychotherapy, the therapeutic process is open-ended, time-unlimited, and exploratory, and it may continue until an unstated end point is reached (most often when the client drops out of therapy). Kelly (1983) notes that unlike the mediator, the therapist assumes responsibility for improving the mental health of the client, expands the exploration of personal meanings and interpretations of feelings and interactions, explores conflict toward resolution rather than managing conflict (as a mediator does), gathers detailed individual histories, and explores the past. She also points out that even therapists who work from a family systems or short-term crisis model differ from mediators in their goals, tasks, and methods by which they work. Irving and Benjamin (1995) further note that family therapy "seeks to produce enduring change while leaving the integrity of the family system intact," whereas family mediation "seeks to alter marital interaction only insofar as this promotes viable negotiation between relatively equal parties" (p. 207).

A therapist typically also has much more information about the couple or family with which to work, is not under any time pressure for resolving the problems (the exception being, perhaps, the restraints of services offered under current managed-care paradigms), and, being out of the "shadow of the law," needs no support from judges or attorneys to carry on the therapeutic work effectively. Furthermore, because of this, the therapist enjoys a reasonable degree of client predictability, both within a given session and between sessions. Hence a great deal of the confusion and stress that mediators experience in their work is typically not present in psychotherapy.

The mediator is in a unique position in relation to both the lawyer and the therapist. She is an advocate for the children but not for either parent. She has an explicit goal to achieve within a clearly designated structure and in a relatively brief time period. She may give support to either spouse, as long as equal support is always offered to the other spouse. And she must always remain impartial, balanced, and objective in all interventions, from the first phone call to the final signing of the written agreement. Emotions are dealt with only to the degree that such intervention contributes to the creation of the final written agreement, but not for any purpose of facilitating personal growth or solving any personal emotional problems. Excessive emotional venting is considered a potentially disruptive event to the mediation process and is channeled into constructive negotiations. This approach is unlike that of therapy, in which such venting might be viewed as a goal in itself.

These differences between mediation and therapy are important to note because of their practical, theoretical, and ethical implications (see also Dworkin, Jacob, & Scott, 1991; Gold, 1985; Haynes, 1992; Saposnek, 1986b). When one is mediating custody and visitation disputes, according to the structure offered in this book, it is very important not to slip into the role of the traditional therapist but to maintain the mediator role throughout the process. Because of the emotionally volatile nature of custody disputes and because the mediator must remain a neutral advocate for the children, it is extremely difficult for the mediator to be concerned with the needs of one or both spouses to the degree necessary for significant psychotherapeutic benefit to them.

It should be noted, though, that within the mediation process with couples who are clearly at an emotional impasse, if the mediator has the requisite skills and training, systemic therapeutic interventions can be selectively utilized to clarify and focus the specific emotional issues underlying the impasse. However, this is not psychotherapy. These are merely brief therapeutic interventions around specific emotional issues with the clear purpose of attempting to prepare a couple emotionally for the negotiation phase of mediation or to get past an emotionally rooted impasse so that effective negotiations can proceed to agreement. Such therapeutic intervention models have been described by Irving and Benjamin (1995), who present a comprehensive therapeutic premediation process that precedes the negotiations, and by Johnston and Campbell (1988), who present a comprehensive therapeutic approach to mediation with high-conflict families called *impasse-directed mediation,* and in less comprehensive form by Milne (1978) and Waldron, Roth, Fair, Mann, and McDermott (1984). (For a fascinating debate regarding the notion of "therapeutic mediation" that occurred in *ConflictNet,* an Internet service that gives access to conflict resolution organizations worldwide, see McIsaac, 1994.)

Of course, with any of these models, if it appears that either or both spouses need more intensive psychotherapy before they will be able to negotiate effectively in mediation, the mediator would make an appropriate referral to a marital or family therapist, preferably one who is knowledgeable about the mediation process and is able to sustain the family systems view while working on the emotional issues.

4

THE STRATEGIC APPROACH

AIKIDO AS A MODEL FOR MEDIATION

THE MODEL OF INTERVENTION put forth in this book is a *strategic* approach, derived from the concepts of strategic therapy, a system of therapy for individuals and families that is based on nontraditional concepts, assumptions, and techniques of change (Fisch, Weakland, & Segal, 1982; Haley, 1963, 1973, 1976; Madanes, 1981; Watzlawick, Weakland, & Fisch, 1974). Haley (1973) most succinctly characterized strategic therapy as follows:

> Therapy can be called strategic if the clinician initiates what happens during therapy and designs a particular approach for each problem. When a therapist and a person with a problem encounter each other, the action that takes place is determined by both of them, but in strategic therapy the initiative is largely taken by the therapist. He must identify solvable problems, set goals, design interventions to achieve those goals, examine the responses he receives to correct his approach, and ultimately examine the outcome of his therapy to see if it has been effective. The therapist must be acutely sensitive and responsive to the patient and his social field, but how he proceeds must be determined by himself [p. 17].

In essence, this approach to change is active, directive, organized, goal oriented, and systemic in its scope, and it requires skill in observing people and the complex ways they communicate; skill in motivating and in-

This chapter is an adaptation of Saposnek (1986a).

fluencing people indirectly by one's own words, intonations, and body language; and acceptance of the responsibility for the clients' behavioral change. The similarities of this early description of strategic therapy to how an effective child custody mediator approaches cases are compelling. In fact, such applications of the techniques of strategic therapy to mediation have now been well described in the mediation literature (Amundson & Fong, 1986; Gadlin & Ouellette, 1986; Isaacs, Montalvo, & Abelsohn, 1986; Johnston & Campbell, 1988; Saposnek, 1983; Sargent & Moss, 1986).

It should be pointed out, however, that not all psychotherapy cases need strategic therapy. Some people come to a therapist simply needing information or support for helping them get through a crisis. They have very little resistance to change; they simply need some expert guidance through it. Similarly, not all mediation cases need strategic mediation. While strategic *thinking* is always useful in mediation, the powerful techniques that derive from it are not always necessary to use in mediation. Some cases are quite benign, involving nonconflicted couples who are in mediation just to have a forum for working out the details of their parenting plan between themselves and to get expert advice on how to optimize the effective coparenting of their children following divorce. They have no particular disputes of substance; they just seek guidance and input from a divorce professional. In such cases, a very straightforward educational approach to mediation is quite sufficient. No fancy or powerful techniques or approaches are needed. Strategic techniques are most useful with cases in which conflict is moderate to high and where the parents tend to lock in to positions that prevent them from achieving their respective goals.

Thinking Strategically

In applying the specific techniques that will be described in the following chapters, the mediator must begin to *think strategically*. This means maintaining an organized and goal-directed but flexible thought process that allows the mediator, in the face of obstacles, to shift gears, change tactics, and continue moving toward a preplanned goal. Watzlawick et al. (1974) observed that when people are stuck in a problem, they often attempt to solve the problem by doing "more of the same." Unfortunately, that tactic simply entrenches the problem further. An adage of brief strategic therapy is that "the problem is the attempted solution." This holds as well for mediators who are trying to help couples resolve their disputes. Thus mediators need to remember what might seem obvious, that when a particular technique does not lead the clients in the direction of the desired goal, one should not do "more of the same" but should instead shift gears and seek an alternate route to the goal. Maintaining a stance of "eclectic flexibility" optimizes the effective use of a range of strategies.

Using a Systemic Approach

A backyard mechanic and a master mechanic both use basic mechanics' techniques for fixing cars. They both use wrenches, screwdrivers, pliers, and electronic scopes. However, when the backyard mechanic applies a screwdriver to remove a rusted engine part and the part will not budge, he may not have an alternative plan and may give up in desperation, feeling hopeless and incompetent. In contrast, the master car mechanic may also begin by using the screwdriver, but when it fails to work, he generates other solutions, perhaps by removing the carburetor and the fuel injector hoses and then using a locking pliers and a small crowbar in combination as he reaches the rusted part from underneath the engine. This solution might never have occurred to the backyard mechanic.

Master car mechanics and master mediators have at least one thing in common: they both approach problems with strategies developed from a systems point of view. Rather than settling on the backyard mechanic's simple goal of "using the screwdriver to remove the rusted part," the master mechanic sets his goal as "removing the rusted part." Eyeing this broader goal, he plans a strategy that takes into account his knowledge of the other systems of the car and eclectically uses whatever specific techniques are necessary to get the job done. The use of specific techniques is not the goal. The techniques are only the means for achieving the larger goals.

Similarly, the master mediator does not use "techniques" in isolation. She uses them in combinations that together formulate a strategy within a larger context of the goals of the mediation. An exclusively technique-based mediation will work for some cases some of the time but will fail with more complex cases unless the mediator can flexibly switch techniques to accommodate the need.

Interventions with a Goal

Another important aspect of strategic thinking is that each intervention by the mediator ought to lead the clients a step closer to the goal. Terminal techniques, those that lead nowhere, are at best wasteful of mediation time and at worst inflammatory. Often mediators will use a technique without having thought out the several possible ways that the client can react to it. Strategic thinking is like three-dimensional chess. Before enacting each intervention, the mediator must think several steps ahead, anticipating the spouse's possible reactions, the other spouse's possible reactions to the first spouse's reactions, and then the position in which each will be upon beginning the next intervention. In effective strategic mediation, every intervention is planned for a certain anticipated reaction. As such, this approach is similar to the lawyers' methods of effective cross-examination in a courtroom. Every trial lawyer knows the wisdom in the motto "Never ask a question to which you don't already know the answer."

The Importance of Timing

Having a thorough knowledge of the process and structure of mediation and a full set of effective techniques, a mediator will be unable to help parents resolve their disputes unless she also has a sense of timing. Timing is the sensitivity to recognize when to move into action with a particular strategy and when to wait. One develops a sense of timing through experience by trusting one's instinctual reactions while making an accurate assessment of the dynamics of the case.

Castrey and Castrey (1987) observed that experienced mediators can sense the key to settlement very early in the process. However, even if the mediator's sense is correct, the solution will not be accepted until the conditions are right. It is crucial to wait for the correct conditions to arise before the potential solution is presented, because if the timing is off, the solution can backfire.

The importance of effective timing is poignantly characterized by a legendary story of a steam-engine train engineer in England. It seems that the steam engine of an important commuter train quit working one day and the train would not run. After having many local train engineers look at it, the train company summoned a well-known retired train engineer. Upon accepting the job, the engineer went to a local hardware store, purchased a hammer, went to the stalled train engine, and, after spending about five minutes looking and listening to the train engine struggling to start, walked over to a certain spot on the side of the engine and, at just the right moment, lifted his hammer and gave it one slight rap. Immediately the engine began running once again. Five days later, the train company received a bill from the engineer requesting a fee of £10,000. The president of the company, dismayed at what he considered an outrageous fee, phoned the engineer and asked, "How can you charge us £10,000 for just five minutes' work?" The engineer replied that he would reconsider and send another bill. A week later, the company received a revised bill that read: "Purchase of hammer: £5. Knowing when and where to use it: £9,995"!

Timing, indeed, is a precious and essential skill, whether one is fixing a steam engine or resolving a custody dispute. As such, it must be respected and nurtured in learning to be an effective mediator.

Strategic Interactional Questions

Direct questions, such as "What is the current time-sharing schedule of the children, Amy?" or "When was your divorce finalized?" are necessary and appropriate for getting factual information at various points in the mediation process. However, interactional questions, such as "Richard, what do you think Sarah felt when you just said that?" or "Sarah, what do you think Richard has been going through since you left the house?" or "Carolyn, how do think Billy feels about his dad?" are questions that ask one person to speculate about what another person thinks or feels regarding a given matter. As such, they are more strategic in nature and can be used to gather purely interactional information (which gives information about the nature of their relationship and thus leverage for influencing the participants toward resolution of the dispute).

These interactional questions, also referred to in the literature as *circular questions* (Gadlin & Ouellette, 1986; Selvini Palazzoli, Cecchin, Prata, and Boscolo, 1980; Tomm, 1985), give the mediator and the couple a perspective on the dynamics of the family system—how each member views and influences each other member of the family. Using such questions may seem to violate the traditional mediation rule of having each person speak only for himself or herself in response to direct questions. However, as Gadlin and Ouellette note, the use of direct questions "can serve to intensify a disputant's attachment to his or her own point of view, to entrench the disputant in the position, to increase the disputant's defensiveness when it is the other party's turn to speak. At the very least, it reinforces an individualistic, cause-effect, win-lose, blame-attributing perspective on the conflict" (1986, p. 109). While there certainly is a solid place for direct questions in mediation, asking interactional or circular questions can serve as a powerful technique for moving a session straight into the underlying dynamics of the custody dispute.

Cross Talk and Side Talk

Similar to strategic interactional questions are two other techniques that are useful. *Cross talk* is a technique whereby the mediator talks about one spouse to the other spouse so that the one spouse can "overhear" important personal information or insights without having to resist it. For example, a mediator might say (to Mother, in the presence of Father), "Fran, you know, it's pretty clear to me that Dave loves his kids very much and that they love him, but I'm not sure that he understands that forcing them to stay at his house when he's not there is very likely to turn them off to wanting to see him. I'm wondering if the children have ever been able to share that with him. I'd sure hate to see him have to learn the hard way, like so many unfortunate parents I have seen in here." At this point, the mediator quickly changes the subject and lets Dave digest what he has heard.

A similar kind of communication, using what we will term as *side talk,* can take place when there are two mediators in the session. At an appropriate moment, one mediator can turn to the other mediator and make the same comment for Dave to overhear.

Strategically Challenging with Support

Throughout the mediation process, there are points at which the mediator must confront one or both parents. These are points at which one or the other parent is being intimidating, threatening, overpowering, stubborn, passive-aggressive, or challenging the mediator for control of the session or when both parents are locked into an unproductive or escalating verbal battle.

There are basically two ways in which the mediator can confront clients. One way is to challenge their words, behavior, or attitude directly. For example, the mediator might say, "Phil, please stop those threats and let's get down to business. Your children aren't going to benefit from that kind of behavior. I know you can do better communicating than that." Though straightforward, direct confrontation can be quite risky. If the mediator knows the client to be reasonable and predictable and can accurately anticipate the likely response, the risks are reduced. However, if the client is not known or is unpredictable, direct confrontation can enrage the client and could result in a face-saving bolting from the room or, worse, a physical assault on the mediator or the other parent.

The second way to confront is indirectly, or strategically. With this method, the client hears the point, with built-in support and therefore with a diminished desire to continue more of the same. For example, the mediator could say, "Phil, I'm really impressed with how much you must care about your children. *(pause)* . . . I bet they'd feel really proud of you for defending what you believe is right for them *(pause)* . . . even if it involves attacking their mother, whom they really love." Or the mediator could say, "Phil, I am really impressed with what a powerful man you are. I wonder if you would be willing to help me learn how you'll be able to get Nancy to hear your point by continuing to use your power in that particular way."

Carl Whitaker, the renowned family therapist, was reputed to be a master at strategic confrontations. In one instance, with a man who was being dishonest with his wife, Whitaker looked at him and said, "Keith, I think you're a damn liar!" When Keith flared up and aggressively challenged Whitaker with "Are you calling me a liar?" Whitaker calmly replied, "No, I don't know if you're a liar or not; I just *think* you are." In this manner, Whitaker make his point strategically while disclaiming that his assertion was a direct confrontation.

Aikido

In an earlier publication (Saposnek, 1980), I drew parallels between brief strategic therapy and the martial art system of *aikido*. The power of both systems for effecting change in behavior, attitudes, and emotions is impressive and unique. Because of their power in influencing change, it seemed worthy to pursue their applications to the more difficult arena of child custody mediation. This discussion integrates the strategic approach detailed earlier in this chapter and presents the parallels between this practical graphic model and mediation practice.

Aikido is a Japanese art of self-defense founded some fifty years ago by the late master Morihei Ueshiba (Stevens, 1985). Derived from a synthesis and adaptation of many martial art systems, it is based on ethical considerations contained in Eastern religious and philosophical thought, but it differs from other self-defense methods in its essential motivations and intents. In contrast to other self-defense approaches, aikido, when used in its highest ethical forms, aims merely to neutralize and harmlessly redirect the aggression of the attacker; nobody is harmed in the encounter. The word *aikido* (composed of three characters in Japanese) means the method or way *(do)* for the coordination or harmony *(ai)* of mental energy or spirit *(ki)*. Because of the strong humanistic and nonviolent values in the philosophical roots of aikido, it serves well as a contemporary model for conflict resolution (Crum, 1987; Dobson & Miller, 1993; Heckler, 1985; Ueshiba, 1984). The applications to mediation are obvious. Before expanding on these applications, it seems helpful to explore the similarities between aikido and mediation.

Contextual Similarities Between Aikido and Mediation

The context of aikido is one in which a person or persons approach the aikidoist with an intended challenge. By his actions, the challenger states,

"I am challenging you to deal with me and to try to change me. I will prove that you cannot and that I am more powerful than you." The aikidoist perceives this challenge not as a competitive or conflictual one but rather as an opportunity both to learn about and to teach the challenger more constructive and less harmful ways of asserting his energy. Hence the aikidoist functions as a teacher, and when the challenger approaches, the aikidoist uses special techniques to teach the challenger that it is futile and unkind to challenge aggressively, and the aikidoist tries to send the challenger away, as briefly and harmlessly as possible, somewhat wiser.

Similarly, when a couple approach the mediator, it is as if the couple were saying, "We are challenging you to try to resolve our custody dispute. We will prove that you cannot and that we are more powerful than you. We are intent on fighting with each other until one of us conquers the other and wins the child." This intense resistance of couples to cease their conflict and free their child from the middle of their dispute is the core challenge to the mediator. Functioning as a skilled teacher, the mediator attempts to educate and maneuver the couple to use their energies to help rather than to hurt their child by developing more constructive interactions with each other.

Figure 4.1 illustrates the basic paradigm of the mediator as aikidoist entering between the struggling couple, turning and removing the child from between the parents, and maneuvering the parents around to a position in which they are side by side and facing their child.

Systems and Interactionist Approach

The aikidoist always views challenges from a systems perspective within a multilevel interactional context. The challenger is perceived in direct relation to the aikidoist, in relation to the immediate surroundings (especially to other challengers), in relation to spatial and temporal factors, and on the most abstract level in relation to all natural hierarchical levels. Moreover, the aikidoist's movements are circular, and the aikidoist always places himself or herself at the center of a dynamic sphere of interactions occurring around the periphery.

In contrast to the more linear judo axiom, "Push when pulled, and pull when pushed," the aikido axiom is "Turn when pushed, and enter when pulled." It is this spherical motion that gives aikido its dynamic and effective variety. The aikidoist spins, twirls, and rotates as he or she blends with and maintains control of the interactions of challengers. The aikidoist's body becomes like a spinning top, exquisitely maintaining its balance and by this motion spinning off or drawing in everything that it

Figure 4.1. Mediator as Aikidoist

touches. This motion has been compared to the natural phenomenon of a powerful whirlwind or whirlpool. By conceptualizing and utilizing forces in a circular, interactional fashion, the aikidoist's strategy no longer has an original cause or an original effect. In fact, it often is not even clear who is the attacker and who is being attacked. An aikido maneuver in action appears like a dance. It is graceful, smooth, subtle, and effective, both functionally and aesthetically. The quick blending of forces makes the cause-and-effect relationships indistinguishable. The only thing that is apparent is the circularity of forces blended together for mutual problem solving, that is, for neutralization of aggression and redirection of energies. Such a systems approach accords with the humanistic ethic of aikido, which attempts to eliminate the concepts of "enemy" and "bad person."

Similarly, viewing the couple's struggle from a systems theory perspective, the mediator perceives them in relationship to the numerous others who are typically involved in their dispute—the attorneys, judges, therapists, stepparents, grandparents, neighbors, and friends who may be actively, albeit unwittingly, fanning the flames of the dispute (Johnston & Campbell, 1986). Problems are viewed as residing not in individuals but in the interactions between the participants, including the children (Saposnek, 1983), in a causal, regularly patterned, systemic sequence of behavior. Once the mediator accepts the challenge of helping a couple resolve their dispute, he or she becomes a facilitator and contributor to the interactional sequence upon which the interventions are focused.

Using the mediator's unique centered position as leverage, the mediator proceeds to direct the ongoing interactional sequences in a more constructive way. The mediator can best be viewed as a verbal spinning top, maintaining conceptual balance while spinning off challenges, using reframing and distraction as well as a host of other techniques, and drawing on the couple's motivation by speaking their conceptual language. After maneuvering the interactions of the couple to a successful resolution of their dispute, the mediator withdraws from the ongoing system of interactions, respecting its integrity. Viewing people from such an interactionist position allows the mediator to function more comprehensively and effectively than he or she otherwise would. It compels the mediator to be aware of the consequences of interventions on the lives of other significant persons in the client's life, thereby increasing the mediator's effectiveness in achieving the best interests of the child and family.

To summarize, the circular view of causality in mediation closely parallels the circular movements and circular orientation of aikido to conflict resolution.

Knowledge of Attacks

The practice of aikido is not based solely on a thorough knowledge and mastery of the aikido techniques of neutralization but is constructed on an equally thorough familiarity with all the possible types and forms of attack, in accordance with the ancient Japanese axiom, "The very first requisite for defense is to know the enemy" (Westbrook & Ratti, 1974, p. 45). Comprehensive knowledge of the various parts, forms, and patterns of attack is essential because the attack contains the very elements that an aikido defensive strategy will use physically, functionally, and psychologically to neutralize the attempted aggression.

Similarly, an effective mediator must know the strategies of human functioning in general and of the participants in custody disputes in particular (Folberg & Taylor, 1984; Johnston & Campbell, 1988; Kressel, 1985; Schwartz & Kaslow, 1997; Saposnek, 1983). The mediator must (1) be able to perceive and assess the functional intents of a variety of verbal and nonverbal behaviors, (2) understand the paradoxical nature of ambivalence and the functional use of emotions in interpersonal relationships, and (3) be thoroughly familiar with and able to isolate and describe a wide range of interactional patterns and strategies that disputing parents use in resisting change and in influencing their spouses, children, therapists, mediators, attorneys, and judges. Such knowledge is crucial because the mediator may use strategies that are similar in form to the strategies used by the couple, but the mediator will extract only the functional aspects of those strategies and use them tactically to resolve rather than to escalate the dispute.

The Process of Defense

Every process of defense consists of three stages: perception, evaluation and decision, and reaction. The effectiveness of any defensive strategy depends largely on the time elapsed between the first inkling that an attack may be imminent and the defensive reaction. Aikido practice aims to train and refine the faculties to such an extent that perception, evaluation, decision, and reaction become almost simultaneous (Westbrook & Ratti, 1974).

In the stage of perception, on the most obvious sensory level, we may see someone preparing to attack, hear the attacker approaching, or feel the physical contact of the attacker's hold. On a more subtle level, we may sense something without being fully conscious of seeing or hearing anything menacing, yet we know that something is wrong. In the stage of evaluation and decision, we analyze the various elements of the attack— its dynamic momentum, its speed and direction—and we make a decision about the most appropriate technique to apply. In the stage of reaction, we use a specific aikido technique of neutralization to implement our decision.

As already noted, in the advanced student of aikido, the three stages are so nearly simultaneous that they seem to be one. The process of defense proceeds smoothly and culminates in the effective neutralization of the attack. A less skilled practitioner exhibits faulty perception, poor judgment, or an insufficient reaction, which does not result in the desired neutralization.

The parallels to mediation practice are evident. When a couple first come to challenge the mediator, the mediator perceives the degree of the challenge by the nature of the referral—is it a hot, emotionally loaded conflict that is ready to explode and that needs immediate attention, or is it a mild disagreement on some fine points of child-rearing practices that is relatively devoid of emotional volatility?

Next, in the evaluation and decision stage, the mediator analyzes the elements of the dispute. The mediator quickly assesses the motives of each parent, the degree to which the children are involved in the dispute, other hidden participants in the dispute, the parents' willingness to negotiate, the degree to which each participant is willing to compromise, the presence of important allegations by one parent against the other (for example, child abuse or alcoholism), the degree to which each parent accepts the divorce, and any other contributing elements (see Chapter Five for an elaboration of these elements).

Finally, in the reaction stage, the mediator selects the appropriate techniques of intervention. These techniques (see Chapters Ten and Eleven)— grouped into four categories of strategies: cooperation-eliciting, conflict-reducing, conflict-diverting, and impasse-breaking—are used by the mediator to neutralize the attack and resolve the dispute. Moreover, they are all conceptually congruent with the basic principles of aikido.

Blending Without Clashing

An aikidoist never confronts or clashes with the challenger. Rather an aikidoist accepts, joins, and moves responsively with the flow of the challenger's energy in the direction in which it is going. Such blending quells resistance because the aikidoist offers nothing for the challenger to resist. The aikidoist makes no use of external force or coercion, only the energy that is already within the challenger. Hence the aikidoist can successfully convert the challenger's potential resistance into free energy that the aikidoist can use to guide the challenger in more positive and constructive directions. This follows poetically from the humanistic and harmonious spirit of aikido: "Aiki is not a technique to fight with or defeat the enemy. It is the way to reconcile the world and make human beings one family" (Ueshiba, 1969, p. 177).

In much the same way, the mediator blends with the stated intent of both parents to resolve the dispute in a manner that is in the best interests of the child. By acting as an advocate for the child, the mediator implicitly accepts the surface concerns of each parent about the child's well-being when the child is with the other parent. The mediator thereby accepts the energy and direction of the couple's challenge and minimizes their resistance to change. By accepting the challenge to protect the child from harm, the mediator offers little or no resistance and can thus utilize the couple's potential resistance as free energy that can be guided responsively into more beneficial directions.

Both the aikidoist and the mediator practice blending and bending, not defending. Yielding to the energy of the challenger gives both practitioners the strength of flexibility. As the practitioner yields, the challenger is given permission to complete his challenge. However, when the challenger is given permission to complete his challenge, the act takes on a different meaning and no longer seems so inviting. The challenger is left feeling disoriented and disarmed.

Extending

After blending with the challenger's movement, the aikidoist allows the movement to reach its natural completion. The aikidoist then extends the movement slightly beyond its natural ending point, which throws the challenger off balance and leaves him vulnerable to an easy shift in the direction of his energy flow by the aikidoist. While the challenger is in this vulnerable stance, the aikidoist has much power and control over the direction in which the particular sequence will go and can effortlessly guide the challenger to a successful resolution. Similarly, after the mediator has blended with the couple's request to achieve what is in the best interests of the child (for example, by saying, "I will serve as an advocate for your child and help you learn what will be in the best interests of your child"), the mediator then extends the movement slightly beyond its natural ending point (". . . and the first thing that is absolutely essential for your child is that the two of you stop fighting over her"). The psychological disorientation and confusion generated in the parents by such a move is parallel to the physical disorientation produced in the aikido challenger at such a point. The parents at this point have been thrown off balance, and they are vulnerable to a shift in the direction of their psychological energy flow.

Leading Control

One of the central principles of aikido is to control the attack by leading it. From the very first moment when an aikidoist perceives an attack, it must be controlled through an appropriate lead that will direct its potentially dangerous and concentrated force into harmless channels. This lead needs to be smooth and continuous and never in direct opposition to the force of the attack, since halting or interrupting the attack would destroy the very momentum that the aikido defense strategy requires. Leading follows the aikido principle of nonresistance or yielding. *Lead* does not mean "force" in the physical sense of pressure, a pull or a push. Such direct action on a person will almost always result in an equally direct reaction. Rather, by spinning when pushed and by entering when pulled, the aikidoist creates a suction that the attacker finds extremely difficult to resist. As the attacker attempts to hit the aikidoist, the aikidoist begins to spin just before the attacker makes contact with the target area, and while blending with, deflecting, and extending the attacker's movement, the aikidoist deflects the oncoming blow away from its intended target into some other direction, often directly back to the attacker. With several attackers, the aikidoist leads the aggressive motion of one attacker around his or her own body, thus creating a vacuum into which the other attackers are drawn, only to send them spinning away across the mat (Westbrook & Ratti, 1974).

For mediation to be effective, the mediator must also establish a sense of leading control. On the one hand, the hostile intensity of many parents in custody disputes means that the mediator cannot afford to be passive, lest she be overpowered. On the other hand, to be confrontive and aggressive with a parent in a forcing way almost always results in a nonproductive clash that hampers or terminates effective mediation efforts. Between these two stances is the stance of active nonresistance or leading control. For example, suppose that a father says to the mediator, "You do understand that I will not allow my daughter to stay overnight with that immoral woman and her new trick, don't you?" If the mediator wanted to clash, the mediator could say, "She's not immoral, and your daughter won't be hurt by her new boyfriend. You are just overreacting and being unreasonable." However, it is easy to imagine the resistance that such a response would generate. In contrast, if the mediator made use of leading control, he or she might say, "How and with whom your daughter spends her time is certainly something that I'm sure both of you are concerned about, and it's nice to see parents who are interested in helping their child become comfortable with new adults in her life. Now, I want to ask you both to think back to the time when your daughter was born and tell me what values you both wanted your child to learn as she grew up." In this way, the mediator can lead the couple away from a potential combative stance to a blending that has a common focus. In doing so, the mediator maintains control of the mediation process while putting the parents in a position to engage in constructive negotiations.

Because disputing parents are often irrational and because the issues in custody disputes rarely have to do with factual matters about the children, attempts by the mediator at direct verbal debate about the content of the dispute often increase the parents' hostility toward the mediator and the mediation process. However, an indirect nonresistance approach that uses techniques of blending, deflecting, and extending allows the mediator to control and lead the process into areas that are conducive to resolution. Leading control is an effective way of being in charge of the mediation process while minimizing parental hostility and resistance.

Centering and Using Leverage

In the centered position that the aikidoist assumes, he or she is able to anticipate and perceive areas in which there is leverage that can be used for facilitating a blended resolution of the challenge. In aikido practice, leverage is almost always found in movement. Since attacks are seen as gifts of energy, kinetic leverage is offered in the challenge and becomes the tool of the aikidoist. Throughout the encounter, the aikidoist focuses on finding the next source of leverage for the next maneuver and on positioning himself or herself accordingly. With practice, this leverage-seeking activity becomes second nature, so that all the maneuvers flow in one continuous but often complex sequence. When aikido is working at its best, the sources of leverage are subtle and inconspicuous, which gives it an appearance of magic. Powerful leverage is typically found in a slight but painless twist of the challenger's wrist, in a sudden reversal of the direction of the challenger's movement, in a slight redirection or deflection of the challenger's linear movement into a curved or circular movement, or in a sudden shift of the challenger's attention from the aikidoist's head to the aikidoist's hand and then to the floor. In each case, the leverage is found by following, pacing, positioning, and redirecting the challenger's energy flow into less destructive directions. By remaining centered and constantly aware of the next source of leverage, the aikidoist is able to maintain control of the encounter and to facilitate harmless resolution with relative ease. To the degree that the aikidoist gets off center, flustered, or emotional, the ability to find the sources of leverage necessary for conflict resolution is decreased.

Similarly, the mediator's main task is to remain centered and in control of the direction that the mediation process takes. Viewing the challenge presented by the parents in much the same way as the aikidoist views a physical challenge, the mediator seeks sources of leverage from the very first moment of encounter, which can be in the first telephone call or in the first few moments of the first mediation session. To maximize the chances of finding the sources of leverage early on in the session, the mediator must develop a dynamic sphere within which everything becomes a source of data that can help identify points of leverage. These data can include passing comments made in the course of a telephone call. For example, a father might say, "I insist on sole custody. . . . I still love my wife and want her back. . . . She really is a very good mother. . . . I guess she's a better parent than me." Hearing the bid for sole custody as a potential reuniting strategy (see Chapter Nine), the mediator knows that she has leverage at the first mediation session for maneuvering the father off his insistence on sole custody by directing the flow of the mediation process to address his hurt and panic about being left by his wife and to assure him of continuing contact with his children. The same data contain leverage that the mediator can use to preempt the mother's panic at the possibility of "losing" her children. This preempting can be accomplished by helping the mother express to the father her reasons for leaving the marriage and her intentions of following through with the divorce. Moreover, the mediator can assure her that her relationship with her children will continue.

Other sources of data for leverage include the referral source, the particular attorneys involved and their degree of support for mediation, the ages of the children, the parents' educational level, and the number of court hearings that they have already attended. Each bit of data suggests new points of leverage to the mediator. Making use of this leverage allows the mediator to maneuver the parents toward the core of the custody dispute. If the mediator remains centered and aware, this can be carried out efficiently without needless and destructive confrontations about who is the better parent.

Maintaining Flexibility

The stance of the aikidoist has been likened to that of a willow tree: supple and flexible yet strong. In contrast, an oak tree, being strong but rigid, will crack and break if it encounters a stronger force. The willow, however, will bend and yield to the force, gathering its strength in its flexibility. Similarly, the aikidoist remains fluid, bendable, and flexible. Based on a rapid assessment of the challenger's particular positions, movements, timing, sequence, systemic interactions, and styles, the aikidoist selects the particular strategies to use for achieving constructive neutralization. Ideally, the nature of the challenge determines the nature of the aikido strategy that is used. If one technique does not seem to create the desired effect, the aikidoist instantaneously switches to another, determined by feedback from the challenger. The aikidoist must be flexible enough to accept any attack or challenge coming from any direction in any form and be able to neutralize the negative energy or redirect it as positive energy.

In a similar fashion, the mediator must remain flexible throughout the mediation encounter. Because parental challengers are typically quite rigid, like oak trees, the mediator must be like the willow: strong yet flexible. The mediator must be able and willing to choose directions, tactics, and perceptions in a completely responsive and fluid manner. Because couples in mediation can be extraordinarily unpredictable, the mediator is often confronted with radically shifting parental challenges. Just when negotiations seem to be flowing along very smoothly and a mediated settlement seems in hand, one of the parents may suddenly launch an attack that brings the mediation to a halt. Or when the mediator is having to remain very firm and assertive on a point, both parents may suddenly yield to the point without a fuss, compelling the mediator to soften up instantly. Such unpredictability and sudden shifts demand that the mediator remain flexible and open. Inflexibility results in clashes and disharmony within the mediation process. Making use of the feedback from clients, the mediator must be firm at one moment, yielding at another, absorbing a negative attack by one parent, bending, turning, and redirecting its energy into a constructive request of the other parent. Rigidity in the mediator usually shows itself as defensiveness resulting from personalization of the attack, not as a gift of energy.

Preempting

A basic technique in aikido is to move before an attack begins, as soon as the challenger mentally gets set to attack. When a challenger is intent on performing a certain action, his mind is committed to a specific challenging movement, and he is unable to react to the aikidoist's move until it is too late. Hence the aikidoist begins to apply the technique when the challenger is raising his hand or pulling back his fist. At this point, the challenger is highly vulnerable, as his energy is drawn backward in preparation for the attack. His desire to challenge has thrown him off balance and out of harmony on both a psychological and a physical level.

In mediation, the very best time to use preempting is before the parents have had an opportunity to take a position on the matter of custody. Typically, by the time parents begin mediation, they each have a position of which they are intent to declare to the mediator and to the other parent. Giving the parents an early opportunity to state their respective positions out loud simply confirms them in those positions and creates unnecessary work for the mediator. However, preempting each parent's position by delivering a monologue before either parent speaks can avert much of the resistance to compromise that parents bring to the first session. The monologue should make use of information that the mediator has already obtained about the parents and the elements of their dispute, and it should be replete with information about the needs of the children of divorce and the structure, process, and goals of mediation. This preemptive maneuver can serve to disarm the parents, or at least it can dissuade them from declaring full-scale war early on in the process of mediation.

For example, using knowledge obtained in a prior phone call that the mother wants sole custody of the child, that she claims the father is irrelevant and probably harmful to the child, *and that there appears to be no substantial or valid evidence to this effect,* the mediator can preempt the mother's as yet unstated position by saying, "You both need to know that our research and clinical experience to date lead us to conclude that most children of divorce do best when they have regular contact with both parents and that even a parent who was not very involved with the child during the marriage can become involved with the child after the divorce in an important and meaningful way." Preempting thus leaves the parent off balance and thus more open to accepting the mediator's direction toward helping their child, since the parent's emotional position must now be much more solidly grounded or given up in the face of the authoritative information that the mediator has just offered. It should be noted that if, in the advance phone contact, there appears to be substantive evidence of a pattern of harm to the child by one of the parents, the mediator would omit this preempt and perhaps design one that would be more protective of the child or wait until more information is generated in the session.

Presenting the Unexpected

A major aspect of the stance and attitude of the aikidoist is that the aiki-doist is evasive, unpredictable, and "invisible." Such a presentation prevents the challenger from planning an effective attack. The aikidoist uses the element of surprise by doing the unexpected. In the moment when the challenger begins to approach with an attack, the aikidoist, with open arms and open palms, welcomes the challenger. The natural, reflexive thing to do when one is threatened with attack is to block the striking hand or weapon or to turn and run away. However, the aikidoist responds quite differently. This different response requires a reframing of the nature of conflict and a trust in the methods of aikido. Rather than viewing the attack as a dangerous or frightening event to be avoided, the aikidoist views it as an opportunity to practice aikido. The attack is viewed as *a gift of energy,* and the transaction is viewed as a creative system of joining rather than as conflict. The aikidoist does not respond reflexively to the challenger in the typical and predictable manner by running away, defensively blocking the attack, or attacking first. Instead, the aikidoist approaches the challenger and, stepping off center from the line of attack, joins the attack form, moves in close, and redirects the challenger into a creative, dancelike encounter, then off into vacant space. Needless to say, the challenger is puzzled and disoriented by the aikidoist's unexpected stance and maneuver. Moreover, the challenger often leaves the encounter unable to explain what happened yet experiencing resolution of the conflict. The effective element of the aikidoist's stance seems to be the open window to suggestion that is created when a challenger experiences an unpredicted or unexpected transaction.

Similarly, the mediator can make effective use of surprise to divert and reduce conflict. While one's natural tendency when one is being attacked or challenged is to respond verbally with fairly predictable defensive patterns, such reflex action usually generates a confrontation and escalates the cycle of attack and defense. The more unnatural but more effective approach, whether to a physical challenge or to a verbal challenge, is to act unpredictably, against the reflexes, thereby breaking the cadence of the attack. To do so, the mediator needs to develop confidence that it is all right to act in an unexpected and seemingly inappropriate manner. Such acting can include suddenly interrupting a parent (stepping off center from the line of conversation) and asking a question that is totally irrelevant to the ongoing discussion. It can include smiling broadly in the midst of a deadly serious dialogue or getting up out of one's chair and doing two or three jumping jacks in the middle of a heated argument. On a more subtle level, after arguing a point with a parent, the mediator might suddenly say, "You know what? You've convinced me that you're right," and quickly change the topic to something totally different. In each of these moves, the timing is critical, because at one moment they might be considered antagonistic or rude, but at another moment they could be skillfully disorienting and effective.

Multiple Challengers

Aikido can be used just as effectively with multiple challengers as it can with one. Approached by six challengers at the same time, the aikidoist does not try to neutralize every challenger at once. Instead, the aikidoist begins by working on two at a time. The aikidoist can turn and shift the direction of the first person's approach to the second person, who in turn makes it impossible for the third person to get near the aikidoist, at which point the aikidoist squats and flips the fourth person over a shoulder. The fourth person rolls into the fifth person, who blocks the sixth person. While spinning in circular, fluid movements, the aikidoist effortlessly uses the challengers' own energy and actions to generate the particular strategies used.

Similarly, the mediator begins the encounter with at least two challengers, the parents. While they perhaps bring the single challenge of resolving their custody dispute, each parent typically presents separate challenges as well. The complexity of overt and covert challenges requires that the mediator remain aware and alert at all times. Each challenge by one parent must be viewed as a potential provocation of the other parent. Once the multiple elements of the dispute have been aired, the mediator must work with each challenge in a way that optimizes her position and leverage for working with every other challenge. As in aikido maneuvers with multiple attacks, the mediator must quickly assess each challenge and carefully and strategically initiate her moves. The timing is critical. The mediator takes on each challenger, working one against the other so as to create a harmonious blend within a constant flow of issues, emotions, and decisions. With this difficult task, it is essential to conceptualize the mediating process as a circular *field of energy* in which the mediator is at the center, flexible, aware, and ready to deal effectively with each challenge, wherever it may arise.

The mediator is often challenged by more than the two parents. As already mentioned, the system of participants involved in a custody dispute can include, besides the parents and children, an array of cross-generational and cross-professional "helpers" as well as neighbors, friends, and other extended kin. To be maximally effective, the mediator must quickly learn who is involved in the dispute. Any mention of relatives, friends, therapists, or attorneys who have privately or publicly sided with a parent can provide the mediator with the information needed to develop appropriate strategies of intervention. Not infrequently, a grandparent or stepparent orchestrates the dispute from the wings by sending out one parental warrior to conquer the other. Before investing all one's energies in fruitless attempts to facilitate a resolution between the two parents, it is helpful to consider whether there are more than two challengers involved. The mediator may need to take on several challengers and maneuver the energy of the various participants into a harmonious resolution so that all are dealt with to the optimal advantage of the children. This effort may involve inviting the other participants to challenge the mediator directly by telephone or in person so that the mediator can use preemptive, reframing, deflecting, and redirecting maneuvers in any combination to neutralize their disruptive effect or to identify the facilitative effect that they can have for the mediation process.

Maneuvering, Not Manipulating

To the uninitiated, it sometimes appears that the aikidoist is manipulating or playing with the challenger. With the paradoxical invitation to the confrontation, followed by the absence of resistance, the confusion and disorientation generated by the circular and often complex movements, and the surprisingly harmless resolution of aggression through indirect, subtle strategies, the aikidoist can seem to be manipulative and deceptive. The distinction that I made in an earlier publication (Saposnek, 1980) between manipulating and maneuvering is helpful here. The connotative distinction between these two terms is one of the *initiator's intent*. The term *manipulating,* which has a pejorative connotation, implies acting in a way that is intended to benefit the manipulator at the expense of the person who is being manipulated. *Maneuvering,* which has a more positive connotation, implies acting in a way that is intended primarily to benefit the person being maneuvered. Using the gentle arts of distraction, illusion, and subtle persuasion, the aikidoist, operating at the highest ethical levels, maneuvers and guides challengers through a series of strategies to achieve the well-intentioned goal of harmless resolution of the challenge. Clearly, these maneuvers are in the challenger's best interests.

Similarly, the mediator's strategies can be viewed as maneuvers intended to achieve what she believes to be in the best interests of the child (which, not uncommonly, in court-ordered cases is the *least detrimental* resolution). When the mediator's strategies are ethically conceived, fully informed, carefully planned, and skillfully implemented, the mediator maneuvers the participants to achieve a feasible resolution of their conflict. If the mediator is careless or exploitative of her own interests, the mediator's strategies may be viewed as manipulative. Such can be the case, for example, if the mediator has a particular bias against one parent and steers the negotiations so as to produce an unfavorable outcome for the disliked parent at the expense of the child. Or the private mediator may unnecessarily prolong the mediation process for her own pecuniary interest.

Aikido-fashioned maneuvers are not always necessary in custody cases. Sometimes, for example, with low-conflict cases, simple, linear explanations and gentle persuasion can be sufficiently effective to reach resolution. However, when there is the necessity to use the more powerful strategies of intervention in difficult child custody cases, it is critical that the mediator assume responsibility for monitoring her own intentions for using the strategies. In addition to abiding by the currently developed ethical guidelines for mediators, the subtle issue of whether one is maneuvering or manipulating is worthy of continual, rigorous self-monitoring.

A Case Example with a Mediator Turned Aikidoist

A father phones the mediator to say, "We've been divorced for almost two and a half years, and my ex-wife has made it very difficult for me to see my five-year-old son. I've recently remarried, and we want to have my son be a full member of our family. I'm suing for sole custody. She can't get away with keeping my son from me!" The mediator perceives the challenge as this: "I am going to punish my ex-wife for keeping my son from me by taking my son from her—and I dare you to stop me!" The mediator then evaluates the elements of the challenge (the father's motives) as a possible power assertion strategy, a retaliation strategy, a strategy for appeasing the new spouse, or some combination of the three (see Chapter Nine). To evaluate the likelihood that the father has the last motive, the mediator asks the father, "How does your new wife feel about the situation?" The father replies, "She thinks I should get full custody of my son and that she will be a better mother for my son." Hearing this, the mediator confirms that the last motive is also operative here and furthermore that this is likely to be a multiple attack (that is, the stepmother is another major challenger). The mediator decides to preempt the attack, then blend with and extend the father's energy so that he is off balance.

The mediator then reacts, centering himself, making use of the leverage inherent in his perceived position as knowledgeable mediator, and saying, "Well, I can tell you from my many years of experience with divorcing families that children certainly need a lot of time with their fathers, just like they need a lot of time with their mothers. You are the father, and the father and the mother together need to make the decisions about how their child will share time between them. Your new wife is very important in your life, and we can hope that your son will be able to enjoy a relationship with her as well. As your mediator, I'll be an advocate for your son to make sure that his relationship with you remains just as important as his relationship with his mother."

In the mediator's first telephone conversation with the mother, she tells him, "He never showed much interest in our son during our marriage, and he hasn't asked to visit him much in the past two years, but now, just because he remarried, he thinks he can suddenly come into the picture. Well, he left me, and he's going to have a fight on his hands if he thinks he is going to get custody." The mediator evaluates the mother's tactic as a possible revenge strategy of frustrating visitation. He proceeds to blend with her center, use her strong emotion of anger as leverage, and preempt her attack by saying, "I know very clearly that you've got serious doubts about his sincerity in becoming involved with your son. Well, if he is sincere, and I'll help you find out if he is, I'm sure that, being the concerned mother that you obviously are, you would be interested in learning how important this possibility of your son's reconnecting with his dad will be. But as an advocate for your child, I'll want to make sure that your son's best interests will be served, and we'll certainly want to find out what his father's getting married again had to do with this whole legal action." With these words, the mediator has successfully centered himself in the mother's emotional sphere, made an effort to preempt her position of keeping the son from the father, and used leading control to maneuver himself into a position from which he can begin the first mediation session with optimal knowledge of the challenges that will be presented.

The mediator begins the first mediation session by setting the context with a preempting monologue that includes information about the needs of children of divorce to have a continuous relationship with both parents who cooperate with each other, the strategies that children use to gain a sense of control over their parents' relationship and thereby over their own survival, and the benefits of mediated agreements over court battles. Then, after gathering a brief history of their marital and divorce relationship, the mediator can ask, "What positive things would you both like to see happen for your son?" That is, by using leading control, the mediator maneuvers the conversation away from attacks on each other toward a blending of common interests. The father says, "I want custody of my son!"—a bold challenge. Before the mother can respond, the mediator swiftly blends with the father and redirects the challenge away from the mother by saying, "So you would like to have your son spend more time with you?" The father responds, "Yes, that's right. I want him to live with me." Perceiving an even stronger challenge, the mediator spins the father around in a disorienting sort of way and redirects him by saying, "Of course, your son should be able to live with both his mother and his father. As I said, that's how children seem to do best after their parents divorce, but your son needs to have his needs addressed by you both. And while we are talking about him, could you each give me a description of what it is that you like most about your son?"

In this way, after blending with the father, the mediator maneuvers him away from a direct challenge to the mother and then uses the son, symbolically, as a buffer and source of distraction to prevent any verbal interactional injury. Such a maneuver prevents the mother from having to defend herself, and it gives the mediator time to reposition the mother so that she will more easily be able to blend with the father.

After hearing positive descriptions of their son, the mediator presents the unexpected by quickly changing the subject. That is, the mediator asks the mother, "What would make it easier from this point on for you to feel comfortable letting your son develop his very necessary relationship with his father?" If the mother replies, "If his father showed a real interest in seeing him," the mediator can quickly extend the mother's position by asking, "What would it look like if he were to show a real interest? How would he be able to show that to you?" In so doing, the mediator positions the father in an open and favorable stance. The mother says, "If he followed through when he says he wants to see him." The mediator then turns to the father, assertively leads him in a semicircular fashion to blend with the mother, and, again using the son as a buffer, asks, "What would it take for you to follow through and show your son that you really want him to have a close relationship with you?" The father responds, "If she wouldn't keep him from me." Quickly, the mediator neutralizes the father's attack and maneuvers both parents into a new position so that they are blending together to offer support for their son by saying, "If the two of you were to begin together to help your son enjoy a healthy and meaningful relationship with both of you, as you both know it should be, then how would you want to begin to set up his time in each of his parents' houses?"

This example details merely one segment of the larger mediation process for this family. Clearly, many issues need to be handled before adequate resolution can take place. These issues include the emotional factors that have maintained the static pattern of their coparenting relationship, the influence of the stepmother in the ongoing dispute, and the child's range of tolerance for different time-sharing structures. However, these factors are generally much easier to deal with after the mediator has centered himself, assessed the challenges to be presented, preempted the challenges that he can, and blended with the emotional center of each parent. Then, systematically remaining centered throughout the interactions and using leading control over the participants, the mediator can deal effectively, skillfully, and efficiently with each new challenge. The result will be a harmonious resolution of the family dispute.

———————— o ————————

To implement any new system of intervention successfully, the practitioner must use the system in his or her own style. While actual on-the-mat practice of aikido can give the mediator a real feel for the power and applicability of this system, it is certainly not necessary to practice this art physically. At the very least, the mediator who uses the attitudes and principles of aikido gains a fresh perspective on the craft of mediation. Moreover, mediators who have used this metaphor in their work have reported feeling much freer to try new maneuvers and less obliged to continue familiar but unsatisfying or ineffective interventions. Certainly, the flexibility and objectivity offered by an aikido approach can be helpful to the mediator both professionally and personally.

PART TWO

STRUCTURING THE MEDIATION PROCESS

5

BEGINNING MEDIATION

SETTING THE CONTEXT FOR NEGOTIATIONS

THE SINGLE MOST IMPORTANT tool of mediation is structure. Because couples going through the crisis of divorce tend to be volatile, a mediation process without a solid, well-defined structure is bound to end in failure. One mediator, for example, who had much experience doing long-term psychotherapy but little experience with mediation, began custody mediation with a couple who were still very emotionally involved with each other three years after their divorce. They could easily be characterized as an *enmeshed couple* (a term suggested by Kressel, Jaffe, Tuchman, Watson, and Deutsch, 1980). As the mediator began to ask the couple about their early marriage, emotions poured forth. Taking this as evidence of their need to express feelings that probably had been repressed for years, the mediator allowed the spouses to vent. After three sessions of such venting, the mediator began to feel as if he were accomplishing a great deal. However, as he then began attempting to focus the couple on the task of developing a time-sharing plan for their child, they just continued to vent their feelings—all the way through session number nine. Needless to say, the mediator felt more and more out of control and unable to focus the couple on any concrete task. Each time he attempted to suggest a resolution, one spouse or the other would divert the topic to an emotional one, which would trigger off the other spouse, and both would become extremely volatile. However, they were no closer to resolving any of the custody issues than when they began mediation. The exasperated mediator finally realized that these spouses thrived on elaborate expressions of their emotions. These were not people who had repressed feelings but a couple whose style of interaction was best characterized as emotionally volatile. Moreover, although their depth of emotional expressiveness was bottomless, they were unable to provide any structure to their interactions that might lead to effective problem solving. Because the mediator began with an assumption of repressed feelings, as is characteristic in traditional psychotherapy, he failed to provide the tight and clear structure necessary in mediation work and hence was unable to lead the couple effectively through the problem-solving process that is mediation. While working with this particular enmeshed couple would be difficult even in a tightly structured situation, the absence of structure leads to almost certain failure in mediation.

To draw an analogy to the nature and scope of the structure and control needed to conduct effective mediation, consider a person who wants to go fishing in the surf. With no concern for structure or control, Fisher 1 might take a stick with a string and hook, cast the line anywhere into the water, lay the stick down on the shore, and wait to see what happens. If a fish gets hooked, this person will rush to pull it in by pulling the stick forcefully toward the shore, risking pulling the fish off the hook. With more concern for structure and control, Fisher 2 would carefully select the right fishing pole of the right length, weight, and flexibility, the right line of just the proper weight test, the correct size hook for the type of fish sought, and the right bait that such fish like and then pick just the right spot toward which to cast. When a fish hooks, he would reel it in as fast as he could before it unhooked, again risking the fish becoming unhooked by the force. Finally, Fisher 3, with optimal structure and control, with the carefully selected equipment of Fisher 2, and with a fish on the line, would sensitively and flexibly reel it in for a while, let it pull out, reel it in some more, let it out, continuing this flexible give take with just the proper timing. Then, just at the right moment, when the fish is resting, he would finally reel it in to a catch. Fisher 3 is most likely to bring in the catch successfully because of the preplanned structure, sensitive and responsive control of the interactions, and artful and flexible maneuvering until resolution.

General Structural Issues

The particular structure that guides the mediation process will be the basis for a variety of decisions the mediator has to make. Let us consider general structural issues before proceeding to specific issues.

Number of Sessions Needed

Mediators tend to split into groups that claim mediation can be accomplished in ten to twenty sessions, six to ten sessions, four to six sessions, or one to three sessions. These differences are a function of a number of contributing factors that can vary the actual number of sessions needed for a particular case. For example, the number and complexity of issues considered in mediation will partly determine how many sessions will be needed. If the mediator is dealing with every aspect of the divorce settlement, including property division, financial distribution, support issues, and tax considerations, in addition to custody issues, he no doubt will require more sessions. Moreover, if the custody issues are intertwined with property division and/or child support issues, more sessions may be required to assist the couple in separating the custody issues from the financial issues. Fewer sessions are needed, however, if the mediator is dealing only with the custody and visitation issues (generally one to three sessions). This may be the case when the financial issues are already settled or are being dealt with separately by a co-mediating or consulting attorney or by the spouses' respective attorneys. It is also the case when financial issues are specifically excluded from the custody mediation work (for example, as specified under California's 1981 mandatory mediation statute).

The nature of the referral also partly determines the number of sessions needed. A private mediator who works with couples that voluntarily seek mediation on an hourly fee basis generally has the opportunity—both temporally and economically—to offer more sessions than a court-connected mediator who may be backlogged with cases and therefore limited in the number of sessions she can offer. Another factor is the amount of experience that the mediator has had in this area of work and his intervention style. In my opinion, more experienced mediators and those who stylistically are more active and structured in their approach generally tend to need fewer sessions to reach settlement than those who are less experienced or less active and structured.

The mediator's view of which issues must be discussed before a satisfactory resolution is possible will also affect the number of sessions needed. At one extreme are mediators who believe that extensive knowledge of the history and dynamics of the couple and their children is essential before the mediator can lead them to agreement. At the other extreme are those who believe that minimal knowledge of the participants yields resolutions most effectively. These mediators feel that prolonged mediation opens a Pandora's box of issues that may forever be unsettled and may in fact aggravate the situation further, making resolution difficult or impossible.

The expectations of the mediator and the motivation and expectations of the spouses will partly determine the number of sessions. If a mediator views part of the task of mediation as helping the couple explore their marital relationship and individual psychodynamics so as to resolve their feelings about each other, the process will go on for a longer time. Occasionally, a couple who voluntarily seek out a private mediator may specifically request such an approach. However, such couples are usually seeking reconciliation and are using the mediation context as a forum for marital therapy, or they may in fact need divorce counseling for help with emotionally disengaging. A mediator who attempts to mediate a divorce and/or custody settlement with a couple who have not really decided to divorce may find her efforts counterproductive. Many sessions may pass by before she realizes that each attempt at clarifying the issues has been frustrated by the strong emotional pull within each spouse for reunification. In such cases, it might be best for the mediator to refer the couple to a couples counselor for what we might call *relationship clarification counseling,* until such time as they have definitely decided either to divorce or to remain together. It should be noted that mediation is sometimes the only face-saving forum that may be available to a separated couple who might reconcile. Larson (1993) warns that mediators all too often assume that couples seeking divorce mediation actually want to get divorced, and the mediator who acts upon this assumption without exploring it can effect a self-fulfilling prophecy. She presents a methodology for exploring reconciliation that shows some promise for saving some of these marriages.

For some couples, mediation presents an opportunity for divorce counseling and for their children to talk to someone who is objective and rational in the midst of parental subjectivity and irrationality. Often the mediation sessions are the only opportunity since the separation or divorce for family members to get together and wrap up the loose ends of the breakup. While an extended number of sessions can occasionally be helpful to families who voluntarily seek mediation, there are circumstances in which extending the number of sessions is counterproductive. For example, extending the number of sessions is risky when one spouse wants to explore the divorce issues more extensively but the other spouse wants the mediation to be short and sweet. This is often the case when one spouse is pursuing a *reuniting strategy* (see Chapter Nine) and the request for more mediation sessions is an attempt to gain more conjoint time to persuade the other spouse back into the marriage. Often this situation reaches the point of one session too many, when the other spouse refuses to continue mediation, resists efforts toward compromise, or demands an immediate and inflexible resolution to the mediation issues. Because this tends to polarize the other spouse, the possibility for a stalemate is great. This situation is also encountered in certain court-ordered mediation cases when neither spouse wants to be there; extending the number of sessions can polarize such a couple even further, forestalling or obstructing a resolution to the custody or visitation dispute.

It is wise for the mediator to heed the warning: mediation is not therapy or counseling. While there may be therapeutic or healing aspects to it, mediation is primarily a structured process for negotiating a temporary or initial agreement from which later decisions can more rationally be made. Very often, the more open-ended the opportunities available for couples in mediation to talk, the greater their chances for justifying their mistrust of each other. Such opportunities can increase the number of negative transactions and thereby increase the difficulty in reaching a settlement. As one therapist put it, "Communication doesn't just mean talking; . . . often couples develop 'communication problems' because they talk to each other too much. For them, communication is increased by not talking to each other so much" (Haley, 1979).

If a mediator views his task as achieving successful resolution to a custody or visitation dispute in as brief and painless a time as possible, then a tight and well-thought-out structure can help accomplish this task in relatively few sessions. The mediator must, indeed, always aim at being in control, and having fewer sessions necessitates greater control.

Length of Sessions

Mediators should generally allow one and a half to two hours per mediation session. Occasionally, a simple case may take as little as forty-five minutes of a single session, but usually it is difficult to accomplish much of significance in a session of less than an hour and a half.

The wide variety of mediator styles, schedules, and circumstances will necessitate different lengths of sessions. Some mediators fit their mediation cases into an hourly schedule in the middle of their regular workload. This can work well if individual sessions are held with each spouse, but it typically is too short a time period to work with the couple together. Other mediators prefer to schedule an entire morning or afternoon for a mediation case. This leaves open the possibility of a marathon session and gives the mediator more flexibility for expanding on the process while controlling its direction.

Time Between Sessions

A key variable for the mediator is the length of time that passes between sessions. Whereas in psychotherapy the tradition has been to schedule weekly sessions for the course of the therapy, in mediation the time between sessions can often determine whether or not a resolution will be reached.

There is an optimal time period between sessions that maximizes the likelihood of reaching a resolution. This period, especially the one between the first and second sessions, needs to be carefully planned by the mediator. If the time period is too short (a week or less), the feelings generated in the first session often prevent the spouses from working on their problems in a rational manner. They remain stuck in protective, adversarial stances. If, however, too much time passes (several months or more), momentum is lost, legal or personal changes will have been numerous, and the complexion of the case is often significantly different by the time of the second session. If, however, the second session is scheduled an optimal length of time after the first session (usually several weeks), there is time for negative feelings to die down following the first session and for each of the spouses to complete some focused thinking about possible solutions to their situation.

An interesting phenomenon often occurs after the spouses leave the first session. Even if the entire first session is devoted merely to understanding the specific circumstances of the couple's situation, there are several significant "firsts" that will also have taken place. For one thing, this is often the first time that the spouses have been together in the same room since their court hearing. For another, it is often the first time since their separation that the spouses have talked together for any length of time without generating more negative feelings toward each other. It is often the first time that the couple have worked on a constructive resolution to conflicts that may have been going on for many years. And it is often the first time that both have experienced equal participation in discussions about their children and their future and the first time that they have experienced equal respect for their particular points of view. All these factors help a couple develop new perspectives on their situation and consequently to think of more cooperative solutions. It is often after this first session that the characteristic unpredictability previously described is first manifested. It is as if the first session has a disorienting effect that temporarily disarms the spouses and makes them open to compromise. Allowing two or three weeks (on the average) to pass until the second session helps the spouses reorient and prepare themselves to engage in more rational problem solving.

Relationship with Attorneys

The relationship between the mediator and any attorneys of the spouses that may be involved in the custody or visitation dispute is very important. The mediator's task is greatly facilitated if the attorneys are knowledgeable about and supportive of mediation. Indeed, attorneys who are experienced with the successes of mediation almost always become quite supportive of the mediator and are a delight to work with. There is great comfort in knowing that a client's threat to talk to his or her attorney about going to court is an empty one.

When one or both of the attorneys in a particular case are unknowledgeable about and/or unsupportive of mediation—as may be the case in court-ordered mediation—the mediator's efforts are vulnerable to being blocked. There are a variety of reasons that a particular attorney might not be supportive of mediation efforts. An attorney who has never experienced or perhaps even considered mediation might simply not believe that it could work. An attorney who is himself in the middle of a bitter divorce might tend to project his unwillingness to compromise onto his clients. Or an attorney might have experienced failure in the only two cases that she sent for mediation and so would remain unimpressed. Finally, an attorney might be so strongly oriented to an adversarial stance that cooperative efforts would seem personally awkward or even professionally unethical. Whatever the reasons, the mediator needs to be aware of potential blockage by an attorney, preferably before starting the mediation process.

If the mediator knows that the attorneys in a particular case are supportive of mediation, the mediator may simply want to make courtesy contact with them before beginning. If, however, an attorney is not known to the mediator or is known to be unsupportive of mediation, a more extensive phone call or personal meeting with that attorney is very important. This contact should be intended to assess the attorney's current beliefs and feelings about mediation in general and for this client in particular. It is also an opportunity to make gestures toward cooperation, either by direct appeals or by offers of information about the mediation process and its potential benefits to the attorney and his or her client. For attorneys, the benefits of this approach include freedom from the angry phone calls from clients that are common in custody cases, having clients who are more satisfied because they worked out the custody and/or visitation issues themselves, and being free to counsel their client about legal matters, rather than having to deal with the raw emotions of marital conflict. Contrary to the implication of Coogler (1978), made in the early days of mediation, that lawyers may sabotage mediation efforts because of reduced financial rewards for them, it has been my general experience that lawyers welcome the opportunity to reduce the level of emotional tension and acrimony in their cases. They appreciate having someone specifically skilled in resolving emotionally laden issues who can take their clients to the point of being rational enough to work effectively within the legal context.

If the confidentiality agreement (discussed later) between the couple and mediator is to be signed, contact with the attorneys should be made before the first session. This allows the mediator to receive from the attorneys any pertinent information about their clients that they choose to reveal, without the mediator's being tempted to reveal any information about the couple to the attorneys. The mediator can open communication by saying, "Is there anything about your client or your client's situation that might be helpful for me to know?" To this question, the attorney might respond in the negative or might indeed share information. For example, the attorney might cite documented allegations or convictions of child abuse, sexual molestation, or dangerous substance abuse or addictions on the part of the other spouse. Or the attorney might point out that her client is a religious fanatic who will not compromise or is dead set against mediation or is extremely young and unable to make mature decisions about children without a lot of help. Given such information, the mediator can be alert to safety issues regarding the children when discussing negotiable parameters in the mediation sessions.

In response to this bid for information, the attorney may attempt to influence the mediator to side with her client and to look askance at the opposing client. A mediator can easily detect this intent by listening to the significance of the content chosen by the attorney. If, for example, the attorney says, "I think the father should not have much contact with the kids because he lets the kids stay up until 10 P.M. and he feeds them hot dogs and he never takes them anywhere fun," the mediator can understand this more as the attorney's fulfillment of her role as an advocate for her client than as serious concern for the safety or well-being of the children. Such an attorney should be respected for the dedication shown to her client and, in time, educated about the really important needs of children and the benefits of cooperative approaches to custody and visitation disputes. If, however, the attorney says that the other spouse has just been released from prison for the third time on felonious child abuse and drunk driving convictions, the mediator must be very cautious when leading the negotiations about child care arrangements.

Before beginning mediation, the mediator should also request that the attorneys refer their clients directly to the mediator if either should consult them during the mediation process. Knowing that both attorneys are supportive of the mediation efforts and the condition of confidentiality (discussed later), the spouses become more willing to commit themselves to participate fully in the mediation process.

Fees

The fees mediators charge vary according to a number of factors. Mediators who are based within a court (such as conciliation court counselors) receive a flat salary from the county to handle all the contested custody and visitation cases and receive no direct fees from their clients. Private custody mediators may also receive direct referral from the court and may be paid by the county on a contract basis per year, per case, or per hour. Private mediators who are not court-connected generally charge on a per-hour basis. When the private mediator is dealing only with custody and/or visitation issues, fees typically are paid at each session. Because of the unpredictability and volatility of higher-conflict cases, some mediators set a policy to be paid *prior* to the session. In that way, if things blow up in the session, the mediator is not left unpaid for the time scheduled for the session.

It is best if half the fee is paid by each spouse, but other arrangements can be made. In some cases—for example, when a modification of custody is requested years after a divorce—there may be a significant discrepancy between the spouses' abilities to pay half the hourly fee each. One spouse may be willing to pay the entire fee or some greater proportion of it, and the other may be willing to contribute an equivalent share in bartered services or a deferred reimbursement to the other spouse. It is best to have each spouse contribute at least a token amount to the total fee in order to emphasize that both parents are responsible for contributing to the resolution of any dispute regarding their children.

When handling all aspects of a divorce settlement, some mediators receive a lump-sum deposit or retainer from the couple at the first session, against which all charges are made for mediation fees, advisory attorney fees, and fees for other consultants needed by the mediator. Any unused money is returned to the clients. Other divorce mediators prefer not to collect a deposit but to receive their hourly fees at each session.

Fees for mediation generally are set in accordance with the usual hourly rates for other work done by the particular professional conducting the mediation. Typically, attorneys who do mediation charge more than mental health professionals, and mediators on the coasts and in large metropolitan areas seem to charge more than those in other locations. Some mediators in both the legal and mental health professions charge a greater fee for mediation than their usual hourly fee for their other professional services. They do this for several reasons: because they have received special training or have acquired special expertise to do mediation, because both spouses are contributing to the fee and therefore can afford a larger fee, or because mediation is generally more demanding of both time and effort than their other work. Moreover, because of the omnipresent threat of lawsuits, mediators are encouraged to carry special malpractice insurance. Malpractice insurance specifically designed for divorce and family mediators first became available in 1982, from Lloyd's of London (Brown, 1982), and is now readily available from a number of sources (contact the Academy of Family Mediators or the Association of Family and Conciliation Courts for information on such sources).

Private mediators also vary in their policies of charging for telephone conference calls. Some mediators charge both parties for all time spent on a case; this is especially true for attorneys, who typically have much greater overhead expenses than mental health professionals do. Other mediators charge only for face-to-face contact time and absorb phone costs as a courtesy extension of their mediation work. Hence some clients may be charged by both their mediator and their respective attorneys for conferences between them, some may be charged by one and not the other, and some may be so fortunate as to not be charged for any services except the mediation sessions per se.

Scheduling the First Session

Based on information gathered on the phone as well as that received from the court, from the attorneys, and from the spouses themselves, the mediator must decide about several structural issues relating to the first session. The first issue—when to schedule the first appointment—should be decided on the basis of several factors. If the spouses were in court for their divorce only yesterday, are still very acrimonious, and are attending mediation reluctantly (that is, by court order or attorney stipulation), the mediator would do well to schedule the first appointment for several weeks hence. This would give the spouses a cooling-off period and would allow them to be more rational when mediation begins. If, however, the spouses have been separated for several years, have been friendly and cooperative with each other over that period of time, and are now filing for divorce and want assistance in making the best coparenting arrangements for their children, the mediator can feel comfortable setting an appointment for the very day or week they call. Although there is no guarantee that the latter couple will resolve their issues more quickly than the former couple, the probability for success in the first case would be increased if they had some time for their anger to dissipate before attempting to cooperate on a plan for their children.

A second issue that needs deciding is who shall attend the first mediation session. Some mediators schedule individual appointments with each spouse before seeing them together, and some schedule the couple together from the start. An advantage of the first approach is that it gives an opportunity for each spouse to vent his or her feelings and concerns before beginning the mediation process. However, there are several disadvantages to this approach. First, there is the potential for stirring up more problems than necessary to facilitate a workable resolution. Second, it may set up client expectations that mediation is counseling or psychotherapy, and they may end up feeling disappointed when the mediator does not follow through with the individualized personal concern characteristic of therapy (see Saposnek, Hamburg, Delano, & Michaelsen, 1984). And third, it seems inefficient, necessitating at least three initial sessions instead of one.

The advantages of seeing the couple together for the first and each subsequent session include the implicit message that this is mediation and not individual therapy, that the problem is to be resolved between the spouses right from the start, that the mediator will not sympathize with either spouse to the exclusion of the other, and that the dispute is to be viewed from a systems rather than individual point of view. Also, the potential for stirring up unnecessary issues and feelings is minimized by the tight structure of the mediation context. And this approach is temporally efficient.

Although seeing the spouses together in every session might appear to have the disadvantage of lacking an opportunity for each spouse to vent feelings, that is not in fact the case. Opportunities to vent feelings arise at various points throughout the mediation process. However, such venting is handled in a constructive manner that leads more easily to resolution than to increased anger and frustration. Moreover, there are to date no clinical or research data suggesting that extensive expression of feelings aids in the resolution of custody and visitation disputes. If the spouses, together or individually, express the desire to have counseling or therapy, a referral is made for them either during or after mediation.

Although factors other than those mentioned may significantly influence the mediator's decisions, careful and strategic planning in scheduling the first appointment can greatly maximize the effectiveness of mediation.

Setting the Context

It has become increasingly clear that the context of mediation is crucial to its outcome. The context is set partly by the nature and source of the referral, partly by the degree of connection with the court system and state and local law, partly by the attitudes of the judges and attorneys involved, and partly by the skills and style of the particular mediator.

The mediator must explicitly elaborate the nature of the mediation context for the couple. This elaboration serves several functions. First, it makes very clear that the mediator is in charge of the entire mediation process and has already worked out how to proceed. This tends to reduce the anxiety level of the spouses, who typically are entering unknown territory. Second, it sets explicit boundaries for the expected conduct of the spouses and the mediator—for example, it specifies that mediation is not psychotherapy; it specifies that there will be no name-calling, accusations, or dredging up the past; and it specifies whether the mediator will make recommendations to the court if mediation is not successful. This allows the spouses to adjust their own expectations accordingly and minimizes the buildup of false expectations or even fear about the proceedings. Third, it gives the couple an opportunity to listen to a significant amount of information about what their children really do and do not need at present and in the years ahead. The conjoint and neutral format for receiving this information decreases the chances that one spouse might later distort what the mediator said. In effect, it serves to preempt much of the resistance to cooperation (Watzlawick, 1978; Saposnek, 1980, 1983). In preempting, the mediator anticipates thoughts, feelings, attitudes, or positions of the client and states them in a neutralizing context before the client has a chance to state them. By preempting these utterances, the mediator minimizes the opportunity for the client to develop and manifest resistance to change or compromise. There are a wide variety of ways for setting the context; the following discussion presents a format that has worked very successfully for me.

Confidentiality Agreement

If the mediator is not expected to arbitrate or make recommendations to the court in the event that mediation is unsuccessful, a confidentiality agreement should be the first order of business. It is very helpful to begin the first session by explaining the purpose and function of such an agreement (see Appendix C) and then to have the spouses and the mediator sign it. The mediator can explain, "In order for us all to talk together in an open and honest manner, without feeling excessively defensive, we need to make an agreement that our conversations in this room will be kept confidential. By signing this form, we agree that anything you or your children say here will not be used against either of you by the other or by me in any future court proceedings, if there are any. Furthermore, I will not reveal any of the contents of our talks to either of your attorneys, to the judge, or to anyone else, unless all three of us agree to it. Moreover, I will not testify for or against either of you, my records will not be subpoenaed, and I will not give any recommendation to your attorneys, to the judge, to a custody evaluator, or to anyone else."

Although there is some controversy as to whether or not such a signed agreement is legally binding, it does seem to have a powerful psychological effect on many spouses, and most judges supportive of mediation will support it. It offers a sense of security and freedom of speech that enables the spouses to achieve at least a minimal degree of trust in each other and in the mediation process. Only rarely has a spouse even questioned the value of signing such an agreement, and I have never had a client refuse to sign it.

In some jurisdictions, in the event that mediation efforts fail, the court rules require the mediator either to function as an arbitrator, who listens to all the input and then renders a binding decision, or to offer recommendations to the judge as to the preferred custodial parent and visitation plan. Within such legal structures, the confidentiality agreement is clearly inappropriate. Advocates of the mediator as arbitrator or recommender point out that after spending many hours in discussion with the spouses (and perhaps with the children as well), the mediator has information about them that would be useful to the judge making the determination of custody and visitation. However, advocates of the mediator as nonrecommender point out the critical importance of the spouses feeling able to be open and honest in their negotiations, even though the information gleaned by the mediator is sacrificed to confidentiality. Such advocates feel that the sacrifice is worthwhile in that it helps maintain the couple's belief in the value of a self-determined approach to solving custody disputes. They feel that when the spouses know beforehand that the mediator will function as an arbitrator, the spouses may limit their disclosures of important information and may be less willing to negotiate. A full debate of the issue of confidential versus recommending mediation in court-ordered cases can be found in McIsaac (1985), representing the confidential argument, and Duryee (1989), representing the recommending mediation argument. Comparative research to date has failed to find any statistically significant differences in client preferences, although there was a slight trend in clients favoring nonrecommending mediation (Depner, Cannata, and Ricci, 1994).

Explaining the Mediator's Role

Not uncommonly, couples begin mediation with the belief that the mediator is to make a decision for them about custody or visitation. Their belief follows directly from the usual legal context, which has made them familiar with a judge's role as an arbitrator and with a custody evaluator's role as a recommender but not with a mediator's role as a facilitator. It is therefore necessary to clarify the mediator's role early in the process as to whether, in the event that no agreement is reached, the mediation will remain confidential or the mediator will make a recommendation to the court. If the mediation is confidential, the spouses will know that they must take full responsibility for arriving at the decisions cooperatively and that the mediator will simply facilitate their doing so. Failure to clarify the mediator's role in advance is now considered an ethical violation, as it can cause the spouses to lose trust in professional help and to feel betrayed.

Benefits of Mediation

Often one or both spouses need to hear specifically how mediation can benefit them and their children. It is useful in such cases to explain the benefits: "From over twenty years of research studies on children and families going through divorce, we've learned that children of divorce did best when their parents continued to cooperate with each other over issues regarding the children even if they did not cooperate over the issues of their own relationship. When parents retain control of the decisions affecting their children, the children benefit because the parents are the ones who best know the needs of their children and the circumstances of their children's lives.

"Mediation was set up to help parents make these parenting decisions together after separation and divorce. The courts have much experience with custody and visitation decisions, and they now know that decisions made by the parents rather than by a judge are more relevant to the specifics of their case, are more meaningful to the couple and their children, are more carefully thought out, and last longer. Also, many years of experience have shown that couples who resolve these issues in mediation typically do not return to court repeatedly, trying to get back at each other, and the children are spared all that conflict. Finally, you will save a lot of money by working out the details between yourselves, rather than paying lawyers for their time negotiating or battling in expensive court hearings.

"To ensure that the two of you will continue to resolve future child-related issues outside the legal system, the last clause that I regularly include in the mediation agreement states that if you are unable to resolve any future disputes about the children between yourselves, you will seek mediation before legal action. This is useful because we have learned over the years that mediation is not a onetime event, as we used to believe. It is more accurately thought of as an ongoing process to which you can return periodically, if you need to, whenever things change in your lives or your children's lives. Mediation allows you to keep modifying your parenting plan as your needs and circumstances change, without resorting to lawyers or court."

On Talking with Attorneys

In the earlier years of mediation practice, it was not uncommon for one of the spouses to talk with his or her attorney, who would then say something from an adversarial stance that had the effect of hampering the mediation process. During those times, it was advisable to admonish clients to refrain from consulting with their attorneys about custody or visitation issues during the course of custody mediation. However, after many years of experience with mediation, most family law attorneys have come to understand the importance of giving their support to mediation efforts, and hence, at this point in the development of mediation, such an admonishment appears unnecessary. Although there may occasionally be an attorney who wittingly or unwittingly sabotages mediation efforts, the benefits may outweigh the risks to a client who needs attorney support through the mediation process. Such assistance may help the client clarify his or her real concerns about the children in a way that can facilitate the mediation process.

General Preempting Statements for Beginning Mediation

Each spouse comes to mediation with a list of adversarial grievances against the other spouse, frequently headed by accusations of that spouse's negative influence on the children. The evidence with which the spouses back up these accusations is often based on their interpretation of the child's behavior on returning home from being with the other spouse or on reports of the child's behavior while at the other spouse's house. Moreover, each spouse comes to mediation believing many myths about what children do and do not need to thrive. If the spouses are given the opportunity to state all these accusations and mistaken beliefs, the mediator is put in the defensive position of trying to persuade the spouses to modify their stated views. However, if the mediator begins the mediation by telling both spouses in an informed and authoritative manner what is currently understood of children's needs following divorce, the parents' resistance can be preempted, often to a significant degree.

If, for example, the mediator presents the finding that children need regular and continuing contact with both parents, it then becomes more difficult for one parent to state that the children do not need the other parent. The particular preempts used in a case are strategically selected, depending on the information learned about the case in advance (from phone calls, fact sheet information, court minutes, and other sources). In easier cases, fewer and less pointed preempts are needed. In more difficult cases, a wider range of preempts that are more specifically targeted to their issues may be needed. The usefulness of presenting these preempts at the start of the mediation process is that they serve as anchors to which the mediator can return later in the session, if more control is needed and/or a different direction needs to be taken. However, the preempts can also be blended in, as needed, at any point in the mediation process in anticipation of nonconstructive resistance.

There are nineteen preempting assumptions from which I choose some or all for their relevance to each mediation case. The particular language that I have formulated to present these concepts has worked well for me. However, it is not critical to use these very words. It is more important for the mediator to clearly grasp the concept of each preempt and then to develop language with which to convey it that fits the mediator's style. The essence of the preempting monologue is to present an authoritative and almost trancelike array of accurate and useful information that seeds the unconscious mind and sets the context for fruitful coparenting discussions and negotiations. Trainees have reported that it is helpful to practice the preempts until they flow into a comfortable, flexible, seamless lecturette.

1. *Assumption of conflict between parents with possibility of cooperation for the children.* "I'm going to assume that the two of you absolutely despise and hate each other and furthermore that each of you wishes the other off the face of the earth." At this point, one or both of the spouses invariably laugh and say, "Well, it's not *that* bad; I don't *hate* him (her)." My assumption is stated in an exaggerated fashion to compel them to moderate the statement, thereby making an implicit move toward

cooperation. To further compel cooperation, I reaffirm the original assumption by saying, "Well, I'm going to assume that anyhow." (Note that I will omit all of this preempt up to this point in cases in which there is compelling evidence of domestic violence, child abuse, or a long-standing history of intractable high conflict between the parents, because this preempt is useful only if the exaggeration actually is an exaggeration. However, the next portion can be useful with all clients.)

I then quickly go on to say, "But we have found, through much experience, that people can hate each other as spouses and still cooperate together as parents in making important decisions about their children. To the degree that you separate the parenting relationship that you share from your spousal relationship, you will be able to make good decisions for your children. It is possible to be a caring and effective parent even if your marital relationship has not been satisfactory. To the degree that you make decisions based on your children's need for parenting rather than on your own need to get even, to gain power, or to satisfy your own needs first, your children will benefit. Remember that children are always easy pawns in marital battles, and they are prime targets for leftover marital conflicts. Keep them out of those battles and you will help protect their psychological health."

These statements give spouses the hope of being able to separate their negative feelings for each other from potential agreements on coparenting. This also begins to disarm them from using the children to get revenge on each other.

2. *Assumption that both parents love the children.* "I'm going to assume that both of you love your children equally well and in your own separate styles and that both of you want the best for your children. Is that accurate?" I find it important for each spouse to verbally acknowledge this assumption at this point, in the presence of the other spouse. This focuses their concern on the children and establishes a neutral territory that is framed in a positive way. It also blocks either spouse from accusing the other spouse of not loving the children. And their explicit assertions of love for the children are an anchor to which I can later return if negotiations take a turn toward self-interest or noncooperation.

3. *Assumption of children's need for both parents.* "I'm also going to assume that your children love and need both of you, even if they are mad at one of you through the divorce process. As I explained, research keeps showing us that children need regular and continuous contact with both parents even if the parents disagree with each other on many issues. Your children can handle the reality of each of you quite well, but when denied a chance to check out the reality of a parent's being, they will fill in the

missing parts with fantasy. And we do know that children's fantasies are very frequently distorted, since children have such minimal experience to draw from in accurately assessing people. Their fantasies tend to be polarized; the absent parent is viewed either as a wicked person who is unfit to care for children or is dangerous to children or, more likely, as a saint who can do no wrong. Often, against the protests of the primary parent, the child's view will be sustained and will only get stronger over time. It may be tucked away in a secret fantasy storage place but will be quickly retrieved whenever the custodial parent challenges the worth of the absent parent."

This assumption and discussion helps decrease the fear that either parent might have of losing the child forever if a compromise is reached. The negative effects of either parent being refused access to the child are explicitly substantiated, which often elicits a smile of relief from one or both parents. They experience momentary relaxation on hearing that the final resolution will assure each of them a significant degree of involvement with the children.

4. *Mediator as child advocate.* "My main concern is for your children. In custody hearings, judges typically deal with children in stereotypical ways and often do not take their individual needs into account. In mediation, though, we have the opportunity to develop a plan that can fit your children's individual needs, as well as your own needs. I am going to keep our primary focus on your children and their specific needs before focusing on each of your needs. I am going to act as an advocate for your children."

This statement serves to reassure both parents of my intent to protect the best interests of their children, in spite of their own motives and confusion. It also serves to reduce the attempts of the spouses to get me to side with each of them by explicitly stating that their interests are a secondary priority.

5. *Effects of putting down the other parent.* "Children seem to have an intuitive sense of justice regarding their parents. In my experience, if one parent puts down the other, more often than not it backfires on the parent doing the talking. The child will come to the defense of the parent who is being put down and will refuse to accept anything negative about that parent. Sometimes this will happen right after a divorce, and sometimes it will happen a few years down the road in the child's development. Trying to convince the child of the faults of the absent parent just leads the child to confirm the absent-parent-as-a-saint fantasy. So even though you may have put down the other parent to your children in the past, it is advisable to refrain from doing so in the future, because it may well

backfire on you." This assumption is intended to prod the parents into supporting each other's parenting role, with the explicit risk that the law of karma—what goes around comes around—may be operating.

6. *Effects of children's strategies.* "While children do not like their parents to put down each other, the children themselves will carry out a variety of behavioral strategies against their parents for some time following their parents' separation. In well-functioning intact families, children almost always play one parent against the other at some time. It is a natural way of learning the limits of their own power and that of their parents. In effect, they are asking several questions about their parents: Will they be in agreement in their decisions? Will they be consistent? Will they act calmly? Will they lose control and hurt or kill me or each other? Will they stay around to love me? Will they still love me and stay with me even if I cause this much trouble? The children will often present their parents with aggressive, demanding, or resistant behavior as a test to see whether their parents will remain united. They hope for the feeling of security that they experience when their parents cooperate with each other for their children's sake.

"Following divorce, children use these same strategies but frequently exaggerate them, even to the point of destructiveness. They will tell Mom the awful things that Dad does and then turn around and tell Dad the terrible places that Mom goes. They will feed your disagreements with each other and will distort and sometimes even lie about events that happened at the other parent's house. All of this is done not because your children are evil but because they seek emotional survival. Partly, they are expressing their anger and frustration about your divorce, but mostly they are asking for clarity about your relationship with each other and your feelings about and commitment to them. These are simply normal behaviors exaggerated to crisis proportions as the children try to take care of themselves through the emotional crisis of divorce.

"So it is important to take what your children say about the other parent with a grain of salt and not jump to conclusions about the unfitness of the other parent. Many a court battle has been initiated by a parent who overreacted to the innocent but distorted words of a child and failed to check out the reality of those words with the other parent." These statements serve to forestall each parent from using the children's verbal and behavioral strategies as evidence for reducing their access to the other parent.

7. *Better parenting when alone with the children.* "In spite of terrible things that your child may tell you about the other parent, and in spite of what you may remember about the ineffectiveness of your spouse's

parenting skills when you were all together as a family, consider the fact that a parent often is more effective with his or her children when alone with them and less effective when the other parent is also present. This is because children will regularly play one parent against the other when both are physically together, but when alone with one parent, this is much more difficult and the children are less motivated to try it. So it is quite possible that each of you is actually more effective with your children, rather than less effective, when the other parent is not there." With these statements, the children's behaviors are put into a normalized perspective, reducing their value as ammunition against the other parent.

8.   *Children's different parental needs at different stages.* "I'd like you to consider the fact that it is rare for one parent to be really effective with children of all ages. Usually each parent is more effective in parenting children of certain ages and less effective with children of other ages. For example, one parent may be wonderful with infants and have a harder time dealing with the challenging and demanding behavior of a three-year-old. Another parent may not know what to do with a child under two but be marvelous with an older child who can talk and reason. Some parents are great with teenagers, and others give their best nurturance to younger children. Parents who are aware of these strengths and weaknesses can best help their children grow up by helping the other get through his or her rough periods in the children's development." These statements allow both parents face-saving protections against accusations by the other that either might have shown ineffective behavior in parenting the children. It also lets one parent ease up on grabbing for custody for now while giving hope for a better parenting scenario later. At the same time, it gives the other parent a developmental foundation for anticipating more effective future coparenting.

9.   *Resisting children's reuniting strategies.* "Children almost always have a secret wish that their Mom and Dad will get back together some day. A well-known family therapist, Carl Whitaker, once said, 'Kids whose parents get divorced stop wishing them back together when the kids are about eighty-one years old.' And your children will often use their behavioral strategies to try to reunite the two of you. Although children do not like their parents to fight, at the same time they often believe that as long as Mom and Dad are dealing with each other intensely, even if that means fighting, there is a chance that they will get back together. But if you play into their game and fight with each other, you actually make it even worse for them by creating more tension and insecurity, which in turn encourages them to provoke you more. This leads to a vicious circle in which everyone loses."

This assumption serves to elicit in the parents an acute awareness of the consequences of their divorce on the children and is intended to influence them to soften the emotional trauma for the children by minimizing further conflict. It also serves as a paradoxical challenge to stay apart by not fighting with each other. By showing that the children take their conflicts as evidence both that the parents have succumbed to the children's manipulations and that they will get back together, this maneuver subtly encourages the parents to reduce their fighting and cooperate with each other.

10. *Individual needs of each child.* "Individual differences among your children are important to recognize. Each child is a distinct person with unique feelings, attitudes, tolerances, behavior patterns, habits, and preferences and as such deserves to be considered in terms of his or her special needs. Your children's ages, sex, and temperament characteristics, such as activity level, attention span, approach to new situations, and adaptability, need to be taken into account, as do their behavioral styles, interests, tolerances, established friendships and relationships with relatives, feelings about their neighborhood, attachment to the family home, adjustment to school, quality of the school they attend, involvement in sports activities, and so forth. Considering all these factors before your own needs will result in the best decisions for your children."

In discussing individual differences of children with their parents, it is particularly helpful for the mediator to be informed about the temperament characteristics of children (see Chapter Two). This assumption about individual differences among children encourages parents to focus on the specific needs of each child. It reduces the tendency to view the children as a package for which to fight, and it gets them to view each child respectfully, as a real and unique person.

11. *Flexibility of the parenting plan.* "A key factor to consider in designing your parenting plan is flexibility. As time goes by, children grow and their needs change. They enter different developmental stages, and they change friends, schools, and interests. Your needs and your life situations will also change over time. It is best to view your decisions about your children as part of an ongoing process, rather than as a once-and-for-all event. Both child and adult development are ever-changing processes, and if we constrain them by forcing onetime decisions to be in effect forever, it will not work effectively. Think of your parenting plan as an organic, growing document that changes to fit your changing lives. Children are constantly changing, so recognize that the coparenting schedule that you come up with now may not fit several years from now. As you flexibly fine-tune it over the years, you will be respecting your children's changing needs.

"Presently both of you are in a crisis and no doubt feel vulnerable, as if you potentially have a lot to lose. Your flexibility is probably not as evident now as it could be, but it is very important to keep in mind as we progress. Some couples choose to make year-by-year or biyearly agreements to meet again, either between themselves or in mediation, in order to reassess the changing needs of each family member. If need be, we can even arrange to reevaluate your plan in six or even in three months."

This statement serves to prevent the parents from viewing the mediation as a crucial, once-and-for-all event and their decisions as ones that must endure forever. Such an attitude encourages intense competition to win, which is contrary to the necessary spirit of mediation.

12. *Reconceptualizing "custody" as coparenting.* "Neither of you owns your children. So the concept of 'custody' is archaic, yet it has tended to guide our perspectives and has encouraged us to view children as possessions. To the degree that you possess your children, you lose them. Both of you are, and will always be, parents to your children, and when you divorce, you simply restructure your family, not abandon or destroy it. It is important to think about the words we use in our negotiations. Phrases like 'getting custody,' 'keeping my kids,' 'giving them up,' and 'having visitations' all imply that the children are owned and loaned. We will begin to use phrases like 'sharing time with the children,' 'being with the children,' 'having the children be with you.' This will help us look at the situation differently—in a more cooperative, sharing way."

These statements lead in to the difficult task of getting the parents to reconceptualize their family relationships using cooperative rather than competitive concepts. This concept must be repeated periodically throughout the mediation process, and the mediator must consistently follow through in using the new language and new concepts in all discussions that follow. The mediator must serve as a convincing and consistent model for the parents of how to think and talk about cooperative coparenting.

13. *Protecting children from psychological harm.* "Young children going through a divorce have two great fears. One is of being rejected or abandoned by one or both of their parents; often they will secretly think, 'If my daddy left, maybe my mommy will leave also.' The other fear is of not being taken care of—that is, fed, clothed, sheltered—and loved on a day-to-day basis. Very often children will not tell you what is upsetting or scaring them, but they cannot help but show it somehow through their behavior, questions, comments, and general attitude. Sometimes they may show their fears by acting excessively clingy or at other times by acting withdrawn and uncooperative. They may also act demanding, challenging, or irritable or show symptomatic behavior such as bedwetting, in-

somnia, stealing, lying, fighting, or poor schoolwork. Sometimes they may not even show their fears and insecurities until years later when they wind up in psychotherapy to try to undo all the damage that has been done. So it is important that you both help them feel as secure as possible by cooperating together to work out a plan for your children to have regular and continuing contact with both of you."

These comments are intended to arouse one of the greatest concerns of most parents: that of psychologically harming their child. It is often very effective to offer the parents such dire predictions of psychological damage as a means of encouraging them to cooperate with each other—and few therapists would question the validity of such predictions. In their therapeutic work with families going through divorce, Isaacs, Montalvo, and Abelsohn (1986) incorporated this notion: "To make the care of the children a priority, we do not hesitate to play upon either the underlying or the exposed guilt of most divorcing parents. We accomplish part of the effective therapy of divorce not only by working with their wish to engage in reparatory and buffering behavior in regard to their children but by heightening and utilizing guilt constructively, modulating it and channeling it into effective avenues of expression. This therapy is possible because it speaks to the couple's deepest underlying wishes to be responsible parents" (p. 12).

14. *Respecting the stages of the divorce process.* "Sometimes people getting a divorce believe that when the judge signs the final papers, the divorce is over. Actually there are often three aspects to a divorce, and each aspect has its own time line. The first aspect is the legal divorce. This occurs when the judge signs the papers saying that you are now legally divorced. In California, there is a legal minimum period of six months, but it can actually take up to several years, depending on the complexity of the matters involved.

"Then there is the social divorce. That involves the dividing up of family and friends—answering the question of who will remain on whose side. This generally takes a few years after the separation to complete. Last, and most difficult, is the emotional divorce. That is the process of emotional detachment from one another, and it usually takes from many years to forever. The person who leaves typically begins this process a year to two before separating, and the person who is left may only begin on the day of separation. So there is often a discrepancy in the time lines between the two people, and it's important to allow the necessary time for the person most recently beginning the emotional divorce process to catch up. Without allowing this time, the potential for conflict is enormous, because one of you will want out quickly and the other will not yet be ready to part emotionally.

"So be patient with yourselves, and don't try to rush through the emotional divorce. You cannot go *around* it—you must go *through* it. And if you try to rush it, it will just take longer." This preempt gives the leaving parent a rationale for slowing down the process of divorce—the risk of generating unnecessary conflict. It also presents a map to the parent who is left that explains why there is a discrepancy in their intensity of feelings, which can minimize attributions to the leaving spouse of being cold, unloving, or uncaring.

15.   *Introducing new partners to children.* "After parents separate, it is very common for one or both to get involved with new partners. Sometimes it is just for companionship and to avoid loneliness, and other times they become intimate very quickly. Often the parent wants the children to like the new partner as much as the parent does. And it is common for a child to come to like the newcomer quickly. New partners are typically very attentive to the children and often bring gifts. And they bring few or no conflicts to the relationship, because they have no emotional history together. The parent may mistake such liking for loving and assume that the child is fine with the new person, and the parent then begins including the child in the relationship, sharing affection, intimacy, and love in front of the child and spending lots of time together.

"If this relationship is built up slowly, over the period of a year or two after the separation, the child may in fact come to love the new partner. However, if the child is seriously involved in the relationship sooner than six months to a year after the separation, the child may suddenly pull back one day and resist seeing the parent. This often occurs at the point when the parent and new partner move in together or announce an engagement or marriage plans. The child suddenly feels that enjoying this new relationship is being disloyal to the other parent. The involved parent then may accuse the other parent of not supporting the child in the new relationship; however, it often has little to do with the other parent.

"Children tell us that they feel really uncomfortable seeing their mom or their dad holding hands with or kissing a new person. They feel especially uncomfortable seeing their parent in bed with another person that is not their other parent. Remember, children want their parents back together, and this new partner is seen as a threat to that fantasy; what's more, they may believe (even in the face of evidence to the contrary) that the new partner is the one who broke up their parents' marriage. So it is important for parents to let their children go through the same year or two of grieving before involving them in new relationships. It is also good insurance for helping your new relationship survive your continuing relationship with your child. The time that your child is with the other parent is an excellent time for you to spend intimate time with your new partner." These statements are intended to normalize a child's reactions to new partners, to inform the prematurely involved parent to take responsibility for the child's reactions without attacking the other parent, and to withdraw the child's involvement with the new partner until its proper time.

16. *The role of stepparents.* "A very common problem that we hear about is the conflicts between parents and stepparents. The fact is that second and third marriages, in which there are children from the earlier marriages, break up more quickly and at increasingly higher rates, largely because of the difficulties that stepparents and stepchildren have with each other. Children who have two biological parents who are actively involved in the children's lives have a lot of trouble accepting a stepparent, especially if the two biological parents don't get along with each other. This places the child in a loyalty conflict. He may actually like the stepparent but feel that the other biological parent does not want him to love the stepparent; and so he feels disloyal, and he pulls back. And so the conflict between households gets started. It's important for stepparents to recognize that their role is, at best, being a *friend* to the child, *not* a replacement for Mom or Dad. The stepparent will never be the child's mom or dad. You two are the child's parents forever! That's how children tell us they want it to be." These statements are intended to diminish the threat that one parent may feel of being displaced by a stepparent. Hearing the "expert" say this in front of the remarried parent helps give implicit support to the single parent's value and position in the children's life.

17. *Alcohol and drug abuse.* "Many couples come in here claiming that the other parent should not be allowed to be with the children because he or she drinks or takes drugs. The fact is that many parents use alcohol and some use drugs, and unless such use can be clearly shown to be directly detrimental to the children, it is not a reason to deprive the children of contact with that parent. However, if the drinking or drug use takes place just before or during that parent's time with the children, it can have a serious impact on the children, and a judge would be very interested in knowing about it. Moreover, both of you need to be concerned about it if your child is, or might be, endangered by the actions of either one of you.

"The problem with drinking or taking drugs around your children is that, first, it puts your child's safety at risk if you get behind the wheel while under the influence or if you are inattentive or fall asleep at home and are unable to supervise your child; children have died starting fires, falling into swimming pools, and running into the street while with a parent who has been drinking or is stoned. Second, drinking or taking drugs while with your children teaches them, by your modeling it, how to deal with stress or uncomfortable feelings by drinking or getting stoned. Over the years children begin to use that pattern for themselves, as they remember how dad or mom dealt with stress or angry or sad feelings by drinking or getting loaded. And we know that children who are genetically prone to becoming alcoholics or substance abusers can be encouraged into habitual drinking or drug use just by seeing someone they care about do it. So if *either* of you has a problem with drinking or drugs, it is a problem for *both* of you." These statements are intended to heighten awareness about the consequences to children of alcohol or substance abuse and to distribute the responsibility for protecting the children to *both* parents.

18. *Joint responsibility versus 50–50 percent custody.* "A lot of parents come in here believing that joint custody means *50–50 percent* time sharing. However, they soon learn that joint custody has nothing to do with percentages; it has to do with each parent having a significant involvement in his or her children's lives. Sometimes parents believe that 50–50 percent custody will magically make them equally important to their children. However, children don't think in terms of percentages regarding their parents. They just want to be able to love and spend time with each of their parents. Most children's lives are not set up to spend exactly equal time with each of their parents. When they do, it's often at some sacrifice to their comfort. Talking percentages is talking about parents' rights, not children's needs. And it also sounds like talking about money, not about children's lives. So let's focus on the needs of your children to have a significant relationship with each of you in terms of specific days and times, not percentages; the ways to support the plan financially can be discussed at another time." One of the toughest positions to undo is a demand for equal time. These statements are intended to soften such a starting position and reframe mediation as dealing with children's needs, not parents' rights.

19. *Domestic violence.* "We have learned a lot over the years about the terrible effects on children of conflict between their parents. The most severe effects on children occur when they are exposed to the extreme of conflict, domestic violence. A lot of parents think that if the children don't *see* it, it won't affect them. However, we now know that even when children *hear* it, it can have devastating effects. Mostly what scares children is that one of their parents will be hurt or killed, and that threatens their very survival. Sometimes parents think that violence is only hitting someone. But children experience violence as anything that is hurtful to their parents—including hitting, pushing, pinching, slapping, poking, and also name-calling, verbal threats, and aggressive or threatening behaviors.

They need you to make life safe for them. If they sense a threat to one of their parents, they cannot trust either of you to keep them safe. Even a single incident can leave a permanent impression on your children—one that they will remember for the rest of their lives. So let's figure out how we can protect your children by minimizing even the opportunity for the two of you to engage in such destructive levels of conflict." This preempt is intended to expand the parents' awareness of the destructive effects of these patterns on the children. Some parents have accommodated to violent patterns of interaction and are surprisingly unaware of the effects on their children.

Divorce education programs for separated and divorcing parents have proliferated over the past several years (Salem, Schepard, & Schlissel, 1996). Much of the content of these preempts has now been incorporated as the basic information presented in such courses (Braver, Salem, Pearson, & De Lusé, 1996). Mediators have acknowledged that when parents attend such courses prior to mediation, they are much more ready to negotiate effectively. And when the mediator then selectively repeats such information in the form of preempts in a planned, strategic fashion, it reinforces the knowledge and enhances the preparation for constructive negotiations in mediation.

Ground Rules

It is helpful to end these preempts by setting the ground rules for proceeding with negotiations. There are two rules that I consider essential:

1. "There is little value in talking about the past, since it only leads to arguments, as I'm sure you both know." (I obtain explicit acknowledgment of this fact from each of the parents before continuing.) "Our focus will be on your children's needs for the future and on how you two can satisfy those needs. I will need some background information for my own benefit, which I will ask for, but unless I specifically request it, we will talk about plans for the future."

2. "In talking with each other, I will encourage you to use '*I*' *messages,* statements that begin with the word *I*, such as 'I want . . .,' 'I need . . .,' 'I get angry when . . .,' rather than statements that begin with *you*, such as 'You are incompetent,' 'You are irresponsible,' 'You always . . . ,' or 'You never. . .' Accusatory statements only cause people to become defensive and angry. That will lead us nowhere in our negotiations. So speak for yourself and about yourself, and we will proceed much more easily."

After the ground rules have been presented, the mediator is ready to begin the first phase of the actual mediation process.

6

PHASES OF MEDIATION

FROM GATHERING INFORMATION
TO REACHING AGREEMENTS

ALTHOUGH MANY DIFFERENT models have been developed for structuring the mediation process, all have in common three phases. Initially, a great deal of information must be gathered regarding the specifics of the particular case. Then, options for resolution are generated and explored. Finally, the proposals are narrowed down to the one that is the most workable for the couple. We will now examine each phase of the process.

Beginning Phase

As every clinician knows, the process of gathering information and generating hypotheses begins well before the first office visit. Short-term, structured intervention approaches require a rapid assessment of the clients and their particular situation. Mediation, which is among the most structured and short-term of all interventions, therefore necessitates the most efficient and rapid assessment of important variables.

Gathering Information on the Phone

The richest source of initial information about the clients' situation can be the first phone call with each spouse. The arrangements for these initial calls are determined by the particular source of the referral to the mediator. In private mediation, referrals may come directly from the spouses or through their attorneys. In the former case, one of the spouses phones the mediator and requests mediation for the couple, who have previously agreed between themselves to seek mediation. In the latter case, an attorney representing one of the spouses phones the mediator and requests mediation for the couple, in accordance with an agreement developed between the attorneys. In both cases, it is wise for the mediator to telephone each spouse and each attorney involved in the case to explain procedures and expectations and to gather essential information. In court-ordered mediation, the mediator may receive the written court order or minutes from a court hearing with the names of the spouses who were ordered to mediation. Typically, the spouses or their attorneys call and provide phone numbers for reaching the parties. The mediator then phones each spouse to explain procedures, answer questions, confirm the time of the first appointment, and gather information.

From these calls the mediator can get basic information, such as the names, ages, addresses, and phone numbers of the parents and children, the names of the attorneys involved, recent and pending court dates, and current custody and visitation arrangements. The mediator can also assess the important issues between the couple; the degree of motivation to negotiate; the degree of resistance to participate; the existence of any special allegations by one parent against the other (such as child abuse, battery, alcoholism, drug abuse, or homosexuality); the interactional dynamics of the couple; the degree and duration of their custody battle; the degree of adversarial attitudes; whether the children have expressed a preference for where to live; whether joint legal custody is a feasible option; the degree to which custody and/or visitation issues are enmeshed with financial, marital, and other matters; the current status of the divorce proceedings; the degree to which each spouse has accepted the fact of divorce; each spouse's level of personal maturity (ability to recognize and deal with the needs of others before, or along with, his or her own); and which issues have already been settled before mediation.

A word of caution is warranted regarding information gathered in the initial phone call with each spouse. Frequently, during these initial calls, each spouse gives slanderous information about the other spouse that goes well beyond what is helpful to the mediator. Such information may bias the mediator or even generate hostility toward the reporting spouse (much as the child might feel when hearing one parent put down the other parent), and it may create difficulty for the mediator in the early sessions. Moreover, by passively listening to such accusations, the mediator implicitly condones the spouse's tactic. However, not listening to such information (including, perhaps, allegations of child abuse, molestation, or neglect) could cause the mediator to overlook or unintentionally screen out important information about the children's safety or well-being.

Hence not listening errs in the direction of missing significant data, while listening encourages distortion, hostility, and noncooperation. The mediator can best handle this dilemma by striving for a balance of input.

Gathering Information in the First Session

The next important information to gather is the nature of the couple's marital and premarital relationship. In asking the spouses to describe the way they met, courted, married, and divorced, the mediator quickly achieves a number of very important steps in gaining essential information. First of all, the immediate emotional climate often changes from hostility to warmth and friendliness as the spouses reminisce about good times past. This frequently stimulates the couple to adopt a more cooperative attitude. Second, the spouses reveal (both verbally and nonverbally) the nature of their best ways of relating and solving problems together. This is useful as a predictor of their potential for cooperation and as an anchor to which to return if they later become too hostile. Third, the mediator gets a quick historical and developmental picture of the stages of their marital relationship, of the long-term marital issues and interactional patterns, of the interactional strengths and weaknesses of the couple, and of their manner of regulating the emotional distance between them (Kantor & Lehr, 1975).

I generally begin the exploration of the premarital relationship by asking, "How and where did the two of you meet?" The couple's demeanor when asked this question is similar to those mildly altered states of consciousness that we drift into and out of all day long, described in the literature as "trancelike" (Erickson & Rossi, 1979; Zeig, 1980). This discussion almost always elicits good feelings between the spouses as they describe what are frequently the best times of their lives. After they describe the beginning of their romance, this next question is rapidly offered: "What first attracted each of you to the other?" This gives further opportunity for the spouses to warm to each other, as each relates the other's most positive aspects. I draw out these descriptions until I sense resistance, at which point I casually summarize and repeat the positive characteristics of each one.

Then I inquire about their predivorce relationship by asking, "How would you each describe the course of your marriage (or relationship, if never married)? Divide it into thirds—a beginning third, a middle third, and a last third. For example, some couples say that it was great at first, then in the middle gradually got worse, and at the end was a disaster. Others say that it was terrific until the day the partner left or that it was horrible from the very first day they met or that it was like a roller-coaster ride, good times alternating with bad times. How was it for you?" I add that "it's not uncommon for each of you to have a very different perspective on it."

They thus are each encouraged to present their personal perspective briefly and in a highly structured manner. From this the mediator gains access to their marital dynamics, which often parallel their stances in the custody battle. Occasionally, one of the spouses resists talking about the early marital relationship, even in very brief form, saying something like, "I thought we were here to talk about custody, not about our marriage." To this, I might respond: "You are right—we *are* here to work out a parenting plan, and you know, over the years I've found that when I get just a flavor for how the two of you got to this point, I'm able to more helpfully guide you both to a plan that could really work for you and your children." Usually this quells resistance to summarizing the history of the relationship. If the parent resists further, I may say, "OK, it sounds like you have some ideas about how we can quickly get your spouse to agree with your position. Please help me understand how we should proceed." If the parent does not relent, the mediator should begin negotiations and backtrack to the relationship history only later in the session, if and when the parent becomes more comfortable.

If the parents agreeably present the relationship history, the mediator can then ask, "How did the decision to divorce (or separate) get made?" Stating the question in this neutral form allows either spouse to respond and implies no judgments or criticisms by the mediator. Often this discussion opens up and clarifies the feelings that each spouse has had and currently has about the other. But since the feelings typically are already very familiar to the couple, they need only be expressed briefly, as reacknowledgment. Paying too much attention to these feelings and their expression may result in an escalation of the negative feelings. The mediator must then take charge, neutralize these feelings, and redirect the discussion.

At this point, it is important for the mediator to explore the degree of finality of the divorce plans and the degree of acceptance of those plans by each spouse. If one spouse is unwilling to accede to the divorce, further negotiations over the custody issues are pointless, since the divorce issue will block any constructive talk about the children. Among the typical reasons that one spouse will resist the divorce are hurt, anger at being abandoned by the other spouse, religious beliefs, love for the other spouse, panic over being alone, excessive dependence on the other spouse, confusion over why the other spouse left, and hope that the estranged partner will return to the marriage.

The mediator should be aware that it is rare for couples going through custody mediation to reconcile their marriage. Generally, by the time they come for custody mediation, one or both spouses have experienced too much pain for reconciliation to be possible. In addition, various postseparation changes typically occur that exclude the other spouse permanently; these may include changed values, a new mate, and numerous other irreversible decisions.

However, because the decision to divorce must be settled squarely before meaningful negotiations about the children can take place, a brief inquiry into this issue is helpful. The mediator asks such questions as "What percentage probability would each of you give as to your getting back together within the coming year? Within the next five years?" "What would it take for you to get back together?" "How likely is it that those changes will happen?" These questions allow the spouses to assess the likelihood of reunification by focusing on the concrete changes required (which they both usually know all too well). Frequently, one spouse states a zero percent likelihood of reuniting. This then functions both as a clarification and as a challenge to the other spouse either to accept this position or to try to persuade the spouse to reconsider. If persuasion is seriously attempted, the couple is requested to go home and think about the divorce decision for several weeks. Usually, allowing time to pass dissipates resistance to the reality of the divorce (if it is a reality) and provides an opportunity for the resistant spouse to reevaluate the situation so as to be able to return to mediation at a later date.

If the decision to divorce is relatively well accepted by both spouses, the mediator proceeds to the next line of questioning, which concerns the children. Either at this time or during the inquiry about the course of the marriage, the question is asked, "How did the decision to have children get made?" This elicits any unusual circumstances surrounding the conception and birth of each child, and it serves as an indicator of the original motivations behind and feelings about the birth of each child. If, for example, one spouse describes never having wanted children and also fails to express any current positive feelings for them, the mediator can hypothesize (and listen for) other motives for wanting custody, such as revenge, assertion of power, or desire to keep a hold on the other spouse.

Then the parents are asked, "What are your children like? Give me a capsule description of each of them." Addressing this question to both parents gives the mediator information about how much each parent knows and cares about the children. The mediator notices which parent initiates the descriptions, the degree to which each parent feels attached to and positive about the children, and how realistically each parent describes the positive and negative characteristics of the children. When parents are asked this question, they almost always have an emotional response that is similar to the one they show when asked about their early courting. Since each parent typically is vying to have the children live with him or her, or at least to maximize their time together, each tends to portray the children in positive and competent terms. Moreover, both parents usually perceive the children in similar ways, except for differences in emphasis on certain characteristics. The similarities of the parents' descriptions provide important leverage for the mediator later in the negotiations. Coming back to the agreed-upon positive characteristics of their children at times when the negotiations are stuck can help the parents get on with cooperative efforts. Moreover, the particular way in which each parent describes each child reveals useful information about the degree to which they are matched or mismatched. This is useful in the middle phase of mediation, when decisions are made about sharing time with the children.

It is important to remember that in intact families, the degrees of positive or negative compatibility between each parent and each child are constantly being expressed. As Thomas and Chess (1977) noted, being aware of the various areas of poorer compatibility allows parents to develop ways of working around them. For example, consider a boy who has a high activity level and whose mother is also very active but whose father likes to sit quietly and read. If the parents chose to facilitate compatibility with these temperament characteristics, the mother and son would probably spend a good deal of time being active together—perhaps playing sports—and would not expect the father to participate. The son and father might well enjoy quiet time together in the evening. However, if the parents expected to fit more traditional sex roles, with the father being more physically active and the mother less physically active, the child's activity might well be viewed by the father as a constant annoyance and by the mother as a frustrating reminder of her own desire to be more physically active. Furthermore, the mother might subtly or overtly encourage the child to be more active, which would further irritate the father and could well cause marital discord.

Hence even when there are difficult temperament matches between a parent and child, if the parents are aware of the potential problems and work together to minimize them, they can share equitably in parenting their children. When the mediator is helping a couple design a parenting arrangement that will approximately equalize each parent's time with the children, it is often useful to discuss temperament differences among the children so that the time-sharing arrangements can be planned with due consideration both to the children's needs and to the parents' tolerance levels. For example, if one of the children has always had particular difficulty in adapting to changes and has been extremely slow to warm up to new situations, the time-sharing arrangements should be designed to minimize transfers between the parents' houses. For that child, alternating houses on a biweekly, triweekly, or even monthly basis might work out best, while for the child's more adaptable sibling a weekly alternation might work out quite well. (Temperament in children is discussed more fully in Chapter Two.)

There are occasions when behavior and temperament are of relatively little importance to the mediation work. For example, when the spouses are very hostile to each other and cannot even consider such issues as temperament matches (as is frequently the case for couples who are in court-ordered mediation), discussion of these issues may backfire and be used tactically by one spouse against the other—for example, "Jennifer cannot handle changes, so I'm going for full custody." In such cases, the mediator must limit the amount of information offered to what the couple can handle constructively. However, if the mediator is obliged to make recommendations in the event that mediation efforts are unsuccessful, information about temperament compatibilities can be useful in formulating meaningful recommendations.

Middle Phase

After the necessary background information has been gathered, the mediation process enters the middle phase, the phase in which the actual negotiations begin.

Describing the Options

To make sure that the negotiations proceed with correct information and to avoid getting caught in conflict based on misunderstanding of the options available for resolving the custody dispute, the mediator should describe those options. While the range of available legal options varies from state to state, I will present those that are available under California law, since this state offers a host of options.

The choices presented for parental consideration are based on the information that has previously been gathered about the needs, preferences, and tolerances of each parent and child. If the parents have agreed that one of them will retain sole legal custody, and they are merely in disagreement about visitation schedules, I may lightly explore the possibility of joint legal custody, or I may not even mention it unless it is brought up by one of the spouses. Not mentioning it can bring up moral issues for the mediator who feels that it is not fair for one parent to have sole legal custody when, for example, there is a judicial preference or presumption of joint legal custody; however, it is more important at times to consider what is *feasible* rather than what is fair. Often emphasizing what is fair serves only to unbalance the mediator's position because it injects the mediator's personal values into the couple's struggle. For example, cases come up in which one parent wants sole legal custody of the children and the other parent wants joint legal custody. In one such case, I spoke of the benefits of joint legal custody as if it were in fact a neutral position. However, this was construed by the mother as evidence of my partiality to the father's position and therefore of my lack of neutrality. As she continued to express her preference for sole legal custody, I spoke further about the benefits of joint legal custody. The father sat back, smirked, and watched me argue with his wife. From that point on, it was very difficult for the mother to trust me to be fair (from her point of view), and she subsequently refused to cooperate further with the negotiations. The importance of looking at the available options from the couple's point of view rather than from the mediator's becomes apparent. This occasionally becomes a full-blown paradox: the mediator who attempts to be fair is perceived as being unfair, while one who refrains from asserting what would seem to be fair is perceived as being fair.

If, as is more often the case, the couple has implicitly agreed to joint legal custody, I describe the range of ways for sharing the children's time, from the most ideal to the most workable solutions. I say, "Joint legal custody means that each of you will have equal privilege and responsibility for making major decisions about your children. Of course, the minor day-to-day decisions need to be made by the parent the children are with at any particular time. We will develop a comprehensive agreement that describes how each of you will share time with each of your children. The design of this agreement is completely up to your creative imaginations. You can literally create any sort of plan that works for you and your children, and as long as it is not inappropriate developmentally, the judge will almost always approve it. So allow yourselves to be flexible, creative, and able to compromise. Consider the needs of the children first; then design the plan to suit both of your schedules and lifestyles. The best plans are actually those that also accommodate the needs of each of you.

"Experience has shown that at first you may both need to have a time-sharing schedule that is highly structured and firmly maintained. If there is any doubt at all as to whether you can agree to minor changes in the schedule without getting into conflict, it is best to keep the dates and times of the schedule set, without changing them. Then, as time goes on, when each of you experiences enough trust and cooperation with the other parent, you can add some flexibility to the schedule. Over time, you may well be able to help each other more in sharing child care responsibilities. When one of you is not available to be with the children, the other parent may be able to spend that time with them, which benefits both of you and your children.

"Think of the possibilities for scheduling in terms of concentric circles of geographical distance from one another. The inner circle is the ideal co-parenting arrangement for children, when parents are cooperative with each other and live at opposite ends of the same block, have bedrooms for the children in each of the homes, and allow much freedom for the children to choose where they will sleep on any particular night, within reason, of course. This allows the children to remain in the same school, stay in the same neighborhood, play with the same friends, see both parents on a regular and frequent basis, and feel the support of both parents maintaining access to each other. The next circle is when you live at opposite ends of town but in the same school district. This will mean more driving and coordination of schedules, but it works as well. The next circle has the parents living an hour or two apart, in different school districts. Clearly, the child must go to only one school for the school year, so time sharing must be arranged somewhat differently. The next circle is when the parents live a half day's drive apart, and the last circle is when it takes a day's drive or a plane ride for the child to see the other parent. These last two schedules involve long-distance parenting.

"Thus the possibilities for how your children will share time with each of you depends first on the distance that you live apart from each other. When living close by, some parents choose to share the children on a daily basis, so that one parent is with them during the daytime and the other with them in the evenings and nighttime. Some parents have the children with one parent three days a week and with the other four days, alternating every other week or month. Some have them with one parent for the weekdays and with the other for the weekends or alternate weekends. Some have the children alternate weeks, every other two weeks or three weeks, every other month or two months, or every other year or two years. Whatever will work for the children and for you can be arranged."

If young children are involved, the parents are given the following advice: "Because young children have a very limited sense of time, it is desirable for them to be able to see each of you on a fairly frequent basis. A common rule of thumb is that a child can comfortably spend one day away from a parent with whom the child is used to being with regularly for each birthday that the child has attained. So a one-year-old child can handle one day away, a three-year-old can handle three continuous days away, a seven-year-old can handle a full week away, and so forth.

If one of you moves far away, it becomes very difficult, though not impossible, for your children to have such frequent contact. So if it is possible for the two of you to remain within the same geographical area until the children are somewhat older, that would be a nice sacrifice for you to make for your children. If that is not possible, your children will still survive. They can maintain a solid relationship through lots of phone calls, faxes, letters, and video and sound recordings of daily and special events. Many parents now keep in touch daily with their children through e-mail. Parents and children can share homework, can communicate on-line in real time, and can leave messages for each other to be read whenever available. This allows regular parent and child contact without one parent intruding into the dinner hour of the other parent's household. In any case, please give these ideas some serious consideration in making your plans."

Cautions Regarding Coparenting

In general, although coparenting to the maximal degree feasible is the ideal goal toward which the mediator should strive, there are circumstances in which the mediator may choose to soften advocacy of this goal and perhaps minimize the elaborations. In addition to circumstances in which coparenting is obviously not possible, such as when one parent is incarcerated or hospitalized for extended periods of time, the mediator should be alert to circumstances in which the best interests of the children would not be served by a high degree of coparenting. These may include situations in which one parent is unavailable to the child for extended periods of the time that the child would be in that parent's care—for example, when extensive travel is necessary in the parent's work or the parent's work hours necessitate leaving the children with sitters for extended periods of time. In addition, when a child tells the mediator of being afraid of one parent's unpredictability or abusiveness (input from the children will be discussed shortly) or when a child consistently refuses to spend time with one parent, the mediator must heed the warning and very cautiously assess the degree to which coparenting may or may not be in the children's best interests.

Obviously, these situations can pose a dilemma for the mediator, especially if her role is exclusive of arbitrating or making recommendations. She must guide and shape the available choices to best serve the children.

As an advocate for the children, she must maneuver the parents to accommodate to the needs of their children while being sensitive to the parents' own needs. If appealing to reason does not suffice, more confrontive suggestions can be offered. For example, consider a parent who works as a traveling salesperson and is on the road five days out of seven. If that parent insists on having the children alternate weeks for an even 50–50 percent split, even though it will involve the children staying with sitters most days and nights, the mediator must convey to this parent the negative effects such a plan will have on the children. The mediator should elaborate on the more workable possibilities for maximizing that parent's time with the children when the parent is available (for example, the two days at home per week, holidays, school vacations, summers), and should inform the parent of the value of children being with the other parent rather than with sitters whenever possible. The mediator may have to help the parents recognize the destructiveness of asserting their parental rights over their children's needs. It may also help for the mediator to venture an experienced guess about how the local court might view such a plan.

In describing the options available, the language that the mediator uses is critical. As Ricci (1980) pointed out, the language that the spouses use largely determines the conceptual way they will deal with each other. By the same token, the way the mediator uses language will determine the way the negotiations proceed. If the mediator continues to use concepts like "custody," "visitation," "the children's home," and "the custodial parent" throughout the negotiations, the spouses will remain in adversarial stances and the mediation process will be bumpy. If, however, very early in the process the mediator begins to shape her language to reflect the change in consciousness from ownership of children to sharing in parenting, the couple will soon follow suit. Although they may, in times of anger and resentment, revert to the older language, the mediator's regular use of the new language will continually reinforce the new conceptual way in which the couple are implicitly and explicitly being encouraged to think and act. Asking the couple how they would like to "share time with their children" and what specific plans they can arrange "for the children to be with their mother" or "spend an extended amount of time with their father" can go far in helping them view their relationships with the children and with each other in a more cooperative manner.

One problematic issue is the frequent parental interpretation of joint custody as meaning the children will spend exactly 50 percent of their time with each parent. If both parents agree to this notion, the mediator can proceed. However, if only one parent insists on it (in spite of the preempt offered on the topic; see Chapter Five) and the other parent resists it, the mediator must strive to get the insisting parent to abandon or at least reconsider this interpretation, since it often leads to an impasse in the negotiations. The psychological implications of exactly equal time are powerful to a resistant parent, and this resistance will hamper the making of more flexible and workable plans. Reminding the parent of the content of the preempt can often help. Moreover, the mediator must remain vigilant to avoid falling into the language pattern of talking about percentages of time spent with the children and must focus instead on specific, scheduled time.

The Children's Input

There are a number of situations in which it is helpful to get input from the children. If one of the parents indicates that the children have consistently expressed a preference for residing primarily at his or her house and the other parent disputes this, the children can be interviewed either separately or together with the parents (or in both circumstances). If one or more of the children have specifically requested to speak with the mediator, that request should be honored. If the parents have been unable to comprehend the destructive consequences to the children of their continued hostility and instead adopt self-righteous attitudes, having the children present in a session with the parents can give the parents the firsthand feedback they need (such "leveraging" of the children is discussed in Chapter Eleven).

Adolescents generally have clear preferences about where they would like to reside and how they would like to share their time with their parents. They should be given the opportunity to express their wishes to the mediator if they have not already explicitly expressed them to one or both parents. Moreover, because of the relative independence of their lives and the importance of their peer relationships and social, school, and athletic activities, the preferences of adolescents should be seriously considered in developing the final parenting agreement.

In contrast, children under the age of five or six will generally abide by the joint decisions of their parents and seldom need to be included in the mediation process. Although the expressed preferences of children of these ages often are transitory and situationally specific (depending on which parent they are with and how they are feeling at the time the preference is expressed), if a child has expressed a consistent preference over a significant period of time, the mediator should take heed, assess the intent and importance of the child's preference, and make certain that it gets conveyed effectively to the parents.

Children between six and twelve years of age are much more varied
both in their desires for input and in their tactical usefulness to the mediation process. Wallerstein and Kelly (1980) concluded that children below
the age of adolescence are not reliable judges of their own best interests
and that their preferences should therefore not be relied on in making decisions about postdivorce parenting arrangements. To support their conclusion, these researchers cite evidence of erratic emotional reactions,
decisions, and judgments regarding parents, especially in children between
the ages of nine and twelve.

Although the Wallerstein and Kelly findings may be valid, the decision
whether or not to include the children in the mediation process must be
made individually for each specific case. There is no doubt that there are
ten-year-olds, and even children as young as seven, who have well-
thought-out, legitimate reasons for preferring one parent's home over the
other's. These reasons need to be considered in the final decisions.

When a mediator decides that it is important to interview the children,
a number of factors become important in planning the approach. If a child
has specifically asked to be interviewed alone, or if the mediator suspects
it will be more helpful for the child to be interviewed without the parents
present, the mediator should get both parents to agree to the interview.
This can reduce the probability that one of the parents will invalidate the
child's preferences by claiming that the other parent primed the child beforehand. Although it happens only rarely, if one parent refuses to give
permission for the child to be interviewed, the mediator should discuss
that parent's concerns in private. The parent may be worried that interviewing the child will be too stressful or that the child might express
something that the parent does not want to hear nor want anyone else to
hear. If the mediator feels that it is important for the child to be interviewed, she must address these concerns. Although she cannot guarantee
that the child will not be under stress, she can reassure the parent by relating her own experience in dealing sensitively with children in such situations. Moreover, the mediator can inform the parent of the approach
that she will take in the interview. The mediator can also assure the parent that she will place any expressed preference of the child within its appropriate context but that if the child has some particularly strong feelings
about how he or she wants to share time with the parents, it should be
acknowledged, or else whatever arrangements the parents make may not
work out. If the parent remains unpersuaded, the mediator can suggest
that the child be interviewed with the parents present. If this is still unsatisfactory, the mediator may have to proceed without interviewing the
child.

When proceeding with an interview, and when there is more than one child at issue, I generally find it more useful to interview all the siblings together. This structure offers several positive benefits: it provides sibling support to each of the children in talking about uncomfortable topics; it gives the mediator data on the interactions, emotional bonds, and general relationships among the siblings; it usually gives the mediator a more accurate assessment of each of their needs and desires, since siblings will tend to keep each other honest and accurate as to incidents, attitudes, and feelings; and it is a more efficient use of the mediator's time. However, it is best to interview the children individually when there is a wide age gap between them, when they have previously expressed clearly different preferences, or when one child is extremely talkative and overpowers the others, effectively preventing them from sharing their feelings when together.

When it is deemed more helpful for the children to be interviewed together with the parents, the parents are instructed to request the attendance of the children by saying, "We'd like you to help us understand your feelings about the arrangements for spending time with each of us so that we can make better decisions for you." It is most important that neither parent directly ask the children to decide which parent they want to live with. Such a request is almost always interpreted by children as being asked to choose the parent they love more. Furthermore, it does not accurately represent the need for the child's input in the mediation process, since it is the parents, not the children, who must make the decision.

Having the parents present when the children are interviewed gives the mediator powerful leverage, for the mediator can orchestrate the children's verbalization or preferences in such a way that the parents will pay attention to them. If the mediator does not know whether the children have strong preferences, she should plan to interview them apart from their parents first and then, on the basis of the information obtained, decide whether to interview them also in the presence of their parents.

Telling their parents directly of their feelings about various time-sharing arrangements is, no doubt, one of the most difficult, frightening, and risky tasks for children, but it is also often one of the most important, since it can open up communication between them.

In all communications with children, building rapport is crucial in order to establish the level of trust required before a child will share feelings that are difficult to express. Talking about the child's interests, skills, friends, and pets is an easy and reliable way to build rapport. Guiding the child to talk about comforting and familiar things is relaxing for the child and also shows respect and support for his or her world. When the child appears reasonably comfortable, the mediator can begin to talk about issues of importance.

The particular language and words used must be addressed to the age of the child. I generally say the following: "As you know, your mom and dad are having trouble talking with each other and making decisions together about how to share time with you. It seems to me that they need to know how you feel about these arrangements. Your feelings are important to know so that your parents can make the best arrangements for you. The final decision about how your parents share time with you will be made by your parents, but it would be helpful if your parents knew first how you feel about it. Even if you don't have any strong feelings one way or another, that would be helpful for your parents to know, too."

As the child begins to elaborate upon his feelings, I gently probe and listen for whether the child has a particularly strong bond with one parent; how comfortable the child feels with each parent for short and extended periods; the nature and duration of neighborhood friendships; the nature and duration of bonds with any relatives who live close to the home; the child's degree of ease in handling changes of homes, neighbors, schools, and other circumstances; the best and worst consequences of extended stays at each parent's home; and rapport with siblings, stepparents, and stepbrothers and -sisters.

If the child is not very verbal or is hesitant to express his feelings about the situation, I attempt to address the child's fear, discomfort, anger, embarrassment, mistrust, and other difficult feelings by telling the child what I know about how other children feel in this situation. I will empathize with the child's feelings, present anecdotes about other similar-aged children, talk about the benefits to the child of helping the parents with their decisions, and generally encourage the child to share at least some feelings, even if it is only how rotten it feels to be interviewed about these feelings. For example, to a six-year-old girl, I might say, "You know, about three weeks ago I saw a girl in my office who was sitting right in that chair that you're sitting in. She was a little bit older than you are—she was, I believe seven years old—or was she only six and a half? I don't remember. Well, her mom and dad got divorced too, and, you know, she was very upset. She told me that when her mommy left, she thought she'd never see her again. But she soon learned that she was going to see her again. Then, you know what she said to me? She said that secretly she was real mad at her mommy for leaving her daddy. She felt confused, and later she felt sad, and she cried in her bedroom a lot. And you know what? She thought that she was the only girl in the whole world who felt that way when her mommy and daddy got divorced. But you know, when

I told her about the many other girls that I had seen who also had those same feelings when their parents got divorced, she was surprised, because she thought she was the only one. And then she didn't feel so all alone anymore. Now, I don't know if you've felt any of those ways or not. *(pause)* . . . Have you felt mad, or confused, or sad about your mommy and daddy not living together?"

At this point, the child usually will tell of similar feelings. A discussion of these feelings can then take place, which can lead to a discussion of her feelings about sharing time between her parents. This topic is very delicate and must be pursued with sensitivity. The timing and pacing of questions about time-sharing preferences must be carefully monitored, and the exact words used must be carefully selected so as to avoid any suggestion that the mediator is pressuring the child to choose between her parents. Oblique questions are much less intimidating to children than direct questions, especially about sensitive topics. For example, the mediator can ask, "What does it feel like when you are with Mommy, at her house?" or "What does it feel like with Daddy, at his house?" Such indirect questions are preferable to such direct questions as "Who do you want to live with, your mommy or your daddy?"

Throughout the interview, I will offer generous amounts of emotional support, give reassurance of the parents' love for the child, and try to explain what it does and does not mean for the child that her parents got divorced. I will also reassure the child that her negative feelings do not mean that she cannot or should not continue to love both parents.

If, after interviewing the children alone, the mediator feels that it would not be productive to have the children express their feelings directly to the parents, the mediator can meet alone with the parents and report the children's feelings, serving as an advocate for them. The wording of such a report is crucial, since the parents are going to feel vulnerable to criticism or rejection by their children. For example, if a particular child says he loves his mother more than his father, the mediator should deemphasize this statement and instead relate things the child said that were favorable to the father. Or if the child's stated preference seems to be based on coaching by one parent or on momentary anger at one parent, the mediator should be very careful in reporting the child's expressed feelings to the parents. Doing so could unbalance the negotiations to a stalemate, with the child gaining nothing but more parental conflict. Hence the mediator must assess very carefully the sincerity, intent, and meaning of a child's stated preference for a particular time-sharing arrangement. Of course, if a child reports being scared to death of a parent or reports that the parent beats him or is always drunk or unconscious when with the child or has been molesting him, the mediator would surely need to confront the parents with this information, but carefully and with tact, to avoid a backlash on the child.

If, after interviewing a child alone, the mediator feels it would be productive to have the child relate his feelings to the parents, the mediator should explain this to the child and get the child's explicit permission to invite the parents in. The mediator should also rehearse with the child several ways that the child might express his feelings. The mediator must always offer support to the child in this task, by saying, for example, "I know this is going to be difficult, but I will help you say what you want to say." The mediator can then invite the parents in and help the child express his feelings to the parents and, if possible, encourage a limited dialogue between the parents and the child about those feelings. The parents are prompted to be supportive of the child's expressions, even if one or both do not like what the child is saying.

It is important for the mediator to be aware that a child may be criticized or punished later by one or both parents for what the child says during this interview. To decrease the probability of this, the mediator should discuss with the parents the negative consequences to the child of their doing so. Obtaining in the child's presence their acknowledgment of this problem and their commitment to refrain from such criticism or punishment can help the child speak more freely. Experience has shown that when the mediator deals with this issue explicitly, most parents respect this need of their children. If criticism is forthcoming, it is usually directed at the other parent, rather than at the child.

The mediator must then decide whether to have the child remain or leave the room while the parents negotiate. This should depend largely on the parents' responses to the feelings expressed by the child. If the parents appear very defensive, hurt, and quiet, it is best to ask the child to wait out of the room while the parents have time to digest what they heard. If, conversely, the parents are very understanding of the child's utterances and there seems to be an affectionate communication between the child and the parents, the child could be encouraged to remain in the room while they all negotiate. In general, however, younger children (under five or six) should not be encouraged to remain during these negotiations, since they are too likely to misinterpret things said during the parents' discussions.

Requesting Proposals

The mediator is now in a position to request from each of the parents proposals for workable coparenting arrangements. The timing of this request is critical, since it is the first point in the process where the parents are asked to offer explicit statements of their respective positions. If this request is made too early, when one or the other parent is still resistant or perhaps upset about something said earlier in the session, the proposal made by one or both parents may be unreasonable. If the request is made too late, there may have been too much opportunity for accusations or expressions of hostility, with the result that the mediation process is further delayed. With experience, a mediator learns to time the request for proposals so that it comes at an opportune moment.

Often by the time this stage is reached, the mediator has some idea of the proposals that will be made. If this is so, the mediator can leave many aspects of the proposals implicit. Doing so can allow the couple to save face. As Haley (1973, 1976) has written, asking clients the obvious about their feelings or beliefs is often just being rude and disrespectful under the guise of being clever and insightful. For example, if the children currently are living primarily with the father and have expressed a consistent desire to remain there, the mediator might entertain proposals by asking the father, in a manner that is indirectly but strongly supportive of the mother, "How do you propose to arrange it so that the children are with their mother on a regular and frequent basis?" Implicit in this question are the facts that the children need regular access to both parents, the understanding that the children are likely to remain residing primarily with their father, and support for the mother's rights in the veiled form of a preemptive challenge to the father to develop a constructive solution.

If, however, the mediator has no idea about what proposals might be offered at this time, the request can be stated: "Now I'd like to hear some proposals about how you two are going to share time with your children." Phrasing the request in this manner implies that both parents will work together on this task and that the children will be shared, rather than competed for or taken from one parent by the other. While such phrasing clearly helps reduce the struggle in which the parents will engage, there is still likely to be a struggle, and one that will persist until both parents feel reasonably secure that their respective needs have been satisfied.

Some mediators prefer to have the parents submit their proposals in writing. Although this does give the spouses more time to think out their proposals, it has the disadvantage of consolidating their defenses early. Social psychology research has demonstrated that people feel obliged to defend a position once it is formulated (Festinger, 1957). Hence if the formulation of the parents' positions can be guided by the mediator within the mediational context, they will feel somewhat more compelled to offer cooperative rather than adversarial proposals from the start. So I prefer that the parents present their proposals orally, under the mediator's guidance.

Ending Phase

Once the children have given their input (if any) and the parents have offered their proposals, the mediator is ready to shape the proposal into a workable agreement. The mediator's role as mediator is most apparent at this point in the process. It is here that the delicate balance between the spouses can be thrown off by one wrong move on the part of the mediator. During this phase, the mediator must utilize all the information gathered in the beginning phase of the process and maintain awareness of the current dynamics and past issues of the couple. The tension is heightened as the couple approaches either resolution or a costly trip to court.

Shaping the Proposal

The mediator needs to offer the couple suggestions of alternative ways to arrange their plan. These suggestions must be fully enlightened by details of the parents' lifestyles, tolerances, feelings about each other, resistant areas, and other relevant considerations. The mediator's suggestions should be geared to be maximally acceptable to both parents. The mediator should support each suggestion offered with an indication of the benefits to the children and to both parents.

The mediator must anticipate the specific issues and details that should be included in a given proposal. Some couples need a fairly lengthy list of very specific agreements, since they are likely to quibble about every detail that is not spelled out in black and white. Other couples need very few areas specifically delineated, since they tend not to argue about details but only about main points. The mediator should offer many suggestions to the first kind of couple and few to the second kind. Offering too few suggestions to the first couple can result in no agreement or a recurrence of conflict in the weeks following the sessions due to the lack of specificity in the agreement. Offering too many suggestions to the second couple can stir up old conflicts and create new conflict between the couple, resulting in no agreement.

The suggestions offered by the mediator often are simple and logical solutions to a particular conflict. It can seem baffling to the beginning mediator why a couple did not think of a particular suggestion before the mediator brought it up. However, with experience, the mediator comes to see how blind a recently divorced parent can be. People going through divorce often experience a kind of cognitive freeze in which rational ideas do not come forth easily. Emotional resistance, too, can prevent the parents from solving even the most elementary problems. So in offering suggestions, it is more important for the mediator to be informed and sensitive to the particular dynamics of the couple than to be particularly creative in the solutions presented.

In attempting to maintain balance when offering suggestions to the couple, the mediator should consider two kinds on which to focus: natural marital balances and mediator-initiated balances. Natural marital balances are those that exist between the spouses; usually, they have existed throughout the marriage. These are based largely on power differences, tolerance differences, and differences in the significance of particular issues to each spouse. Any stable pattern of balances between the couple will manifest itself during the negotiations, and the mediator simply needs to note the decisions that result naturally from it. For example, if a father proposes having the children stay at his house six days a week and the mother and children do not seem to object, the mediator should think twice before suggesting, for example, that the couple split the week in half between the mother and the father.

Mediator-initiated balances, by contrast, develop when the mediator makes a suggestion that tips the balance from an extreme spousal position to a more moderate or equal position. Using the same example, if a father proposes having the children with him six days a week and both children and mother strongly object, the task of the mediator is to present to the father the benefits of a more equal sharing of time with the children. The mediator can use research information, clinical experience, and the expressed feelings of the children and the mother as backup, all the while supporting the father for his obvious devotion to the children. The mediator can reemphasize the importance to the children of more frequent access to both parents and also stress the importance to the father of having time to himself. In essence, if there is an uncomfortable imbalance between father and mother, the mediator must initiate a more reasonable balance to achieve a satisfactory resolution.

Getting Agreements

The mediator should choose the path of least resistance and seek agreement on the easier issues first. Typically, these are issues like arrangements for transporting the children between the parents' homes, arrangements for the children to have phone access to both parents, selecting the particular clothes and children's belongings to be regularly transferred between the parents' homes, and sharing of special days. Usually the parents will inform the mediator, either explicitly or implicitly, which are the easier issues. In spite of the many disagreements that a given couple may have, there are usually at least several issues upon which they agree. Initially, their agreements may be based on a desire to relieve some of the tension by settling something. Still, an agreement of any kind is helpful in that it seems to reduce the couple's general resistance to engage in discussion.

As the spouses come to agreements about these issues of lesser importance, and they often realize how much easier it is to agree than to disagree, they may still maintain some resistance as a form of self-protection. The mediator should proceed to the next issue as if there were no resistance at all. It is always better to move into another area of potential agreement than to get stuck arguing with a parent who is resistant in one area.

In the event that one parent offers resistance to a comprehensive or long-term plan, the mediator should suggest a temporary agreement. This can be either the same comprehensive agreement plan already proposed or a scaled-down version, but enacted in either case for a limited period, anything from one year to as short as two weeks. If need be, this can be framed as an *experimental* or *probationary* period, depending on what concepts are needed to help the parents feel safe and justified in acquiescing to the temporary agreement. Offering such a temporary agreement almost always functions to reduce the parent's resistance. A temporary agreement serves several purposes: it gives the resistant parent an escape clause, by offering a sense of security and control, and helps the parent save face in submitting to the compromise; it yields an agreement, which serves to defuse the present power struggle; and it allows a real-life test of a cooperatively made plan for sharing the children. Moreover, experience has shown that on reevaluation at the end of the designated time period, the temporary agreement is rarely thrown out entirely; typically, it is modified slightly to be more effective. In fact, most often, once the parents have reached a temporary agreement, they do not even need to renegotiate. The reasons for this are not clear, but it is likely that over time, life events change perspectives so profoundly that the original power struggle no longer seems important or worth the effort.

The "Last Issue"

Occasionally, after all the minor issues and most of the larger issues are settled, one or two holdout issues persist. These are the issues that one parent hangs on to until the very end—the last stronghold of resistance. Years ago in California, this issue was often the designation of legal custody. However, since joint legal custody is now considered the norm in California (Kelly, 1993a), most parents no longer quibble over this particular issue any longer. However, in jurisdictions where parenting disputes do not commonly result in joint legal custody, parents may still argue intensely about the designation of legal custody as the last issue.

Saving this issue until the very end serves several purposes. It allows the couple to experience cooperative efforts in finding areas of agreement before tackling the tougher issues, it gives the mediator time to reinforce the couple's cooperativeness, and it gives the mediator the leverage of the couple's earlier successes to use in encouraging the final agreements.

By far the most effective approach for settling this last issue is for the mediator to remain subtle and indirect. If the mediator draws too much attention to this last point, one of the parents may feel challenged to take a rigid stance, bringing the mediation process to a standstill. The psychological and symbolic connotations of the concepts of sole legal custody and joint legal custody are often greatly disproportionate to their real significance. Sole legal custody connotes that there is a winner and a loser, a competent parent and an incompetent one, a loved parent and an unloved one, while joint legal custody connotes cooperation, compromise, and balanced power. One parent may dread joint legal custody, while the other may fear sole legal custody, and each may feel that the wrong designation will result in irreparable harm to the children. However, the direct ramifications of legal custody seldom determine the psychological well-being of a child. The parent with legal custody has a say in the major life decisions of a child, but the day to-day decisions—which are, in fact, much more psychologically meaningful to a child—are made by the parent with whom the child happens to be staying on any given day. The mediator can usually minimize the importance of the exact designation used by providing an appropriate perspective on the issue. It is often helpful to remind the parents that the degree of postdivorce parental cooperation is a much more important determinant of the psychological health of the children.

If all the earlier agreements look cooperative, the mediator can assume that the parents are implicitly agreeing to joint legal custody. At this point, the mediator can say something like, "So we will call this joint legal custody, all right?" Usually, if asked in this fashion, both parents will agree. If, however, the mediator were to present this final decision as a major and difficult one, it could be predicted that if either of the parents wanted to have one last issue of contention, he or she would seize the opportunity to stalemate the process.

An inexperienced mediator may feel quite disheartened when a couple works out all the details of a parenting agreement and then gets unexpectedly stuck on this last symbolic issue. If, after exploring each parent's understanding of and concerns about the legal custody designation (see Chapter Seven), neither parent will budge, the mediator can try using one or more of the impasse-breaking strategies presented in Chapter Eleven. If nothing seems to work, a partial agreement can be written up (see Chapter Seven), and the issue of legal custody can be sent back to the attorneys and/or the court for a decision.

Fortunately, however, couples seldom fail to resolve this issue and end up back in court. With the settlement of this last issue, the mediator gets to experience one of life's pleasures, the resolution of human conflict.

DRAFTING THE
MEDIATION AGREEMENT

AGREEMENTS REACHED through the mediation process are formalized in a written mediation agreement. This document represents all the hard work of both the couple and the mediator. As such, it must be relevant, clear, and useful. It must stand as a lucid statement of the parenting arrangements to which both spouses have agreed.

Many couples, before entering mediation, have already made parenting agreements with each other that have failed. These may be oral or written. Both types typically break down for some or all of the following reasons: absence of a mutually acceptable context of cooperation; hidden motives that can lead to sabotage of the agreements; differing interpretations of the agreed-upon clauses due to lack of precision and clarity of wording; inclusion of inappropriate, insensitive, imbalanced, or unworkable clauses; exclusion of certain appropriate and necessary clauses; absence of an agreed-upon format for making future modifications.

Oral agreements often break down the first time one parent irritates the other. For example, suppose that for the second or third time in a row, a father returns the children home an hour later than the orally agreed time. The mother confronts the father, who then retorts, "I didn't know that you really meant five o'clock; it didn't sound like it was that important when we talked about it." The argument often escalates because the fact that nothing was put in writing leaves open the possibilities for distortion by both parents to justify their respective interpretations of the agreement.

Written agreements about parenting arrangements, while clearer and more definite than oral agreements, typically have been made either by court order or by attorney stipulation. Such agreements often suffer from excessive rigidity and insensitivity to both marital dynamics and the spousal strategies for sabotage. Because the context in both of these circumstances is adversarial, there is ordinarily no precedent for flexibility or cooperative modification of the agreement should circumstances change. As instruments of the legal system, these agreements usually cannot deal very responsively with the children's and parents' needs and circumstances.

In contrast to these agreements, the mediation agreement derives from a supportive, cooperative, nonadversarial context, within which the marital dynamics, hidden motives, needs, and less guarded desires of the children and the parents have been systematically taken into account. Moreover, the agreement itself is born out of a direct communication between the parties involved, rather than by court imposition or by the indirect, almost inferential process of adversarial negotiations. This provides the couple with a sense of direct control over every detail of the agreement. It frequently gives a psychological boost of mastery to the parents, in the midst of feelings of helplessness. Hence if the mediation process is done well, the mediation agreement is the most valid and useful kind of agreement about parenting that is possible to achieve.

As every therapist knows professionally and as all of us know personally, interpersonal conflict is increased by disorganization and the absence of mutually acceptable rules of conduct and is decreased by organization and structure. Before such conflict can be reduced, there has to be a common focus on the elements of structure that are necessary to create order out of disorder. Focusing is recognized as an important element of self-healing as well as a tool for behavior and attitude change across a multitude of therapy approaches (see Budman, 1981; Saposnek, 1984). Whether it be the acupuncturist's needle, the behaviorist's assigned behavioral task, or the hypnotist's repeated words and images, the point of focus serves to create ease out of dis-ease, order out of disorder, and harmony out of disharmony. The mediation agreement serves as the common focus for the conflicting spouses. Through sensitive and responsive design, it directs the attention of each spouse to the specific issues that have in the past led to conflict, and through careful wording, it offers concrete and workable resolutions to this conflict.

Structure of the Agreement

Different mediation agreements are written up for different types of referral. For the self-referred couple who draw up their own divorce settlement and consult a mediator solely to assist them in making coparenting arrangements that will best meet the needs of their children, the written agreement can be in the form of a simple typed list of clauses to which they agree. They each receive a copy, and the mediator keeps a copy for his records. Since spouses who choose these self-divorce procedures are usually quite amicable, it is often not even necessary for them to sign the written agreement. The document serves as a simple clarification of what they already agree to in principle and in spirit, and they usually follow through quite successfully. If there are any issues that might require legal perspectives or advice (for example, financial issues), the mediator should refer the couple to one or, if need be, two consulting attorneys to review the agreement.

A second type of mediation referral is the divorcing couple who have each retained an attorney to work out their dissolution and are in conflict over custody and/or visitation issues. As part of their negotiations, the attorneys stipulate to private mediation for the custody and visitation issues, and the spouses come to mediation with varying degrees of willingness. The written document that results from this mediation should be in the form of a *memorandum of understanding* that includes the agreements reached and a brief discussion of the issues over which no agreement may have been reached. The spouses may sign the memorandum, and the attorneys can submit it with its language intact as part of the marital settlement agreement. Or the attorneys may rewrite its content directly into the more comprehensive marital settlement agreement.

Then there are the couples who have been ordered by a judge to attend private mediation following a court hearing on an order to show cause (OSC) regarding custody and/or visitation. In these cases, the judge usually requests a written mediation agreement. If the mediator is known by the court as willing to serve as an arbitrator and make recommendations in the event that mediation fails, the court may request these recommendations as to the custody and visitation arrangements that the mediator thinks would best serve the interests of the children. If agreements are reached, it may be helpful but not necessary for the couple to sign the document before sending it to the judge.

Mandatory mediation laws result in several types of referral. In some cases, there is an automatic referral by the court at the time of an OSC hearing regarding modifications of custody and/or visitation. Under California's mandatory mediation law, some counties instead allow attorneys to stipulate to mediation before a court hearing, thus saving court costs. Some counties even allow divorcing or divorced spouses themselves to stipulate to mediation simply by filing with the court a signed one-page petition and paying a nominal filing fee, saving both attorney and court costs. In each of these cases, the mediation agreement is signed both by the spouses and by the mediator, with copies going to the judge, to each attorney, to each spouse, and to the mediator. In the event that no agreements are reached, some counties require the mediator to send recommendations to the court and to the attorneys, and other counties allow the mediator to retain the privilege of confidentiality and simply send a statement back to the court and attorneys that says "No agreement reached—referred back to court" with no further details of the content of the mediation sessions.

Partial Agreements

Occasionally cases are referred under mandatory mediation in which the couple are able to reach agreement on many or most issues but not on all. The mediator can then write up a *partial agreement*. The clauses are written up in the same order and fashion as in a full agreement, but at the end a separate section is included that describes the issues on which no agreements were reached. To retain a positive, cooperative stance, this last section can begin: "Because the parents are unable to reach agreement on issue X (or on issues X, Y, and Z), they agree to request that the court make the decision for them on this issue (on these issues)."

If the mediator is able to help the parents formulate a number of possible options to resolve a particular issue, even if they cannot agree on which option to choose, these can be included. For example, the agreement can state: "The following possible plans for sharing the children were developed by the parents: plan A, plan B, and plan C. Because the parents were unable to decide among these options, they are requesting that the court decide this matter for them."

Although a partial agreement still may necessitate a court hearing (albeit brief), the benefits of a partial agreement over none are several. First, there appears to be a psychological advantage to the couple in signing a statement that includes any agreements at all, even if some matters remain unresolved. This gives them at least some hope that further cooperative efforts may be possible. Second, it saves time, money, and stress for the couple by reducing the number of issues needing to be argued by their respective attorneys. Third, it facilitates the work of the attorneys and judge by separating the issues of contention from other issues.

Clarity of Wording

The importance of words in shaping our thoughts, beliefs, attitudes, emotions, behaviors, and relationships cannot be overstated. Human history has been significantly influenced by the strategic use of language (see Watzlawick, 1976). More recently, words have been discovered to have therapeutic potential for dealing with problems of both physical and psychological origin. The crafts of the diplomat, the politician, the lawyer, the poet, the therapist, and the mediator are basically grounded in the precision of word choice. The greater the precision of words used, the more influential the person can be.

An agreement as significant as the one developed in mediation must be written very carefully. The exact wording chosen for the various clauses of this document is a delicate matter and can make the difference between a workable plan and one that escalates old marital conflicts. Four aspects of the wording are particularly important: the clarity of the clauses, the degree of detail in the clauses, the balance of spousal concessions, and the attitude and perspective connoted.

For the mediation agreement to be more workable than previous oral or written agreements, the conditions of each clause must be spelled out clearly. For example, a clause written "Father will get the children every other weekend" allows many possible misinterpretations. The father may interpret this as meaning Friday after school until Sunday bedtime or even Monday morning, while the mother may interpret it as meaning Saturday morning until early Sunday afternoon. If, instead, the clause is written to reflect days and times that are convenient for both spouses, there is little or no possibility for differing interpretations. For example, "The children will be with father on alternate weekends beginning the weekend of January 1, 1998. On his weekends, he will pick the children up from their mother's house between 4:30 and 4:45 P.M. on Friday and will return them to their mother's house on Sunday between 6:30 and 7:00 P.M. If he ever anticipates being late for either of these transfer times, he agrees to call the children's mother at least one-half hour before the pickup or drop-off time." Because conflict so often arises over the pickup and drop-off times, it is generally a good idea to negotiate and write down a time period within which the transfer of the children will take place. This gives some room for lateness and helps keep the issue from inciting conflict. The time period must be negotiated between the spouses until it is acceptable to and truly workable for both spouses before entering it on the written agreement.

Degree of Detail

A second important aspect of the agreement's wording is the degree of details written down. As a general rule, the more detail included, the less the spouses will have to fight about later. However, too much detail can be counterproductive. For one thing, excessive detail may unintentionally convey the message to the spouses that there will be debilitating conflict if they do not include a written exposition of every last transaction to be made between them. Such a message can effectively destroy the potential for a cooperative joint custody arrangement. The spouses may be left feeling that unless they carry their mediator around with them at all times, there is no hope for a cooperative coparenting relationship to develop.

Another reason for avoiding excessive detail is that some spouses are offended by highly structured arrangements, viewing them as rigid. Following mediation, such a spouse will often systematically and subtly sabotage each clause of the agreement, not because the clauses are unworkable, but because their rigidity triggers rebellious feelings in the spouse, who may be yearning to be free after the divorce. To such a spouse, an overly detailed agreement may also feel demeaning and condescending. He or she may feel that the intent of the mediation process—to give control back to the parents—has actually backfired and that the mediation agreement has become even more restrictive than a judge's decree. Moreover, the potential for spousal conflict may rise even higher if the other spouse uses the written agreement as a weapon of revenge against the rebelling spouse and sticks rigidly to each detail.

Some couples require very little detail in their written agreement. These are generally couples who have a fairly smooth and organized child-sharing routine worked out, either by chance compatibility on this matter or by previous private negotiations between themselves. They typically come to mediation over a single major issue or just a few minor issues, such as a need for clarification of the specific days that the children will be with each parent, a need for a plan to share holidays equitably, or a need for written acknowledgment that both parents agree to consult each other before moving out of the area. Typically, such couples have a basic trust in each other's parenting abilities, and they respect each other's right and need to stay significantly involved in the children's lives. Although they may have strong negative feelings toward each other, they seldom have many doubts about the welfare of the children while in each other's care. Moreover, they have usually maintained a level of postdivorce communication such that they can negotiate directly with each other to work out the necessary details for sharing their children. For instance, once the number of regular days that the children will spend at each of their homes has been settled, they frequently have no need to include a written plan for sharing holidays and special days with the children. By mutual consent, they maintain that they will have no difficulty in developing their own workable plan outside of mediation. Since the mediator can trust their declarations, such details need not be included in the written agreement.

Some couples, however, have such basic disagreements, mistrust, or doubts about each other's intentions, abilities, and resources for taking care of the children that it is necessary to include great detail in the agreement. Each spouse may insist that his or her long list of conditions be included before agreeing to the conditions of the other spouse. While such details often appear quite petty to the mediator, they may have great significance to the spouses, both personally and strategically. For example, in one case, the spouses needed to include a plan for dividing the baby clothes and baby pictures of their teenage children before they could agree on a joint custody plan. After forty-five minutes of negotiations, they finally were able to resolve the issue by developing a plan for joint custody of the baby clothes such that they would alternate possession of half of the clothes every six months. Moreover, copies of the baby pictures were to be made from the original prints, for which each spouse was to pay half. However, because the copies would not be as clear as the originals, the couple agreed to have a neutral third party randomly assign half the originals and half the copies of all the pictures to each spouse. Then, because one spouse had negatives for about one-third of the pictures, it was decided that whichever spouse had the copy of a particular picture after their random division to the spouses would be entitled to personally claim the negative. This spouse would then have the option to have a print made directly from the negative, at his or her own cost. Even though these issues were closer to property division than to child-sharing concerns, their symbolic significance, which related to the resolution of their feelings about sharing their children, was so strong that the mediator felt it was important to include these details in the agreement. (Examples of agreements with differing amounts of detail are presented in Appendix F.)

Balance of Concessions

The third important aspect of the written agreement's wording is the balance of spousal concessions. Just as it is crucial for the mediator to maintain a balance between the husband and wife throughout the negotiations, so is it critical to preserve this balance in the final written agreement. Because the mediation process requires both spouses to compromise to some extent if it is to be successful, the agreements that are included in the written document represent a list of concessions made by each spouse. If, however, the concessions made by one spouse significantly outweigh the concessions made by the other spouse, renewed conflict may erupt.

Sometimes a single concession by one spouse can be equivalent to several concessions by the other. For example, a wife yielding sole legal and physical custody of a child and reluctantly agreeing to joint legal and physical custody with a spouse for whom she feels a great deal of mistrust may feel recompensed by an extensive, detailed list of provisions for the care, welfare, and education of the child when in the husband's care. Hence the importance of achieving a balance of spousal concessions does not necessarily mean including one concession by the wife for every concession by the husband; rather, it means including an equivalent value of concessions for each spouse.

Occasionally, one spouse refuses to be singled out on disproportionately many conditions even when those concessions are balanced by a single major concession on the part of the other spouse. This is especially true if the spouse allegedly has been involved in alcohol or drug abuse, child neglect or abuse, violence, or the like. In these cases, the mediator must carefully monitor the number of concessions that the accused spouse can tolerate in the written agreement. Occasionally, one too many concessions asked of this spouse will trigger heavy resistance and possibly refusal to complete mediation. If this happens, the mediator must back off and negotiate a way for this spouse to concede these points in a face-saving way. One technique is for the mediator to word the one spouse's concessions in a way that is tactfully inclusive of both spouses and focuses on the children's welfare. For example, instead of writing, "Father agrees to refrain from using cocaine or alcohol while driving the children or while in the presence of the children," the mediator could write, "Both parents agree to protect their children by not exposing them to any use of drugs or alcohol while the children are in the care of each parent, and they agree not to drive the children while under the influence of alcohol or any illegal drug." Sometimes the other spouse will resent being included in such a clause if he or she does not partake in substance abuse. In such cases, the mediator can usually negotiate an acceptable phrasing between one that singles out one spouse and one that includes both spouses.

Cooperative and Child-Centered Focus

The final point to remember in wording the written agreement is the importance of emphasizing the cooperative attitude and child-centered perspective of the mediation approach to custody and visitation decisions. Whereas the legal wording of such written documents almost always takes the point of view of the *parents' rights and privileges,* the mediation agreement can and should be written largely *from the perspective of the child.* For example, the traditional wording of a court-ordered custody and visitation plan is something like the following: "(1) The parties shall have joint legal custody of the minor child. (2) Physical custody is awarded to the mother. (3) The father shall have visitation with the minor child alternate weekends, on Wednesday of each week, and alternate holidays."

The mediator, however, can shift the perspective by writing it up as follows: "(l) Both parents agree to share joint legal custody of their child, Alicia. (2) Alicia will share her time with her parents according to the following schedule: (a) She will be with her father from Friday after school at 3:00 P.M. until Sunday evening between 7:00 and 7:15 P.M. on alternate weekends. She will also be with her father from 4:30 P.M. on Wednesday until her father takes her to school on Thursday morning, each week. (b) She will be with her mother from Sunday evening until Wednesday afternoon and then from Thursday after school to the following Wednesday, except on the alternate weekends that she will spend with her father. (c) Alicia will share her holidays with her parents by spending the first seven days of Christmas vacation with her father and the remaining days with her mother this year . . ."

In this example, the focus is on how the child will share her time with each parent. This represents a conceptual shift from *parents owning their children* to *children sharing their parents*. Such a shift is in the true spirit of mediation. Such wording may also help reorient the perspectives of the attorneys and judges involved in the case. While some attorneys and judges still prefer, or even insist, that any legal document be worded in legalese, perhaps enough examples of child-centered coparenting agreements can eventually modify the spirit of the law, at least on these particular domestic issues.

Content of the Agreement

The primary goal of child custody mediation is to develop a plan that will reduce spousal acrimony and increase cooperative decision making, and the secondary goal is to maximize the children's access to both parents. To achieve these goals, the final document needs to include five areas of content: a designation of legal custody, a plan for regular time sharing of the children, a plan for sharing time on holidays and special days, adjunct clauses to facilitate cooperative time sharing, and a clause that specifies the procedure for future modification of the mediation agreement.

Legal Custody

The first clause included in the mediation agreement (but the last clause negotiated) states how the spouses have decided to designate legal custody.

Except for the traditional designation of sole custody (which implies both legal and physical custody) to one parent and reasonable visitation to the other parent, other designations of custody have had few clear legal definitions. Generally, it is assumed that legal custody entitles the legal custodian to make decisions about the child's educational and religious upbringing and to give consent to medical, dental, and psychological treatment for the child. Moreover, physical custody is assumed to entitle the custodian to the companionship of the child (MacGowan, 1981). However, controversy continues over the actual demarcation between legal custody and physical custody, in terms of the real nature of parental influences on the child. The controversy is especially great over the designation of joint custody, which, as a general term, implies shared legal and physical custody. However, as Clingempeel and Reppucci (1982, p. 103) note, "Practically speaking . . . this may translate into a multitude of variations and does not mean that physical custody is necessarily divided evenly between parents or that there is an equal sharing of childcare responsibilities. The pattern of alternating between parental homes (including the duration of stays with each parent and the frequency of environmental changes) varies widely so that one parent may have physical custody a greater percentage of the time (and thus have greater responsibilities with regard to daily care and activities . . .)."

Unless the actual daily care and daily responsibilities for the children are shared relatively equally, the designation of joint legal custody may be limited in its practical significance for the child's upbringing. However, some fathers' groups have asserted that unless there is joint physical custody in the idealized sense for the father (equal time with each parent), joint legal custody is not really meaningful to them. Nevertheless, as mentioned earlier, the psychological benefit to a parent achieving joint legal custody, with its connotation of equal legal power, may be extremely important for certain parents and should be seriously considered by the mediator.

Other designations of legal custody that may be approved by a court are *alternating* or *divided custody* and *split custody*. Alternating custody permits each parent to have one or several children for a part of a year, for alternating portions of a year, or for alternating years. Each parent alternately assumes the responsibility given to a sole custodian during the time period when the child is with that parent. Reciprocal visitation rights are given to the noncustodial parent. It should be noted that alternating custody is not joint custody, since the parents never have *simultaneous* legal custody of any particular child. Split custody, which applies only to families with two or more children, allows each parent to be the sole legal custodian of at least one child all the time. For example, the mother might assume custody of one child and the father of the other two, and each parent would have visitation rights for the child or children not in his or her custody.

Of the legal custody designations available, joint custody remains the most controversial in terms of its ambiguity of definition; its legal, theoretical, and practical significance; and its sociological implications. In spite of its problematic nature, however, it appears to reflect the ideal spirit of shared parenting that is implemented, in varying forms, by mediation. As such, joint legal custody generally seems to be a more desirable legal designation than sole, alternating, or split custody, unless specifically contraindicated by circumstances, as previously noted.

Regular Time-Sharing Schedule

The next clause included in the mediation agreement is the plan for how each of the children will share time with each of the parents. This written plan will stand as the descriptive substitute for the legal designations of physical custody and visitation. While such designations may be required in the formal court order of particular jurisdictions, the connotations of ownership of children and of the insignificance of the visiting parent are contrary to the spirit of shared parenting. They also seem contrary to the intent of a joint custody preference or presumption currently held in a number of states. When such legal designations are necessary, the mediator can begin the wording of the clause as follows: "Both parents agree to share physical custody (and visitations) of their children according to the following schedule: Jessica will be with her mother on . . . and with her father on . . . ." With such wording, the focus shifts back to the child after the required legal opening.

The variety of ways for divorced parents and their children to share time with one another is limited only by their individual schedules. If the couple have difficulty coming up with possible ways to share time, the mediator can suggest a variety of ways that reflect the greatest degree of sharing that the couple seem able to tolerate. These can range from the children having total open access to two homes within walking distance of each other to the children staying in one home and the parents alternately moving in and out of the house according to a set schedule to the children spending equal or disproportionate amounts of time at each parent's home. Or, if the couple need something more traditional, the children can spend the school year at one home and part or all of vacations at the other.

When the children are going to spend the great majority of their time at one parent's house (for example, during the school year), weekend times should be carefully considered. The mediator should alert the parents that, next to holidays and vacation times, weekends are typically the most flexible periods for children to spend time with either parent since most parents do not work (and the children do not attend school) on weekends. If at all possible, it is generally advisable for parents to share the weekends in some sort of alternating fashion, with the children spending at least one full weekend per month with each parent.

Holiday and Vacation Schedule

Included next in the agreement is the plan for sharing special times during the year with the children. These include regular school vacation times, national holidays and their occasional extended weekends (New Year's Day, Presidents' Day, Easter, Memorial Day, Independence Day, Labor Day, Veterans Day, Thanksgiving, Christmas), special festive days (Valentine's Day, St. Patrick's Day, Mother's Day, Father's Day, Halloween), special personal days (family members' birthdays and unanticipated special occasions), and special religious and cultural days (Martin Luther King Jr.'s Birthday, Good Friday, Cinco de Mayo, Rosh Hashanah, Yom Kippur, Chanukah, and so on).

Most couples do not celebrate or find personal significance in all such special days. Moreover, most court-ordered decrees primarily specify schedules for regular school vacation times and, occasionally, national holidays, since these occasions usually include days off from work and school that parents and children can spend together.

In developing a plan for holidays and special days, the mediator first needs to ask each parent which holidays or special days are of particular personal significance. For example, one spouse may traditionally spend a particular holiday with the extended family, while for the other spouse that holiday does not have any special significance. Many of the major holidays can often be divided up equitably according to the parents' personal preferences. Then the special days that are not particularly special to either parent can be subsumed under the regular time-sharing plan.

For the holidays and special days on which both parents want to share time with the children, the mediator can suggest several workable solutions. The most traditional solution is to alternate the holidays during a year, reversing the alternation every year.

Another plan is to divide the longer holiday periods into two phases so that the children spend part of each holiday with each parent. For example, Easter week can be divided in half (or into two separate weeklong periods, if there is also a spring school break), and Christmas vacation, which is typically two weeks long, can be divided so that the children can spend the first portion (through Christmas Eve) with their father and the second portion (Christmas night through New Year's day) with their mother. The schedule can remain the same every year or switch every other year. A third, less desirable plan is to have one child with one parent and the siblings with the other parent for a particular holiday and then switch every other holiday or year. This can work if the siblings do not enjoy each other's company or if each parent insists on having at least one child present on every holiday. However, this plan deprives the siblings of contact with each other during times that are usually fun and special.

Summer Schedule

Summers can be shared in a more flexible way, since the time available for the child to spend with each parent is almost completely a function of the parents' availability. Summer is the ideal time for a child to share more extended periods of time with each parent, particularly one whom the child may be with less frequently, or not at all, during the school year.

Depending on the time-sharing arrangements made for the school year, the child can spend large portions of the summer with each parent, on a rotating basis—for example, six weeks (or four weeks) with one followed by six (four) weeks with the other. Occasionally, summers can be divided by the child's scheduled summer activities. For example, the father may want to take the child on a camping trip for the first three weeks of summer vacation, and then the mother may want to take the child to her parents' home for four weeks and then return home to enroll the child in two weeks of swimming lessons at the neighborhood pool. This kind of arrangement best accommodates both the child's opportunities and the parents' schedules.

Because of the flexibility usually possible during holidays and vacation times, the mediator should try to optimize creative solutions in the written plan for these times. This gives an extra sense of control to the parents as it expands the available options for everyone involved.

Clauses Regarding Conduct

In two kinds of cases, the mediation agreement needs to contain additional clauses to be workable. In the first kind of case, spouses who have been in significant conflict in a wide variety of areas regarding time sharing with their children may need the additional structure provided by adjunct clauses that will regulate their conduct with each other and with the children. In the second kind of case, a spouse who has made a very large concession to the other spouse may need the security of knowing that the other spouse will be expected to fulfill a number of extra conditions before the concession will go into effect.

In both of these cases, the adjunct clauses do not relate directly to scheduling but rather to issues that are of concern to both spouses or to one spouse about the other. These typically include the children's phone access to their parents ("Both parents agree to allow access by phone for both children to call either parent at any time"); communication about a child's health ("Both parents agree that each will call the other at any time if there is any special health concern regarding Patrick"); communication about a child's whereabouts ("Father agrees to provide Mother with an itinerary and phone numbers for any trips with Caitlin out of the county"); child care responsibilities ("Both parents agree that the parent with whom Jonathan is scheduled to be is fully responsible for arranging and paying for child care in the event that that parent is unable to care for Jonathan"); safety ("Father agrees to keep Sara away from his workshop and welding torch whenever she is in his backyard"); health ("Mother agrees to take Richie to a doctor immediately if he is injured or sick"); cleanliness and neatness ("Both parents agree to return the children to the other parent's house bathed and dressed in clean clothes"); shared resources ("Mother agrees to send all requested items of the children's clothing to Father's house, to remain there for the children to use on subsequent stays at Father's house"); restraint from harassment ("Both parents agree to remain in their respective cars during transfer of the children to each other's houses and not to enter each other's house uninvited by the other parent"); restraint from drug or alcohol use ("Both parents agree to use no illegal drugs or alcohol in the presence of the children, especially prior to or while driving"); and restraint from verbal degradation ("Both parents agree to refrain from putting each other down to the children or to anyone else while in the presence of the children").

When discussing these clauses, the mediator should attempt to elicit a balance of concerns from both parents while being careful not to push too deeply into sensitive terrain. As stated earlier, too many clauses can trigger off resistance in one parent; too few clauses could leave the other spouse feeling excessively vulnerable.

Future Modifications

As mentioned, the mediation agreement should not be viewed as a final decree but rather as a growing and changing document. Hence provisions must be made for future modifications of the agreement should any of its clauses prove untenable for any reason. If necessary, the mediator should include a clause that states: "Both parents agree to reevaluate the above plan in one year's time [or any other reasonable interval] in order to reassess the changing needs of the children and the living situation of each parent. This will take place in a discussion between the parents or, if necessary, with the assistance of a mediator." Interestingly, not many couples return for this follow-up session. The expectation that in a year's time they will return to mediation rather than to court may well set a context for the parents to take responsibility for resolving future problems on their own. This hypothesis is supported by the findings of Frank (1974, 1978), who confirmed that expectancies have a powerful positive effect on potential psychotherapy clients and can elicit improvement in them without treatment. The expectation of help alone often induces change.

To encourage the couple to continue solving their problems in a cooperative rather than an adversarial mode, the last clause in the agreement should read: "In the event of any future dispute regarding the children that the parents are unable to resolve between themselves, both parents agree to seek mediation before legal action at the request of either parent, and the costs will be shared equally or otherwise by agreement." When the first edition of this book was published, couples rarely returned for such mediation. However, over the past fifteen years, presumably as a result of greater public exposure to the benefits of mediation, about one-third of the cases return for more mediation, making this clause a very useful one. Occasionally, a parent will phone the mediator with a minor question or problem, which the mediator can usually resolve satisfactorily on the phone. If a mediation session is deemed necessary, the mediator can usually begin at the ending phase of mediation (see Chapter Six) and proceed directly to negotiations. Needless to say, resolution typically is reached much more quickly the second time around.

It is important that the mediator inform the parents that if they modify their agreement on their own, it is advisable to put the modifications in writing in the form of an addendum to the mediation agreement. This document should be dated and signed by each parent, and copies should be sent to the mediator, to the court (for inclusion in their file), and to each of their attorneys (for their records). This will ensure that such modifications are formally acknowledged and that each parent has a clear agreement in hand in the event that the other parent has a change of heart later and violates the agreement or tries to deny that the agreement was made. Moreover, by filing it with the court, the doctrine of *parens patriae* (which requires the court, as the legitimate representative of the state, to approve any custody arrangement) is legally satisfied.

Financial Linkages

When negotiating and designing the mediation agreement, the mediator should be aware of the broader context within which custody mediation takes place, which may involve certain financial matters. In addition to cases in which property settlement and custody may be linked (see Chapter Five on talking with attorneys), the mediator will most likely encounter cases in which the financial issue of child support is intertwined with custody and visitation issues. This link is usually present for one of two reasons, according to Mnookin and Kornhauser (1979). First, each parent may be willing to exchange some amount of time with the child for an increase or a reduction in income. Second, one parent may keep the child from spending designated time with the other parent in order to enforce the collection of support payments. And conversely, the other parent may withhold support payments to ensure maintenance of the time designated to be spent with the child. While such bargaining over children may seem offensive to some people, Mnookin and Kornhauser suggest that it may well be preferable to going to court as a way for couples to enforce support and visitation. These authors further suggest that withholding support payments to ensure that the other parent will not interfere with court-ordered visitations is not as potentially damaging to the child as the legally sanctioned alternatives of having the sheriff take the child from the custodial parent or of filing a contempt order that would put the custodial parent in jail until the designated visitation time is fulfilled. In most states, parents are not legally permitted either to cut off visitation if child support payments have not been made or to withhold support payments on the grounds that the custodial parent withheld visitations. Hence the parents often are left to their own informal tactics to maintain an equality of bargaining leverage between themselves. When one parent shifts the balance by initiating a court action for enforcement of a promise to comply, an escalation of many peripheral issues often ensues, presenting the mediator with a challenging bundle of issues to unravel.

Links between financial and custody or visitation issues also arise when there is an agreement between parents for equal time sharing, yet the parent with the larger income is still expected to make child support payments to the other parent. Often these parents (typically fathers) resent having to pay child support when the time shared with the children is exactly equal. Moreover, they feel that they are being exploited by the other parent. Their preference for everything being equal (including financial support of the children) is based on not wanting to put out more than the other spouse rather than on wanting to share proportionately in the financial support of their children. This resentment may present itself to the mediator in disguised form, as strategic resistance (see Chapter Nine).

Yet another financial link exists when one parent, because of low income, is receiving money under the federal government's Aid to Dependent Children program, as part of welfare benefits. Since this program was developed before joint custody arrangements were legally sanctioned, welfare regulations have not been specifically developed to accommodate newer custody arrangements. In facilitating a time-sharing arrangement that gives the child equal time with each parent, the mediator may unwittingly be terminating welfare support money for the children because such benefits can be issued only to a parent who has primary custody of the children. If the parents share equally in physical custody, neither parent may be eligible for such aid. For example, the regulations may require that one parent have the children at least 51 percent of the time in order to retain eligibility. This imbalance may be unacceptable to the other parent, who may not only insist on sharing time equally but also want to be the recipient of the welfare benefits.

In light of the possibilities for such financial links, the mediator should be informed about local regulations and practices regarding such matters and should help the spouses separate time-sharing issues from financial matters. Moreover, there are advantages to excluding financial questions from the mediation agreement. For one thing, some jurisdictions (for example, those under California's mandatory mediation) restrict mediation exclusively to time-sharing arrangements and leave financial problems and child support to the attorneys and judge, who typically are more skilled at negotiating such issues. For another, it seems tactically preferable for the mediator to keep negotiations about parenting and child sharing separate from the bargaining inherent in money negotiations. This helps the parents focus more exclusively during mediation on the psychological, emotional, and social needs of their children. Financial arrangements can then be accommodated to the child-sharing plan, rather than vice versa.

PART THREE

STRATEGIES USED BY CHILDREN, PARENTS, AND MEDIATORS

8

HOW CHILDREN CONTRIBUTE TO CUSTODY DISPUTES

CHILDREN'S LIMITED COMPREHENSION of the meaning and implications for them of their parents' breakup creates terrible confusion and emotional upset and generates characteristic attempts to cope with the disruption. However, the limited means they have for expressing their needs makes it difficult for their parents to accurately recognize and address those needs.

For example, in her attempts to control her fear of losing both her parents, four-year-old Kirsten tells her father at his visitation time, "Mommy doesn't have any more food in the 'frigerator—could you come over tonight and bring us peanut butter and jelly sandwiches?" In a characteristically childlike way, Kirsten is trying to convey to her father that she is afraid she will be completely abandoned, no longer fed or cared for (she feels that since Daddy left, maybe Mommy will also). To assure her continuing survival, she tries to mend her parents' relationship by getting her father to offer nurturance (food) to her and her mother while reuniting them at the family home. However, the parents are unable to understand the emotional basis or functional intent of Kirsten's utterance; instead they interpret it in accordance with their mistrust of each other. Her father takes Kirsten's comment as evidence of her mother's parental incompetence and neglect. Her mother takes it as evidence that Kirsten's father is continuing to spoil her by letting her think she can get anything she wants from him. As a result of their respective misinterpretations, Kirsten's father may file a court petition for sole custody and Kirsten's mother may file a counterpetition for a reduction of visitation times—each believing that he or she is doing what is best for Kirsten.

It is these very fights over differing interpretations of their child's needs and behavior that frequently drive spouses to court. The complications that arise from these disputes are for the most part not due to parents being callous or uncaring about their children's needs. The vast majority of parents are very concerned about the emotional well-being of their children and are able to set aside their own needs so that they can try to satisfy the needs of their children first. Even when faced with the pain and anger of divorce, these parents still maintain a sense of fairness, understanding, and compassion and may even convert the trauma of divorce into a growing experience for each of the family members. However, some parents who become involved in custody or visitation disputes have difficulty focusing clearly on the needs of their children. Often the stress of divorce narrows their perception of their children's needs, and their anger at the ex-spouse clouds their ability to separate their own needs from those of their children. This is particularly the case with couples who are ordered to mediation by the court, but it may also be true of couples who attend mediation voluntarily. Let us now attempt to clarify what becomes so problematic for these families by exploring the nature of the strategies that children use to express their needs.

Children's Strategies

In intact families, there are some occasions when a child willfully provokes conflict between his or her parents. There are other occasions when a child is merely an innocent victim of parental disputes. However, a third and even more common occasion, in accordance with family systems theory, is when a child is an *innocent but functional contributor* to conflict between the parents. From this perspective, it appears that the child, in attempting to get his or her needs met, initiates and participates in a behavioral sequence that results in overt parental conflict. The child's action is neither clearly willful nor clearly an instance of victimization but partly both—hence the term *innocent but functional contributor*. Such a conceptual formulation does not aim at making children blameworthy but rather focuses on the perspective that within a family system, all the members are contributors to the interactional process. By maintaining such a view, the intervenor (whether therapist or mediator) has the decided advantage of neutrality over fault finding and side taking and maximizes her leverage as a result of her more comprehensive view of the functional rules of the family system. So, for example, when a mother accuses the father of turning the child against her and subsequently refuses to let the father see the child, the mediator may be able to defuse this accusation by pointing out the innocent but functional part that the child may have played in telling his mother that he wanted to live at his father's house.

Early theories of the etiology of child and marital problems assumed unidirectional cause-and-effect relationships. That is, it was always presumed that dysfunctional marital relationships caused dysfunctional behavior patterns in children. However, contemporary formulations within the field of developmental psychology point to the unmistakably circular nature of causality in family interactions (Ambert, 1992, 1997; Lerner & Spanier, 1978; Chess & Thomas, 1984). And family systems theorists and therapists have developed such interactional theories to quite sophisticated levels (Haley, 1976; Madanes, 1981; Minuchin, 1974; Minuchin & Fishman, 1981; Nichols & Everett, 1986; Watzlawick & Weakland, 1977; Watzlawick, Weakland, & Fisch, 1974).

From this systems perspective, it appears that children and parents tend to express distress during times of natural developmental family crisis (such as the birth of a sibling, the beginning of adolescence, or leaving home for independent living) and that each family member subsequently responds to the responses of the others in a circular rather than linear fashion. If these interactions are based upon clear communications, understanding of each other's needs, empathy, and the absence of overreactions, the natural developmental stresses are resolved in a constructive fashion. If, however, the situation is characterized by unclear or distorted communications, lack of understanding or empathy, or blatant overreactions, the stresses escalate into crises that are greater than those typically experienced during these transitional stages in family life. It is out of these negative, escalating, interactional loops that serious family conflicts and, specifically, child behavior problems most often arise. The child's behavior functions as a strategy to communicate distress and to escalate the family conflict to a climax and resolution. Hence what may seem irrational, self-defeating, and antagonistic behaviors on the part of the child when viewed from an intrapersonal perspective appear as functional strategies when viewed from a family systems perspective.

The extraordinary crisis of divorce elicits all the strategies that children normally use, but in exaggerated form, to cope with the unpredictable and uncontrollable aspects of divorce. Wallerstein and Kelly (1980) detailed the various characteristic ways in which children responded to the separation of their parents initially, after eighteen months, and after five years. Their responses were clearly developmentally linked and expressed the emotional issues typical of each age range. After the initial marital separation, children three to five years old primarily manifested behavioral and emotional regression (thumbsucking, bedwetting, whining, clinging to caregiver). Children six to eight years old primarily expressed pervasive grief (crying, sobbing, yearning for the departed parent). Older children (nine to twelve years old) primarily manifested intense anger at the parent whom they perceived as responsible for the divorce, as well as a variety of psychosomatic complaints. Adolescents aged thirteen to eighteen expressed grief and anger in a more sophisticated and dramatic manner, blaming their "selfish" parents for leaving them prematurely and hence removing the opportunity for the reverse and more natural developmental event to occur, the children leaving their parents.

These characteristic initial reactions tended to subside within eighteen months and to diminish significantly within five years as more integrated acceptance of the reality and permanence of the divorce took place. However, most custody and visitation plans are made within the first year following the separation, and hence it is on the children's initial expression of their needs that parental negotiations are typically built. Moreover, while the Wallerstein and Kelly findings have shown us that it is normal for children of divorce to manifest these characteristic responses for up to the first year and a half following the separation, most parents are unaware of this fact. Not uncommonly, each parent will interpret such behaviors as evidence of harm to the child caused by the other parent.

Added to the children's general manifestations of emotional distress are more specific and individualized reaction patterns, to which we refer here as *coping strategies*. These strategies are the manifestations of a combination of factors, which include the emotional needs of the child, the social and intellectual skills of the child, the temperament of the child, and the child's awareness of the emotional triggers of each parent.

To reiterate, these strategies are functional but not necessarily intentional. Their significance lies in the conflict that results from the parents' interpretations of their meaning. In general, the clarity of meaning of children's strategies is age-linked. The younger the child, the more ambiguous the meaning of the child's behavior and the more open to differing adult interpretations. However, it is not infrequent that older children (even those well into adolescence) will show behaviors that are ambiguous and open to conflicting interpretation. This can be the case when, for example, the child changes his mind several times about his preferences for living arrangements or when an older child does not easily express herself verbally and consistently says, "I don't know." Such instances of ambiguous meaning will often polarize parents.

Because of the importance to the mediator of understanding children's strategies, I will discuss some of the more typical ones. Although the examples presented here are not comprehensive in scope, they are representative of the common strategies dealt with by mediators.

Reuniting

As stated earlier, it is common for children of all ages to wish to get their parents back together. Even in intact families where there is marital discord, children will attempt a variety of strategies for keeping their parents together even if it necessitates developing symptomatic behavior so that the parents have to remain together to solve the child's problem. Children of all ages (but especially younger ones) would often rather have their parents fight than have them separate. The child reasons, "As long as my parents are dealing with each other, they are more likely to remain together." This is a family variant of the more widely acknowledged emotional wisdom of childhood, "Negative attention is better than no attention." The desire for parental reunion is most intense for the children of divorce, and the strategies for attaining it are quite diverse.

For very young children who do not have the verbal sophistication to express their needs, their behavior is their means of expression.

> EXAMPLE
>
> *Behavior:* A three-year-old boy, on returning to his mother from an overnight stay with his father, wets the bed, sucks his thumb, clings to his mother, and is excessively whiny and prone to tears.
>
> *Underlying emotion:* Fear of abandonment, anxiety about his own survival without his mother and father together.
>
> *Function:* The emotional distress should appeal to both mother and father and urge them to reunite to make child feel better.
>
> *Mother's interpretation:* Contact with father is disruptive and destructive to the child; child feels insecure when with father; contact with father should be terminated.
>
> *Father's interpretation:* Child misses his father very much and deeply loves him (perhaps more than his mother loves him); mother is not caring well enough for the child; contact with father should be increased.

For school-age children, reuniting strategies are more active yet often still disguised.

> EXAMPLE
>
> *Behavior:* An eight-year-old girl tells her mother how her father has changed: "He's so nice now, he has lots of money now, he doesn't yell anymore, and he takes us to nice places."
>
> *Underlying emotion:* Sadness and grief at loss with hope of parental reunion.

Function: Child's description of perceived changes in father should attract mother to father once again and result in reuniting them.

Mother's interpretation: Father is trying to buy the child's love; he is pretending to show real interest in the child but is not sincere; he is conveying a false image of himself to the child; he should have limited contact with the child until his life gets settled and the child can see him for what he really is.

Father's interpretation: Child really wants to live with him; child will continue to be poisoned against her father if she continues to live at her mother's house; custody should be given to father.

With adolescents, reuniting strategies are even more active and intense, though, again, often disguised.

EXAMPLE

Behavior: A thirteen-year-old girl reports to her father that her mother is very unhappy and that she is afraid her mother will not be able to take care of herself or her household responsibilities.

Underlying emotion: Fear of losing nurturance and fear that she will not be provided for.

Function: Father should feel worried about mother and should return home to take care of her.

Mother's interpretation: Child is just manipulating the parents to get out of doing her chores; she needs firmer discipline, unlike what her father provides.

Father's interpretation: Mother is unfit and incompetent to parent. She obviously is suicidal once again and it will be harmful for the child to be around her; child should live with the father and have minimal or no contact with the mother until she seeks treatment and is certified by a competent psychiatrist as not suicidal.

Reducing Separation Distress

For some time after the marital separation, young children often experience separation distress each time they make the transition between their parents. Each time such a child leaves one parent to go to the other, he experiences the emotional loss of the parent he is leaving, even if he is going for just a day. Often such a reaction reflects a particularly close bond with both parents, but it can also be reflective of the child's own

adaptability. Children who are less adaptable tend to have a more difficult time dealing with the transition from one parent's house to the
other's. Because of the increased emotional stress following divorce, ten-
dencies toward nonadaptability are likely to be exaggerated.

> EXAMPLE
>
> *Behavior:* A four-year-old girl cries each time she is transferred
> from her mother's to her father's care (or vice versa); child appears
> to be happy while in the care of each parent, after the transition
> time.
>
> *Underlying emotion:* Child reexperiences intense separation anxi-
> ety each time she has to make this change from one caretaker to
> another.
>
> *Function:* To signal distress about these changes so that parents
> will somehow reduce the number of changes or help her decrease
> her discomfort in dealing with such changes.
>
> *Mother's interpretation:* Child is crying when leaving her because
> she doesn't like having to leave her mother so often; she cries upon
> returning to her mother because she is upset at having to stay at
> her father's so much, and she no doubt has a terrible and stressful
> time with her father; contact with father should be reduced until
> child feels more comfortable around him.
>
> *Father's interpretation:* Child cries when leaving him because she
> does not want to go back to her mother's house so soon. She cries
> upon coming to her father because her mother probably has told
> her bad or frightening things about him; contact with father
> should be increased in frequency and duration so that child can
> enjoy even more time with him.

Detonating Tension

Very often, the tension between hostile separated parents feels to the children like a volcano waiting to erupt. In intact families, such marital tensions are often resolved or at least temporarily reduced by the child
providing an excuse—such as disturbing behavior—for both parents to
yell and even strike out, thereby diffusing the tension between them. In
effect, the child unconsciously (and sometimes consciously) offers himself
temporarily as a scapegoat to divert the hostility between his parents.

Children of divorced parents utilize this strategy as well, but in different ways.

EXAMPLE

Behavior: A seven-year-old boy tells his father that his mother has been sleeping with two different men at the house within the same weekend.

Underlying emotion: Fear that father's chronic jealousy and anger at mother may result in mother and child getting hurt or killed.

Function: To get father to blow up once and for all; the reality would be easier to handle than the fantasies that the child has generated in response to the chronic tension over his father's jealousy.

Mother's interpretation: Child is just angry at mother for the divorce and is jealous that his mother shares her attention with other people in her life. Child needs to refrain from telling father about her personal life, and father needs to keep out of her life. Now there is even more reason to be guarded in dealing with father, since he is so intrusive.

Father's interpretation: Mother is an immoral person and an incompetent parent; child's contact with her should be limited or restricted until she gets her life straightened out. She should not be allowed to set such an example for his son.

Testing Love

Wallerstein and Kelly (1980) have pointed out that both parents are frequently emotionally unavailable to their children for about a year following the separation. During this phase, children often feel emotionally neglected and will occasionally test their parents' love for them.

EXAMPLE

Behavior: A five-year-old boy who lives with his father calls his mother on the phone frequently and, in a driven manner, repeatedly tells her he loves her. Throughout his stays with her, he repeats this utterance.

Underlying emotion: Fear of rejection by his mother for wanting to stay with, and feel love for, his father.

Function: To find out, in a child's characteristically backward fashion, whether his mother still loves him. The statement is really intended as the question, "Do you still love me, Mommy?"

Mother's interpretation: Child desperately wants to live with mother; he is probably afraid of his father or is not being nurtured enough by the man; custody should be changed to mother, since father obviously cannot satisfy the emotional needs of a young child.

Father's interpretation: Child is just trying to make mother feel better because mother has been complaining to the child how unhappy she is. Mother must stop encouraging and using the child to satisfy her own needs. Contact between child and mother should be restricted until she stops burdening the child with her own problems.

Proving Loyalty

The emotional unavailability of both parents can frighten a child enough to sacrifice a relationship with one parent, at least temporarily. The child feels tremendously torn between her parents and feels that she cannot love both of them if they do not love each other. She feels that she has to choose between her parents, withdrawing love from one and investing it all in the other. She allies with that parent and proves her loyalty by actively participating in the ongoing marital conflict. This results in the development of a dysfunctionally close relationship with one parent and a dysfunctionally distant one with the other.

EXAMPLE

Behavior: A nine-year-old girl refuses to have any contact with her father and spends a lot of time and energy disparaging him to her mother and agreeing with and supporting the mother in her own disparagement of the father.

Underlying emotion: Fear of being totally neglected by both parents.

Function: To prove to her mother that she will fully support mother in her feud with father, in exchange for being taken care of and loved by mother. Child also assumes that her father will somehow understand and be patient until she feels reassured of her mother's love, at which time she can then reestablish an affectionate relationship with him.

Mother's interpretation: Child knows the truth about how rotten her father is; contact between father and child would be seriously destructive to the child and should therefore be terminated.

Father's interpretation: Mother has poisoned the child's mind against him and should be forced to stop this; custody should be given to the father so that he can undo the damage and normalize his relationship with the child.

Seeking Fairness

Children of almost any age will often attempt, to the point of self-sacrifice, to make everything come out exactly even between their parents. They will take it upon themselves to monitor fairness for both their parents no matter how embroiled the parents may be with each other. They feel burdened with the task of keeping parental peace and pressured to balance concessions to each parent. They fear confrontation between their parents and repress their own needs and sense of individuality in order to keep their parents from overt conflict.

> EXAMPLE
>
> *Behavior:* A fourteen-year-old boy insists on staying exactly one week at his mother's house and one week at his father's, even though his parents live a sizable distance apart; this creates considerable inconvenience and distress for the boy, and his schoolwork and friendships suffer markedly, but he maintains the preference.
>
> *Underlying emotion:* The boy wants both his parents to keep loving him equally well; he is afraid of losing one of them.
>
> *Function:* To make the time-sharing arrangements so perfectly equal that mother and father will stop fighting over the boy and resume showing their love for him.
>
> *Mother's interpretation:* Son is unquestionably afraid of confronting his father because father may have a temper tantrum and intimidate him; boy's own life is suffering from this bouncing back and forth between houses, and the arrangement must be changed; boy should live at his mother's house and visit his father every other weekend only if he wants to.
>
> *Father's interpretation:* Son understands what is fair and loves both parents equally; his problems at school and with friends are natural for children following divorce and have nothing to do with the time-sharing arrangements; the arrangements should remain as they are.

Protecting Self-Esteem

Unfortunately, some parents are quite insensitive to the feelings of their children. Because children often hide their own feelings, some parents mistakenly assume that children either do not have significant feelings or are so resilient that they can easily recover from any hurt feelings. In the case of divorce, when parents are just looking for places to vent their anger, children are easy, available targets. And if such anger is exacerbated by a parental style that is already insensitive to children's feelings, the emotional ambiance for a child can be quite threatening. This problem is complicated further by the fact that children often have difficulty identifying, let alone vocalizing, the source of their discomfort when around a parent who threatens their self-esteem. Hence they will commonly resort to strategies that protect their self-esteem.

EXAMPLE

Behavior: A ten-year-old girl resists going to her father's house and develops psychosomatic illnesses whenever time with him is anticipated; when asked why it is that she resists, she says, "I just don't feel like going today."

Underlying emotion: Child fears being criticized and teased by her father; she loves him but always feels uncomfortable and guarded around him.

Function: To protect child's self-esteem and hopefully persuade father to change his style of dealing with the child.

Mother's interpretation: Father is denigrating child just the way he used to denigrate mother; child should not have to tolerate such abuse from someone whom she does not even care about; until father changes, contact between father and child should be restricted.

Father's interpretation: Mother is once again poisoning the child's mind against him; child and father used to have a very good relationship, which mother is clearly trying to sabotage; child needs more contact with father to get her away from her mother's influence.

Protecting Parents' Self-Esteem

Children often are acutely aware of the fragility of their parents' self-esteem, especially following a marital separation. Partly out of genuine empathy and love for each parent, but mostly for their own emotional survival, they will make efforts to protect the self-worth of each parent. Such efforts are particularly characteristic of children who tend to be more sensitive to their parents' feelings and thereby get "caught in the middle." Children using these strategies generally are not aware of the resulting inconsistencies of their actions toward their parents.

EXAMPLE

Behavior: An eight-year-old girl, when with her father, tells him that she really wants to live at his house and see her mother once in a while. When with her mother, the girl tells her that she really wants to live at her house and see her father once in a while.

Underlying emotion: Child feels badly for each parent and is scared that something bad will happen to each of them unless the child emotionally supports them; also, child fears being emotionally abandoned by either or both parents.

Function: To boost self-esteem of both parents so that they will remain emotionally strong enough to care for and love the child.

Mother's interpretation: Child wants to live at mother's house and is afraid to tell father; father should give child to the mother.

Father's interpretation: Child wants to live at father's house and is afraid to tell mother; mother should give child to the father.

Permissive Living

A mediator may occasionally come upon older children and adolescents who appear to deal with the divorce by manipulating the marital dissolution to their own immediate advantage. They appear to be in little or no emotional distress and state preferences for their living arrangements that tip the marital balance into conflict. Although these youngsters may actually have repressed their emotional distress over the divorce, it is very difficult for the mediator to ascertain this. The motivation for their strategies may be a lack of any particular bond with either parent, an exceptional degree of manipulative skill or self-centeredness, a simple withdrawal in response to feeling trapped between conflicting parents, or any combination of these. In any case, these youngsters appear to push a decision that will work to their own advantage.

EXAMPLE

Behavior: A sixteen-year-old boy consistently states a preference to live at his father's house and see his mother every other weekend. When asked why, he gives a variety of inconsistent reasons.

Underlying emotion: The youth has withdrawn his emotional investment in his parents and now wants the most comfortable lifestyle that he can get.

Function: To structure his postdivorce living situation so as to maximize his financial resources and minimize daily responsibilities and demands for conforming behavior.

Mother's interpretation: Father clearly has made unrealistic promises that life will be easy for his son if he lives with him. This is just another of the father's tactics to get revenge on the mother; father sets no example of discipline for his son; the son should live at his mother's house, where he will learn responsibility and self-discipline.

Father's interpretation: Son loves his father more than he does his mother and does not want to live with her; he is old enough to make his own choices and should live with father if he so wishes.

o

Certainly, each of the children's behaviors in these examples is open to differing interpretations. Still, they exemplify the vast range of misinterpretations of which conflicting parents are capable. The unfortunate consequence for the children is the pain and anguish they must suffer as a result of not having their real feelings recognized or their emotional needs met. Moreover, the children may unwittingly contribute actively to the leftover marital feud by fanning their parents' flames of wrath and mistrust with behaviors that are confusing and unintentionally provocative to the parents.

The mediator is in a position to utilize this information to reduce acrimony between parents. By offering a thorough, detailed explanation of the general nature of children's strategies and by discussing the particular ones used by their child, the mediator can help parents unravel the sequence of events that led up to the present custody or visitation dispute. Sometimes it is most effective to carry on this discussion after interviewing the children, to confirm the data and muster further confidence in the mediator's perspective. It is not uncommon for a couple to be drawn together somewhat by a shared recognition of their child's innate cleverness in initiating these strategies. It should be repeatedly emphasized by the mediator that children's strategies are *not malevolent or blameworthy* but merely their way of taking care of their own needs. This emphasis is intended to reduce any tendency in a parent to displace his or her anger at the ex-spouse onto the child for contributing (however innocently) to the dispute.

It is of great significance that the parents' various misinterpretations of their children's behaviors are exactly the arguments that would be utilized by the parents' respective attorneys in court. The lawyers build evidence to support each misinterpretation and then construe this as reality. They then portray this construction, built on distorted assumptions, as "in the best interests of the child."

It should by now be clear that such legal maneuvering frequently has little to do with what is in the best interests of the child and much to do with what is in the best interests of the adult client. Ultimately, however, even this approach is likely to backfire on the parents, for if the legal argument presented by the parent's attorney is based on false assumptions of the child's needs, pursuing that position in court may yield an unhappy child. Certainly no parent, no matter how motivated by anger, could feel satisfied at winning such a bitter victory.

Once in a while, the mediator has occasion to observe children who are in such severe emotional distress that they seem in need of psychological treatment. However, before making a referral for such treatment, the mediator should consider several factors. While it is possible that the child's emotional difficulties predate the divorce, it is more probable that they are a reaction to or have been exacerbated by the ongoing parental conflict. Treatment for the child alone may therefore be of only minimal help if the spousal feud continues. In fact, because a child would have some implicit hope that the therapist will make things better, when the conflict between the parents remain unresolved even with therapy, the child may lose hope that anyone can help and perhaps even lose trust in helping professionals altogether. Moreover, the child's therapist may unknowingly add to the problem by siding with one of the parents (typically the one who brings the child for therapy), thereby escalating the conflict.

Because the child's problems are embedded in the family's dynamics, it is important that those problems be viewed in the context of the family system. Thus if therapy seems appropriate, it is helpful for the mediator to refer the child to a therapist who will deal with the child within the family perspective. Ideally, the therapist should be sensitive to and experienced with the systemic nature of custody and visitation disputes. This will help ensure that the therapist will remain neutral with respect to the parents while treating the child's distress. A sensitive, knowledgeable therapist can support the child through the crisis of the divorce and custody dispute. In addition, if the parental feud continues, the therapist may be able to help the child develop coping strategies that take a less severe psychological toll than the ones the child may already be using. Finally, support groups for children going through divorce have been quite helpful, as talking with other children going through similar experiences can be therapeutic. These groups typically use an educational approach incorporating age-appropriate games and activities to help the children learn most effectively (Di Bias, 1996).

9

PARENTS' MOTIVES AND METHODS IN CUSTODY DISPUTES

THE EMOTIONS EXPERIENCED by divorcing spouses have been thoroughly detailed by other authors (Ahrons & Rodgers, 1987; Kaslow & Schwartz, 1987; Schwartz & Kaslow, 1997). Among the many difficult feelings experienced are hurt, rejection, anger, loneliness, depression, anxiety, lowered self-esteem, and guilt. Although many of these emotions are transitory, there is a great deal of variation from one person to another in terms of the intensity and duration of each of these feelings. In one person, the rejection, hurt, and anger may be experienced for only a few weeks or months following the separation and then be processed in a relatively healthy way, freeing the person to begin the task of building a new life. In another person, the rejection and hurt may turn into a lifelong vendetta against the ex-spouse, and the anger may persist as chronic bitterness, affecting new relationships and other aspects of the person's life.

Two factors tend to keep negative feelings alive and are central in spurring the spouses to take up adversarial postures following the decision to divorce. One is the almost universal presence of varying degrees of mistrust between the spouses; the other is the traditional legal process for reaching divorce settlements, which actively encourages this mistrust by restraining the spouses from communicating directly.

Mistrust, which builds rapidly after the divorce decision, arises as a result of the traumatic breach of interpersonal security in suddenly losing a mate. During the last phase of the marriage, there typically is a breakdown in communication between the spouses and therefore in their trusting that they could resolve their conflicts together. Even when conflict resolution skills break down, they might at least be able to trust each other's commitment to being a "married couple," with the inherent security that comes with maintaining the semblance of their social and financial lifestyle. At the point of the divorce decision, however, even this commitment is breached, and the spouses often can no longer trust each other to negotiate for their common interest. They may suddenly become adversaries, at a time when they are feeling most vulnerable. Moreover, they may project their own vulnerability onto their children and fight intensely to protect the image of their children thus created, even if such actions are not in the children's best interests by any objective standards.

Levels of Impasse

Johnston and Campbell (1988) described three levels of impasse that keep parents stuck in disputes during divorce. At the *intrapsychic level,* a custody dispute may be an expression of an emotionally vulnerable parent's inability to manage feelings elicited by the divorce (of humiliation, sadness, helplessness, and guilt). For example, the divorce may trigger abandonment issues or profound feelings of loneliness left over from childhood that prevent the parent from letting go of the marriage or sharing the children. (The psychodynamics behind extreme intrapsychic impasses that result in high conflict and violent divorces are elegantly elaborated by Johnston and Roseby, 1997, and Roseby and Johnston, in press.)

At the *interactional level,* the dispute expresses the habitual and dysfunctional patterns of relating to one another within the marriage that continue through the divorce. The parents are easily able to trigger each other into old familiar, predictable patterns of responses, or "interactional reflexes," and prevent new ways of relating necessary for effective coparenting. At the *external-social level,* disputes are fueled by family, friends, new partners, and even lawyers and therapists. These external participants typically mean well but form alliances with one of the divorcing parties and reinforce their negative views of the other person.

To Johnston and Campbell's paradigm, I would add another category of impasse: *reality-based impasses.* These are impasses that are rooted in normal reactions or feelings brought about by divorce. They may be caused by temporarily disabling sadness at the anticipation of being alone for the first time in one's life or of being away from one's children for the first time since their birth, or they can stem from a genuine disagreement between the parents about what truly is in the best interests of their children. If normal but temporarily disabling feelings are causing the impasse, some brief therapeutic work within the mediation session can be of much help in facilitating the parent through some of the grief so that negotiations can effectively begin. If the grief is too deep, of course, a referral for counseling for that parent can be of much use before attempting the mediation negotiations. If the impasse is based in disagreements about the best interests of children, the mediator can offer current information about the needs of children (see Chapter Two) or direct the parents to the relevant literature or to other appropriate, informed professionals before beginning the negotiations.

Some spouses (more often those voluntarily seeking mediation), in spite of their negative feelings toward the ex-spouse, are able to contain their hostility and mistrust enough to consider the legitimate needs of their children as well as the needs of each other. During mediation, they may want to discuss such reasonable and important concerns about their children as safety and health; social, emotional, and cognitive development; behavioral styles; interests; and tolerances. These spouses are typically expressing reality-based impasses. However, many spouses entering mediation (largely those court-ordered to mediation) have not drawn such clear boundaries between the valid needs of their children and their own hostility toward and mistrust of each other. Furthermore, they may have a great deal of difficulty coping with these negative feelings within themselves. Confused and overwhelmed by the negative feelings that erupt following the separation, they grapple with their ex-spouse to gain some sense of security, personal power, and dignity. Often they feel disillusioned at the actions and reactions of their ex-spouse following the separation, and they may even be surprised and disheartened by their own reactions. This may be accompanied by a sense of personal failure and guilt over their own actions leading up to the divorce, and they may displace these feelings onto the ex-spouse. Such feelings interact with their individual emotional styles to yield a wide array of responses. Some spouses can utilize their insight into these feelings to check their expression; others appear to have little control over the expression of negative reactions. For these latter spouses, the mediation process becomes an arena for protecting their own vulnerable feelings under the guise of seeking what is in the best interests of the children. These interactional maneuvers with a hidden personal agenda are similar to the functional strategies of children discussed previously. Because adults have more sophisticated cognitive abilities, their strategies generally appear to be more consciously motivated, albeit unspoken. However, if such a strategy is pointed out to the spouse by the mediator, the spouse typically denies any hidden motive and even more firmly proclaims the maneuver to be solely in the best interests of the child. Typical strategies (some at the intrapsychic level and most at the interactional level) manifested by spouses before, during, and, unfortunately, even after mediation are given in the following sections.

Reuniting Strategies

In most cases, one spouse wants a divorce and the other spouse does not. This often leaves the remaining spouse with little or no leverage over the departing spouse. However, custody mediation does provide a forum for attempting to persuade the other spouse to return to the marriage. In assessing the degree to which each spouse wanted the divorce (see the sections of Chapter Five on gathering information), the mediator should listen for any extreme position taken by a spouse—for example, "I'll do anything to get her back." Such an assertion should alert the mediator to the possibility of reuniting strategies initiated by that spouse. Although it is rare for couples reaching the stage of custody mediation to reunite (McIsaac, 1981), even though, potentially, there may be more couples that could with encouragement from the mediator (see Larson, 1993), spouses will attempt a variety of strategies in the hope of bringing about a reconciliation.

Requesting Extended Mediation

Under the guise of having many issues concerning the children to work out, a spouse may request mediation. In the first phone contact with the mediator, this spouse indicates that his wife left him and the children are unhappy. He says that they need to see their mother more often and that he wants to work out a schedule with her, but she has been unwilling to talk with him since she left. When told by the mediator that she will meet with the two of them for one or two sessions to work out these issues, the man expresses distress, saying, "I had hoped we could meet for more sessions—she needs you, or someone, to explain to her that she's making a terrible mistake in going through with the divorce."

In the mediation sessions, the husband persistently tries to talk about the marriage, bringing up issues that elicit talk of the past. Even in the face of repeated clarifications of the wife's determination to end the marriage and of repeated requests by the mediator to refrain from talking about the past, the husband persists in eliciting talk of feelings rather than proceeding with the task of negotiating coparenting arrangements. He may try to convince the wife that she really still loves him, or he may try to induce guilt feelings by telling her that the children are suffering greatly and need their father and mother together. If all else fails, he may threaten that she will never be able to make it on her own.

Because of the wife's determination to divorce, his strategies are met with resistance, determination to hasten the divorce, and increased reluctance to participate in further mediation sessions. If the mediator allows the husband to continue expressing his feelings about the marital relationship, the wife may well get up and walk out or at least be extremely reluctant to cooperate in any coparenting agreement.

Pursuing Sole Custody

If a husband feels that appealing to his wife's feelings is futile, he might initiate a reuniting strategy by declaring that he wants sole custody of the children. Once in mediation, he presents a host of reasons that the children should live with him and remain under his legal control. Although the reasons may seem valid, they are put forth in a context of bitterness and refusal to compromise. Further inquiry may elicit a statement such as "Just because you want your freedom doesn't mean that the family must split up. We will stay together, and when you are finished doing your thing, we would like you to return to the family."

With this strategy, the husband attempts to maintain unilateral control over the children and the family, with an eye toward coercing the wife to reunite with him or lose her controlling interest in the children and be excluded from the family.

Pursuing Joint Custody

Sometimes a husband tries to reunite with his wife by insisting on joint legal and joint physical custody and presenting the plan as in the best interests of the children. Previous to the divorce decision, this father had little or nothing to do with the children, but suddenly he is extremely interested in sharing time with them. It should be noted that in their longitudinal study, Wallerstein and Kelly (1980) found that the interest of fathers in their children, postdivorce, was unrelated to their relationship with them during the marriage. Fathers who had been distant with their children during the marriage often began visiting them after the divorce with surprising regularity. The clue for the mediator to whether a particular husband's pursuit of joint custody is motivated more by a genuine interest in the children than by a reuniting strategy is the nature of the particular plan proposed by the husband. If, for example, he proposes daily contact with the wife and, against her protests, persists in trying to convince her of the importance of regularly sharing information about the children between themselves, then the latter motive may be safely inferred.

This strategy is aimed at giving the husband another chance to prove his marital worthiness to the wife by setting up frequent contacts between them. The husband hopes that he will be able to use such contact to re-open the marital relationship and eventually persuade the wife to reunite with him.

Yielding to All Demands

If active strategies do not seem likely to work, a husband might take the approach of giving in to all of the wife's demands, which may be quite specific regarding the care of the children when they are with the husband. Even when some of these demands are unreasonable, the husband offers no resistance and agrees with each one exactly as it is presented by the wife.

The mediator may be surprised at the husband's total lack of resistance but soon notices that he is not taking any of these demands too seriously because he wants and expects to get back together with his wife. Her demands are irrelevant to him, but he appeases her in as sincere a manner as he can in the hope that she will eventually realize that she and he belong together. His strategy of yielding keeps down the marital conflict while he waits for the reunion.

Refusing to See the Children

This uncommon strategy is typically used by husbands who are less emotionally mature. If the husband wants a reconciliation but direct efforts have failed, he may refuse to see the children unless his wife reunites with him. The effectiveness of this strategy relies on the wife's feeling strongly about the importance of continuing contact between the children and their father. The mediator can recognize this strategy by observing the wife's response to the husband's threats. If she becomes worried and upset, the husband's (implicitly coercive) threat of psychological damage to the children may indeed function as an effective tool for attempting reconciliation. This tactic, however, rarely achieves its goal of reconciliation. As the wife comes to realize her own leverage in not succumbing to her husband's threat, she neutralizes his strategy.

With all reuniting strategies, the mediator must repeatedly clarify the degree of certainty that the divorce decision is final. Often it takes numerous repetitions of this fact throughout the mediation process before the unwilling spouse can accept it. Sometimes the spouse cannot acknowledge it in the presence of the other spouse and simply needs more time apart to process the painful reality. Scheduling sessions many weeks or even months apart can help resolve this emotional block, which otherwise often prevents agreements from being reached. Occasionally, it is helpful to refer the spouse who desires reunion to a counselor for help in accepting the divorce before further mediation efforts are attempted.

Emotionally Disengaging Strategies

Although it is easy to get a legal divorce, it is extremely difficult to get an emotional one. It is probably a truism that one is never completely emotionally divorced from a spouse. Carl Whitaker (1982) stated it even more poignantly, saying, "Divorce does not exist." By this he meant that spouses (or even young lovers) who have had a deep emotional attachment will never completely lose that feeling, even if the primary feeling that lingers is the intensification of all the anger and pain experienced in the relationship. Nevertheless, having such deep feelings, whether positive or negative, is very different from having no feelings either way.

It is striking to see couples who have been divorced for ten or fifteen years come to mediation for modification of custody or visitation arrangements and reengage the negative aspects of their emotional relationship with (according to the clients) the same intensity that existed at the time of divorce. Clearly, time sets no boundaries for such emotions. To a spouse who wants to divorce and get on with life, the lingering intensity of negative feelings can feel like a curse—or, as one spouse put it, "like being condemned to a life sentence of anger, frustration, bitterness, and general misery." Especially when they have young children at the time of the divorce, spouses can feel overwhelmed at the thought of having to maintain regular contact with the ex-spouse for up to eighteen more years. Each contact with the ex-spouse may reignite their negative feelings, generating repeated reminders of their unhappiness in the marriage. Even when a spouse understands the benefits to the child of regular contact with both parents, the emotional response to the idea of such contact can generate defensiveness. Emotionally, one spouse may wish to be rid of the other spouse forever. As one woman put it, "I know that my son needs his father too, but I wish deep in my heart that the man would move to the other end of the country, get remarried, have some of his own kids, and leave us alone forever."

Whether fresh from the divorce or many years down the line, people use a variety of strategies to emotionally disengage from the former spouse. In some ways, the disengaging strategies of one spouse can be complementary to the reuniting strategies of the other.

Taking or Giving Sole Custody

In an attempt to minimize contact between the spouses, one spouse may enter mediation insisting on sole custody. Initially, she argues that it would be too disruptive to the young child to have to deal with the confusion of two sets of rules and with changing back and forth between houses, as would be the case with joint custody. As the negotiations proceed, she adds that she would have an extremely difficult time dealing with her ex-spouse on any more frequent a basis than visitation times every other weekend. She further insists on being the one to receive sole custody, explaining that she is clearly the superior parent for the child. However, she enters the second mediation session declaring that she has decided to give sole custody to the father and that she will retain visitation rights every other weekend. While maintaining that joint custody would be worse than sole custody to the father, she berates the ex-spouse even as she offers him sole control over the child.

There may be several reasons for such a switch. In one case, the wife rightly interpreted the husband's efforts to work out a reasonable solution involving coparenting as his attempt to remain emotionally engaged with her. The threat that she felt from this bid for closeness (since her own ambivalence may have been tipped in the direction of reuniting) was noticed by the child during the interim between mediation sessions. The child then displayed a reuniting strategy of her own, telling her mother that she wanted to live with her father, which compounded the mother's feelings of threat. The mother's response was a desperate attempt at disengaging. Her initial motive to protect the child became displaced by her need to be emotionally at peace and truly divorced from her ex-husband. She was willing to sacrifice legal and physical control over her child in order to distance herself permanently from her ex-husband.

Such desperation typically subsides over time, as the freshness of the divorce trauma fades and time mellows chaotic feelings. Scheduling extended time periods between sessions often helps in these cases.

Labeling and Invalidating the Spouse

It is well known that when we apply a negative label to a person—such as "thief," "drug addict," "pervert," "schizophrenic," or "liar"—we are able to distance ourselves emotionally from that person (Aronson, 1994). This principle may be taken up by a person who wants to discount the ex-spouse. For example, a husband who repeatedly refers to his wife as crazy or a wife who, throughout the mediation sessions, refers to her husband as violent may each be attempting to invalidate the other as a person worthy of regard. Within the arena of custody negotiations, these labels function as attempts to enlighten the mediator about the unfitness of the other spouse for parenting responsibilities. Typically, the accusations are generalizations from previous difficulties between the spouses that are extended into assumptions about parenting competence. But even though a marital relationship may evoke violent or crazy behavior between spouses, there is no necessary or direct connection between such behavior and each spouse's relationships with and caregiving to the children.

Through labeling, one spouse builds an emotional case for not trusting the other spouse. Such mistrust then functions as a defensive strategy for maintaining emotional distance from that spouse. If she is crazy, he wants less to be involved with her. If he is violent, she has good reason to stay away from him.

Spouses frequently present reasons to mistrust each other and may well expound on this mistrust all the way through mediation. However, mistrust does not necessarily preclude development of a workable parenting agreement. Often the expressions of mistrust can be translated into something like "If I trust you at all, then I might be pulled back into a spousal relationship, which I do not want." As long as the mediator views these labels as strategies for emotionally disengaging rather than as charges to be investigated (assuming that the charges are unsupported), the mediator can guide the process to a successful agreement in spite of the labels.

Buffering

A spouse who is unable to maintain emotional distance from the other spouse in any other way may resort to a strategy of forcing the other spouse to communicate only through other people—the children, a new spouse, a lover, a lawyer—who function as interpersonal buffers.

For example, a husband might propose that all arrangements between his ex-wife and children be made through his new wife. Or with older children, a wife might insist that her ex-husband make arrangements directly with the children. Although such arrangements occasionally work out, it is usually necessary for the ex-spouses to deal directly with each other, especially during the first year or two following the separation. Moreover, further problems are likely to emerge as a result of the miscommunications and misinterpretations that frequently occur when spouses deal with each other through third parties, since each of these other people has vested interests that may differ from those of the spouse in charge of the children. Hence buffering strategies for preventing emotional involvement between the ex-spouses make for difficulties in constructing a workable plan for coparenting. Moreover, because a buffering strategy prevents direct exchange of information between the spouses, it increases the probability that the other spouse will become resistant. The mediator must try to maintain the highest level of direct communication between the spouses that feels satisfactory to both.

Sabotaging Visitations

If all other methods of emotionally disengaging fail, a spouse may attempt to sabotage visitations between the children and the ex-spouse in the hope of driving the ex-spouse away. If a wife, for example, is successful with this strategy, her need for emotional distance from her ex-husband will be satisfied, albeit at the cost of severing their father from the children's lives.

During mediation sessions, a husband may complain that the children always seem to be sick or busy with a planned activity or to have just left to go somewhere whenever his visitation time comes around. The wife retorts, "Well, the children *do* get sick, and they *are* very busy." In such cases, the mediator must help the wife understand the importance for the children of regular contact with both parents and must help the spouses work out a plan that minimizes contact between them while maximizing contact between the children and each of them.

Emotional Survival Strategies

The pain that parents experience in suddenly being apart from their children for extended periods of time is less apparent than the pain that children experience following the separation of their parents. Indeed, the mediation process has as its central goal to reduce the suffering of children following parental separation by maximizing access to both parents. This is a necessary priority because children do not on their own have the power or resources to arrange continuing contact with their parents. But it is also true that just as children need access to their parents, so do parents need access to and continuing contact with their children.

Many parents, especially mothers, who have built their lives around their children throughout their marriage, will, on being informed that their spouse is leaving, cling ever more tightly to the children. Frequently, they have never cultivated adult friends other than their spouse and have not worked outside the home for many years, if at all. Hence the only significant relationships remaining for them are those with their children.

Moreover, the thought of being completely alone, without either spouse or children, is more than they can bear. When mediation begins, these spouses often panic and develop rigid strategies for their own emotional survival.

Resisting Mediation in Favor of Court

One strategy that these spouses attempt is flat resistance to mediation. In the first phone call from the mediator, these spouses typically say things like, "I am not giving up my children; my children want to stay with me. I am keeping custody, so there is nothing to mediate." When the mediator suggests that mediation is almost always a more constructive approach for deciding parenting arrangements for children, such a spouse may say, "Well, I've already decided on the parenting arrangements—I'm keeping my children. Besides, I'm sure that any judge would let me keep my children—a judge wouldn't let him take them from me, so I'd rather go to court."

Usually, with further explanation of the mediation process, this spouse can be persuaded to attend a first mediation session. The mediator must deal sensitively with a mother's emotional panic at the prospect of losing her child by rephrasing the idea as "keeping your child but also allowing the opportunity for your child to keep his father."

If the mediator cannot persuade the spouse to attend even a first mediation session, a phone call to her attorney will usually resolve the problem. However, on occasion, the spouse will attend the first mediation session but will either not participate sincerely or resist all reasonable offers by the other spouse during the negotiation phase. In such a case, the mediator must delicately probe the nature of the resistance. If such probing reveals an emotional survival strategy, the mediator must sensitively help the spouse by framing the negotiation efforts as an opportunity for opening ways for the children to share time with both parents and by discussing the consequences of sharing the children. If, conversely, probing reveals that the spouse's attorney advised her to attend mediation but not agree to anything, the mediator must confer with the attorney to explore the reasons for the attorney's resistance to mediation. Sometimes the attorney may need more information about the process of mediation, and sometimes the attorney may need more of a sense of participation. If the latter seems true, then the mediator can invite both attorneys with their clients to the next mediation session in order to elicit explicit cooperation from the attorneys (see Chapter Eleven).

Demanding Sole Custody

A demand for sole custody may persist in spite of all the mediator's efforts. The reasons offered by the spouse are likely to be weak and inconsistent and may not even be accompanied by any particular accusations about the other spouse as a person or as a parent. With further probing, the mediator usually elicits tears and unveils the spouse's panic at losing the children. At this point, the other spouse typically backs off and responds sympathetically to the panic. A husband may offer affirmation that he has no desire to take the children away but that he does want to maintain involvement in their lives. The wife may then soften her stance and appear more ready to negotiate an agreement.

Manipulating or Invalidating the Children's Preferences

When children have indicated a preference for living with one parent, the other parent, feeling hurt and abandoned, may attempt to manipulate or invalidate the stated preferences of the child. This strategy takes several forms. The father may refuse to bring the children to the mediation session when requested, saying he does not want them traumatized by having to answer painful questions. Or he may agree to bring them but show up without them, saying, "I forgot that they had Little League practice today." In this instance, the father knows that the children would express a preference for living at their mother's house, but he does not want to face it. He may even say that the children have told him they want to live with him—and the children may actually have said so, in an attempt to protect either themselves or their father.

Another form of this strategy is for the father to insist that he bring the children to the mediation session. He may also claim a particular day as the only time he has available for that session—which just happens to be on the last day of a stretch of time during which the children will have been with him. Of course, he does not state his hidden agenda, but he is exploiting what we may call the *recency effect*—the tendency of children (particularly young ones) to express a preference to live with the parent with whom they most recently spent time.

A last and more desperate form of this strategy is enacted after a child states a preference at the mediation session to live with the other parent. The threatened spouse may refuse to accept the expressed feelings of the child, claiming that the child has been brainwashed by the other parent or was too uncomfortable to state her real feelings or didn't want to hurt the parent's feelings. The spouse might even blame the mediator for providing such an artificial setting as an office for the child to talk about difficult feelings.

All of these strategies are challenging for the mediator to counter, since the spouse tends to invalidate any perspective offered by the mediator unless it supports that spouse's own perspective. Sometimes the support of a counselor, a sensitive attorney, or even a trusted clergyperson can help the spouse accept the child's real needs and desires.

Financial Survival Strategies

Along with a divorce come radical changes in lifestyle due to financial stress. Both spouses experience the economic crunch, but in different ways. Not uncommonly, the wife's spousal support alone may be inadequate for her to live on comfortably, and she may become acutely aware that she needs the children to live with her if she is to survive financially.

The husband may also experience financial difficulties in having to pay out a significant amount of money in child support and spousal support. Often he feels cheated because he is forced to make regular payments to his ex-wife, toward whom he may have very bitter feelings, and for his children, whom he may see only infrequently. Hence he is often motivated to develop more financially advantageous arrangements for himself.

While financial survival strategies may be used by a spouse for self-serving ends, they are also used when there is a legitimate need to establish or modify spousal support or child support payments. This is especially true for mothers, who, notwithstanding well-intentioned court orders to provide her with adequate financial support, may receive less than adequate support following a divorce and whose earning power is considerably less than that of their ex-spouses because of underdeveloped job skills (see Kitson & Morgan, 1990; Schwartz & Kaslow, 1997). When such financial needs are not dealt with elsewhere, they sometimes enter into the custody negotiations.

Wanting Primary Physical Custody

Although the parent utilizing a financial survival strategy usually seeks sole physical custody, legal custody is not usually an issue. For example, a wife may be quite willing to have joint legal custody as long as the children primarily reside at her house. Only when challenged by the husband or the mediator might the wife reveal the real reason for her position: that she will not be able to survive financially without the child support payments.

The husband's parallel strategy of requesting physical custody is rooted in his belief that it would be less costly to him to be the primary caregiver than to make the payments to his ex-wife. For him also, the issue of legal custody is irrelevant as long as his child support costs are minimized by retaining physical custody.

Because of the negative impression conveyed by a parent who makes postdivorce parenting arrangements primarily on the basis of financial concerns, neither parent is straightforward about motives. Instead, their discussion centers on which parent can offer better caregiving to the children and on other appropriate issues. Sooner or later, however, a connection between money and time with the children is usually established. Such a connection should cue the mediator to the hidden agenda.

Wanting Shared Physical Custody

This strategy is typically employed only by the husband. Using the excuse that the children need to spend time at both houses, the father attempts to significantly reduce his child support payments, since the wife would have the children only about half the time. This strategy is again rooted in the belief that being the primary caregiver for even half the time is less costly than making the equivalent child support payments to the ex-spouse. Again, the cue to the mediator is the frequent mention of money issues while discussing optimal living arrangements for the children.

Wanting the Children Most of the Summer

The wife who is financially dependent on child support payments may argue for the children being with her through the summer, except for two weeks or at the very most one month with the father. She may claim that the children have all kinds of summer activities planned and really want to be with her for the summer. Her hidden agenda is a fear of reduced child support payments if the children were to spend the summer with their father.

Conversely, the husband may argue for having the children with him for the whole summer because they don't see enough of him during the school year. Father's hidden motive is the hope that he will not be required to make child support payments during that period.

Both these strategies are weakened by the fact that even if the children do spend the entire summer with their father, he will still be required, by most judges, to pay a significant proportion of the regular support payments. Courts do recognize that the mother's bills keep coming in even during the summer.

Because these strategies can color the negotiations over the parenting agreement, the mediator must remain aware of financial motives behind the spouses' positions. If it appears that the couple are able to reach an agreement that is constructive for the children in spite of the fact that their primary motives are financial, the mediator need not intervene. If, however, financial concerns prevent the couple from even considering the needs of their children, then these issues should be dealt with separately by a consulting attorney, by the spouses' respective attorneys, or by the mediator, if appropriate. After the financial issues are clarified and perhaps negotiated to the point where the parents are able to consider parenting arrangements on the basis of their children's time-sharing needs first, time-sharing negotiations can resume. As previously noted, financial considerations can and should be arranged to accommodate such parenting decisions, not vice versa.

Power Assertion Strategies

While most spousal strategies have some inherent element of a power struggle, there are a number of strategies in which an assertion of power is the primary goal. These strategies proceed from any of several motives. A spouse who felt dominated by the other spouse throughout the marriage may view custody mediation as the first opportunity to assert his or her own power in a manner that is equal to or greater than that of the other spouse. This view may be encouraged by the spouse's attorney. With the confidence inspired by the attorney, the spouse may feel strong enough to prove to the other spouse that he or she will no longer be pushed around. Conversely, if one spouse has been the dominant partner throughout the marriage, he or she may try to preserve that status following the divorce by staking out an aggressive claim regarding the custody issues.

Wanting to Win Sole Custody

There are occasions when one or both spouses retain an adversarial stance throughout mediation and consider some or all of the issues in terms of winning and losing. They each arm themselves with aggressive, high-powered attorneys, and the content of what they win is less relevant than the win itself. In some cases, a spouse will push for sole custody until he or she wins over the other spouse and then will turn around and allow the other spouse to retain custody of the children. The trigger for such behavior may be the initial divorce, a remarriage by either spouse, a move by one spouse out of the state, or any number of more minor incidents. In each case, the urge to dominate the other spouse is strong. Occasionally, these spouses are able to work out every aspect of the parenting agreement except the designation of legal custody. If they each appear too concerned with winning such a symbolic victory, it is advisable for the mediator to send this one issue back to their attorneys. Sometimes, unfortunately, the craving to win will be satisfied only by a judge's decree, in which case they must go to court for a decision.

The 50–50 Percent Split

In another kind of strategy, one spouse (typically the husband) will insist on joint custody in an absolutely literal (but, again, not legally accurate) interpretation of the term. Although the mediator may explain that joint custody really means 50 percent legal responsibility, not 50 percent ownership, and that the parents can design a time-sharing arrangement so that each of them is with the children for significant amounts of time, this spouse continues to argue for an exact 50–50 percent split in time sharing even though it will be inconvenient for the children, for the wife, and even for him.

A father using this strategy may argue that the children need him as much as they need their mother. Even after it is revealed that because of his work schedule he will be able to be with the children only infrequently and that they will be staying with sitters much of the time while at his house, he does not budge from his position. In effect, his intention is to assert to his ex-wife his equality of power in parenting the children, even if he, the children, and the ex-wife all suffer as a result.

If the husband cannot be persuaded to stop thinking in terms of percentages and if the wife will agree to an even split for the time being, then a short-term agreement can be developed that specifies a reevaluation in three months to a year. The mediator's goal would be simply to get past this particular power struggle and hope that over time the husband will relax his strategy. Moreover, other circumstances that may well change can allow for a more flexible arrangement in future months. Sometimes the initial arrangement eventually works itself into a satisfactory permanent arrangement, and sometimes, unfortunately, the children have to suffer some distress before the father will reconsider.

The 51–49 Percent Split

A couple may be fairly open and flexible in negotiations about all aspects of sharing their children. They may even agree to joint legal custody and to the idea of equitable sharing of time with their children. However, as the details of the number of days that the children will spend at each parent's house become apparent, one spouse begins to resist and deadlocks the negotiations.

In one such case, the couple worked out a compromise to within three-fourths of one day's difference in their respective time with the children each week. However, the wife subtly kept resisting working out the final details as to specific days. Because there seemed to be no apparent motive for such resistance, the mediator probed her reasoning. She then revealed her motive, relating a conversation she had had with her attorney. In their discussion of strategies for future custody battles, her attorney had advised her to keep more than 50 percent of the time spent with her children so that if she ever moved out of state, she would stand a greater chance of retaining physical custody, since the children would have become more attached to her.

Clearly this advice was incompatible with mediation efforts. And in fact, this wife was perfectly willing to share her children equally with her ex-husband, and she had no intention of moving from the area. Yet she was in an intense conflict between her own desires and her attorney's advice to keep the leverage on her side for future court contests. The resolution of this issue entailed inviting both attorneys to the next mediation session, where the wife's attorney was obliged to give her explicit permission and encouragement to compromise.

Use of Clichés for Justification

Clichés give an impression of wisdom and sanctimony and make the person uttering them appear confident and decisive. The only problem is that there are many clichés that contradict each other, and a spouse can simply pick the ones that support his or her desires and ignore the ones that contradict them. Furthermore, clichés are not open to rational discussion, only to argumentative debate.

These are some of the typical clichés used by spouses in mediation:

Young children need to be with their mother.

Young children just need any loving parent.

Girls need their mother.

Boys need their father.

Children need one primary parent.

Children need both their parents.

Children need one place to call their home.

Children are adaptable.

Children need one consistent lifestyle and cannot handle bouncing back and forth between two homes.

Children are resilient.

Quality of time shared is more important than quantity.

Children need extended periods of time with a parent to develop a really close relationship.

When clichés are being used as justifications, the mediator should point out the overgeneralized nature of their truths and stress the importance of considering each child as a unique person with unique needs. Ideally, such clichés should be preempted by the mediator's opening monologue in the first mediation session (see Chapter Five).

Changing the Child's Last Name

On occasion, a mother who feels particularly bitter toward her ex-husband will assert her power in a subtle but powerfully symbolic fashion by changing the child's last name. Usually the change is from the father's last name to her own maiden name, or it may be to the name of her new husband. With this action she attempts to stake out an exclusive claim on the child and at the same time negate the father's claim on the child; she may also be trying to protect herself against the negative emotions associated with the sound of his name. Typically, this occurs in cases in which the mother, at least temporarily, has sole legal and primary physical custody of the child and is in mediation at the father's initiation to increase his time with the child. During mediation, the mother may compromise on many aspects of the parenting agreement, apparently despite the deep bitterness that she feels. Then, in between mediation sessions, the father learns indirectly from the child's school or some other source, or directly from the child, that the child is being called by the mother's or her new husband's last name. Needless to say, the father comes into the next mediation session incensed and resistant to any agreements. He may then force an impasse by insisting that the child retain his last name. In such a case, the mother's unexpected cooperation is due to the fact that she has already secretly and symbolically asserted her power by depriving the child of the father's name. Had the father not discovered the name change during the course of mediation, a workable parenting agreement might well have been reached. However, when the father eventually discovers this fact, the agreement will no doubt break down and require further mediation.

If the conflict over the name change does not escalate beyond the possibility of negotiation, the mediator may suggest a more contemporary resolution—a hyphenated last name, combining those of both parents. If this is not an acceptable compromise, the issue can be referred to the attorneys for negotiations or to the court for a judge's decision.

Secret Phone Calls

A spouse will occasionally attempt to gain some power by phoning the mediator on the sly. If the call is made before the first mediation session, it may be to reveal incriminating information about the other spouse's habits and treatment of the children. If the call is made between sessions, it may be to denigrate what the other spouse said and to reveal what was omitted in the previous session.

The goal of such phone calls is to gain relative esteem in the eyes of the mediator and consequently to gain power by biasing the mediator in one's favor. Such strategies will not be resorted to if the mediator consistently expresses disinterest in hearing accusations about either spouse and declares that there will be no secrets withheld from either of them.

"Holier Than Thou" Impression

Another way of attempting to bias the mediator in favor of one of the spouses is by the strategic use of "impression management" (Goffman, 1959). To convey an impression of being self-assured, in good self-control, rational, and reasonable, a spouse dresses neatly or even formally for the sessions and consistently keeps cool during emotionally laden discussions. One goal of this strategy is to provoke the other spouse to lose control and appear enraged or parentally incompetent, inappropriately emotional, irrational, or even crazy. Such behavior is then used as evidence of unfitness to care for the children.

Thus provoked, an ex-wife, for example, may decide to break the rule against talking of the past and tell how the ex-husband's previous life included drugs, wife battering, sexual perversions, or a criminal record, right up until a few weeks or months earlier, when, for example, he underwent a religious conversion. The wife then berates him for his holier-than-thou attitude, asserting that he has not really changed a bit. The mediator should ignore all such accusations, refrain from judging the validity of either spouse's claims, and refocus the couple on the task at hand.

Retaliation Strategies

Whereas strategies of power assertion are aimed at proving oneself as strong as or stronger than the other spouse, the sole intent of retaliation strategies seems to be a desire to hurt the other spouse. They are by far the most unpleasant of the strategies with which the mediator has to grapple.

Sole Custody as Revenge

In a typical case, a previously uninvolved father vigorously seeks sole custody upon being divorced by his wife. Even though he admits to not being very close to the children and not having much time to spend with them, he insists on sole custody nonetheless. In probing further, it becomes clear that he is seething with anger at his wife for leaving him, and although he is fully aware that his wife would feel deeply hurt by being separated from the children, he feels that she deserves it. So he uses some cliché or rationalization to contend that the children would be better off with him.

It is helpful for the mediator to facilitate a discussion of the husband's hurt and resentment in such a way as to stimulate a controlled and face-saving venting of feelings. Sometimes this helps stabilize the husband enough so that he can get on with reasonable negotiations. However, if he appears too overwhelmed by his feelings and seems unable to negotiate in a reasonable manner, a referral for counseling can be helpful. It may also be helpful for the mediator to alert him tactfully to the likely outcome of a court decision if he wants to push the issue that far. Knowing that a judge is unlikely to favor him, the father may be persuaded to reconsider his position by the next mediation session.

Point-Counterpoint

A classic strategy is a retaliation move provoked, for example, by a wife's taking her ex-husband to court to request an increase in child support payments. Feeling threatened, insulted, and angry, the husband files a counterpetition for sole custody of the children. As the story unfolds in mediation, he explains that his wife just pushed him one step too far. He proceeds to elaborate on his plans for having the children live with him.

Once the mediator probes the husband's motives, his anger usually reveals his retaliation motive. Some sensitive clarification of the situation by the mediator can often persuade the wife to offer a more compromising way to satisfy her need for more money and the husband to back off from his rigid position. Often he then acknowledges that he is not really prepared to have the children live full-time with him anyway. A compromise is soon reached, and the strategy is ended.

Joint Custody as Revenge

Occasionally, an embittered spouse (usually a husband) will push for joint legal and joint physical custody while at the same time manifesting no real intention of being actively involved with the children. As he discusses his plans for regular and frequent contact with his ex-wife, she appears horrified—continuing contact with her ex-husband is the last thing she wants. It may be that she left him for another man, and consequently his primary intent is to punish her—perhaps for years to come. Usually, at some point, the wife expresses real distress and refuses to go on with mediation if she will have to deal with her ex-husband so regularly. If the mediator then deals sensitively with the revenge motive and suggests a method of sharing the children with minimal spousal contact, the husband will usually back off. Even though he wants to taunt his ex-wife, he does not really want much contact with her either, for it only regenerates his own feelings of hurt and anger.

"Bait and Switch"

Sometimes, at the outset of mediation, a husband will offer a cooperative sharing of custody and time with the children. The wife is pleasantly surprised, since the husband had previously been uncooperative. However, in the second session, as her hopes are up to finalize the cooperative plan, he suddenly switches gears and decides that he wants sole custody and will go to court if necessary. His ex-wife is puzzled and upset by this sudden move, especially as he refuses to give her further information about this sudden shift in his position.

On probing, the mediator usually is able to reveal that in the interim between sessions, the husband started to feel resentful of the idea that he should even consider sharing anything with the woman who left him. Moreover, he is not going to give her the satisfaction of having it easy. With help from the mediator in discriminating between spousal issues and child-related issues, the husband will usually reverse his position once again and work out a reasonable compromise.

Frustrating Visitations

The strategy of frustrating the spouse's visitations is used mostly by wives who already have sole custody of the children. It often arises in situations in which a husband who had not been involved with the children for some time since the divorce files a petition to clarify his visitation rights. The wife resists such visitations in every way that she can and resists efforts in mediation to work out a plan to accommodate the children's schedules to the visitation plan proposed by the husband. Using a litany of excuses—ballet practice, gymnastics, playing with friends, birthday parties, camp, doctor's appointments—she blocks all efforts.

In such situations, the mediator often finds that the wife wants to punish the husband for leaving her to raise the children all by herself. As one woman put it, "I don't want to share the kids with him—he left me, and I always just wanted to be a mother. I'm working full-time now only because I have to—I'd rather be a full-time mother. He doesn't deserve to see the kids." Although these feelings may be intense, the mediator is usually able to help resolve them by pointing out that the children are the ones being punished and that the woman needs to consider the possibility that her former husband may now be ready to help her by participating in the children's lives.

Another common motive for frustrating visitations is to punish the other spouse for not keeping current with child support payments. The wife may feel that if the ex-husband is unwilling to fulfill his responsibilities for financial support of the children, then he does not deserve to see them. If such a motive is revealed, the mediator should alert the wife to the illegal nature of her action and also inform her that it is not in the children's best interests, psychologically. Moreover, visitation is not only a right of the parent; it is also a right of the child. The mediator should then help the wife deal with time sharing and support as separate issues. Often such a discussion gives the husband an opportunity to clarify his reasons for being in arrears on support payments, and the spouses can then work out a plan for solving the two problems independently.

"Pushing to Lose" Strategies

Following a divorce, spouses sometimes feel pressure from their extended families, friends, neighbors, and even society at large to fight for custody of the children. Not uncommonly though, upon divorce, an individual finally feels free to live as a single person, unencumbered by spouse or children. If he or she succumbs to the social pressure to pursue custody, it is often with much ambivalence. Such ambivalence frequently leads the spouse to use strategies that are almost certain to result in a failure to gain custody of the children.

Typically, these strategies involve an initial declaration to the judge, the ex-spouse, and the mediator of an intent to obtain sole legal and physical custody of the children. However, from the time of the initial separation all the way through the mediation process, this spouse fails to establish suitable housing for himself or herself and the children, fails to find or keep a job with which to provide for the children, and fails to spend any significant time with the children. In spite of having been informed of the importance of these factors, he or she makes no changes in lifestyle while still declaring the intention of gaining sole custody. When the other spouse refuses to agree with such an obviously unsuitable proposal, the first spouse responds with one of two strategies: a martyrdom strategy or a face-saving strategy.

Martyrdom Strategy

The essence of the first strategy is to present oneself as a wronged victim. Upon receiving the expected refusal by his ex-wife, the husband expounds on how difficult his life has been, how his own parents never gave him enough love or support, and how he always gets fired from his jobs for insignificant and unexplained reasons. If he plays out this strategy to the end, he may appeal to his ex-wife not to take away the "only things that matter to me—my children." Upon her refusal even to consider joint custody, he accepts her decision with a show of defeat and passively signs the agreement giving his ex-wife sole legal custody and leaving the general visitation plan open and conditional upon his finding a job and suitable housing.

Face-Saving Strategy

The husband who employs this strategy is much more aggressive in his pursuit of sole custody. Throughout the mediation process, he pushes his position to the maximum, attempting to prove to his ex-wife and to the mediator his sincerity in wanting to be the sole custodial parent. However, the living situation for this husband usually is not unlike that of the husband employing the martyrdom strategy. Although he keeps reiterating his plans to get a house and job, they never reach fruition.

Typically, this husband forces the dispute out of mediation and into the courtroom. Once in court, he presents his case aggressively, even though the odds are unmistakably against him. And he loses—but feeling that at least he gave it his best shot.

With both strategies, the husband more or less unconsciously sets up the situation so that his chances of losing are great. The real intent of his display is to prove that he at least tried to fulfill his role as a concerned father. His failure was not unintentional; rather, it served his need for freedom in a manner that allowed him a sense of self-respect and a temporary relief from guilt.

Strategies for Appeasing a New Spouse

Although most spousal strategies are motivated by the dynamics of the divorcing couple, some are motivated by a new spouse or new partner.

When a woman marries a recently divorced man who is still emotionally enmeshed with his previous wife over custody and visitation issues, she often suffers from a feeling of insecurity about her new husband's loyalty to her. A husband's emotional investment in his previous wife, even if it is primarily negative, is quite threatening to the new wife. Moreover, if the children, in playing out their own reuniting strategies, create conflict between their father and stepmother, she is likely to feel an even greater threat to the solidity of the new marriage. As a way of coping with these threats, the new wife may put subtle or overt pressure on her husband to resolve her insecurity either by pursuing sole custody or by pulling away.

Sole Custody for the New Spouse

The husband who attempts to claim sole custody of the children typically presents a very straightforward argument on his own behalf, such as being able to offer more resources for the children, a larger home, better schools, and someone who can be home for the children all day (the stepmother). Occasionally, he may offer some mildly negative facts about his ex-wife, but usually he does not push his position beyond a simple presentation of facts.

When confronted by the outrage of his ex-wife over the threat of having her children taken from her, he usually remains rational and objective. The mediator's probe of his motives reveals a lack of any personal emotional commitment to the children. He is not really able to justify taking the children from their mother's primary emotional care. At this point, the mediator is often able to work out a compromise that includes more time for the children to be with their father.

Because it would be far too threatening for the husband to reveal his real motive—appeasing his new wife—he never offers a solid justification for pursuing sole custody. Over the course of the year following the signing of the mediation agreement, the husband typically reduces the frequency of his contacts with the children to less than it was before mediation. While this may be due to other factors as well, the primary reason usually appears to be his original lack of real commitment to involvement with the children.

With this strategy, the husband attempts to help his new wife satisfy her territorial needs and prove herself a better mother than the ex-wife. However, his efforts at gaining possession of the children typically are not fruitful. Unfortunately, all too often, the children are eventually disappointed by a dwindling relationship with their father.

Pulling Away

Sometimes, when ex-spouses have been grappling over custody and visitation for some time, the husband's new wife puts pressure on him to end the struggle by either getting sole custody or moving away. After the husband makes his bid in mediation for sole custody and his ex-wife refuses, he informs her that he will be moving away from the area (often out of state) very soon. He then settles for some minimal contact with the children, perhaps on a holiday or two and during a small portion of the summer.

The fact that he did not more actively pursue his original position is the key to recognizing this strategy. In probing, the mediator usually finds out that the husband feels caught between the ongoing struggle with his ex-wife and his new wife's intolerance for it. He then explains that he has been forced to make a choice. Once again, unfortunately, the children wind up losing frequent contact with their father.

There usually is little that the mediator can do in these situations, since the only available solutions seem to be for the father either to lose his new wife and remain in the area to continue struggling with his ex-wife or to keep his new wife, move, and lose significant contact with his children. It is a very difficult dilemma indeed for the father and for the mediator.

○

Although it is essential for the mediator to know the individual strategies of spouses as described in this chapter, the real challenge lies in working effectively with the complex matrix of multiple strategies that spouses actually present in mediation. Often one spouse's strategy will elicit a complementary strategy on the part of the other spouse. For example, a husband's reuniting strategy is often complemented by a wife's emotionally disengaging strategy. A wife's strategy for emotional survival may be complemented by a husband's power assertion strategy. For the mediator, the challenge resides in the complexity of the multiple strategies used. In the next two chapters, we turn to ways of meeting this challenge.

10

STRATEGIES FOR
ELICITING COOPERATION
BETWEEN PARENTS

THIS CHAPTER WILL DELINEATE the strategies for inducing cooperation between the spouses, and Chapter Eleven will discuss strategies for handling conflict. Although many of the strategies can be used at numerous points in the mediation process, they generally are used sequentially, in the order presented here.

In the opening phase of negotiations, the mediator's central goal is to develop cooperation between the spouses. Because it is virtually impossible to begin negotiations that lead to resolution while overt conflict rages, the first step is to establish a cease-fire. The mediator can achieve this using strategies that are functionally incompatible with open conflict. It should be noted, though, that these strategies will not permanently prevent overt conflict, for such conflict will almost inevitably rear its head at some later point in the mediation process. However, a cooperative ambiance at the beginning of mediation serves several purposes: it optimizes the spouses' readiness to attend and listen to the mediator's opening presentation; it gives the spouses a period of relative calm in which to reflect on their struggle and defuse some of the angry feelings generated by the presence of the other spouse; it gives the mediator a chance to observe the degree of each spouse's impulse control and the way the spouses relate to each other; and finally, it gives the mediator an opportunity to prove his or her positive intent by producing a beginning atmosphere of hope, cooperation, and interpersonal respect, which the mediator can anchor and refer to as needed in later, more conflict-laden phases of mediation.

Establishing Control and Trust

By far the most important aspect of the mediator's interventions in eliciting cooperative efforts is maintaining flexible control over every phase of
the process. The mediation process needs to be carefully designed to yield
just the right emotional and attitudinal climate, topic choice, and sequence
and timing of topics. And the mediator needs to maintain a strategic flexibility so as to sensitively and responsively direct the flow of events to the
final resolution—the mediated agreement. Inefficiencies and blockages in
the process occur if the mediator does not strictly adhere to the structure.

Some level of trust must be established between the spouses before any
cooperative agreements can be developed. However, couples almost always begin mediation with little or no workable level of trust; moreover,
throughout mediation they may be unable to believe that trust is possible.
Even the most trusting couples experience intense mistrust during mediation. Trust requires letting go of the negative experiences of the past;
however, the past is all there is on which to base predictions for the future. Because these couples have no maps for the future, their anxiety level
tends to be very high. To cope with this anxiety, they seek some security
by hanging on to the past.

Dealing with mistrust is a real challenge for the mediator because it is
not something that can be argued against logically, and if challenged too
forcefully, it will simply increase in intensity. One must deal with it indirectly. Acceptance of the mistrust by the mediator is an important start.
The mediator should always assume that there is and will continue to be
mistrust until the spouses have rebuilt trust by following through on their
agreements. Paradoxically, by accepting the presence of mistrust within
the sessions, the mediator facilitates trust building.

It is helpful for the mediator to initiate the growth of trust by offering
a positive perspective. Often the only trust that the spouses have in each
other is the trust that they both love the children very much. Throughout
the mediation process, the mediator can refer back to this basic area of
agreement whenever the spouses begin to argue about issues out of mistrust for each other. The mediator may say, for example, "It would be a
very loving gesture for you both to offer your children the possibility that
the future might be better than the past. In spite of how you feel now and
in spite of the past, just consider the possibility that people can change
and that by avoiding prejudging and by staying as flexible and open-
minded as you can allow yourselves to be, you can help your children develop emotionally in healthier ways. With your help, they won't have to

remain stuck at the point at which you two are now." If the spouses cannot even agree on their shared love for their children, the mediator can request that they just assume it to be true for the time being so that each can eventually give the other an opportunity to show his or her love for the children. This is consistent with the notion in behaviorist theory that changes in behavior can elicit changes in thinking and feeling, with the Alcoholics Anonymous adage "Fake it till you make it," and with Cloé Madanes's "pretending" technique from strategic therapy (1980, 1984).

From the very beginning of the process, the mediator should persistently affirm the fact that in spite of their mistrust of each other as spouses, they can still develop sufficient trust to coparent effectively. The mediator should search for even the smallest areas of trust regarding parenting, from the beginning of their relationship with their children until the present. He can then take whatever evidence is presented, elaborate upon it, and refer to it repeatedly throughout the negotiations. The mediator might remind the couple that children typically can trust each parent more easily than the parents can trust each other.

The mediator should be aware that this alone will do little; the only way that trust can develop is if the spouses act in trusting ways with each other. The mediator can seed the beginnings of trust by establishing several minor agreements that will be kept. If mistrust is particularly high in the first session, a structured task to which both spouses agree can be assigned. The task should be completed before the next session and should be similar to one they have already been able to carry out, even if it involved some conflict. However, the mediator's task should have a slightly different twist, designed to prevent conflict. For example, the parents could be asked to arrange two days and times of child transfer to take place at a new, agreed-upon place and time. This task can be presented as a challenge for each spouse to prove to the other that he or she can and will follow through as agreed. This assigned task is best accomplished before the second mediation session, serving as a first step in trust building and perhaps also as a first item to include in the final parenting agreement. If the task is not carried out successfully, the details can be discussed, while still fresh in the minds of both spouses, as material for building time-sharing arrangements that will work. In the first case, the problem is solved, and in the second, a problem is objectively identified in such a way that solutions are more easily forthcoming.

There are, however, occasions when a mediator is confronted with a facsimile of trust between a couple. For example, one couple came into mediation requesting help in working out a joint custody arrangement that would be best for their young children. Both spouses were extremely pleasant, cooperative, and seemingly receptive to the ideas of the mediator. During the information-gathering phase, the husband said, "We still love each other very much." The wife agreed, adding, "We will probably get back together in the near future." When asked why they were getting a divorce, the husband replied, "Well, we both definitely want a divorce now so that we can do our own things for a while." He then added, "We both have done really well in sharing the kids." To the mediator, this case looked like a piece of cake. However, their apparent trust and respect was revealed as false as soon as they got down to discussing details of the joint custody plan. At that point, the husband utilized a 50–50 percent power assertion strategy, the wife utilized a 51–49 percent power assertion strategy, and the negotiations broke down into accusations and assertions of mistrust. It was as if the mediator had been walking through a hall of mirrors, cautiously at first and then, seeming to see a clear path through, forged ahead to the exit only to be confronted abruptly by a solid mirror. Such an unexpected event can be disorienting and frustrating, and if the mediator pushes on the mirror, it may well shatter and destroy the possibility of mediated settlement.

Had the mediator been more skeptical about the couple's initial display of trust and respect, he might have been able to reveal their underlying agenda before attempting to solidify a final agreement. However, because the display was so unusual and refreshing, he was taken off guard and succumbed to it. To avoid such traps, the mediator must be wary of any situation that appears too easy.

Specific Strategies

The process of eliciting cooperation from the couple requires that the mediator have a set of versatile and effective strategies at his disposal.

Preempting

Certainly the best strategy for dealing with undesirable conflict is to prevent it in the first place. Effective preempting of conflict depends heavily on information gleaned by the mediator before negotiations begin. For example, suppose that in the first phone call, a husband tells the mediator that he is furious with his ex-wife and elaborates on all the terrible things that she has done but then subtly adds that he still loves her and will do anything to get back together with her. He then proceeds to tell of his goal to "keep the children from seeing her because she is too unsettled." Armed with the knowledge that this husband really wants a reconciliation and that he is prepared to utilize reuniting and retaliation strategies, the mediator can preempt some of these moves in the first mediation session. He can emphasize that it is very difficult for spouses to think about their children objectively and to make plans for sharing them if they are not yet emotionally divorced from each other and can point out that while it is perfectly natural for a spouse who does not want a divorce to punish the other spouse by wanting to withhold the children, actually doing it will hurt the children. The mediator can then inquire about the degree of certainty of the divorce decision and explore the feelings and expectations around the divorce decision. It is important that the mediator address these comments to both spouses equally (turning toward and making eye contact with each of them for equal periods of time) so that the comments do not appear to be critical of either spouse singly (of course, both spouses are aware that the comments are more appropriate to one of them—in this case, the husband). Thus the mediator preempts the reuniting and retaliation strategies of the husband in a way that allows face saving but clarifies the couple's differing expectations regarding the divorce decision.

To take another example, suppose that in the first phone call, the wife informs the mediator that she is not going to allow the husband to have any further contact with the children because he is irresponsible, does not discipline the children, and returns them home dirty. She rants about all the years that she had to put up with his antics. On calling the wife's attorney, the mediator then hears that the wife has said that she really feels the husband is a good father and that even though he makes many mistakes, the children need contact with him and she wants him to be more involved with them. However, she has filed a petition to restrict visitations in order to get him to listen to her. Having determined that the attorney's information is probably valid, the mediator then sets out to preempt conflict.

In the first session, the mediator can elaborate on the benefits of mediation as follows: "This format gives each of you an opportunity to clarify what you expect of the other in sharing your children. Sometimes it's hard to make clear to each other the things that get in the way of sharing your children. Sometimes it might even feel easier not to have to deal with each other at all, but you both know that your children need both of you." Then the mediator can ask, "What things do you each need the other person to do to make sharing your children easier for you?"

Here the mediator cuts right through the conflict that would probably arise if he dealt directly with the wife's initiating a petition for restricting visitation. Had he instead asked the wife why she wanted to cut off her ex-husband's visitation rights, she would likely have uttered her list of accusations in such a manner as to justify her action, which would doubtless elicit defensive retaliation from the husband, who would perceive her actions as an insult and a power play. Instead, the mediator simply refuses to deal with the superficial legal threat and proceeds as if it were clearly understood that the husband would continue sharing time with the children. Typically in such cases, the couple immediately begin to make constructive requests of each other to facilitate sharing of their children.

Preempting, then, is a sophisticated tool for circumventing polarized conflict and saving face for both parties simply by going directly to a level where a concordance of opinion is likely to exist.

Giving Information and Hope

Much of what underlies conflict between people is a lack of information about their situations. When people pass through a major life crisis such as a divorce or a custody dispute for the first time, they find that there are few road maps with any guarantees of reliability. As a result, they feel scared, insecure, and vulnerable. It is comforting at such times to be offered an authoritative description of what they are going through and what others in similar situations have gone through and a perspective on how these crises are most effectively resolved. Just knowing that it is possible to come out of such a crisis relatively intact and rational can bring great comfort—and out of such comfort come reductions in acrimony and defensive maneuvering.

Often in a first phone call, a spouse will tell the mediator, "I don't know about mediation. I'm sure that there's no way it could work or that you could help. You don't know my ex-wife; she's totally irrational and unpredictable, and she won't stick to any agreements—you can't even talk to her." In response, the mediator can say, "I know that it may seem impossible for you to imagine your ex-wife being reasonable, but every couple that comes into mediation starts off feeling that way about each other. That's our usual starting point, but we have a pretty good track record. In fact, I've even had some couples in very high conflict with each other, but they still came to agreements about sharing their children." This tactic invariably elicits a comment like "Really? Well, our situation isn't that bad." Learning that people whose mutual animosity is greater than theirs have successfully worked out parenting agreements in mediation provides a glimmer of hope as well as a challenge for the couple to give mediation a try.

If no separate divorce education class or orientation program precedes mediation, the mediator must also, early in mediation, offer information about the stages that people typically go through from the time of separation until several years later, about the normal reactions of children following divorce, and about the new forms that family dynamics take when parents in two different homes share their children, as well as the hopeful message that things typically improve and negative feelings subside over time. Once couples develop a new structure for relating to each other as ex-spouses, they typically start to get along better, with less conflict and less anger over sharing their children.

This educational information that a mediator gives a couple about the nature of divorce is certainly helpful in reducing their anxiety and anger and consequently in eliciting more cooperation. However, this is only one aspect of the mediation process, and although it shares similarities with more formalized divorce counseling (see Kaslow, 1981, 1995; Sprenkle, 1985), the in-depth discussion of these points that takes place in divorce counseling is inappropriate to mediation. Giving information and hope is a useful strategy for anchoring out-of-control feelings, but it should not be used by the mediator as an opening to the process of divorce counseling. Unless both parties request it, an unsolicited imposition of such counseling will probably backfire, as one spouse asserts, "I don't want to dwell on the divorce; I just want to settle the custody problem, so let's get on with it."

Complimenting

When praise is given, most people feel disarmed and even somewhat embarrassed. It is a very rare individual who can feel angry and defensive while being flattered. This makes the use of praise particularly effective in mediation. Because spouses entering mediation frequently have been devalued and humiliated by each other, favorable and even flattering words coming from the mediator tend to disarm them. Moreover, to have complimentary things said about them in the presence of the other spouse further enhances their self-esteem. Indeed, this may be the first time anything positive has been said about either spouse since well before the separation.

Because of the sensitivity of both spouses to evaluative comments, any praise or flattery needs to be carefully chosen. Avoidance of all areas of contention is essential. Taboo areas may include parenting skills, availability to and emotional involvement with the children, resources available to the children, and personal qualities that may be linked with areas of contention, such as flexibility, self-control, spontaneity, or honesty. Safe areas generally include the competencies and positive traits of the children ("Your five-year-old is already reading? Gosh, what a bright child!"), physical attractiveness of the children (the mediator can ask to see wallet pictures if the children are not present and then volunteer, for example,

"Gee, what beautiful blond hair—looks like she got it from both of you"), and the competencies of each spouse in areas unrelated to their relationship, such as work, sports, or hobbies ("What's it like to fly a plane? I understand it takes a great deal of skill—and courage! How did you master the fear of heights that most of us earthbound folks have?"; "How do you carry all those meals on one arm without dropping them? It must take a lot of skill. I've always admired how many things a waiter can handle all at once. I think I would forget all the things I needed to do. You must have a fine memory"; "You've run several marathons? Gee, you must be in great shape—how long did you have to train to achieve such an admirable goal?").

Particularly helpful are compliments to both spouses for jointly contributing to their children—for example, "I think your children are really lucky to have you two as parents. It's a valuable gift to your children that you decided to remain living in the same area so that they could continue to enjoy their relationships with both of you, uninterrupted."

In offering compliments, the mediator must remain within the bounds of sincerity and moderation. Insincerity can backfire on the mediator, resulting in greater resistance and mistrust and a loss of the mediator's credibility in the eyes of the flattered spouse. Moreover, flattery of one spouse can result in a perception of mediator bias on the part of the other spouse ("You were taken in by my ex; you were conned and blinded, just like so many other people who don't know him very well") and in a loss of the neutrality necessary for the mediator to be effective.

For some mediators, complimenting other people with sincerity is a natural behavior. For other mediators, who are not used to offering compliments, this strategy will require some practice. If one has good intentions, practicing giving compliments will soon yield sincerity. Furthermore, the practice of finding good in other people can only enhance one as a mediator and as a person. Finally, complimenting one's clients can counteract the effects of therapists and lawyers, who over time can come across as judgmental, critical, and cynical.

Reframing

Another powerful strategy is to redefine a particular concept so as to give it a more constructive interpretation. The process by which we label feelings, thoughts, attitudes, behaviors, and events has a great influence on the way we perceive reality. In essence, we construct our own reality largely on the basis of the *frames,* or points of view, that we impose on the world of our experiences (Watzlawick, 1976, 1978; Watzlawick, Weakland, & Fisch, 1974). Moreover, these frames guide our behavior

and persist even when they result in self-defeating or even destructive behavior patterns. When such perspectives are altered, we have the opportunity to get unstuck from old behavior patterns and to try new behaviors.
It has been said that "organization inhibits reorganization." In essence,
then, any efforts to disrupt habitual patterns of behaving or thinking allows the possibility to reorganize the behavior and/or thinking into more
constructive patterns.

Reframing is especially useful in mediation for changing adversarial
perspectives into cooperative ones, particularly when the couple are talking about their child-sharing plans. For example, when one spouse says,
"I want to keep custody of my children," the mediator can reframe it as
"You would like the children to share a significant amount of time with
you." When one spouse says to the other, "You can visit the children every
other weekend," the mediator can reframe it as "The children will be able
to share time with their father for two weekends every month." Finally,
if a spouse says, "I don't care if we live three blocks away from each other,
I want custody of the children and you can see them once a week," the
mediator can reframe it as "So it would be hard for you to give your children the opportunity to share lots of time with both of you." Even though
these word and syntax changes are subtle, the differences in connotation
are profound and can set the stage for more cooperative negotiations. The
rephrasing effectively shifts the perspective from that of the parent to that
of the children, which helps keep the children's needs foremost in the
awareness of the parents. Moreover, after the mediator reframes their language a few times, it is not uncommon for the spouses to begin imitating
the mediator's language and hence thinking patterns.

Anecdote Telling

Telling stories is a powerful way of conveying information. If the story involves someone else, and the situation happened some time ago, and the
content is only tangentially related to the couple's present situation, it is
relatively easy for angry and suspicious spouses to accept the message.

For example, the mediator might say to a very mistrustful couple, "I
saw a couple, way back about a year ago, who were so suspicious of each
other that they had developed many tactics for spying on each other. The
husband secretly taped all his wife's phone conversations with her mother,
and the wife drove to his place of work every day to make sure he wasn't
running around with other women. When they got divorced, they each
called me to warn me of the lies that the other would doubtless tell me in
mediation. Well, when they got here, they were still paranoid about each
other's every word and move. They fought over every single issue until sud-

denly one of them stopped and began to laugh. When the other asked what the laughing was about, that spouse was told, 'I'm laughing because I realize how absurd this all is. We both love our children and hate each other. So we should just work it out for them—let's not make them miserable too.' And you know, after that they worked out a parenting agreement that's still working very well a year later . . . and they still hate each other."

When stories are told in a more allegorical fashion, the message speaks directly to the unconscious mind (Combs & Freedman, 1990; Gordon, 1978; Haley, 1973; Johnston, Breunig, Garrity, & Baris, 1997; Zeig, 1980). This way, both the threat of the message and the resistance to it are practically nonexistent. An example of this form of anecdote was told by a mediator to a couple who were extremely hostile to each other. The mediator said, "My daughter came crying to my wife and me last night. It seems that she had a nightmare about some rabbits, and she was very upset by it. She dreamed of three rabbits who lived in a small bush by a meadow. Whenever the baby rabbit started to go out and play, the mother rabbit would pull it back into the bushes by its rear legs. The father rabbit, though, didn't like the way the mother rabbit made the baby stay around the nest, so he would pull on the baby rabbit's ears to get it away from the mother's grip. The baby rabbit would squeal and cry, and the mother and father rabbit would drop the baby rabbit and start biting each other. The next day, the same thing happened—and then it began to happen more and more frequently. After some time, the baby rabbit's ears were very long from being pulled at, and its rear legs were very long from being pulled at too. And the baby rabbit's fur was pulled out in patches and its body was all bloody and scarred. The baby rabbit cried and cried, because now that its ears were so long, it was supersensitive to noise and it could not help but hear every sound of every argument of its mother and father. And now that its legs were so long, it could only move awkwardly, and now that its fur was so bloody and blotchy, it looked very ugly. The baby rabbit felt awkward and ugly and worthless and unloved, and the saddest thing of all was that its mother and father did not even notice because they were too busy biting each other. The baby rabbit cried and cried."

Sargent and Moss (1986) suggested another story intended to emphasize cooperation. The mediator says, "I am reminded of the two thirsty mules tied together by a length of rope. Each wanted to drink at a separate watering hole. The harder the one pulled away from the other, the thirstier they both became. Finally, one of them got smart and went along side the other mule to *his* hole, and they both drank" (p. 91).

After telling such anecdotes, the mediator can simply move on to another subject, letting the metaphoric impact of the story sink quietly into the unconscious minds of the spouses.

The telling of anecdotes is a very powerful technique for eliciting from the parents an attitude of cooperation in mediation. Mediators are encouraged to develop their own stories, based upon actual mediation cases, relevant personal experiences, legends, allegories, or myths.

Using Physical Metaphors

Using physical objects as metaphors can have the same effect as verbalized anecdotes in shifting the spouses' perspectives toward cooperation. For example, the mediator can pull out a braided straw "Chinese finger puller" and have each parent place a finger in an opposite end. The couple are then requested to pull their respective finger away from each other and try to get out of the device. The couple soon discover that the only way for them to release their fingers is by each moving the finger toward each other in a gesture of compromise. This symbolic exercise typically makes its point.

Shattuck (1988) describes the use of a "tear bear" (a Velcro teddy bear designed to tear in half when pulled on by both parents), which is offered to couples in conflict. As the parents each pull, they suddenly realize, symbolically, what continuing their fight might accomplish.

George Ferrick, a mediator in Los Angles, once told me about a technique he has used for sensitizing parents who are in dispute about whether their child needs to have a relationship with the other parent. With the child present in the room, he pulls out several jump ropes and gives one end of each rope to the child, and the other end of rope A to the mother and the other end of rope B to the father (a third rope may link the child with a stepparent, grandparent, and so forth). He then describes, using language addressed to the particular level of the child's age for emphasis, how the child has a "close tie" with each of the people on the other end of the ropes, even though they do not have ties with each other. In this simplified and graphic manner, the parents can more easily accept the child's need for the various family relationships to continue.

Resisting a "Time Squeeze"

As mentioned earlier, there seems to be an optimal time frame for each couple within which the mediation process is most successful. When this time frame is compromised, mediation efforts can be sabotaged.

There are two situations in which a mediator may have to resist pressure to complete mediation too rapidly. One arises, usually in the first mediation session, when one spouse demands that the other decide about coparenting arrangements on the spot. The spouse may add, "I want your decision right now, so I can sell the house (get a loan, take my new job, move out, plan to rent a place to live)." In response to this time squeeze, the other spouse freezes up. The mediator must persuade the demanding spouse to back off and give more time so that a workable decision can be made. Usually this spouse is pushing to get things settled because of the pain suffered in the divorce. If the mediator gives encouragement to slow down, the spouse will usually do so.

The second such situation arises when one spouse's attorney responds to threats made by the other spouse as a challenge to be dealt with aggressively and immediately, rather than gently over time. In one case, for example, a couple had just separated and filed for divorce; both were distraught. The wife, who was in shock after her husband suddenly left her for another woman, threatened that the husband would never see their children again. Challenged by the wife's threats, the husband's attorney tried to gain leverage to establish the husband's visitation rights by attempting to arrange for an immediate mediation session. When the mediator talked on the phone to the spouses, it was clear that neither of them was ready for mediation. The wife had sought counseling on her own to help put herself back together, and the husband wanted to wait to start mediation because he was afraid his wife's emotional state would prevent rational agreements. When the mediator informed the attorney that mediation would not begin for a month, the attorney threatened to file a petition ordering immediate visitation. Even after the mediator explained the marital dynamics, the attorney had difficulty seeing beyond the fact that his client's legal rights were being threatened. After the month had passed, mediation was, in fact, not even necessary, as the wife voluntarily arranged a workable visitation plan directly with the husband. She told the mediator that it just took her some time to realize that she did not want her anger at her husband getting in the way of the children's positive relationship with their father.

Clearly, if the mediator had succumbed to the attorney's time squeeze, the marital conflict would have been exacerbated, perhaps forcing the spouses into a standoff. Many times, attorneys operate out of a sincere interest in asserting the legal rights of their clients. However, on occasion an attorney may take a wife's threat as a personal challenge to prove her weak or call her bluff. Either way, the attorney can benefit by learning to appreciate the psychological aspects of such matters. Respecting the natural course of emotional changes after a separation can facilitate cooperative settlements; ignoring it or wielding legal sledgehammers will only create problems that did not exist before.

11

SKILLS AND TECHNIQUES FOR MANAGING CONFLICT

IN SPITE OF THE MEDIATOR'S best efforts at preventing conflict and setting an atmosphere of cooperation, there are almost always some points in the mediation process where overt conflict erupts. For mediation to proceed, the mediator must have a set of tools for dealing with such disruptions. In general, from the first phone call on, the mediator must establish his authority. This comes across in the firmness of the mediator's words and tone of voice, in the confidence of his bearing, and in the ground rules as to what the spouses can and cannot say or do in the mediation sessions. When the mediator projects confidence and authority, the spouses will show respect. When the mediator projects ambivalence and weakness, the spouses will make more than the usual number of attempts at power assertion and intimidation. In many ways, the mediator must act as a parent figure to the parents, since their struggles are often not unlike those of siblings squabbling over joint possessions.

General Aspects of Conflict Management Strategies

Once the structure and context for cooperation is set, then the mediator must operate from a general theoretical approach guided by pragmatic principles for managing conflict. We will now explore these important aspects of conflict management.

Questions Asked

Unlike traditional psychotherapy, in which the process is guided largely by the client, the mediation process depends on the structure set out by

206

the mediator. The mediator delineates this structure both by making statements and by asking questions. The questions themselves have at least two primary functions: seeking information and giving it. Asking a question lets the responder know what information is of importance to the asker.

Rather than asking questions that lead nowhere constructive for the mediation task, such as "Why do you feel so angry when he returns the children a half-hour late?" or "What do you think makes him drink so much and act so violently when he picks up the children?" the mediator can ask more useful questions, such as "What specific time would you like the children returned from being with their father, and what needs to happen for that time to work out for each of you?" or "What specifically do each of you need to do in order for the transfer of the children to go smoothly and uneventfully for both of you?" These questions imply both that elaboration of the parents' feelings during conflicts with each other is counterproductive to mediation efforts and that the mediator is interested in the parents' ideas for solutions to the problems at hand.

Scheduling of Sessions

Another way in which the process of mediation is a function of the structure is the mediator's use of scheduling to regulate conflict and create an opening for solutions to develop naturally. A large part of the mediator's task is to apply a brake (or a break) to the couple's conflict so that intervening life events can influence the mediation process.

This awareness that daily life events tend to change people's attitudes, feelings, and behaviors far more frequently and fully than therapy can is the basis of the contemporary practice of brief strategic therapy (see Bergman, 1985; Fisch, Weakland, & Segal, 1982; Gadlin & Ouellette, 1986; Gilligan, 1986; Haley, 1973, 1976; Rossi, 1980; Saposnek, 1980; Watzlawick, Weakland, & Fisch, 1974; Zeig, 1980). In this therapy approach, clients are given behavioral tasks intended to hasten the natural resolution of their problems. The client is sent out with a slightly new perspective that is reinforced by the events that occur between sessions, typically resulting in changed behaviors by the next session. The goal of this approach is to change unproductive behavior patterns. By strategically utilizing interim periods of time—from a week to a month (Selvini Palazzoli, Boscolo, Cecchin, & Prata, 1978) between sessions—the goal is more easily attainable.

Behavior Change First

From the mediator's perspective, the emotional conflicts of a couple, whether married or divorced, are dilemmas, that is, inherently unsolvable problems. The mediator who views them as solvable is courting frustration. Emotional problems displayed in mediation may be resolved *after* an agreement is reached but not before. It is only when couples begin to behave in trustworthy and trusting ways that they can develop insight about themselves and each other. Milne and Folberg (1988) point out that mediation is a process of "conflict management" rather than "dispute resolution," distinguishing between the presenting dispute and the underlying conflict. It is quite possible to resolve the dispute while not necessarily eliminating the conflict. In custody disputes, often the couple has a long history of underlying emotional conflict that is highly unlikely to get resolved in mediation. So if one of the mediator's goals is effective management of the conflict, mediation can create and sustain a constructive environment for coparenting the children over the long run.

Maintaining Neutrality

A mediator must always maintain neutrality with respect to both spouses. This is often difficult to achieve, because being neutral with respect to each spouse is more a function of their respective *perceptions* of the mediator's neutrality than of any objective reality. For example, a spouse might assume that the mediator will inevitably favor the parent of the same (or the opposite) sex. Or a spouse may feel that if the mediator ever previously met or talked to either spouse, even with no memory of such contact, neutrality is impossible. Or a spouse may fully accept the mediator's verbal declaration of neutrality, regardless of a history with the other spouse. Each spouse's perception of the mediator's neutrality must be assessed before proceeding, for if one spouse perceives partiality and this is not revealed until late in mediation, a gradual buildup of resistance may already have jeopardized the mediation process.

Sometimes what may seem to the mediator a neutral perspective appears to one spouse as clear evidence of partiality toward the other spouse. As noted in Chapter Three, a mediator who advocates joint custody when only one spouse wants it may appear biased to the spouse who does not desire joint custody. Similarly, a mediator might in good conscience emphasize the necessity of predictability and regularity for the healthy development of young children in a case where one spouse has been accusing the other of unpredictable and irregular behavior. Such advice ordinarily makes much sense; however, within the context of custody or visitation negotiations, it creates an impression of partiality. In one such case, a husband had been accusing his ex-wife of changing her lifestyle too much and not being predictable or structured enough during her time with the children. The mediator then gave a lecture, addressed to both spouses, on the importance of predictability for the emotional security of young children. Upon hearing this, the husband overtly agreed, nodding repeatedly and showing signs of approval. The wife became very defensive and accused the mediator of siding with the husband against her. She insisted that she was not unpredictable and that the husband's perception was faulty. Each time thereafter when the topic of predictability came up, the wife would attack both the husband and the mediator, bringing the mediation to a standstill. Even though the mediator eventually recognized the pattern and tried to divert the discussion to another topic, it was too late. The wife had already deemed the mediator biased, and further mediation efforts were futile.

To help maintain a position of neutrality, the mediator must early on learn an important lesson: to forgo the search for *truth* and adopt a relativistic perspective. A mediator who focuses on truth will inevitably slip into judging the spouses and will soon exhibit a bias in favor of one spouse and against the other that will sabotage effective mediation efforts. Of course, an exception to this position (and to the examples that follow) should be made if there is compelling evidence that a spouse has been or is currently being abusive to the other spouse and/or the children, in which case that truth must be dealt with before further mediation efforts can be safe and productive.

The Dilemma of Relativity

If we consider how a mediator might assess the reasonableness of a particular spouse's behavior, we will find that there are at least three different perspectives on which to base it: (1) the view of one spouse about the other spouse's behavior, (2) the view of the mediator about that other spouse's behavior, (3) and the view of the mediator about the marital system. The wife may view the husband's actions as unreasonable while the mediator views them as reasonable. Or the wife may view the husband's behavior as reasonable while the mediator views it as unreasonable. By the same token, the interactional system between the husband and wife may strike the mediator as perfectly complementary, to the point that the issue of reasonableness no longer applies.

The first two standards are used by lawyers and judges in court custody battles, and the third is used by family therapists. The mediator must use all three but lean toward the third so that neutrality is maintained while the interests of the children are always safeguarded. With few exceptions, there are no angels and no devils in custody and visitation disputes, but there are "double conspiracies," in which both parties play their complementary parts in the ongoing conflicts. From this systems perspective, there are no better *sides,* only better *balances.*

Since the original edition of this book was published, several researchers have voiced exceptions to the advisability of a mediator taking a rigid "systems" view of disputing couples. Kressel, Butler–De Freitas, Forlenza, and Wilcox (1989), for example, have documented the existence of what they refer to as an "IDP" (interpersonally dysfunctional parent) whose personal psychopathology (which parallels a narcissistic personality disorder) disrupts the mediation process and potentially prevents the other spouse and/or the children from getting their needs met in any mediated settlement. Kelly, Gigy, and Hausman (1988) further point out that "the presence of certain psychopathologies, such as depression or passive-aggressive behavior, in one or both of the parties may also hinder or distort the mediation process" (p. 472). In essence, these researchers are alerting us to evidence that there are in fact bad and better parents entering mediation, and to operate on the assumption that all parents are equally good may be risky for both the process and the outcomes of mediation. These observations are worthy of serious consideration and of further research. Given that this book presents the mediator as an advocate for children, such data are especially relevant because the children of mediated settlements may well be adversely affected by the presumed equality of parent safety and effectiveness. For the theoretical purposes of this book, the strategies that follow operate on the assumption of a family systems view, mindful always of the need to protect the children from obviously harmful parental influences whenever possible.

Specific Strategies

The specific strategies the mediator uses to deal with conflict fall into three categories: conflict-reducing strategies, conflict-diverting strategies, and impasse-breaking strategies. In the discussion that follows, the strategies are generally arranged sequentially, from the mildest to the most potent. The mediator should utilize them in a similar fashion, always beginning with the mildest strategies that are likely to effect results for a particular couple and using more potent strategies as necessary until one is found that achieves the desired results. Obviously, there are cases in which none of the strategies is helpful for reaching agreements. In such cases, the couple should be referred to their attorneys or to court for resolution of their disputes.

Conflict-Reducing Strategies

In order for mediation to proceed effectively, the level of conflict must be at a minimum. Five strategies have proved effective for directly reducing the level of conflict.

REFLECTIVE LISTENING. By reflecting to the spouses the feelings behind their words, the mediator attempts to take the emotional charge out of the conflict. If, for example, a wife begins a tirade that the husband is completely uncooperative and never listens to or follows through on any request she makes, the mediator can cut through the content and address the feelings directly. He can say, "It sounds like when you've got something important to say to him and he doesn't seem to listen, you feel really angry and frustrated." Then, if the husband says, "But she always tries to talk to me when I'm furious about something," the mediator can say, "It sounds to me like you have a hard time hearing her when you are angry but could probably listen much better when you are calmer."

This strategy will work if many of the conflicts of the spouses are grounded simply in poor communication skills. If these skills are underdeveloped, reflective listening can at least build enough clarity of communication for a parenting agreement to be negotiated. Surprisingly, this is all that some couples need to reach workable agreements.

ABSORBING. Sometimes when a spouse is expressing anger and frustration, reflective listening does not help and may even be an irritant. In such cases, the mediator can simply listen and try to absorb that anger. This is much easier to do if only one spouse speaks while the other spouse listens. The mediator can safely allow the venting of feelings by the angrier spouse because steering those feelings away from the other spouse and onto the mediator reduces the need for that spouse to be defensive. And when the calmer spouse maintains a quiet, nondefensive demeanor and appears to be sincerely listening, whether out of guilt or a real willingness to cooperate, the mediator can often successfully absorb the rage from the angry spouse. This can be followed by rational negotiation.

There is a risk to using this strategy, however. If the other spouse actively challenges the assertions uttered by the angrier spouse, an escalation of the conflict may well ensue. Or if the angry spouse is just manifesting a habitual over-reactive behavior pattern, the venting may continue indefinitely. In either case, if the mediator allows the venting to continue, the conflict that is likely to ensue will either sabotage the mediation efforts or necessitate that the mediator change strategies.

BLOCKING AND SOOTHING. When conflict escalates to the point where milder strategies are unsuccessful, the mediator can block it by interrupting and taking charge of the discussion, converting the dialogue to a monologue, and slowing the pace. If done skillfully, this technique allows the mediator to maintain sole control by delivering, in an almost trance-inducing monotone, a monologue about anything that will keep the conflict quelled. This gives the couple a chance to cool off, since the more the mediator talks, the less opportunity the spouses will have to talk. In such cases, the mediator should allow the spouses to talk only insofar as their talk is productive.

In a conversation we had about reducing conflict, George Ferrick offered another approach that he uses for more literally blocking the spouses from one another. He graphically illustrates for the couple the debilitating effects that their ongoing conflict has on the mediation process by placing a partition (made out of any sturdy material, such as an old cardboard refrigerator packing box) between the conflicting spouses such that he can see and talk with each of them but they cannot see each other. In the frustration of not being able to communicate in their familiar, face-to-face, destructive way, they gain a valuable insight that often reduces the level of conflict for the duration of the mediation session.

TAKING AN ASSERTIVE STANCE. If the conflict does not respond to more indirect efforts, the mediator can assertively request that the spouses stop their verbal assaults. This may mean raising his voice and saying, "Stop," standing up between their chairs and blocking their view of each other, or engaging in some other unexpected behavior, such as jingling a string of bells (some mediators keep a set of bells in their office for this purpose).

If the couple respond to this, the mediator needs to follow up with a reminder about the ground rules of no talking about the past and speaking about one's own feelings only in the form of "I" statements rather than "you" statements. The couple can also be advised that if they are unable to conduct themselves civilly, the session will end immediately and their attorneys will be required to be present at the next session to assist them in remaining rational. It should be added that they each will be responsible for paying their attorneys' hourly fees to sit in the session with them.

If these efforts do not reduce the conflict, the mediator can admonish the couple that he will need to send them back to court if they want to continue arguing. Such an admonishment can work strategically only if one or both spouses dread court.

LEAVING THE ROOM. As a final strategy, the mediator can simply get up out of her chair and announce to the couple, "I am not interested in listening to you two argue—arguing is for the courtroom, not for mediation. Please continue your argument until you are finished. I will be in the waiting room; when you are done arguing and are ready to do mediation, please let me know." The mediator then walks out of the room, closes the door, and reads a magazine. Usually within five minutes or so, one of the spouses sheepishly opens the door and announces that they are finished arguing and are ready to resume mediation.

Most mediators have a difficult time carrying out this bold strategy the first time, but after doing so once, each occasion thereafter is much simpler. The unexpectedness of the action throws the spouses off balance and startles them into realizing how unproductive their behavior has become, and thus it functions as an effective message to the verbally sparring spouses.

It should be noted that this strategy is inadvisable if there is any doubt as to the potential for violence between the couple. If there is the slightest danger, the mediator must stay in the room and utilize other strategies, to protect both parties from physically getting out of control.

Conflict-Diverting Strategies

After talking with a couple for some time, the mediator gets a sense of the degree of conflict that is likely and of the specific topics most likely to trigger it off. Once the mediator has a sense of these factors, he can use one of several strategies to divert conflict at the first warning of its presence.

CONVERTING ACCUSATIONS TO REQUESTS. A useful technique to use when one spouse begins to make accusations about the past behavior of the other is to turn the accusations into requests for the future. For example, if one spouse accuses the other of never cleaning or bathing their child and of returning her dirty, the mediator can instruct the spouse to put her accusation in the form of a request: "I would like you to bathe our daughter once a day and return her with clean skin, clean hair, and clean clothes." Only rarely will the other spouse refuse to agree to such a straightforward, unthreatening request, and this can then be an item to include in the written parenting agreement.

If, however, the accused spouse springs to defend himself, the mediator can say, "Whether or not it happened that way in the past is not important, and I would have no way of knowing for certain anyway, but will you agree to respect this request for the future?" Only rarely will a spouse refuse to agree to this.

DIVERSION PROBLEM SOLVING. Another technique for diverting conflict is for the mediator to lead the couple from the topic of contention to a topic of common concern that would bring them onto the same side of the issue. For example, one couple had two younger children over whom they both vied for primary physical custody, and their negotiations would regularly escalate into a heated argument whenever they discussed these children. However, they also had an older teenager who had developed some problems as a result of the divorce. Since both parents were equally concerned about that child and had no contention over his primary residence, the mediator steered the discussion away from the younger children and onto the older child. The spouses discussed this child for about forty-five minutes, until they had formulated plans to seek counseling for that child. Having made this joint decision, they were then able to cooperate enough to develop a satisfactory coparenting agreement for the younger children. This diversion strategy can be used to detour the couple onto any nonconflictual topic—Grandma, the family house, the family pet, or any other topic about which the parents have similar and concordant concerns.

In another version of diversion problem solving, Shattuck (1988) describes a technique for diverting a spouse who justifies an impasse position by the injustices in the system. The mediator agrees heartily with the parent when he claims that the courts are not fair to fathers and then goes on at length to say "starvation in Ethiopia is not fair, napalming babies is not fair, drunk drivers killing children on the way to school are not fair, income taxes are not fair . . ." (p. 202). This puts the victim's frustration into perspective and allows him to move on to address his particular child's needs.

SUDDEN POSITIVE SHIFTING. When spouses become entangled in arguments, they often rigidly persist in discussing more of the same while knowing full well that their conflict will merely escalate. A useful strategy for getting them unlocked from their negative pattern is to suddenly shift the topic to a positive one. One way is to shift the couple's focus in time to past, present, or future, depending on where they seem stuck. For example, if spouses are arguing about present coparenting arrangements, the mediator can shift them to the past by suddenly asking, "When you two were first married, how did you make decisions?" After they respond, the mediator can follow through by asking, "Do you remember how you felt about each other at that time?" Of course, the mediator would shift the conversation to the early marital relationship only if he was certain that it was a positive period for both spouses.

Sargent and Moss (1986, p. 97) offer other versions of this line of questioning. They suggest that the mediator ask, "'Do you remember when you had a parenting disagreement that was resolved?' If the parents say yes, then the mediator can direct them to discuss how they solved it. They can rediscover the tools and resources that they have as individuals and as a couple for conflict resolution." With more resistant couples that refuse to remember a time of resolution, the mediator can ask, "'Can you remember a time when you cooperated with anyone in solving a conflict?' Who could answer no to that question? The next question to ask is, 'What were the ingredients in that process of resolution?'" This intervention also gives hope for an eventual resolution by focusing the couple on their mutual or individual successes in the past.

Alternatively, with a couple who keep slipping into arguing about the past, the mediator can suddenly shift the focus to the future by asking: "When your children are teenagers five or six years from now, and you two are well past your divorce and your present angry feelings and are each settled into new relationships, how would you like your children to feel about their parents?" The mediator can also shift to other topics. If, for example, the spouses begin to argue about finances, the mediator can suddenly ask, "Tell me, what do you like most about your children?"

In each of these examples, the shift is effective because its suddenness is disorienting. As one observer noted, these shifts are like pulling the carpet suddenly out from under the parents. As such, this technique has similarities to the well-known hypnotherapist Milton Erickson's "confusion technique" (1964), in which the therapist suddenly utters something out of context, creating momentary instability and confusion, leaving the client open to a new idea, perspective, or behavior. In an effort to reestablish equilibrium, people quickly search for and easily accept whatever explanations are offered. When the mediator's moves are more unpredictable than those of the spouses, the mediator is able to control the direction of the sessions.

Other examples of this confusional technique for diverting conflict were suggested by Sargent and Moss (1986). In one example, a couple were arguing about who would transport their four-year-old child on visitation from San Diego to Los Angeles. The discussion began to deteriorate.

Mother, accusing the father, said, "You never helped with the children." Father retorted, "You're the one who is moving to Los Angeles to screw that bozo every night" (p. 93). The mediator intervened by suggesting loudly that they should let their child hitchhike. The parents stopped arguing momentarily, confused as to why their responsible mediator would make such an irresponsible suggestion. Finally it dawned on them how unproductive they themselves were being, and they then began to renegotiate in earnest about how to share the driving.

In another example, Sargent and Moss (1986, p. 93) describe a mediator's response to a mother who needs help resisting her husband's attack. The mediator firmly says to her in front of him, "Don't cooperate with him . . .," and then pauses. As the husband looks up at this apparent attack and breach of mediator fairness, the mediator continues, ". . . until you remember the ways in which he has been a good father. He has helped the children learn their music. In fact, you said you married him partly because you loved dancing with him and loved listening to him play the flute." (Of course, the mediator must have prior knowledge that any statement he makes is accurate.)

DEFLECTING. Part of the mediator's task is to prevent the spouses from saying things to each other that are so hurtful that irreparable harm is done to whatever trust each may have had in the other. Contrary to the prevalent belief of beginning psychotherapists, it is not useful to allow conflicting spouses to share all their feelings. For example, it sometimes happens that one damaging remark uttered at the wrong time will permanently close communications between a couple. No matter what the reasons were or how apologetic the attacking spouse later appears, the other spouse will never forgive or forget.

Hence there are times when the mediator must deflect one spouse's words from the other before such harm can occur. The mediator's intervention could be in the form of a clarification or rationalization that helps the attacked spouse interpret the other spouse's comment. The other spouse may pick up the mediator's cue and phrase the comment in a less provocative way. For example, in the middle of a heated exchange, a wife said to her ex-husband, "You never paid any attention to the children, then you left me, and you're not getting the children now or ever." Before the husband had a chance to respond, the mediator deflected the comment by saying to the wife: "The anger and hurt that you feel right now is not unusual, and it is very understandable. And it's also not unusual for a parent who was not involved with the children before a divorce to decide to become sincerely involved after the divorce. Allowing that opportunity will give your children a chance to get to know their father in the future in the way that you wanted it in the past. But give yourself plenty of time to get through those difficult feelings."

Hearing this, the husband kept quiet, for he knew that the mediator's remark implied support for his continuing relationship with the children yet presented it in a way that allowed both him and his wife to save face. He then tearfully expressed his sincerity in wanting to become more involved with the children. The wife cried and was able to constructively express her hurt feelings at being left by the husband. Negotiations then became possible.

SIDESTEPPING. Sometimes the conflict that needs diverting arises between a spouse and the mediator. Typically, one spouse presents a rigid position that is not in the best interests of the children. This spouse's manner is self-righteous and provocative, and the other spouse appeals to the mediator to intervene. Because the mediator feels a compelling urge to argue the challenging spouse out of the inappropriate position, a response is critical at this point. If the mediator gets pulled into debate with the spouse, he loses his neutral stance and will thereafter be viewed by that spouse as one-sided. If he restrains himself, he can continue to be neutral.

The strategy of sidestepping is intended to help prevent the mediator from succumbing to such provocation. Instead of responding to a challenge, the mediator simply lets the issue drop and goes on to another topic. For example, in one case, a husband said to the wife and mediator, "My children do not have to follow any rigid rules. Children need to be free; they know what's best for them. They've already been harmed by your rules, and I'm not going to impose any more on them. They are almost six and five years old, and they can go to sleep whenever they are tired and eat whatever they like whenever they are hungry and wear whatever they want to wear." The wife looked at the mediator incredulously and said, "Would you tell him what children really need?" The mediator, sensing a trap if he were to debate the point, sidestepped the issue by saying: "The differences the two of you may have about ways to raise children are important to consider, but let's put that off for now because I want to ask you about the kinds of things that your children enjoy doing together with each of you."

In this way, the topic of contention is labeled in a neutral fashion, its importance is acknowledged, and a transition is made to a topic that is not emotionally charged. Later the mediator may return to the issue of child-rearing differences, but from a perspective that is within his control.

Impasse-Breaking Strategies

During the period of negotiations over workable agreements, there are often points where the couple reach an impasse and are unable to negotiate any further. The problem at these points is not overt conflict but rather resistance to workable compromises. Unless the mediator actively initiates some strategy to overcome the impasse, it may eventually force the couple into court.

The strategies used by the mediator in this particular phase of mediation are somewhat controversial; because they are expedient, there are certain risks involved in using them. The central risk is that they could backfire, making the situation worse for both parents and children. It appears, however, that the risks are usually outweighed by the potential gains in reaching compromised agreements.

OFFERING SUGGESTIONS. Certainly the least risky of these strategies is the straightforward offering of suggestions for a compromised agreement. However, the term *straightforward* must be qualified; because the mediator must maintain a balance between the spouses, suggestions can be offered only if they support each spouse equally. If the mediator suggests that one spouse compromise more than the other, that spouse may then feel the urge to resist the mediator as well as the other spouse.

Offering suggestions is helpful because spouses typically are aware of few alternatives to the usual time-sharing formula—every other weekend, alternate holidays, and a month in the summer—or the 50–50 percent joint custody formulas portrayed in the popular media. Moreover, even if a spouse does have alternatives in mind, he or she often is reluctant to be the first to suggest a compromise. In other cases, spouses are so angry that they are locked into defending narrow positions. In both situations, the spouses can much more easily agree to a third person's suggestions for compromise if such suggestions seem equitable and balanced.

Suggestions can be offered in a very direct form or through examples from other couples' creative solutions to similar problems. For example, one couple could not come to an agreement on how to share time with their two children. The husband said the children should not be separated, and the wife said she would like to have at least one child living with her. At this point, the mediator said: "Some couples with two children have worked out this kind of situation by having each child spend some time with each parent alone and some time with each parent together with the sibling. That way, the children are together for significant amounts of time, and each parent also gets the chance to know each child as a separate person—and the children usually love the special attention they receive from each parent during their one-on-one time."

In another case, the mediator offered a direct suggestion to a couple in which the wife was leery of trusting the husband enough to share physical custody with him. He had not been very involved with the children before the divorce, and the wife wanted him to prove his intentions before allowing the child to share equal time with him. The mediator offered this suggestion: "Since the two of you are fresh from a divorce, and we know that it takes some time to rebuild trust in each other, how about setting up a plan in which over the next six months you gradually increase the amount of time that the children spend with their father. This will give the children and you, Phil, a chance to build a stronger relationship, which does take time for most children, and it will give you, Sarah, time to build more trust in Phil."

Such suggestions are, of course, offered only when the mediator has prior evidence that they will be feasible for the couple. Offering unfeasible suggestions can destroy any hope for future cooperation, as the couple may well conclude, If the expert can't come up with a workable alternative, how can we?

LEVERAGING THE CHILDREN. When a couple reach an impasse, the mediator can utilize the children's input and impact to unblock the negotiations. This is an extremely sensitive maneuver because of the potential for emotional trauma to the children. If it is handled skillfully, however, the children can teach their parents an important lesson.

When children are brought into the mediation session at a point of impasse, they are always uncomfortable. They may look and feel sad and scared, they may verbalize their discomfort, and they may even cry. It is rare for a parent not to react to this in some fashion. When the children's main contribution is simply an expressed desire for the parents to stop fighting and settle the custody battle, the parents are confronted with a powerful challenge. One exceptionally mature four-year-old said poignantly, with tears in his eyes, "Mommy and Daddy, I wish you would just stop fighting; you act more babyish than me!" When the child left the room, the father, who was the more resistant of the parents, said, "I care enough about Billy and the pain that he is going through that I will make a sacrifice for him. I'll agree to having him live for the school year at his mother's house."

Before using this strategy, the mediator must seriously consider whether the risks are too great for the children or the ongoing negotiations. The risks are several. For one, the discomfort manifested by the children can be interpreted by one of the spouses as evidence of the destructive effects of the other spouse's presence on the child. Second, a spouse may take the children's upset state as evidence of insensitivity on the part of the mediator. One such spouse said to the mediator, "You are torturing my children. I can't stand to see them tortured, and I don't think it's fair or necessary for them to be here." While such an interpretation may seem difficult to counter, it is frequently the case that these children witness similar scenes at home on a daily basis, with no relief in sight.

If the mediator decides to proceed, she must carefully guide the session to protect the children from excessive pain while making sure that the parents hear the children's feelings about the issue. Even though this intervention can be extremely uncomfortable, if it can motivate the parents to stop their fighting, the strategy can finally bring the children some relief.

PERSUADING WITH DRAMATIC ANECDOTES. If the mediator has evidence that one or both of the spouses are worried about some particular aspect of an unsuccessful mediation outcome, the mediator may be able to use this as leverage to overcome an impasse. For example, a mediator may be able to facilitate an agreement by supplying vivid stories of other couples' traumatic experiences of court custody battles, of their near financial ruin from lawyers' fees and court-related expenses, of the damaging psychological effects to children of testifying in court, and of the endless cycle of court battles, which typically repeat year after year.

The anecdotes selected should be related directly to the areas of most psychological concern to at least one of the parents. For example, before telling of traumatic court battles, the mediator should already have determined how badly each spouse wants to stay out of court. Some spouses are very willing to compromise if they know that court will be the next step, and traumatic stories of court battles will enhance that willingness. Other spouses are so driven by power assertion and revenge motives that they would love to have their day in court, and the mediator's intended warnings function instead as incitement to go to court. Naturally, it is important that the particular story selected by the mediator be presented in a balanced manner so that neither spouse feels unduly pressured. The mediator must modulate the degree of vividness and pointedness in content so that the intent of the story is not perceived as a biased persuasion of just one spouse. Addressing the stories to both spouses also allows a face-saving format for the target spouse (if there is one) to hear the message. With sensitivity, tact, and professional and personal clarity and judgment of its ultimate good, a mediator can often leverage spousal concerns into constructive agreements.

LEVERAGING WITH ATTORNEYS. There are several ways in which attorneys can be useful if a couple reaches an impasse. For example, it can be useful to consult with an attorney by phone if the mediator knows the attorney to be supportive of the mediation approach or suspects that the attorney is discouraging a mediated settlement. As previously noted, not all attorneys are supportive of mediation.

If the attorney is supportive of mediation, the mediator can suggest that the attorney discuss with her client the likely outcomes of a court-rendered decision and the advantages of mediation over court. Often merely this show of support can unblock the impasse. If, however, the attorney is skeptical of the mediation approach, the mediator can discuss with the attorney the long-range benefits to the children of a mediated settlement. If the attorney still seems unpersuaded, the mediator had best not request her direct assistance in the mediation efforts.

Sometimes requests for assistance by an attorney who appears to be supportive of mediation can backfire. In one case, for example, the mediator called the husband's attorney, with the client's permission, and explained that mediation was at a stalemate because the attorney's client was not yet willing to accept the fact that his wife was really divorcing him, even though she had filed the papers, followed through on every step, and gave no evidence of reconsidering. The attorney was requested to talk with the client and help him realize that the divorce was really happening. The attorney agreed to assist the mediator in this way. However, the husband came to the next session enraged at the mediator. He explained that his attorney had met with him after talking with the mediator, adding, "My attorney made fun of me. He laughed and criticized me for hanging on to my child to keep my wife. I was humiliated and insulted. That is not what I'm doing." The upshot was that the husband was even more resistant than before.

Hence the mediator needs to be extremely careful about the specific type of assistance requested of attorneys, since the mediator has no control over how the request will be carried out. When a mediator requests help from an attorney who is not cognizant of the family systems perspective of the mediator, the request may get translated from a psychological to a legal framework and become distorted in the translation.

Another way the mediator can seek assistance from attorneys for breaking an impasse is to arrange for them to be present in the next mediation session. Again, this can be helpful only if the mediator is certain that the attorneys are supportive of mediation. Before the session, the mediator meets briefly with the attorneys without their clients. He discusses the expectations of each concerning what would constitute an acceptable agreement and explains the ground rules for mediation, focusing on how they differ from legal methods. Each attorney's purpose in the session is to be the link between his or her client and the other spouse, and they are encouraged to stress compromise and to temporarily suspend advocacy for their own clients.

When the attorneys carry out their task, an agreement is almost always reached during the session. If one attorney slips into an adversarial position, the task is more difficult, but it may still be possible to salvage an agreement. Either way, the extra effort required to steer the attorneys away from adversarial positions usually pays off, since such sessions usually produce workable agreements.

Because of the added expense to the spouses in having their attorneys present, this strategy should be saved as a last step, to be used only if absolutely necessary. However, this strategy is still less expensive than a court appearance. It is highly unusual for a spouse to refuse to continue mediation just because of the extra expense.

Success and Failure in Mediation

In the first edition of this book, the elements of success and failure in mediation were described and illustrated through ten case studies—five successful cases and five unsuccessful ones. Cases that are successful are characterized by parents who trust in each other's parenting intentions and skills, are willing to compromise, exhibit relatively consistent and predictable behavior patterns, engage in at least some ongoing communication about coparenting, and generally agree on basic child-rearing values. These, also, are the same elements that are important for effective parenting in intact families.

Our original hope for mediation—that it would be able to resolve all conflict—turned out to be far too ambitious. Research over the past two decades has confirmed that mediation is a more limited enterprise (see Irving & Benjamin, 1995; Kressel, 1985; Kressel & Pruitt, 1989; Pearson, 1991). Irving and Benjamin's comprehensive and integrative review of the research on family mediation led to the conclusion that there is no consensus among researchers as to the best predictors of mediated agreements. Certain types of disputes will not be resolved by mediation even when the most sophisticated techniques are applied by an experienced mediator. Among the elements that appear to contribute to failure in mediation are chronic hostility and mistrust between the spouses that does not cease or ease up with structured intervention; strong religious, moral, or culturally based convictions on the part of at least one spouse, which lead to uncompromising beliefs about the needs of children even in the face of research and clinical evidence to the contrary; consistent allegations by one spouse of severe misconduct on the part of the other, including violence, substance abuse, and sexual abuse; consistent allegations by one spouse of the other's unfitness to parent for reasons of immaturity, neglectful or erratic behavior, or ambivalent intent to follow through on any mediated agreement; and refusal to abandon incompatible spousal strategies that lead to impasses.

As the complexity and level of conflict of cases referred to mediation have increased, in the past fifteen years, an array of conflict resolution procedures beyond mediation have been developed to serve the families that fail initial mediation efforts. Since these other approaches are beyond the scope of this book, the reader is referred to Irving and Benjamin (1995) and Johnston and Roseby (1997) for descriptions of this spectrum of dispute resolution processes.

In this new and revised edition of the book, two new illustrative case studies will be presented that will zoom in on the mediation process and more specifically demonstrate for the reader the strategic approach to mediation—the focus of this book. The first, in Chapter Twelve, is a simpler case, with fewer complicating elements, and the second, in Chapter Thirteen, is a more complex case, with various elements that make it more challenging for the mediator.

To assist the reader in understanding the thinking behind each strategic intervention, a commentary will be offered followed by an aikido image of the interactions, providing both a cognitive map and a physical metaphor to illustrate the particular maneuver. And because mediators may have restrictions on their time available with a particular case—in court settings as a result of heavy caseloads and in private settings as a result of limited client income or client tolerance—the case scenarios will be further developed within the context of such typical time restrictions.

PART FOUR

TWO CASE STUDIES

12

CASE STUDY 1

A LESS COMPLEX CASE

JIMMY, AGE THIRTY, a new-car salesman, and Rhonda, age twenty-seven, an unemployed credit office clerk, were referred to mediation by the court after Rhonda petitioned to have the time-sharing schedule for their five-year-old son, Jessie, modified.

Intake Information

The following information was gleaned from the initial phone interview with each spouse and the intake sheet filled out by the couple.

Rhonda's Statement

Rhonda indicated that she and Jimmy had been married for six years and had been separated for a year and a half at the time of this referral. She indicated that since their separation, Jessie had been sharing time weekly with her from Saturday afternoon to Wednesday morning and with Jimmy from Wednesday morning to Saturday afternoon. She is now requesting that Jessie be with her from Monday through Friday and with Jimmy on the weekends. Her stated reason for requesting the change at this time is that she wants Jessie to have a "stable home during the school week" when he begins school in the fall. She further indicated that there has never been any problem with domestic violence, drugs, alcohol, or child abuse either in their marriage or since their separation.

Jimmy's Statement

Jimmy reported the same basic facts as those reported by Rhonda. (This does not always occur in mediation cases; it is not uncommon for each parent to report very different basic factual information about past and recent events.) He indicated that the current schedule of time sharing is working out just fine for him and Jessie, and he does not want to change it. Moreover, he indicated that his days off work are Thursdays and Fridays, which he cannot change. He worries about deteriorating the quality time he currently spends with Jessie by seeing him only on the weekends as Rhonda is requesting.

In the commentary section of the intake sheet, Jimmy added that Rhonda is presently five months pregnant by her boyfriend, Verne, whom she is planning to marry. He further added that "she is emotionally unstable and doesn't tell the truth." He finally noted that "she is a very good mother, but she doesn't live with reality about money."

Beginning Hypotheses

In thinking out, *strategically,* the possible dynamics of this case, we can consider the following points:

- On the manifest level, Rhonda's stated reasons for requesting modification of the existing time-sharing plan sound reasonable. She may know something about Jessie's particular needs to remain in one home for the school week as he begins school. This option must be balanced against Jimmy's flexibility in considering such a change. If Jimmy is amenable to changing the schedule, it seems a reasonable option, and negotiations could proceed rather easily. However, if Jessie is in fact doing fine on the current schedule and Jimmy is adamant about keeping the status quo, Rhonda's request needs to be questioned and explored further.

- Jimmy's information about Rhonda's pregnancy and impending marriage may suggest a latent level to Rhonda's request (particularly since she did not mention this important fact on the intake sheet). She may be trying to recast Jessie as a central member of a fantasized "complete new family," as she anticipates her new marriage. If so, her request for modification may be more for her own needs (or perhaps even to satisfy her boyfriend's needs) than for Jessie's. Moreover, Jimmy's assertion that Rhonda "is unstable and doesn't tell the truth" may lend further support to the notion that

Rhonda has a hidden agenda that reflects her own needs more than those of Jessie. However, this is partly countered by his statement that Jimmy believes she is a "good mother."

○ Jimmy may also feel threatened by Rhonda's new boyfriend as a potential stepfather and may resist any change in the schedule that would diminish his time or his control in his role as Jessie's father.

From the information obtained so far, five outcomes are possible:

1. Maintain the current schedule until such time as Jessie's behavior evidences some distress, according to the notion that minimal change is best for children.

2. Modify the current schedule to weekdays with Rhonda and weekends with Jimmy, based upon the premise that resolving the parental dispute is more important than the particular schedule change and that Jimmy can and will in fact change his work schedule if such options can be shown to be available and important.

3. Modify the current schedule to weekdays with Jimmy and weekends with Rhonda, if Jessie merely needs one home and the parents can agree that it does not matter which home it is.

4. Discover some other schedule that would fit for Jessie and suit the needs of Jimmy and Rhonda.

5. Realize that the couple have reached an impasse and require arbitration of this dispute.

Ideally, prior to beginning the mediation process, Jimmy and Rhonda would attend a divorce education class that provides them with information about the needs of children through divorce, would be given relevant handouts about sharing children after divorce, or would be requested to watch any of a number of good videotapes about postdivorce parenting relationships and the benefits of mediation. (Such resources are available through the Association of Family and Conciliation Courts and the Academy of Family Mediators.) The mediator then makes phone contact with each parent, gathering essential information about them and their situation (see Chapter Six), and setting the first appointment time.

Resolving the Case in One to Two Hours

In most court settings where mediation is conducted, the high case loads may necessitate limited time offered per case, often one or two hours. In order to assist the reader who works in such a setting in using this time well, the cases presented here will discuss how the mediator might best utilize this limited time period, given the data presented. In reviewing the facts of the present case, the mediator assumes that, barring unforeseen circumstances, it would require no more than two hours.

Phase One: Setting the Context

Upon greeting Jimmy and Rhonda, the mediator begins the session by informing them about confidentiality and its limits (regarding mandatory reporting laws for child abuse, danger to self or others, and so forth, if appropriate), and then has them sign the confidentiality form (see Appendix C). The mediator then briefly explains her role as a neutral facilitator of their discussions, the benefits of mediation over litigation, and the time allotted or likely needed for their mediation. Information is then given about the procedures for formalizing any agreement that they may reach and the procedures in the event they are unable to reach an agreement.

The mediator then briefly reviews, in a strategic fashion, using modifications of the appropriate preempts (see Appendix D for a complete list or Chapter Five for verbatim presentation of the full preempting monologues), some of the information about children that is relevant to this case. This is intended to elicit cooperation from the parents and set the stage for more resistant-free negotiations. Given the apparent history of cooperation between these parents, the preempts could be limited to versions of these four:

○ Assumption that both parents love the children
○ Assumption of children's need for both parents
○ Mediator as child advocate
○ Flexibility of parenting plan

"In beginning our mediation, I'm going to assume that both of you love your child equally well, in your own styles, and that both of you want the best for your child. Is that accurate?" Both parents nod their heads.

"I'm also going to assume that your child loves and needs both of you. As you saw in the videotapes and read in the handouts, research has consistently demonstrated that children need regular and continuous contact with both parents even if the parents disagree with each other on many issues.

"My main concern is for your child. In custody hearings, judges typically deal with children in stereotypical ways and often do not take their individual needs into account. In mediation, though, you have the opportunity to develop a plan that can fit your child's individual needs, as well as your own needs. I am going to keep our primary focus on your child and his specific needs before focusing on each of your needs. I am going to act as an advocate for your child.

"A key factor to consider in your decisions is flexibility. As time goes by, children grow, and their needs change. They enter different developmental stages, and they change friends, schools, and interests. Your needs and your life situations will also change over time. It is best to view your decisions about your child as part of an ongoing process, rather than as a once-and-for-all event. And it is also important to consider the importance of stability and predictability in your child's life. Children generally do best with the fewest major changes in their lives. So balancing their needs for stability against the necessary changes in your lives is challenging but necessary."

Commentary. These particular preempts (which take up only about five minutes) were selected on the basis of the case information generated so far. The first two are intended to preempt the possibility of Rhonda asserting that Jimmy's fathering is less necessary for Jessie than is her mothering. The third is intended to reassure both parents that someone objective will be helping them protect Jessie's best interests, so that neither of them need worry about the other proposing something destructive to Jessie. The fourth is intended to authoritatively validate both starting positions but add the importance of flexibility to both parents' thinking, so that each parent may begin to view the validity of the other's position by understanding the interests behind their respective positions.

Aikido Image. The aikido image is of the mediator moving forward toward the child in the middle to initiate a maneuver that engages both parents before either is positioned to strike the other.

The ground rules (see Chapter Five) are then recited and acknowledged, and the mediation enters the next phase.

Phase Two: Gathering Essential Information and Assessing Family Dynamics

To test out the beginning hypotheses, the mediator must strategically gather essential information about this couple in such a fashion as to validate which of the beginning hypotheses are the basis of their impasse (or if others are revealed). Knowing this information then allows the mediator to optimally steer the negotiations to a positive outcome.

MEDIATOR: I understand that you two were married for six years and have been separated for about a year and a half. Is that right? *(Mediator scans both parents for visual and verbal acknowledgment.)*

JIMMY: Yes. It'll be eighteen months tomorrow.

MEDIATOR: In order for me to help you with your parenting plan, I need to get a little bit of information about how you both got to this point. Please tell me *(looking at both)* in one sentence why your marriage ended. And I realize that you may well each have a very different point of view about it.

Commentary. Because of the time constraints, the mediator concisely requests information about the divorce decision—in one sentence. This not only saves time but also compresses their answer into a relatively neat and simple conceptual framework that can be quite revealing of the nature of their relationship. This can also be the first time that the spouse who was left hears a clear statement of why the other spouse left the marriage. This can often help the left spouse begin the emotional process of divorce and loosen up the impasse to allow for meaningful negotiations toward a parenting plan.

With more time available, the mediator can always expand their answers, but with little time, one at least gets a clinical glimpse of how they each viewed the breakup and how, if at all, this may be influencing the present impasse.

RHONDA: We just didn't get along. We argued a lot. We had a lot of marital therapy, but it just didn't work out.

JIMMY: I was gone at work a lot. She felt that I wasn't around enough. I tried to change, but it apparently was too late. She had already decided she wanted out.

Commentary. Their answers clearly suggest that they each have already adequately processed the reasons for their divorce.

Aikido Image. The aikidoist invites both parents in to test if they will move to grab for or strike each other. Neither moves.

MEDIATOR: What is the percent chance that each of you would give of the two of you ever getting back together again? Say in a year or in five years.

RHONDA: Zero! I wouldn't go back. Besides, I'm getting married soon.

JIMMY: She's pregnant!

MEDIATOR: *(to Jimmy)* If she weren't pregnant, would that change things between the two of you?

JIMMY: No. We're finished with each other. I wouldn't go back with her. It just wouldn't work. I need to move on in my life.

Commentary. This line of questions is intended to ferret out any present fantasies of reconciliation that may be fueling the impasse in the form of a reuniting strategy. Their answers suggest that both have accepted the divorce and that the impasse is probably related to other issues.

Aikido Image. The aikidoist once again invites them in to test whether either has any intention to reengage with the other.

MEDIATOR: *(to Rhonda)* Who are you marrying?

RHONDA: His name is Verne. We've been seeing each other for about seven months.

MEDIATOR: *(to Jimmy)* Do you know Verne?

JIMMY: Yeah. We've talked a lot before.

MEDIATOR: What is your impression of him?

JIMMY: He's a nice person, and Jessie really likes him.

MEDIATOR: *(to Rhonda)* How does Verne feel about your request to modify your parenting plan?

RHONDA: He stays completely out of my dealings with Jimmy. He supports me in whatever I feel is right to do.

MEDIATOR: So he wouldn't care what happens here today?

RHONDA: Oh, sure, he cares. He wants me to be happy—and I'll be happy when I can have my son Mondays through Fridays!

Commentary. The mediator pursues the hypothesis that Rhonda may be making the modification request to appease her fiancé and that Verne is an active participant in the impasse. The mediator asks Rhonda direct questions about Verne's possible involvement in her bid for modification, and indirectly through Jimmy (using the *cross talk* technique), she attempts to cross-validate Rhonda's answers and also get a reading on how Jessie feels about Verne. Rhonda's answer suggests, and Jimmy's answer validates, the fact that Verne is not an active or strategic participant in the present dispute.

Aikido Image. The aikidoist assesses the direction of energy of each parent and scans around to see if there are any other contenders in the surrounding energy field with which the aikidoist must deal in the planning of her intervention.

JIMMY: Yeah. It might make *you* happy, but what about Jessie, huh? What about what makes *him* happy? I think you are being selfish. I want . . .

MEDIATOR: Wait a minute. Hold on! Before we get into too many details, I need to get a little bit more information from you two. What is Jessie's birth date?

Commentary. The mediator senses that the discussion is leading rapidly into conflict and so, using the technique of *deflecting,* steers the subject off the hot one to some neutral topic—of factual information gathering. This is also a version of the strategy of *sudden positive shifting.*

Aikido Image. The aikidoist effects a wrist hold and shifts the energy of the father into a different direction, alongside the mother, so as to pre-empt a strike and slow the energy down to a standstill.

RHONDA: He just turned five.

MEDIATOR: When is his birthday?

JIMMY: June 7.

MEDIATOR: *(to both parents)* Tell me about Jessie. What is he like?

(Both parents describe him very favorably and without any apparent problems.)

Commentary. The mediator pursues asking about Jessie both as a follow-through to the deflection technique and also as a nicely timed opportunity to learn each parent's perspective about Jessie. The mediator is looking for how each parent feels about Jessie by their respective descriptions of him. The responses of both parents suggest that they each know Jessie well and are deeply connected with him.

Aikido Image. The feedback from the aikidoist's last move is that neither parent is intending to let Jessie get hurt in their interactions, so the attacking energy is not likely to be destructive and can be dealt with by gentler maneuvers.

MEDIATOR: So for the past year Jessie has been successfully sharing time between the two of you on a Saturday-to-Wednesday and Wednesday-to-Saturday schedule?

Commentary. The mediator attempts to indirectly highlight (mostly for Rhonda) that the current schedule is working just fine for Jessie, on the basis of positive phone intake information about Jessie's adjustment from Jimmy and the absence of negative information about Jessie from Rhonda.

JIMMY: Yes, and I want to keep it that way.

Commentary. Unfortunately, Jimmy picks up on the mediator's leverage and expands it, leaving the mediator somewhat imbalanced between the parents.

Aikido Image. Father begins to position and grab for Mother, which signals the aikidoist to join with the grab so as to redirect its energy.

MEDIATOR: How has Jessie been doing with that schedule?

Commentary. The mediator attempts to recover by focusing more emphatically on Jessie. She sets out a probe by attempting to get each parent to acknowledge that Jessie has in fact been doing fine. This is an attempt to see if Rhonda will ease up on her pressure to change the schedule, in the event that Jimmy won't budge.

Aikido Image. The aikidoist tests Mother's stance to see if she can be moved off point by the aikidoist so as to turn out of reach of Father's grab.

RHONDA: I'm concerned about when he enters school. I want him with me on the school days.

MEDIATOR: *(to Rhonda)* But how *has* he been doing for this past year?

RHONDA: Fine.

MEDIATOR: *(to Jimmy)* How would *you* answer that question?

JIMMY: He's had no problems, and he told me that he likes his schedule and wants to keep it that way!

MEDIATOR: So you both agree that Jessie has been doing fine so far. Is that right? *(Both parents nod in agreement.)*

MEDIATOR: I want to commend you both for being well ahead of most couples in your situation. Somehow, you have managed to cooperate with each other in a way that has allowed Jessie to have lots of time with each of you and not to have to deal with constant conflict between his parents. That's the *most* important thing for children of divorce. When you have been this cooperative this far, the rest is just fine tuning.

Commentary. After overemphasizing Jessie's positive adjustment to the current schedule, the mediator *compliments* both parents on their cooperation, in an effort to join them in a common view and also in an effort to help Rhonda save face if she decides to concede her demand.

Aikido Image. Mother moves in the same direction as Father and the aikidoist move, whereupon the aikidoist turns both Mother and Father to be side by side; then the aikidoist smiles and points to the child and their more positive, cooperative future ahead.

JIMMY: Well, we *do* have our spats, but we make sure that Jessie is never around when we argue.

RHONDA: I believe that's really important!

Commentary. Both parents affirm the mediator's anticipation of their continued cooperation, but Jimmy saves face with a distancing comment.

Aikido Image. The parents accept the position that the aikidoist placed them in, but Father takes one step back to keep his safe distance from Mother.

Phase Three: Generating and Exploring Options for Negotiations

In some cases, this phase in the mediation process begins very clearly when the mediator requests proposals. However, in this particular example, the mediator subtly slips into this next phase.

MEDIATOR: *(anchoring back to one of the preempting statements in the opening monologue)* As I said earlier, stability and predictability are really important for children, and you two have managed to keep these going for Jessie by each maintaining a stable relationship with him. Now *(to Rhonda),* you were saying that you would like to change the schedule to have Jessie be with you Mondays through Fridays. *(to Jimmy)* What are your thoughts on that?

Commentary. The mediator uses the technique of *reframing* to reconceptualize Rhonda's belief that Jessie needs *stability in one household* into the notion that Jessie needs *stability in two relationships.* In the same utterance, the mediator indirectly confronts Rhonda with a restatement of her request for a change. This creates the tension of contradiction within her. Letting her sit with this tension, the mediator turns to Jimmy and gives him the opportunity to respond either by following the lead of the mediator's opening or by modifying his position and conceding to Rhonda.

Aikido Image. The Aikidoist opens the field to test if Mother will still assert her attack on Father's position but redirects Mother's energy from where it was headed in order to avert her striking Father. Then the aikidoist invites Father in to see how he will respond to Mother's intended but redirected attack.

JIMMY: I'm about to become supervising salesman in the car lot, and I need to work on the weekends—those are our biggest sales days. I have Thursdays and Fridays off, and I spend the whole day with my son. We have a really good time together. He really loves spending it with me!

RHONDA: But when school starts, Jessie won't be with you on those days. He'll be in school.

MEDIATOR: What will be his school schedule?

RHONDA: Well, he'll be going from 8:15 to 11:30 A.M. They're on a split day.

MEDIATOR: So Jessie would be free from 11:30 in the morning each day?

Commentary. Jimmy maintains his position and chooses not to concede to Rhonda's position. The mediator, knowing that kindergarten is only a half-day, then utilizes an opening to assess once again the determination of Rhonda's position by leading her to recognize the possibility of keeping the status quo, in an attempt to preempt her positioning.

Aikido Image. Father positions himself to resist Mother's attack, and the aikidoist continues to move Mother in a circle directed away from Father, repositioning her out of attacking distance and position.

RHONDA: I want him with me every day.

JIMMY: You aren't looking at Jessie's needs.

Commentary. Rhonda gets the point and retorts defensively. Jimmy jumps into the fray and begins to attack Rhonda.

Aikido Image. Now Mother assumes a threatening posture to intimidate Father. Father responds by running toward Mother to attack her.

MEDIATOR: Let me ask you this, Rhonda. What does Jessie tell you about the times he spends with his dad?

RHONDA: He says he has fun. He loves his father, but I want him with me during the week.

MEDIATOR: What does Jessie tell you, Jimmy, about his times with his mother?

JIMMY: He feels very comfortable with her. She's a very good mother. But I'm also a very good father!

Commentary. Sensing the danger of a pending attack, the mediator proceeds next to quickly *deflect* Jimmy's comment and replace it with an indirect and softer question. This is an another attempt to preempt Rhonda from staking out a position before considering other options. The mediator hopes that it might lead Rhonda to seeing the value of keeping Jessie's time with Jimmy intact. The mediator gets Rhonda to acknowledge the value and importance of Jimmy's relationship with Jessie and then, to balance things out, gets Jimmy to acknowledge Rhonda's value as well. (The mediator was quite certain ahead of time what their answers would likely be.)

Aikido Image. Aikidoist quickly interrupts Father's attack by moving Mother alongside Father and Father alongside mother, whereupon each parent threatens to attack the aikidoist in a reflexive self-defense reaction.

MEDIATOR: *(to both parents)* So Jessie really enjoys spending his time with Dad just as he enjoys spending his time with Mom? Is that right? *(Both agree.)* Jessie is a really lucky kid to have two loving parents as you two obviously are. Rhonda, since you no doubt understand how important it is to offer Jessie the most possible good time with his mom and with his dad, what do you know about the possibilities of Jimmy changing his days off?

Commentary. The mediator once again emphasizes the point and *compliments* both parents for being loving and generous in sharing. Then she challenges Rhonda to discover directly whether Jimmy can change his work schedule.

Aikido Image. With Mother and Father side by side, the aikidoist pats each on the back, smiles, bows to them both, and then, gliding between them, grabs each of their arms and moves them forward, maneuvering Mother slightly ahead of Father, to whom she must hang on to keep her balance, placing him off balance.

RHONDA: He could ask for the weekends off. He used to do that when we'd go on vacation when we were together.

JIMMY: You don't understand. In a month I'm going to be in charge of the entire car lot. *I have to be there on the weekends!* I'm not going to be able to change my days anymore!

MEDIATOR: *(to Jimmy)* So before, you had more flexibility in your schedule, but soon you won't have any choice? That must be rough on you, working while Rhonda and the rest of us get the weekends off. If Jessie were with you on the weekends, what would you do with him?

Commentary. Jimmy clears up Rhonda's misunderstanding of his options to change his schedule. The mediator indirectly reiterates the point and then gently places him in a one-down, less enviable position and challenges him to reveal to Rhonda the consequences of following her request.

Aikido Image. Father begins to stabilize his position in a potentially threatening way, so the aikidoist joins him, leads him off balance, and then swiftly shifts his energy into a direction that heads him straight to the mat while watching to see where Mother will go.

JIMMY: I guess I'd have to hire a baby-sitter for the weekend, or I'd have to take him to the dealership all day with me. He can play in the office.

RHONDA: I don't want him going to the dealership. He hates it there. He tells me he gets bored.

MEDIATOR: *(to Rhonda)* So you would prefer that when Jessie is with his dad, he should get his dad's undivided attention?

Commentary. Jimmy neatly provides a very undesirable consequence, to which Rhonda reflexively reacts negatively. The mediator then, *converting accusations to requests,* quickly leads Rhonda to her other desire, that Jimmy pay attention to Jessie when with him. This is the opportunity for her to draw her own conclusions about the best alternative arrangement available.

Aikido Image. Aikidoist allows Mother to enter, but as she begins to attack Father, the aikidoist redirects Mother away from Father to look toward the child, giving Father time to get up.

RHONDA: He's going to do to Jessie what he did to me—always working, always gone!

MEDIATOR: You really missed out on spending the time with Jimmy that you needed for a healthy marriage. And now you know that you don't want Jessie to have to repeat the same experience with his dad. Is that right?

RHONDA: Yes. I don't want Jessie to have to wonder all the time, "When is my daddy coming home?"

MEDIATOR: So you want Jimmy to really be with Jessie when they are together. *(to both parents)* How can we work this out?

Commentary. The mediator and Rhonda pursue and develop the lead through their dialogue.

Aikido Image. Aikidoist continues supporting Mother in harmless but repetitive circular movements as she tries, ineffectively, to strike out at Father. Father observes the seriousness of Mother's attempts.

JIMMY: The current schedule is fine. Let's not mess with it. I also don't want to miss out on my time with Jessie. I love him very much, and he loves me.

MEDIATOR: I don't think there is any question about that. But I wonder if there are any other days besides Thursday and Friday that you could take off that might be more convenient for Rhonda?

Commentary. Jimmy again threatens to create resistance and defensiveness in Rhonda. The mediator deflects it by turning the energy around and challenging Jimmy to try harder to concede rather than to attack Rhonda. This maneuver also serves to balance the interactions by putting some pressure on Jimmy so that Rhonda is out of the hot seat for a while.

Aikido Image. Father begins to position with a defensive but threatening gesture. Aikidoist joins him and moves him in harmless but vigorous circles, challenging him to be more flexible.

RHONDA: It doesn't matter. All the weekdays are the same.

MEDIATOR: So if Jimmy took off Monday and Tuesday, for example, it wouldn't make a difference?

RHONDA: No. *(She begins to cry.)*

Commentary. The mediator restates the obvious. Rhonda acknowledges the attempt and accepts the logical conclusion. However, she expresses sadness and frustration about her dilemma.

Aikido Image. Mother begins to walk away from the interactions, rather than attack further. Aikidoist turns Father in the direction of Mother to observe her withdrawal, hoping that he will ease up on his resistant energy.

MEDIATOR: Jimmy, do you know why Rhonda is crying now? What do you think she's feeling right now?

JIMMY: Probably frustrated.

Commentary. The question, in the form of *cross talk* strategy directed at Jimmy, is an attempt to sensitize him to Rhonda's feelings in a way that she can observe.

Aikido Image. Aikidoist moves Father next to Mother to experience her very nonthreatening energy.

MEDIATOR: Is that right, Rhonda?

RHONDA: I just want Jessie to have a nice stable home life.

MEDIATOR: From what I've heard from each of you so far, it sounds to me like he already does—a nice stable home life at the homes of each of his loving parents.

Commentary. Again the mediator positively reframes Rhonda's meaning of *stable.*

Aikido Image. Aikidoist gently leads both parents, side by side, toward the child.

RHONDA: *(to Mediator)* Let me ask you, don't you think kids need to be in one home during the school year?

MEDIATOR: Well, different kids do well with different arrangements. Some kids do better in one home and can't handle the changes between households too easily. Other kids really like being with each of their parents throughout each week and do quite well on a schedule like Jessie has with you two. Some of those kids begin to do poorly if they are deprived of contact with a parent they're used to being with a lot. It all depends. The only way to know is to try different arrangements. But all else being equal, the best time to try a new arrangement is when a child shows distress over his current schedule. Then systematically trying different options makes a lot of sense. But, as the old saying goes, "If it ain't broke, don't fix it."

JIMMY: Rhonda, let's just leave the schedule the way it is for now.

Commentary. Rhonda tries to get the mediator to side with her. The mediator does not accept the challenge but rather *sidesteps* the issue by offering educational information with many options and built in safeguards for Jessie. This allows Rhonda to save face in making her concession. Jimmy once again jumps in with pressure on Rhonda.

Aikido Image. Mother attempts to grab the aikidoist to push her into Father. Aikidoist steps aside and lets Mother go right by her and then grabs Mother's arm and leads her in circles, shifting orientations in space and ending up next to Father, looking toward the child.

MEDIATOR: Kindergarten is usually not very demanding of a child, but once a child hits first or second or third grade, sometimes the school demands are stressful for that particular child, and then keeping the households the same during the week makes a lot of sense. If you both agreed to let Jessie continue enjoying the amount of time he currently spends with each of you until he shows either of you that it isn't working for him, I would recommend that you return to mediation at least next spring. That way, we could assess how he has been doing, and you could change the schedule if he isn't handling the current one anymore.

Commentary. The mediator elaborates on the status quo option through more developmental information to further allow Rhonda to save face.

Aikido Image. Aikidoist extends both parents' energy toward the child.

Phase Four: Negotiating to Resolution and Drafting the Agreement

At this point, Rhonda seems to have conceded to leaving the schedule as it stands. The mediation process then enters the final phase, in which various issues are negotiated, loose ends are tied up, and a written agreement is produced.

RHONDA: I want him assessed in December. I don't want to wait until spring!

MEDIATOR: Jimmy, what are your thoughts on Rhonda's suggestion?

Commentary. Rhonda asserts another position to aid in her face saving. The mediator checks out possible resistance in Jimmy.

Aikido Image. Mother begins to attack the aikidoist and Father. Aikidoist spins Mother so her energy is redirected next to Father.

JIMMY: I'd agree to that. Besides, I don't know what my job situation will be like at that time anyhow.

MEDIATOR: It could change even before the fall term begins?

JIMMY: It could, but I doubt that it will.

MEDIATOR: Would you both agree to return to mediation if your work schedule, Jimmy, changes even before school starts in the fall? *(Both parents agree.)*

Commentary. Jimmy acquiesces and offers the mediator another opportunity to balance the challenges by saying that there is hope in the near future for Rhonda's position to become operative.

Aikido Image. Father does not attack Mother as she goes by him but rather suggests by his movement that he is not intending to attack her anymore. Aikidoist invites both parents to relax. They do.

RHONDA: That would be fine with me. I just don't want Jessie having any problems when school starts.

MEDIATOR: So you are both agreeing to let Jessie keep his current schedule until either he shows some problems with it or Jimmy's job situation changes, whichever comes first. And you also agree that the two of you will return to mediation in December, to see how things are going for Jessie. I may also want to interview Jessie at that time.

RHONDA: That would be great if you would. I'd like you to talk to him and see if he's doing OK.

JIMMY: Sounds great to me.

Commentary. The mediator expands the opening and further *offers hope* to Rhonda that if Jessie does develop problems, the mediator will pick up on it (through the proposed interview of Jessie).

Aikido Image. Seeing that both parents have relaxed, the aikidoist walks over to Father and acknowledges to both parents that she will protect the child from further harm.

MEDIATOR: Now, what about summers and holidays?

RHONDA: We've been able to agree on those. We share them.

JIMMY: I want to take him this summer on a camping trip for two weeks.

RHONDA: I think two weeks is too long.

Commentary. Jimmy presents a plan, and Rhonda resists it, perhaps to save face for conceding on the schedule.

Aikido Image. Father begins to posture for an attack on Mother. Mother goes to attack Father.

MEDIATOR: What's the longest that he's been away from either of you so far?

Commentary. Mediator looks again for a status quo starting point for negotiations.

Aikido Image. Aikidoist preempts Father's attack and neutralizes Mother's attack, positioning them both side by side facing the child.

JIMMY: About eight days.

MEDIATOR: You might want to consider his comfort level in being away from either parent at his age of five.

RHONDA: Two weeks is too long. I think one week is OK.

JIMMY: But my vacation is two weeks, and I want to go to Yosemite with him.

MEDIATOR: *(to Rhonda)* What would help you feel more comfortable that Jessie would be OK with his dad for two weeks?

Commentary. The mediator explores Rhonda's conviction in her point.

Aikido Image. Aikidoist moves Mother away from Father, preventing her from getting near him.

RHONDA: If he called me every few days.

JIMMY: There aren't any phones in the forest!

MEDIATOR: There are forest ranger stations and recreation centers. It is true that children Jessie's age do miss the other parent when away from them for too long—generally about three or four days. You may find Jessie crying for his mom in the middle of the forest, Jimmy. I wonder if you would consider arranging for Jessie to make a phone call to his mom every few days during your trip.

Commentary. Jimmy shows too much rigidity, so the mediator, using the strategy of *persuading with dramatic anecdotes,* challenges him in an attempt to balance the concessions between the parents.

Aikido Image. Father begins to position for attack again. Aikidoist preempts his attack and moves him forcefully to Mother's side but in no striking position.

JIMMY: Yeah, I guess I could do that.

RHONDA: I won't agree to two weeks.

MEDIATOR: How about ten days?

RHONDA: I guess I could live with that.

JIMMY: All right, but you can only have him for ten days for *your* vacation too!

Commentary. The mediator facilitates negotiating with Rhonda, reaches an agreement, and then Jimmy tacks on a further face-saving demand of his own.

Aikido Image. Mother and Father swipe at each other. Aikidoist maneuvers both their arms to harmless positions.

MEDIATOR: And I'll assume that the same agreement about the phone contact every three or four days holds true when Jessie is with his mom for her ten days. Right? *(Both parents agree.)*

Commentary. Rhonda concedes, and the mediator expands the concession just a bit further to even out the balance between the parents.

Aikido Image. Aikidoist moves Mother through one more circle to even out the maneuvers and positions both parents side by side, facing the child.

MEDIATOR: OK. Are there any other clauses that you want in your agreement?

RHONDA: *(to Jimmy)* I want him wearing a seat belt whenever you take him *anywhere.*

JIMMY: I know that. I always buckle him in now, even since I had a really close call—to be perfectly honest with you, it scared the hell out of me, and now I'm real careful about that sort of thing.

RHONDA: I sure hope so.

Commentary. Rhonda asserts one final demand. Luckily, it is an easy one that the mediator can support and Jimmy can easily concede to.

Aikido Image. Mother and Father grapple lightly and then calm themselves down, with no further maneuvers needed.

MEDIATOR: All right, I'll go ahead and write up the agreement and then you can both sign it and then be on your way.

RHONDA: Thank you for your help.

Written Agreement Reached

1. Both parents agree to share joint legal custody of their son, Jessie.
2. Jessie will share time with his parents according to the following schedule:
   a. He will be in his mother's care from Saturday at 9:00 A.M. until Wednesday's return to day care at 10:00 A.M.
   b. He will be in his father's care from Wednesday at 10:00 A.M. until Saturday at 9:00 A.M.
   c. Father agrees to return Jessie to Mother's house on Saturdays, and Mother agrees to return Jessie to day care on Wednesdays.
   d. During the summer, Jessie can spend a continuous period of up to ten days with each parent for special vacation trips. During those trips, to prevent Jessie's distress over missing the other parent, each parent will arrange for Jessie to make a phone call to the other parent every three or four days, no matter where Jessie may be.
3. Both parents agree to return to mediation in December 1999 or anytime before then if (a) Jessie shows any problems in school or

home as a result of his current time-sharing schedule or (b) Father's job situation changes in a way that changes his work schedule.

Case Intervention Summary

The impasse in this case is probably best viewed as a *reality-based impasse* because it was fairly simple and was resolved in a fairly straightforward manner at a brief session. Had one or two hours not been enough time to resolve the issue, or had the issues expanded, the mediator could have gone further into the latent causes of the impasse. But there was little psychological complexity to the case, and so little in the way of therapeutic interventions was necessary to reach agreement. Whereas in this particular case, an hour and a half proved to be sufficient to resolve the dispute and reach agreement, two to three hours could be helpful in consolidating the changes. It is very unlikely that more time would be needed for this case, seeing that the issues were limited in scope, there were no complicating allegations, and the parents were positively responsive to this very brief intervention.

Resolving the Case in Two to Three Hours

If the mediator had two to three hours to work on this case, what might be different in her approach? If we look through the transcript carefully, we note that there are several points at which more "educational" and/or "therapeutic" interventions would be appropriate. With more time available, the following issues could be discussed and explored further, with a goal toward expanding the awareness of each parent and fostering healthier postdivorce family structures:

○ Clarify further Rhonda's worries about Jessie developing school problems within the current schedule. Explore whether there is anything that Jimmy could agree to or the mediator could do that would help alleviate her concerns.

○ Explore both Rhonda's and Jimmy's expectations and goals for Jessie in the future and how they both could help him to achieve them.

○ Help them clarify the role of stepparents, half-siblings, and "our kid and your kid," since Rhonda is expecting a baby and about to venture into a new marriage. Educate them about the natural sibling jealousy that will likely arise when Rhonda gives birth and how both Rhonda and Jimmy (and Verne as well) can help Jessie through that process. The discussion should include clarifying lines of authority for disciplining Jessie while at his mother's house and ways to increase cooperation across households.

If these further clarifications did not lead to resolution of the present dispute, several other hypotheses as to Rhonda's motives for requesting the change could be checked out:

- That Rhonda might be wanting an increase in child support
- That Rhonda might be wanting to set a precedent of increased time at her house as a prelude to moving out of the area with her "new family"
- That Rhonda might be resentful of Jessie's getting the attention from Jimmy that she never got from him in the marriage. (This hypothesis is not likely, but exploring it might prove productive.)

Special Issues in This Case

The mediator decided not to interview Jessie because he did not seem directly relevant in resolving the dispute and also because he was quite young. It would, however, be advisable to interview him if he manifested symptomatic behavior that seemed related to the dispute or the current time-sharing arrangement, if he expressed a strong preference for a particular schedule (as reported by either of the parents), or if the parents were in high conflict and the mediator needed demonstrable leverage of its effects on Jessie to break their impasse.

Also, in exploring her own biases in this case, the mediator began by neutrally entertaining the possibilities of either parent's position being viable for Jessie. As the session proceeded, the mediator felt that Jimmy had compelling reasons for his position (his job hours and his sincere desire to maintain the close relationship that he had established with Jessie). She also felt that Rhonda's reasoning behind her position was not clear, except for her worry about the future, which seemed ungrounded in light of Jessie's excellent adjustment to date. Moreover, since Jimmy was more resistant to changing his position and Rhonda was more easily persuaded, the mediator let the stream flow toward the status quo as the resolution. This, being a known quantity in terms of Jessie's adjustment, felt like a positive outcome for Jessie's best interests at this time.

13

CASE STUDY 2

A MORE COMPLEX CASE

LLOYD, THIRTY-ONE YEARS OLD, and Joanne, thirty-three, were referred to mediation by the judge after a court appearance in which Joanne
filed to restrict Lloyd's visitation and had Lloyd served with a temporary
restraining order. In seeking this order, she alleged that he had been verbally abusing her on the phone and in person over the past two months
since the court set a visitation schedule.

Intake Information

The following information was gleaned from the initial phone interview
with each spouse and the intake sheet filled out by the couple.

Joanne's Statement

Joanne and Lloyd have two children, LeeAnn, seven years old, and Danny,
four. They had been married nine years and had been separated for three
months at the time of referral. Joanne, a cosmetologist, stated that they
had gone to three different marriage counselors off and on for the previous four years, but nothing was resolved. Lloyd had been physically abusive of her on several occasions during the marriage, and for the past
several years and increasingly since the separation Lloyd had been verbally abusive to her in front of the children. Joanne claimed that he did
not use alcohol or drugs, but he had a very hot temper.

Lloyd has refused to accept the divorce. He has regularly begged Joanne
to return, and, whenever she declines, he begins swearing at her and

threatening her. She has always been willing to accommodate to his schedule but is fed up with his changing plans at the last minute and then verbally abusing her when she declines to take the children. She is requesting primary custody of the children, and she would like the children to be with him only on weekends. She asserted that she has a letter from LeeAnn's therapist recommending that LeeAnn spend less time with Lloyd. Moreover, Joanne said that Lloyd's attorney told her that to get what she wants, she would have to be psychologically examined in a custody evaluation. Joanne has no attorney; she used paralegal services to file her petitions.

Lloyd's Statement

Lloyd, an aggressive high school football coach, reported that his work schedule is very erratic, due to the many football practices and traveling games that he must attend. He stated that he needs his schedule with the children to be flexible, just as it has always been. He wants to keep a basic schedule of having the children with him Monday through Wednesday and on Sunday whenever there is no game or practice. He also went on at length to describe the "incompetent therapists" that he and Joanne have seen and revealed that he is suing one of them for "alienating his wife's affection from him." He declared firmly that he does not want this divorce. Moreover, he wants the court mediators to "help his wife come to her senses and get the family back together!" He further alleged that Joanne had an alcohol problem and comes from a severely alcoholic family. He added that Joanne's alcoholic father has been very influential in encouraging Joanne to divorce, and he does not want the children to see the man. Lloyd further notes that Joanne has recently become heavily involved in a fundamentalist church group and has been preaching for him to accept Jesus and be saved. He requested an immediate appointment.

Beginning Hypotheses

As we try to anticipate the possible dynamics of this case, the following points stand out from the information collected so far.

○ From the intake information, we can speculate that reaching agreement on a comprehensive parenting plan with this couple will take some time. It is clear that Lloyd has not yet accepted the divorce and that he is likely, at this time, to resist efforts to finalize a parenting plan, let alone a divorce. Moreover, the couple have a long history of marital problems that remained unsolved even with extensive professional help. Joanne's alleged recent involvement in a fundamentalist church suggests that she has had a difficult time separating from Lloyd and needed an external anchor to help her pull away. Also, the fact that Lloyd is suing one of their past therapists for supporting Joanne's decision to divorce bodes poorly for rapid success in mediation. Finally, the addition of domestic violence to the picture further dims chances for early success.

○ This case appears, at first glance, to involve an impasse at the *interactional level* (Joanne's emotional *disengaging strategy* countered by Lloyd's *reuniting strategy*), with elements of the *intrapsychic level* (Lloyd's reluctance to divorce) and *external level* (the involvement of the grandparents, the therapist, and the lawyer) as well. The issues seem more about their dysfunctional relationship than about a parenting schedule per se. Hence a likely productive focus of the first session would be on assessing and unbundling the marital dynamics from the parenting issues.

○ If the mediator can help Lloyd let go of the marriage and begin the emotional process of divorce, it is likely that the impasse over the schedule will loosen up. This assumes that Joanne, who is struggling hard to pull away from Lloyd, is indeed ready to proceed with the divorce—an assumption that needs to be explored.

As with Rhonda and Jimmy in the case study presented in Chapter Twelve, ideally, prior to beginning mediation, the couple should have been given a wide range of educational information on divorce and the needs of children after divorce (in the form of classes, handouts, videotapes, and so on). Because of the domestic violence allegations, the mediator asks Joanne by phone if she would like to have a separate session first, which she declines, and so a joint mediation session is scheduled. The mediator further asks her if she feels the need to have a support person present during mediation. She declines, saying that she will feel safe enough with the mediator in the room.

The mediator phones Lloyd's attorney to inquire about the information conveyed to Joanne about the need for an evaluation. The attorney replies, "This is a very difficult case, and I don't have much hope for success in mediation; I was just spelling out the next likely step for Joanne." This action could be interpreted as an overreaction by a naive attorney; however, the mediator happens to know this particular attorney to be a strong adversarial advocate and so concludes that the action was more likely a tactical ploy to intimidate Joanne, who has no attorney and is therefore somewhat vulnerable. The mediator engages the attorney in a discussion about the critical need for attorney support to give mediation a chance to help Joanne's children, pointing out that legal clients are much more satisfied when their divorce minimizes damage to their children. The attorney agrees to offer such support to her client. The mediator thanks the attorney and tells her he will call again if the mediation process should break down and he should needed the attorney's further support in reaching an agreement.

Resolving the Case in One to Two Hours

A number of indicators suggest that this case will require more than two hours to complete, so, if working in a time-restricted court setting, the mediator must plan carefully in advance how he will use the typical one-to-two-hour time period available. The following is a reasonable plan within this time framework:

If feasible, because of the pressing emotional dynamic leading Lloyd to request an immediate appointment, it would be advisable for the mediator to *resist the time squeeze* and delay scheduling the first appointment for as long as tolerable by the parents. This could increase the chances that Lloyd would use the extra time processing his emotional divorce and thereby increase the chances of success in mediation. If this is not feasible, however, the mediator can use the first session to get acquainted, get some background on the marriage and divorce, briefly explore the issues at impasse, and plan to use the rest of the time to talk about the need for divorce counseling for Lloyd and perhaps for Joanne as well. Giving educational information about the stages, process, and dynamics of divorce (see Chapter Five) could be a good way to introduce them to a referral for private divorce counseling (explicitly *not* marital counseling), and it would be a valuable use of the first hour's time. Helping both parties see the value of working through the emotional process of divorce at least to the point that both have accepted its reality can be of much benefit in setting the stage for effective mediation at a later date. It can also be of immediate indirect benefit to their children.

It would be ideal to reschedule the couple for another session of an hour or two some months later, after some divorce counseling has taken place. Again, the chances are greater that the couple would be more amenable to mediation at a later point in their divorce process. Trying to jam this couple through the full mediation process in an hour at this time would likely be a waste of time for the mediator and frustrating and self-defeating for the couple, and it would discourage the couple from using mediation services at a later time when they could really benefit from the process. (Remember, Lloyd is ready to sue therapists who were unable to help him to achieve his inflexible and seemingly unattainable goal of re-uniting with Joanne.)

If the couple can be persuaded to agree to maintain the current schedule until after they have completed a round of divorce counseling, the case could be placed on hold for a few months. If, however, the couple will not agree to maintain the current schedule, then the mediator could suggest developing a partial agreement that they seek divorce counseling and then attempt to develop a temporary, time-limited agreement regarding the parenting schedule until they return for "real" mediation. If they are unable to agree to any schedule, the mediator could suggest that they request the court to issue only a temporary time-sharing schedule until their return to mediation after divorce counseling.

The particular elements of this case as described here suggest that the mediator should not anticipate failure merely due to the fact that the case cannot be resolved in one hour. This couple does have the potential to reach agreement, given more available mediation time. Sending them into a full evaluation mode at this time would likely aggravate their dispute further by placing them prematurely into an adversarial context. In such a process, the elements of their emotional impasse could well fuel an unnecessary full-blown dispute of the "tribal warfare" variety.

Resolving the Case in Two to Three Hours

Because of the greater complexity of this case, it could be assumed that a minimal time of two to three hours would be needed for the couple to reach an agreement.

Phase One: Setting the Context

Beginning the mediation process with a first one-hour session, the mediator plans to spend about ten minutes presenting educational preempting information applicable to this case. The particular preempts selected, based upon the information obtained from the intake sheet and phone calls so far, include the following (see Appendix D for a complete list or Chapter Five for verbatim presentation of the full preempting monologues):

○ Assumption of conflict between parents

○ Assumption that both parents love the children

- o Assumptions of children's need for both parents
- o Mediator as child advocate
- o Effects of putting down the other parent
- o Respecting the stages of the divorce process
- o Effects of alcohol and drug abuse
- o Effects of domestic violence

All the applicable preempts do not necessarily have to be presented at the very beginning of the mediation process. Preempts can also effectively be inserted at any point in the process at which they seem to be appropriate.

The session begins. As the mediator is presenting the "assumption of the children's need for both parents," Lloyd, who has been staring intensely at Joanne to this point, interrupts:

LLOYD: Joanne, the children need us back together. It's the only way they should be raised . . . as a family!

MEDIATOR: Lloyd, we are going to talk very soon about what children need in these situations, but first I need to give you both some other important information.

LLOYD: I'm sorry. I just really don't like what has been happening.

MEDIATOR: I hear you. We will get to the details of your situation in just a little while. Please bear with me.

Commentary. Lloyd's anxiety erupts, and he tries to gain control by engaging Joanne at the outset. The mediator *deflects* his comment, joins him in his concerns, and assertively leads the discussion back to the context-setting comments. This diverts a likely escalation of conflict, and it establishes for both Lloyd and Joanne that the mediator is in charge of the session and in control of the agenda and the process.

Aikido Image. Father interrupts the energy field by grabbing for Mother. Before he secures his grip on her, the aikidoist intercepts his grasp and turns him away from Mother, then gently places him down on the mat.

LLOYD: Go ahead.

(Mediator completes the preemptive monologue.)

Phase Two: Gathering Essential Information and Assessing the Family Dynamics

When the preliminary context-setting comments have been made, a shift to questions about the situation at hand marks the start of the assessment phase.

MEDIATOR: So, how and when did the two of you first meet?

JOANNE: We met in college. We were in the same chemistry lab.

LLOYD: *(utters longingly to Joanne)* You are still just as beautiful as you were back then.

JOANNE: *(to Mediator)* Do I have to listen to this?

MEDIATOR: *(to Joanne)* Tell me how your relationship progressed after you first met.

Commentary. Lloyd again erupts with his impulses, and Joanne reacts defensively. The mediator converts her defensiveness into cooperation by offering *her* the control to answer the question to which she objected.

Aikido Image. Aikidoist engages both parents in eye contact. Father once again attempts to reach for Mother. Aikidoist blocks his move, redirects him away, and then turns to invite Mother in.

JOANNE: We were deeply in love. I thought he was the greatest—good-looking, strong, and so clear in what he wanted in life. Now I realize I was probably mistaken—he's really controlling and abusive.

LLOYD: *(looks and points at Joanne and then addresses Mediator, in a booming voice)* Well, tell him about *your drinking!"*

MEDIATOR: *(to Lloyd)* Would *you* like to tell me about her drinking?

JOANNE: I used to drink when Lloyd was gone a lot. I stopped when we separated, and I now attend AA regularly.

LLOYD: Well, I didn't make you drink. It was your *own* damn responsibility. You never . . . *(voice escalating)*

MEDIATOR: *(taking an assertive stance)* Hold on here! If you want to do what's best for your children, let's just slow down here and take some time for me to learn about how you got to this point—and remember to use "I" statements, not "you" statements. *(He pauses and slows the pace.)* Now, have you two had any prior counseling together?

Commentary. Each time Lloyd tries to engage Joanne back into the relationship, she pulls back defensively and/or humiliates him. Each time that he hears her reject him, his panic escalates, and he expresses it in attacking rage. The mediator intervenes rapidly. Using the technique of *blocking and soothing,* he deescalates the interactions by talking progressively more slowly and deliberately. It should also be noted that the mediator took full notice of Lloyd's allegation about Joanne's drinking and, if it surfaces again, will check it out later in the session, when it can be explored outside a context of escalating anger.

Aikido Image. Mother invites Father in and then provokes him by pulling away. Father responds by reaching to attack Mother. Aikidoist swiftly moves in on Father, deflects his grasp, spins him around, slowing down the pace, and sets him at rest facing his children across the room while turning to invite Mother in.

LLOYD: Yes we did. Plenty of incompetent therapy. I'm going to sue the last therapist we had. He saw my wife alone and told her she should get a divorce from me. Don't you think he overstepped his professional boundaries?

MEDIATOR: It sounds like you were very upset hearing a professional tell your wife to leave you.

Commentary. Lloyd tries to set up the mediator to side with him, but the mediator *sidesteps* the attempt, and by using *reflective listening,* he effectively empathizes with the feeling without answering the question directly.

Aikido Image. Father, still enraged at Mother, begins lashing at the air around him, then tries to grab the aikidoist to support him in getting closer to Mother. Aikidoist absorbs his energy, moves beside him, and supports him against his side while they turn toward Mother.

LLOYD: You're damn right, and I'm going to sue that bastard.

MEDIATOR: Lloyd, let me ask you this. What do you think Joanne would have done if that therapist hadn't told her that?

JOANNE: I still would want a divorce!

Commentary. Lloyd continues expressing his displaced anger. The mediator indirectly challenges his belief about the therapist being responsible for the divorce decision. Joanne clarifies the point.

Aikido Image. Father once again begins lashing out at the air. Aikidoist maneuvers him toward Mother while inviting Mother to make her next move. She turns to walk away.

LLOYD: *(to Joanne)* You're just quitting. You're just a quitter! I was taught *never* to quit. That's how I became such a successful football coach. *(to Mediator)* You know, we just won the Western Regional Championships and are heading for National.

MEDIATOR: You must be really proud of your team.

Commentary. Lloyd reveals part of the reason for the impasse: that divorce goes against his view of himself as *persistent no matter what the odds.* He prides himself on becoming successful in sports through persistence and is mistakenly applying the same formula to his marriage. The mediator simply uses *reflective listening* and *complimenting* to defuse Lloyd's anger at this point, with the intent of picking up this theme later in the mediation process.

Aikido Image. Father continues lashing out, trying to reach Mother. Aikidoist maintains centered control and moves Father's energy around in a harmless circles, making sure Father does not reach Mother or hurt himself.

JOANNE: If only he put in the time with his family that he put in with his team, we might still be married today.

LLOYD: We *are* still married, and I know I made a mistake by working so hard, but I'm ready to really be married now. After this season, I'm going to hire my assistant coach to cover a lot of my time, so I'll have time for us to be together.

Commentary. Joanne offers her view of the trouble in the marriage. Lloyd further reveals his resistance to accepting the divorce and then asserts his half-committed plan for reaching his goal.

Aikido Image. Mother provokes Father again and stirs up Father's intent to grab Mother again.

JOANNE: You're still married to football, not to me!

LLOYD: I can't just quit my profession. I have to make a living. You want blood from me? I can't give that, but I will go the distance.

Commentary. The couple continue discussing the issues leading to Joanne's divorce decision. Each time the discussion gets off course and into accusations, the mediator relentlessly *deflects* and refocuses the discussion on their relationship, the goal being to help Lloyd understand why Joanne left the marriage. After some time, the mediator calls the question.

Aikido Image. Mother and Father harmlessly spar with each other. When too much contact is made, the aikidoist deflects the dangerous moves.

MEDIATOR: What would it take for this relationship to get back together?

JOANNE: It would take too much work. It's just not worth it.

LLOYD: It *is* worth it—for the kids!

MEDIATOR: *(to Joanne)* What if he is very sincere about making any changes you wanted?

LLOYD: I am!

JOANNE: He would still have to come to the Lord.

LLOYD: But you *just* got involved with that religious stuff. *(to Mediator)* And she's been telling the children that I'm a sinner, 'cause I don't believe as deeply as she says she does.

JOANNE: It just won't work out. I don't want to be married to you.

LLOYD: There you go, quitting again. Why can't you just give it a chance?

MEDIATOR: Lloyd, I don't think you *should* accept this divorce . . . *(long pause as both Lloyd and Joanne look at the mediator, astonished)* . . . until you are fully ready!

Commentary. As they continue arguing in this fashion, the mediator uses a *confusion* technique to disrupt the cadence of their arguing.

Aikido Image. As the parents continue to spar, the aikidoist finally moves in on Father, spins him around, and then suddenly shifts his direction and, using a no-touch throw (as Father is running forward, at just the right instant the aikidoist suddenly places his index finger an inch in front of Father's eyes, startling him into falling instantly and reflexively backward onto the mat, flat on his back).

MEDIATOR: As I hear you two discussing this matter, I'm reminded of the owner of a basketball team that was in the NBA playoffs a number of years ago. His team was having a very hard time scoring, and the other team kept getting basket after basket. He remembered his best teacher telling him, "Don't quit until the buzzer rings, but when the buzzer rings, quit." After years of staying really furious for a long time whenever his team lost a game, he finally understood what his teacher meant, and then, instead of getting depressed long after the game was over, he simply played his team hard until the end and accepted the loss and then immediately began preparing for the next season, a whole new game ahead. *(pause)* Now, I would suggest that we end this session today and schedule another appointment to continue our discussion. I'm assuming that you two can leave the time-sharing schedule the way it is until our next session, when we can really get into looking at the schedule.

Commentary. Having Lloyd's attention, the mediator proceeds to use a strategy of *anecdote telling,* which metaphorically addresses, within his own area of interest, his strong feelings regarding quitting the marriage.

Aikido Image. Aikidoist spins Father around in a variety of disorienting but harmless circular moves, attempting to drain off his energy from attacking Mother, while Mother remains quiet.

LLOYD: That's fine.

JOANNE: But I don't want him taking the kids to his football practices.

LLOYD: They're OK. They enjoy it. But if you want, I'll hire a sitter.

MEDIATOR: OK, fine. Let's get more into the particulars in the next session. But before next session, I'd like to ask each of you to think about something. Joanne, I'd like to ask you to think about what you believe it would take for Lloyd to truly accept the fact that you really do want to divorce. And Lloyd, I'd like you to think, only to yourself and without talking to Joanne, about what you'd have to do to get Joanne to change her mind about the divorce decision and get back together with you. OK, we'll meet in six weeks, and I'll see you both then.

Commentary. The use of the *confusion* technique brought both Lloyd and Joanne to attention and punctuated the point that final clarification and acceptance of the divorce decision is crucial to a settlement. Then, while they were still somewhat psychologically disoriented, the mediator further elaborated the point by *anecdote telling,* in an attempt to influence the unconscious mind. Finally, he brought this point home by assigning the paradoxical task to be completed before the next session (intentionally scheduled many weeks later to give them time to process the discussion in this session). He asked each of them to consider the complement of the other person's question, further focusing them as a couple, but asking them separately to work on this critical issue of the divorce decision. The goal is to have them each do introspective work between sessions so as to speed up their emotional process in preparation for negotiations next session.

Aikido Image. As the parents are both back up on their feet, the aikidoist moves them side by side and then forward together, giving them the experience of harmony. He then separates them to continue forward at a mutually developed distance from one another.

At the second session, scheduled to last an hour and a half, the mediator needed to assess what had transpired since the first session; what communications, if any, took place between the parents; and how much they each were able to process the emotional issues from the first session. Generally, it is helpful to initiate the second session with open-ended questions focused on assessing these areas of concern.

MEDIATOR: So, let's see. It's been about six weeks since our last session. Have you two had any discussions with each other since last session?

LLOYD: Yes we have. I decided to buy her out of the house.

MEDIATOR: *(to Joanne)* How did that decision get made?

Commentary. With his utterance, Lloyd indicates that he may have made some progress toward accepting the divorce decision. The mediator again attempts to empower Joanne (to balance Lloyd's aggressiveness) by letting *her* explain how this negotiation took place.

Aikido Image. Aikidoist invites each parent in to test their level of aggressiveness, and when Father declines to attack, turns to specifically invite Mother in, testing whether she will provoke Father.

JOANNE: He made me an offer that seemed reasonable. I checked with the paralegal and my father first, and I accepted his . . .

LLOYD: I probably offered it too soon. She's having second thoughts about leaving.

Commentary. Lloyd's comment suggests to the mediator the hypothesis that Joanne may indeed have been ambivalent about the divorce decision and that since the last session, she may have shifted back to wanting a reconciliation. The mediator proceeds to check it out directly with Joanne.

Aikido Image. Father faces Mother and opens. Mother faces Father as if positioned to reach for Father.

MEDIATOR: *(looking at Joanne, who sits motionless)* Is that accurate?

JOANNE: Absolutely not! I am *not* interested in staying in this marriage.

Commentary. Joanne disconfirms the hypothesis. The mediator proceeds to clear up the misunderstanding so as to get back on track with a mutual understanding about the marriage ending.

Aikido Image. Aikidoist invites Mother in, and she turns around and decisively walks away.

MEDIATOR: *(to Lloyd)* Where did you get that information?

LLOYD: Her brother told me last week. He said he was talking with her and she was crying and saying that she was so confused.

JOANNE: I *am* confused, but not about my decision. I don't know where I'm going to live, and I need to get a job really fast because he said he wouldn't pay me any alimony.

LLOYD: You could have all the alimony you want if you'd come back!

MEDIATOR: *(to Joanne)* So, you *haven't* changed your mind? You *still do* plan to follow through with a divorce?

JOANNE: Absolutely. I packed up the last of my stuff and moved it all out. I went . . .

Commentary. Joanne clarifies the confusion. Lloyd tries again to persuade her back into the marriage, using coercion. The mediator uses Joanne as leverage (with the technique of *cross talk*) to let Lloyd hear once again of her intent to divorce. (Rather than arguing with Lloyd to accept the divorce, it is best to utilize more natural leverage within the family system and help Joanne restate her intentions repeatedly in many different forms until Lloyd finally gets the message.) The mediator then punctuates Joanne's declaration by restating it one more time.

Aikido Image. Sensing Mother's intent to disengage, aikidoist invites Father to approach Mother to see if she will accept him. Mother invites Father in and then effectively proceeds to throw him across the room.

LLOYD: She moved in with her father, the drunk.

MEDIATOR: Hang on a minute, Lloyd! *(pausing and slowing down the pace)* . . . I know that Joanne's moving out must have been the worst experience of your life and must leave you feeling devastated.

Commentary. Lloyd, in his panic, tries to derail the conversation into accusations. The mediator proceeds by *blocking and soothing,* changing the pace, and preempting the escalation by using *reflective listening* to try to defuse his panic.

Aikido Image. Father leaps up and heads toward Mother for an attack. Aikidoist moves in, preempts Father's strike at Mother, slows down his pace, and takes him down to the mat slowly and supportively.

LLOYD: She's quitting. She's just quitting! *(becomes quietly tearful)*

MEDIATOR: Joanne, I know that you can understand how hard this is for Lloyd and that it may be even harder for him to understand how hard this has all been for you. So now I'm a little confused. You say you have moved all your stuff out, you are staying at your dad's place, and you're looking for a more permanent place to live?

Commentary. Lloyd's panic erupts again, threatening to escalate the interactions. The mediator responds by *deflecting* the allegations and keeping focused on the emotional issues. After empathizing with and labeling Lloyd's pain for Joanne to overhear, Lloyd for the first time reveals tears, showing his fear and sadness over the reality of the pending loss. The mediator lets him sit with his feelings, turns to Joanne, and, in a message that is both challenging of her (for Lloyd to overhear) and supportive of her (for her sake) at the same time, mutualizes the pain that both are feeling. Rather than ending the message there, the mediator proceeds in the same sentence to lead the couple to clarify the living arrangements further.

Aikido Image. Aikidoist engages Mother in movement, spins her in a half-circle, supportively, and then launches her off to assume a position near Father, waiting to see what her next move will be.

JOANNE: No. I just stayed at my father's house for a few days. I have my own place with the kids now. We moved in two weeks ago.

LLOYD: Where is it? The kids didn't tell me. Where is it?

MEDIATOR: So Lloyd doesn't know where you live?

JOANNE: I prefer that he not know. He keeps harassing me.

LLOYD: I want to know where my children are living. *(to Mediator)* Don't you think I have a right to know?

Commentary. Joanne's clarification of her living arrangements and prohibition against Lloyd knowing the location of her residence provokes Lloyd, who feels even more out of control. The mediator attempts to test out Joanne's resistance to revealing the location. She maintains her secrecy. Lloyd responds by trying to leverage the mediator, self-righteously, onto his side.

Aikido Image. Mother moves alone toward the children. Father struggles to get to her. Mother postures to discourage Father's attack. Aikidoist blocks Father and invites Mother in to test whether she intends to maintain her position. When she does, Father grabs for the aikidoist to leverage him against Mother.

MEDIATOR: I know, Lloyd, that you're concerned that your children are OK, and Joanne, it sounds like you don't yet trust that Lloyd can let go of you.

Commentary. The mediator *sidesteps* the provocative question and, for face-saving purposes, *reframes* Lloyd's panic of being out of control into "concern for the children." Then, in the same sentence, the mediator challenges Joanne in a supportive way that *reframes* Lloyd's harassment as "difficulty in letting go of the marriage."

Aikido Image. Aikidoist steps aside, letting Father go by him, then turns Father in the direction of Mother and moves with him toward Mother and the children, then spins Mother safely out of the way.

LLOYD: I'm done with her! I don't want to ever see her again. Let's just get the schedule done and get out of here.

Commentary. Lloyd reacts self-protectively, but in the right direction for negotiations to proceed. He clearly is not finished with this issue. However, the question of the divorce decision is perhaps clarified and encapsulated enough that negotiations of the parenting schedule can begin.

Aikido Image. Father begins to see that he can get close to the children but still is unable to get near Mother.

Phase Three: *Generating and Exploring Options for Negotiations*

This phase begins at the point when the emotional impasse issues have been dealt with sufficiently so that the mediator can temporarily suspend them and move forward with the mediation process. These issues may well resurface to re-create an impasse at any point in the mediation process. If that should occur, the mediator can relabel and compartmentalize the emotional issues, perhaps individually caucus for a few minutes to attempt further clarification of the feelings that are resurfacing, and/or suggest divorce counseling to work on those issues further. Then the mediator can often simply continue work on the parenting plan.

At this point in the session, negotiation options are explored.

MEDIATOR: *(to Joanne)* How have the transfers taken place if he doesn't know where you are living?

JOANNE: We've been doing them at the police station, but the kids get scared there, and he even harasses us there. . . . We can do the transfers at day care—we don't need to see each other.

MEDIATOR: So you two can transfer the children at a neutral place that would probably feel safe for the kids? Good! That will cut down on the hostility between you. A lot of parents make transfers at day care. It feels safe for the children. And as I said last time, it's really crucial that the children not witness any further conflict between you two—it's for their emotional survival.

LLOYD: That's fine. I don't need to see her. I don't want to see her.

MEDIATOR: Good, then I'll write in your agreement that you both agree to transfer the children at day care. Now, what about the days of transfer?

Commentary. The mediator uses Joanne's statement to expand and clarify the need to reduce conflict between the parents, and then he uses Lloyd's self-defensive retort to expand into one of the clauses of the soon-to-be-developed agreement. The decision made at this time to move beyond the emotional issues into negotiations was made partly because of the time constraints of the session and partly because Lloyd has at least verbally acknowledged (although not yet emotionally resolved) that he appears finished trying to persuade Joanne to reconcile (at least in front of the mediator) and is ready to move on to negotiations.

Aikido Image. Aikidoist, using leading control, moves Mother and Father together back and forth across the room, firmly separated by the aikidoist's body but heading in the same direction, ending with them facing the children.

JOANNE: The kids are supposed to be with him from Tuesday to Thursday and Saturday and Sunday, but he rarely has taken them on the weekends.

LLOYD: I've had practices and games out of town on the weekends for the past month or two. You know, she never wanted me to be a coach, since we got married.

MEDIATOR: Well, how much in advance do you know your practice schedule?

LLOYD: That's the problem. It all depends on whether we win or lose, how many practice sessions we need. Sometimes we need to spend the whole weekend. She needs to be flexible!

JOANNE: I've got my own life too, you know. I can't sit around and wait for you to tell me Friday night that you can't take the kids Saturday. I've got plans too, you know!

MEDIATOR: Let's see if I can understand how your schedule works. Does it change in different seasons?

Commentary. Joanne presents a problem, and Lloyd fires back an accusation. Before letting Joanne respond, the mediator *deflects* the accusation and begins to clarify details of the pragmatic issue at hand. The sequence repeats a second time.

Aikido Image. Mother stops, positions, and begins to attack Father. Father prepares to attack back. Aikidoist preempts both strikes by deflecting and moving both parents side by side once again, disabling their attacks. They once again go through the same sequence.

LLOYD: Yeah. During football season, and for two or three months before, my schedule is booked up pretty tight. Then other parts of the year I am freer, except for the summer, when I get a chance to go to Canada for two months—my team won an opportunity to practice with the "big boys," pro ballplayers. . . . I was the only coach on the West Coast given that honor.

MEDIATOR: That must be exciting for you. So your kids can't be with you during that time or during weekend practices.

Commentary. Lloyd takes the opportunity to boost his self-esteem by bragging about his honors. The mediator *reflectively listens,* to keep his cooperation, and then expands to clarify the implications for the children's time with him.

Aikido Image. Father prepares to defend himself. Aikidoist circles him and supports him, then flings him off across the room to test what he will do next.

LLOYD: Well, they could be. They could sit around and play.

JOANNE: No, they can't. They tell me they want to be with me.

MEDIATOR: Lloyd, since kids like to spend time with each parent when that parent is directly available to them, I wonder if you could work out a plan that allows the kids to be with you when you are available *exclusively* for them—that way you could give them your hundred percent!

Commentary. Joanne makes a potentially inflammatory comment. The mediator *deflects* the comment with general information about children's needs, framed in language that is directly within Lloyd's "athletic" conceptual framework.

Aikido Image. Father comes back at the aikidoist. Mother attacks Father along the way. Aikidoist deflects Mother's attack and turns Father around heading back in the direction of the children.

LLOYD: I can't say exactly when that would be—during the middle of the week I'm fairly free, but on the weekends I'm very busy with my team. My players need me. Joanne just has to be flexible.

MEDIATOR: So the Tuesday-through-Thursday times have worked out OK? *(Both parents agree.)*

JOANNE: The kids enjoy their time with him, but they hate it when he disappoints them.

LLOYD: I want my weekend times with the kids.

MEDIATOR: It sounds like it's been hard for you to free up time from your responsibilities to your team to give your all to the kids on the weekends. I wonder if you could come up with a strategy for being available at least some regular time on the weekends, when the kids would know that you will come through for them for sure.

Commentary. The mediator explicitly establishes the acceptability by both parents of the Tuesday-through-Thursday arrangement. The mediator makes a mental note of the fact that while Lloyd's intake information request was for Mondays through Wednesdays, he did not even mention this during the session. This can be taken as evidence that Lloyd is going to be flexible in negotiating about the schedule and that he is not likely to take a hard line. Joanne offers support to Lloyd's importance to the children, but with a tagged-on criticism. Lloyd defensively gets grabby. The mediator *reframes* Lloyd's behavior of disappointing the children as "difficulty in breaking away from his important responsibilities." The mediator, using a version of the strategy of *converting accusations to requests,* then challenges Lloyd to "come up with a strategy" for resolving the problem. Note the particular language used, designed for a coach. Note also that the mediator has seemed very supportive of Lloyd to this point. The intent is to elicit his cooperation as much as possible until such time as the issues get resolved or Joanne challenges the mediator. If challenged, the mediator would lean more heavily on Lloyd soon thereafter, shifting the balance back to neutral.

Aikido Image. Father looks back and wrestles to get free. Aikidoist circles Father back toward the children. Mother moves in to push Father off balance. Father reaches out to strike Mother, but the aikidoist deflects his move and redirects him back toward the children.

LLOYD: I could set aside time either Sunday or Saturday, but I really need to spend at least one and a half days with the team, at least until the season is over.

JOANNE: I want the kids to go to church with me on Sundays.

MEDIATOR: *(to Lloyd)* Would Saturdays work out?

LLOYD: That would be fine.

Commentary. Lloyd finally offers a clear statement of his possibilities. Joanne throws in a slight wrinkle, but Lloyd accedes.

Aikido Image. Both parents are facing the children but trying to grapple with each other while side by side. Aikidoist deflects each attempt.

Phase Four: Negotiating to Resolution and Drafting the Agreement

This phase emerges when the impasse in the basic schedule has been resolved and the road is fairly clear for working out the final details of the agreement. This does not presume that earlier issues will not crop up, merely that the preparatory work completed so far has broken up the big boulder into smaller, more manageable rocks that can now be rearranged until they fit into the desired design.

MEDIATOR: *(to Lloyd)* So we could say that the kids would be with you on Saturdays and also on Tuesday and Wednesday and you would return them on Thursday? From what times to what times?

JOANNE: We've been doing it from Tuesday at 9 A.M. to Thursday at 9 A.M. And Saturday can be 9 A.M. to 7 P.M.

MEDIATOR: *(to Lloyd)* Will that work for you?

LLOYD: Yeah, but I'd like to have them on Sundays sometimes.

MEDIATOR: Well, how would you work it out so that you let Joanne know enough in advance so as not to spoil *her* plans?

Commentary. The mediator consciously attempts to regain balance between the couple by supporting Joanne's needs. This is to compensate for the previous negotiation in which the mediator appeared to attend more to Lloyd's needs. Maintaining balance throughout the negotiations is crucial for success.

Aikido Image. Father begins a move to strike Mother. Aikidoist blocks Father's attack, moves Mother out of the way, and then moves him back next to Mother.

LLOYD: I would just tell my team what day I'm taking off.

JOANNE: If I get at least two weeks' notice, that would be OK, if it's just once in a while.

LLOYD: It will be. Most of my practices are on Sundays.

MEDIATOR: *(to Joanne)* Am I right in assuming that Lloyd has your phone number?

JOANNE: He has it.

MEDIATOR: OK, then, so I can write it up that you'll give Joanne two weeks' notice if you will be available to be with the children on a Sunday.

LLOYD: Fine.

MEDIATOR: Now, what about the transfers on the weekend? I assume the kids are not in day care on the weekends.

Commentary. It is important for the mediator to anticipate any loose ends that might later become problematic for the couple. Sometimes parents overlook an obvious logistical problem that can kill the agreement at a later time. This anticipatory action of the mediator must, of course, be balanced with restraint from opening up potential cans of worms that best be left unopened.

Aikido Image. Aikidoist maintains each parent's position to be side by side, facing the children, while checking for tensions in their respective energy fields, which would indicate more aggressive intentions toward each other.

JOANNE: I'll pick them up from his house and return them to his house.

MEDIATOR: *(to Lloyd)* Will that work for you?

LLOYD: Fine, but I thought you didn't want to see me.

MEDIATOR: I wonder if there is a third party whom you can both agree to that you can use for the transfer on weekends.

Commentary. Lloyd again reacts defensively and attacks Joanne. The mediator *deflects* the comment. Then, because of the potential volatility of *any* future contact between the parents, the mediator *offers suggestions* in attempts to expand the possible options for transfers to one that would be safer.

Aikido Image. Mother begins to move assertively. Father defensively prepares to attack her, and the aikidoist once again deflects the attack and, with leading control, redirects them both toward the children.

JOANNE: We already tried to find someone neutral, and we couldn't agree. It will work if he stays in the house and I stay in my car. I just don't want him coming out to my car.

LLOYD: Have I ever done that? Huh?

JOANNE: He hasn't yet. I think it will work out.

MEDIATOR: How about trying that out, and if a scene starts to develop, you can return to mediation and we'll figure something else out. It's really important for your children that they not be subjected to any more scenes. Do you both understand how important that is? *(Both say they do.)* You two are still pretty fresh into your separation. If all goes well, the transfers should get better and better. It takes some time to cool out all the anger and mistrust. Be patient with yourselves, and just follow the agreement the very best you can. That way you will rebuild trust in each other and not have to continue such rigid rules in sharing the kids. But for now, it is important to set up these rules, to protect and guide your children and yourselves.

Commentary. The mediator, by *giving information and hope,* tries to build in levels of protection against difficult and/or violent encounters between the parents, given their history of aggressive behavior.

Aikido Image. As the final grappling takes place, the aikidoist gives reassuring support to each parent by keeping them side by side but a comfortable distance apart.

MEDIATOR: OK, so weekend transfers will work out. Now about the summer, what will happen?

LLOYD: I'll be gone to Canada. They'll have to stay with her.

JOANNE: That's fine with me.

MEDIATOR: What contact will you have with the children while you are in Canada?

LLOYD: I plan to call them every few weeks.

MEDIATOR: Because of their young ages, it might be better to consider talking with them more frequently, since their sense of time is still limited. They might feel rejected if they don't have more frequent contact with you. Even a five-minute phone call can go a long way toward maintaining the relationship during that long stretch of time.

Commentary. As an advocate for the children, the mediator *offers suggestions* about children's needs even though the parents did not ask for it.

Aikido Image. Father tries to pull away from facing the children. Mother remains still. Aikidoist circles Father around, with a supporting hold, and firmly leads him back toward the children.

JOANNE: I agree. They need to hear from you, but I don't want to talk with you. You can call the kids whenever you want, as long as you don't harass me.

LLOYD: Fine. I'll call them every couple of days.

MEDIATOR: *(to Joanne)* What time of the day is best for him to call?

JOANNE: Mornings are best, so their bedtimes are not disrupted.

LLOYD: OK. That's fine.

MEDIATOR: Now what about holidays?

LLOYD: We agreed when she left that they'd be with me half of Thanksgiving weekend and Christmas Eve or Christmas Day and part of Easter week, every other year.

JOANNE: I think we can work that out. *(The parents clarify the details.)*

Commentary. The parents nicely continue working out each issue. The mediator needs to intervene only to expand the discussion in anticipation of potential problem areas.

Aikido Image. Aikidoist continues to monitor the tension level between them as they look at their children.

MEDIATOR: Are there any other clauses that either of you wants included in this agreement?

LLOYD: Yeah. I don't want the kids being baby-sat by Agnes Johnson. She's too old to be driving and she's not safe.

JOANNE: I don't have any other child care person to use.

LLOYD: Well, she's not safe with my children!

MEDIATOR: *(to Joanne)* What are your thoughts about Agnes?

JOANNE: He's right, she *is* old and isn't too good a driver. I also worry about the kids' being with her. She's very nice and all, but doesn't have good judgment with the car.

LLOYD: Don't get me wrong. I like her too as a person, and she's always been there for the kids, but I don't want her driving the kids.

JOANNE: Well, how about if I talk to her about not driving the kids— just keeping them at her house?

LLOYD: But she likes to take them shopping with her, and the kids enjoy it.

JOANNE: I'll agree to talk with her about that and ask her not to take them anymore.

Commentary. The mediator initiates a *diversion problem-solving* strategy, by inquiring about Agnes. The couple nicely engage in the discussion and temporarily pull together in their ambivalence about the woman. This serves to generate more cooperation in completing the agreement.

Aikido Image. Mother and Father do one last grapple, and the aikidoist takes each on some spins that has them circling around one another but never colliding. Then the aikidoist maneuvers them back to a side-by-side position, facing their children.

MEDIATOR: Fine, I'll include that in the agreement. Anything else? *(Parents shake their heads no.)* Next year, when Danny begins school, you may need to modify the agreement. So come back to mediation before that time if you need to, OK? *(Parents agree.)* OK, I'll write up the agreement and you both can sign it.

Written Agreement Reached

1. Both parents agree to share joint legal custody of their children, LeeAnn and Danny.
2. The children will share time with their parents according to the following schedule:
   a. They will be in Father's care from Tuesday at 9:00 A.M. until Thursday at 9:00 A.M., when he returns them to day care.
   b. They will also be with Father on Saturdays, from 9:00 A.M., when Mother will bring them to Father's house, until 7:00 P.M., when Mother will pick them up from Father's house.
   c. They can also be with Father on occasional Sundays, if Father gives Mother at least two weeks' advance notice.
   d. They will be with Mother during all other unspecified times.
   e. During the holiday times, the children will share their time between their parents as follows: In odd-numbered years, they will be with Father on the Thursday and Friday of the Thanksgiving holiday and with Mother on the Saturday and Sunday. In even-numbered years, this pattern will reverse. They will share

    Christmas Eve, Christmas Day, and Easter vacation and Easter Day between the parents, with the details to be determined by mutual consent of the parents.

3. During weekend transfers, Mother agrees to remain in her car and Father agrees to remain in his house, while the children walk from the driveway to the front door. If this arrangement should lead to overt conflict between the parents, both parents agree to either hire a third neutral party to be the transfer person or to return to mediation to develop another plan.

4. During summers that Father is out of the area, the children will be with Mother. During these summers, both parents agree to the importance of maintaining the children's contact with Father by phone. Father agrees to call in the morning at least every three or four days, and Mother agrees to support and encourage the children to talk with him.

5. Both parents agree that the children will not be driven by Agnes Johnson in any motor vehicle.

6. Both parents agree to return to mediation before school begins for Danny, if they need assistance in modifying the parenting plan.

7. In the event of any future dispute regarding the children that the parents are unable to resolve between themselves, both parents agree to return to mediation before seeking legal action, at the request of either parent, and costs will be shared equally.

Resolving the Case in Four to Six Hours

Although the parents in this case very probably could not have reached agreement in just one hour, they were able to do so in two and a half hours. If more time were available, the mediator could have explored a number of other possible underlying issues—for example, the degree to which Joanne's intense involvement with the church spills over in her dealings with the children in potentially harmful (extremist) ways, the alleged influence of the maternal grandfather on Joanne and the children, the influence on the children of Lloyd's past violent and aggressive behavior toward Joanne, the concerns expressed in the letter from LeeAnn's therapist, how the children are faring with the separation and pending divorce, and the influence that Joanne's alleged drinking problem may have had on the children. (It is significant that after the initial intake allegation, Lloyd never brought this issue up again. While the mediator must always remain vigilant about such issues, he can usually treat early charges as unsubstantiated allegations unless they are brought up in the sessions.)

Several considerations arise here. If one's goal in mediation is to cover enough issue bases to reach a reasonable agreement, the issues dealt with in this case were sufficient to explore, since neither parent appeared to pursue them beyond making the initial allegations. However, if one's goal in mediation is to develop postdivorce family structures and roles that may better sustain the family's ability to traverse the struggles of the divorce process, these issues could be selectively and carefully uncovered and worked with if one has sufficient time in which to work. This decision is partly reflecting the mediator's values, partly the clients' desires, and partly the time available to the mediator.

Special Issues in This Case

Because of the intensity of Lloyd's attachment to Joanne, it was critical to take the time to get him to the point where, somehow or other, he could begin to accept the reality of Joanne's divorce decision. The mediator spent about one and a half hours dealing, largely in a "therapeutic mode," with just this issue. The intervention strategies with the couple were aimed at the simple goal of moving Lloyd along in the emotional process of divorce. While time in and of itself would likely have accomplished this same goal, carefully crafted strategic interventions can facilitate the job more quickly. It will take much more time before Lloyd truly accepts the divorce (if ever), but it became clear in mediation that once he was unstuck on the manifest level, negotiations could proceed.

Because of the intensity of the divorce decision issue, meaningful talk about how the children were doing was probably premature. The goal at this early phase of a hostile divorce impasse can only realistically be to reduce conflict and get the beginnings of a coparenting structure in place. Later, more mediation work can be done to refine and fine-tune the parenting plan.

PART FIVE

CHALLENGES AND PROFESSIONAL ISSUES

14

SPECIAL CIRCUMSTANCES AFFECTING MEDIATION

IN THE NORMAL COURSE of mediation work, a number of issues present special challenges to both the mediator and the local courts of jurisdiction. Interestingly, since the original edition of this book was published, some issues that were of concern to mediators then have diminished in their impact, while others have increased over the intervening years. In this chapter, we will discuss some of the significant contemporary issues mediators face.

When a Parent Moves Away

One of the issues that has increased in significance for practicing mediators over the past fifteen years is dealing with what have been termed "move-away" cases. Due to such factors as corporate employees' increased mobility resulting from mergers and relocations and the increase in remarriages and multiple divorces and their associated geographical moves, the problem of move-aways, both during and after divorce, has been challenging mediators and the courts.

Mediating custody disputes when one parent is moving a long distance away from the other brings up a number of special considerations. The prospect of a significant geographical separation typically represents a major threat to all family members. As Ricci (1980, p. 206) noted:

> There are two bottom lines to big geographic separations. First, distance feels final, and gives tangible proof that the parents are separated. If one member of the family has harbored, however unconsciously, a sense that the old family feeling or the old marriage was not finished, long distance will bring that hope painfully to the

surface. Second, the physical separation hurts. Many miles means no way to hug, to brush back a forelock of hair, to drop in on football practice, or to watch a first book report being written. The parent separated from the child feels this pain, and so does the child.

The threat represented by a major move increases the probability of an escalation of the parents' and the children's strategies in the custody dynamics, which contribute to the complexity of the presenting dispute. The mediator must assess the motives and reactions of the family members extra carefully, since the stakes are higher for all concerned. As part of this assessment, the mediator needs to know the intentions and circumstances of the parent's decision to move.

In years past, the criteria that courts considered legitimate for a parent to move out of the area with the children seemed simpler. For example, MacGowan in 1981 pointed out that moving for better employment was "unimpeachable" and probably would not sway a court to impose sanctions. However, in recent years, a number of states have grappled more intensely with this issue, attempting to clarify and sophisticate the criteria for legitimate move-aways.

A parent may wish to move away following a divorce for reasons of economic opportunity, remarriage, health, emotional and financial support, or to escape domestic violence or continuing conflict within the postdissolution family. One parent may oppose a move by the other because it interferes with existing patterns of parenting, including the elimination of midweek visits, a decrease in the frequency of visits, and an inability to participate in the child's school and extracurricular activities (Nachlis, 1996).

State courts have long grappled with developing clear legal guidelines that would assist judges with the difficult decisions in move-away cases. Generally, courts have not looked favorably upon relocation of a parent because it deprived the noncustodial parent of contact with the child (Schwartz & Kaslow, 1997). In New York and California, a three-tiered burden of proof had developed, with the threshold question based upon statutory language (grounded in the early research by Wallerstein and Kelly, 1980) that presumed that *frequent and continuing contact* between the child and both parents was in the best interests of a child. First, the nonmoving parent was required to show that the move would be disruptive to the frequency and continuity of the relationship between that parent and the child. Then the burden of proof switched to the moving parent to demonstrate that the move was "necessary" (in New York, an even stricter burden of proof was used, requiring the existence of "exceptional circumstances" that justified the move). If the moving parent met this second test, of necessity (or exceptional circumstances), the court would finally look at "the best interests of the child." In 1996, within three weeks of one another, precedent-setting test cases were heard by trial courts, appellate courts, and supreme courts, shifting the standards used for deciding these cases. In New York, two consolidated cases known as *Tropea* (1996 N.Y. Lexis 300) essentially eliminated the use of any presumptions and instead generated a pure "best interests" standing, which gave trial courts the freedom to weigh all appropriate factors on a case-by-case basis. In California, the *Burgess* case (*In re Marriage of Burgess*, 1996, 13 Cal.4th 25, 51 Cal. Rptr. 2d 444), set a new presumption for move-away decisions: that *stability and continuity in the primary custodial relationship* are in the best interests of the child. (This change in presumption was significantly influenced by the testimony of Wallerstein herself.)* Moreover, *Burgess* set up three rules that are applicable in all move-away cases: (1) the parent with sole physical custody can move without being required to show necessity for the move, (2) frequency and continuity of contact is only one factor to be considered, and (3) the wishes of the children should be considered (Nachlis, 1996).

As the implications of these rulings are being sorted out in further court decisions, one is struck with how daunting a task it is to attempt to set a consistent legal standard that can effectively and fairly cover the wide range of variables in move-away cases. It is important for the mediator to keep current on the shifts in thinking by the courts regarding issues as complex as move-aways and to be guided by the most current precedents, knowing full well that the standards are likely to change again.

---

*In the *amicus* briefs submitted by Tanke and Willemsen, attorneys for *amica curiae* Judith Wallerstein, the argument was made that Wallerstein's own longitudinal research and her review of the research literature revealed that the long-term outcome of children of divorce was essentially related to the *stability and continuity of the custodial relationship* and that the *frequency and continuity of contact with the noncustodial parent* is *not* a significant factor in the children's psychological development (she also specifically cites Furstenberg and Cherlin, 1991). Interestingly, this position contrasts sharply with her views in her 1980 book with Joan Kelly, *Surviving the Breakup*, views that were seminal in the development of California's joint custody statute. Moreover, Nachlis (1996) notes that no opposing viewpoint to Wallerstein's was presented in the *Burgess* hearing before the California Supreme Court.

Most jurisdictions do expect a parent who proposes a relocation to have motives that benefit the child in some clear way. If the parent cannot give a valid reason for moving or the reason is to deprive the other parent of contact with the child, the mediator should alert the parent to the legal and psychological consequences of such a move. The legal consequences, of course, will vary, depending on the particular jurisdiction.

If the proposed move is being made to relieve the child from continuing exposure to unrelenting high conflict between the parents, the mediator should help the parents consider the positives of this option for the children and for the parents (see Johnston, Kline, & Tschann, 1989; Weissman, 1994).

The psychological consequences of a prolonged separation from a parent (as described in Chapter Two) should be discussed with both parents. Particularly if the move is motivated by bitter feelings, the child could suffer greatly. Without the opportunity to communicate and maintain regular contact with the absent parent, the child can easily misinterpret a distant move as sure evidence of rejection and abandonment. The parent who is moving needs to be fully informed of these consequences. Not uncommonly, after learning about these factors, the parent is persuaded to delay or even abandon the plans to move. Moreover, by presenting these consequences in the presence of both parents, the mediator can often dissuade a move for inappropriate reasons by indirectly providing the remaining spouse with leverage for retaining a continuing relationship with his or her children.

If the move is being made for valid reasons, the mediator must then consider the ages, preferences, and needs of the children involved, the nature of the parent-to-parent and parent-to-child communication that will be possible over a distance, and the financial circumstances for supporting such communication, be it by phone calls, faxes, letters, e-mail, or travel.

With school-age and older children, time sharing must depend first of all on a plan for spending the school year at one home. Periods of more extended contact with the other parent can be arranged in the summer and during Christmas and Easter vacations. Individual differences among children should be assessed so as to maximize good matches of temperament, interests, available resources, and other factors (see Chapter Two). With these factors in mind, the parents can proceed to make a plan to last a year or two, with periodic reevaluations built in to protect the needs of the children.

With infants and preschool children, the decisions become much more difficult. Questions arise: At what age is it advisable for a very young child to stay with a noncustodial parent for the whole summer? What are the consequences for a ten-month-old infant of being away from the primary caretaking parent for four weeks? How often should a custodial parent call a three-year-old child when the child is with the visiting parent for six weeks, given that this is the only contact during the year with the visiting parent? Many of these questions are the very ones asked of mental health professionals when called to testify in court. The answers are complex because they involve a wide range of variables, beginning and ending with the support and explanations offered the child by the parents.

A central task for the mediator in dealing with issues regarding very young children is to emphasize the importance of supportive communications between the parents and to try to optimize such communication. Moreover, it could be argued that if two parents are genuinely respectful and supportive of each other's importance to their child, they can make any sharing arrangement work well for their child. And to the degree that this ideal is less attainable, the mediator must help build structures that will safeguard the child's emotional and psychological well-being.

Galper-Cohen (1989), Ricci (1980), and Twilley (1994) all provide useful guidelines to facilitate coparenting when one parent moves far away.

Stepparents

Inclusion of extended family members in the mediation process offers additional possibilities for resolving deadlocks and for maintaining agreements that are reached. However, the inclusion of extended family members entails certain risks, and both risks and benefits must be duly considered before deciding whether and how to include them in the mediation process.

Stepparents frequently play a significant role in the lives of children and parents of divorce. If the circumstances of the remarriage are positive—as is most often the case when the remarriage is not a contributing factor to the divorce and occurs a considerable length of time after the divorce—the stepparent can become a helpful ally to the new mate. By offering a more neutral perspective and a leveling of the spouse's emotions, the stepparent can facilitate the negotiation process. The stepparent can also help the children by listening dispassionately to them and supporting them through the stresses of divorce. The stepparent can also provide alternative and sometimes more constructive parenting practices to supplement those of the children's parents. Finally, the stepparent may become a facilitative ally of the ex-spouse—for example, a stepmother can offer the children's mother help in dealing more effectively with the father.

Generally, stepparents who play a positive role in the lives of the disputants are best brought into the mediation process at the point of an impasse where other mediator strategies have proved unsuccessful. Inviting them in as consultants to the mediator can provide fresh perspectives that can be useful in reaching an agreement. Moreover, including stepparents in the mediation process may facilitate the maintenance of the agreement over time.

Several factors, however, suggest that a mediator should be cautious about involving stepparents in the mediation process. First of all, a spouse may seek a divorce specifically to remarry. In such circumstances, the new wife, for example, may be regarded by the former wife as the "other woman" who broke up the marriage and by the children as the "wicked stepmother" who took Daddy away from both Mommy and them—effectively scapegoating her as a person to avoid. If such scapegoating has occurred, including the new wife in the mediation process may serve only to escalate the antagonism between the parents.

Second, a stepparent may be the force behind a petition for modification of custody. If, for example, a father petitions for sole custody as a strategy for appeasing his new spouse, the former wife usually suspects this and becomes hostile to the stepparent. Bringing them together in the mediation room would then be counterproductive.

Third, if only one parent is remarried, including that parent's new mate in a session with both parents may unbalance the negotiation process so that the single parent feels outnumbered and intimidated. That will increase resistance and decrease the probability for reaching a mediated settlement.

Grandparents

Similarly, grandparents who have been significantly involved in the lives of the children can offer a mature perspective to the couple and serve as family consultants to the mediator. In this role, they express an historic tradition in families, offering experienced advice on how to conduct one's life, how to raise children, and how to relate as marital partners. If this advisory and mentoring role is respected by the parents, involving the grandparents in the mediation process can be very facilitative. Every state now has legislation affecting grandparent visitation (Elrod, 1993); it gives grandparents the right to petition the courts for visitation privileges that can be enforced over the parents' objections (Thompson, Scalora, Limber, & Castrianno, 1991). However, the actual leverage that they have in asserting their visitation is guided, within the courts' view, by the best interests of the child. So grandparents who are seen as lovingly connected to the children have stronger standing in gaining visitation, when all the factors under the best interests standard are considered. Kruk (1994) advises mediators to actively inquire into the involvement of grandparents in the children's lives. If the relationship has been positive, the mediator should consider inviting the grandparents into the mediation session or should at least encourage the parents to negotiate the role the grandparents might have in the parenting plan that is being developed.

Unfortunately, grandparents can also be less than ideal in their contributions to resolving custody disputes. If they have taken sides with their respective children, they simply add to the adversarial atmosphere. They are each then viewed by the opposing parent as a critical enemy. If grandparents have become overinvolved in the custody battle, the mediator needs to think twice before inviting them into the mediation process.

Parental Sexual Conduct

In the earlier era of fault divorce, the sexual conduct of parents heavily influenced awards of child custody. Trial courts have generally frowned on sexual behaviors or relationships that did not conform strictly to traditional norms. However, owing to the legitimation of no-fault divorce and the increased use of the best interests standard for custody decisions, the other parent more often bears the burden of showing that such parental behavior per se is detrimental to the children (Hyde, 1991). This approach has been followed by a number of American appellate courts (see Dooley, 1990), as well as Canadian courts (see Fowler, 1995). This is not to dismiss the frequently acknowledged prejudices and personal biases that still guide judges in custody decisions.

Nevertheless, the mediator not infrequently encounters the issue of sexual conduct in the form of allegations by one parent against the other. Several specific concerns are regularly expressed.

It is not uncommon for one spouse to refuse or resist letting a child visit overnight with the other spouse if that spouse is cohabiting with a lover while unmarried. Such concern can spring from a religious conviction that this kind of relationship is sinful, a fear that the relationship is psychologically harmful to children, or any of a number of strategic motives, such as reuniting, emotionally disengaging, power asserting, and retaliation.

If the concern stems from a religious conviction, the other spouse will usually respect it. The mediator must respect such convictions in all cases or forfeit neutrality. One cannot persuade a person, with logic, to give up or suspend a deep religious belief.

If the concern is about psychological harm to the children, the mediator can probe the specific worries and present pertinent information about how children experience a parent who has a new mate. This information should include the fact that children at different ages will experience the very same objective event in radically different ways and that because of the wide range of individual differences among children, different children of the same age will also have very different experiences of the same event. Moreover, the significance to a child of a circumstance such as parental cohabitation is largely a function of what it does and does not mean for the child. For example, a young child may interpret his father's sleeping with a woman to mean that his mother is no longer his mother and therefore does not love him any longer. Or a child may interpret her mother's sleeping with a man to mean that the mother will not care for her any longer. If both of the child's parents were to explain clearly and periodically that cohabitation does not mean that the child is unloved, will no longer be provided for, or will lose one of her parents, the child could well accept cohabitation as a reality of life.

If the other parent's allegations about cohabitation are strategically motivated, they will tend to diminish in importance as other issues are dealt with. By not drawing too much attention to such concerns during the mediation process, the mediator can discern the sincerity of the parent's concern. If the concern holds up consistently through the first phases of the mediation process, it should be faced squarely and dealt with in terms of its motivation.

As one immediate result of a marital separation, a spouse may begin to express his or her sexuality in a flagrant and open manner. Partly out of a need to "burst free" of the restraints of the marital bond and partly out of a need to prove that one is still sexually attractive, a parent may engage in openly affectionate and overtly sexual behavior with new partners in the presence of the children.

Typically, the other spouse finds out about such conduct from the children after they return home from spending time with the other parent. Children may report such behavior out of several motives, depending on their developmental stages. A preschool child may feel jealous of the intimate attention being given to the other person and worry about not getting enough attention and love for himself. An older child may simply feel embarrassed or confused about the nature of such intimacy. A young teenager may feel overly excited and stimulated at seeing overt displays of sexuality and may report the incident as "disgusting" or "gross" in an attempt to defend psychologically against her own sexual impulses. An older teenager may view such behavior with contempt because it represents a blatant betrayal by one parent of the other parent. Finally, children may express concern about such behavior out of such strategic motives as reuniting the parents, detonating tension, and proving loyalty.

In planning the best way to handle such concerns, the mediator must carefully assess the children's concerns developmentally, as well as the accusing parent's motives. As with the cohabitation issue, a parent may make allegations of sexual indiscretion out of a variety of strategic motives as well as out of genuine concern for the welfare of the children. Solid developmental information given to both parents about children's interpretations of adult sexuality should alleviate unwarranted worries or put them into perspective and should inform the sexually expressive parent about the benefits to children of showing discretion and restraint. Agreements to refrain from overt sexual expression in the presence of children can be helpful in minimizing such concerns in the future. Unfortunately, however, the accused parent will frequently deny such allegations, which forces the other parent to choose between trusting the parent and trusting the children. The mediator can also sometimes help clarify incidents and interpretations that have been distorted so that the negotiations can move on to other, less volatile areas.

Parental Homosexuality

Among the sexual issues that may arise in custody disputes, homosexuality has historically been the most unacceptable of parental sexual conduct. The 1974 deletion of homosexuality from the American Psychiatric Association's categories of mental disorders and its acceptance of homosexuality as a valid sexual orientation was a significant beginning toward changing societal views. Increasing numbers of gay and lesbian parents have been awarded custody of the children from their prior marriages. However, while society's tolerance for homosexuality has definitely increased, there is evidence that courts still look with disfavor upon gay or lesbian parents (Bryant, 1992; McIntyre, 1994). According to Fowler (1995), rationales that are typically used by courts to deny custody to homosexual parents focus on five specific areas: (1) psychosocial development; (2) societal stigmatization, harassment, and intolerance; (3) fear of exposure to the AIDS virus; (4) exploitation or molestation by the homosexual parent; and (5) inability of homosexuals to be good parents.

In dealing with the issue of homosexuality, the mediator must be able to inform both parents of the factors that are truly relevant to child rearing. The myths and generalizations have to be dismantled, and the particular circumstances must be fully explored so that the parents can make informed and intelligent decisions about child sharing. Moreover, the mediator should be informed about the current attitudes of the local courts toward parenting by homosexuals in case she needs to leverage the negotiations so that they stay within the parameters of likely court decisions.

The mediator should be aware of the following information to balance parents' (and courts') typical concerns regarding the influences of gay and lesbian parents on children. The information is organized around Fowler's five categories of concern.

1. *Psychosocial development.* A central concern for the heterosexual parent is the way in which the children's psychosexual and social development will be influenced by the homosexual parent. While there is no consensus among the experts about the causes of homosexuality, compelling evidence suggests that genetic, biological, and hormonal factors play significant roles in its etiology (Maccoby & Jacklin, 1974), and as with so many other human conditions, it is likely that homosexuality does not have a single origin but results from a variety of contributing factors.

It has now been well documented that the children of homosexual parents are no more likely to become homosexual than are the children of heterosexual parents (see Golombok, Spencer, & Rutter, 1983; Hoeffer, 1981; Suseoff, 1985). Moreover, as the renowned child expert Benjamin Spock noted, almost all homosexuals are the children of conventionally heterosexual parents. It is also the case that children learn sex-role behavior from people of the opposite sex as well as from people of the same sex and that people other than parents, such as teachers, friends, and relatives, can contribute significantly to a child's sex-role development. Moreover, as Greene, Mandel, Hotvedt, Gray, and Smith (1986, p. 182) pointed out, "children spend more time watching television than watching their parents." Finally, Gonsiorek and Weinrich (1991) noted a New Jersey judge who, when hearing an argument about the purported risks to a child raised by gay parents, said that the only effect he could predict would be that the child would grow up to be a more tolerant individual.

2. *Societal stigmatization, harassment, and intolerance.* Another typical concern of the heterosexual parent is that the child living with the homosexual parent is likely to have to face peer ridicule and harassment. However, it is a fact that all children experience harassment in some form at some point in their childhood, whether it is for being too short, too thin, too uncoordinated, too intelligent, or too poor or for having a black stepparent, an Asian mother, a Jewish father, or any of a myriad of other differences. Children who have a gay or lesbian parent do not appear to feel any more stigmatized by it than they do by any number of other childhood differences.

3. *Fear of exposure to the AIDS virus.* The parental concern that a child living with a gay parent may have greater exposure to human immunodeficiency virus (HIV) can be dealt with by citing the well-known medical claim that there is no evidence that HIV is transmitted through casual contact. However, this is not always a sufficient explanation. For example, the intensity of this type of concern was brought to light in a recent mediation case in which a gay father wanted his eleven-year-old daughter to live with him. The mother protested vehemently. When asked why, she told how her daughter, who had reached puberty, needed to shave her legs while at her father's apartment. She had left her razor at her mother's house, so she used the father's gay partner's razor that was on the sink in her father's bathroom. She complained to her mother that it was "yucky" because it had some blood on the edge, but she used it anyway. Upon hearing this, the mother became extremely distraught, worrying about the possibility that her daughter had been infected with HIV-tainted blood.

Despite the facts that the current medical literature documents the statistical improbability of contracting HIV without intimate contact and that it is no longer primarily a disease of gay men (in whom new cases have dropped dramatically) but is increasingly a disease of the heterosexual population (in which the number of cases is growing rapidly), the mediator needs to listen carefully and sensitively to the parent's concerns. Being knowledgeable about the areas or circumstances in which HIV transmission has a higher probability for children can help the mediator educate the parents about protecting their children from such risks. Once such discussions have taken place, negotiations about shared parenting can often continue fruitfully.

4. *Exploitation or molestation by the homosexual parent.* There is a myth that gay and lesbian parents are more likely to molest children than are heterosexual parents. Courts have denied custody to gay parents in fear that they will molest or sexually exploit the children (Gonsiorek & Weinrich, 1991). However, social science research has concluded that sexual exploitation of children by gay parents is virtually nonexistent (Miller, 1979; McIntyre, 1994) and that "sexual molestation is essentially a heterosexual male act" (Falk, 1989, p. 944). Reassuring a parent of these data can usually move the mediation negotiations along.

5. *Inability of homosexuals to be good parents.* In general, the homosexuality of a parent can be a relatively insignificant factor if he or she is a loving, responsible person who shows consistency, stability, and other qualities of good parenting on which all children thrive. However, if the homosexual parent shows poor parenting characteristics, parenting

effectiveness is bound to decrease, and the best interests of the children may be compromised, not because of the homosexuality per se but because of other factors in the overall conduct of that parent. For example, if the parent is indiscreet about his or her sexual life or expresses generalized hostility to the opposite sex in a way that is insensitive to the needs and feelings of the children, this could adversely affect their well-being. The mediator should deal with such difficulties in much the same way that he or she deals with sexual indiscretions on the part of heterosexual parents. The parent should also be alerted to the effects on the development of children's self-esteem when they are exposed to categorical hostility toward all members of one sex or the other.

If the parent is effective and sensitive and remains supportive and respectful of the other parent's importance to the child, homosexuality per se need not be an issue. However, the mediator must be very careful to remain objective in assessing the implications for the children of these circumstances. Because of the typically loaded nature of these situations, it is all too easy for the mediator to succumb to personal prejudice rather than stick with real child-related concerns. Keeping abreast of developmental research in this area can facilitate the mediator's effectiveness.

Substance Abuse

Allegations of substance abuse made by one spouse about the other are increasingly encountered by mediators. In a California statewide study of 1,669 mediation sessions of family court, a sample that included 93 percent of all custody and visitation disputes mediated under the California mandatory mediation law during a two-week period, substance abuse allegations were raised in 36 percent of the sessions (Depner, Cannata, & Simon, 1992).

Such allegations typically include, in more serious forms, alcoholism, heroin addiction, and amphetamine, barbiturate, and cocaine addictions and, in less serious forms, chronic or recreational use of marijuana. Because of the personal and seemingly victimless nature of these abuses and because substance abusers characteristically deny their addiction (unless they are already in recovery), the accused spouse frequently denies the allegations. Or the spouse may not deny use of these substances but may deny that it presents any danger to the children. This is best characterized by the frequently heard assertion, "I'm in control, and I know exactly what I'm doing when I drink, so there's no need to be concerned."

When substance abuse is presented as an allegation in court custody disputes, it is a difficult issue to deal with. Producing admissible evidence of alcohol or drug abuse, other than hearsay, is often difficult. If substantial evidence exists, it must be demonstrated to the court that the drug or alcohol abuse renders the particular parent unable to care adequately for the child and results in detriment to the child's best interests. Because the only evidence that may be available is the child's report to the other parent, such allegations are often dropped as unsubstantiated, especially when the child refuses to talk to any professionals about it in an attempt to protect the substance-abusing parent.

Even when there is enough evidence to suggest judicial concern, a judge is often limited in ways to respond to it. The judge can order abstention from drugs or alcohol while the parent is in the presence of the child and can order random drug testing. This frequently results simply in the parent becoming more circumspect while continuing the substance abuse. If drug screening comes out negative, the judge has little legal recourse. If it comes out positive, the judge can order supervised visitation. If a pattern of positive screenings develops, a judge can then cut off all contact between the child and the parent. Schwartz and Kaslow (1997) point out that children often retain a strong attachment to the positive aspects of the parent and still want to be with the parent when that parent is not drinking or using. These authors urge mediators and other divorce professionals to be mindful of the fact that cutting off all contact with such a parent often makes the child feel that half his identity is lost, since children tend to view themselves as half Mom and half Dad. They further urge judges and mediators to develop a plan to reunite the parent and child, even if contact is cut off for some period of time.

The mediator faces the same kind of dilemma. Without any way to investigate the truth of allegations of substance abuse, the mediator is left to treat them like any other allegation, by remaining as neutral as possible. However, in a case involving substance abuse where the alleging parent persists and the children confirm the allegations, the mediator, as a child advocate, has a duty to confront the issue. Discussing the effects of parental substance abuse on children in general can be an informative and relatively nonthreatening way to make the point. The mediator can talk about the direct risks to children of being unwittingly exposed to dangerous circumstances at home (for example, fires, poisons, falls, other medical emergencies) while the parent is in an altered state of consciousness. And the presence of the substances themselves can also constitute a hazard, such as children eating crack cocaine or drinking straight tequila and ending up dead. Or he could talk about the serious risks that children face while in a car with a driver who is drunk or drugged. He can add to the impact of this perspective by telling a few graphic horror stories emphasizing the severe legal and personal consequences to parents who, unwittingly, injure or kill their children while under the influence of drugs or alcohol.

The mediator can then talk about the indirect effects on children of parental substance abuse. These include children feeling scared, insecure, and confused when around the parent. Over time, the children may well refuse to be with the parent at all. Moreover, their own self-esteem can be weakened by the lack of security they feel around a neglectful or unpredictable parent. Finally, there is the indirect effect of modeling negative behaviors for the children. When children repeatedly observe their parent engaging in some self-gratifying behavior, whether it be smoking, drinking, or pill taking, they may well be learning to use the same behaviors as they get older and confront their own life stresses.

As a last resort with a well-documented substance-abusing parent, the mediator can suggest the benefits of supervised visitation with that parent. The mediator can say, "You know, John, it seems like you really want to be with your children, but every time you are with them alone, their mother could claim that you were drunk or using. To protect yourself from these allegations, it might be a good idea to have someone else present to attest to your being sober. That way, she couldn't accuse you of things that you weren't doing. After a while, if you kept it up, she'd have no more basis for resisting your being alone with your children. Let's see if we can find someone that you both agree could be with you and your children. The best might be a professional monitor who could tell the court how well you were actually doing."

Because parents going through a divorce are under such great stress and because our society is so drug-oriented, it is difficult to be certain that a parent will refrain from substance abuse when with the children. However, the mediator who informatively, tactfully, vividly, and sincerely presents the real risks to children of exposure to this behavior and includes clauses of self-imposed restraints in the agreement has done all that is possible to protect the children. Enforcement of such restraint agreements is clearly out of the mediator's domain.

Allegations of Child Sexual Abuse

The California statewide study (Depner et al., 1992) revealed that child neglect was alleged by one parent against the other in 38 percent of the mediation sessions, child physical abuse in 18 percent, and child sexual abuse in 8 percent (although in Thoennes and Tjaden's 1990 national sample, this last figure was reported as 2 percent). Even though California law requires the reporting of child neglect and abuse, mediators generally contend that these allegations often do not meet the criteria for mandatory reporting and that when investigated by child protective services, the allegations are dismissed by overworked staff who write off the allegations as impossible to prove, not serious enough, or assumed false just because they are family law cases (Johnston, 1994).

Whereas the more widely made allegations of neglect and physical child abuse are often difficult enough to prove, child sexual abuse, even though it is alleged less frequently and is considerably more difficult to prove, has a very powerful impact on the mediation process, as well as on the lives of all the family members involved. During the 1980s, child sexual abuse allegations appeared to run rampant, perhaps fueled by media-sensationalized preschool molestation cases (such as the McMartin case, the Little Rascals case, or the Old Cutler case) and notorious child custody cases involving sexual abuse allegations (such as the Dr. Elizabeth Morgan case).

Accurate data on the actual incidence of such abuse are difficult to come by, as there is a wide range of conclusions and interpretations. The media and some of the professional literature have reported an alarming rise in such cases, most involving divorcing mothers who falsely accuse fathers (Thoennes & Tjaden, 1990). When the dust settled and more solid studies were completed, Ceci and Bruck's review of the research (1995) suggested that, notwithstanding conflicting data, more false allegations are made in the heat of custody and visitation disputes. Although only 4 to 8 percent of such allegations are thought to be deliberate and malicious false reports (see Everson & Boat, 1989; Faller, 1991; Jones & McGraw, 1987), Ceci and Bruck contend that the characterization "false allegations" should also apply to cases in which the allegations turned out to be *unfounded* (reports made in good faith but that turned out to be wrong), since they encompass children's reports that reflect the distorting influence of interviews by the parent and other adults. This would raise the incidence of false allegations to somewhere between one-fourth and one-third of all sexual abuse allegations. Ceci and Bruck's argument is based upon research on the suggestibility of children when interviewed by unskilled or biased interviewers and the questionable credibility of their testimony. Nonetheless, these authors note, "we also feel that it is important not to automatically discount reports that emerge during custodial battles or during divorce disputes. The data from the above studies indicate that as many as 50 percent of the reports are valid" (p. 33).

Reasons that have been suggested for actual increases in sexual abuse during the crisis of divorce include the fact that fathers are lonely and depressed and children need comfort, and they mutually obtain affection, which becomes sexualized; alcohol and drugs used to numb the emotional pain may create disinhibition of sexual impulses; inadequate sleeping conditions may force child and father to share one bed; and absence of clear guidelines for single fathers regarding appropriate touching. Reasons suggested for the mother making false allegations include retaliation and revenge for the father leaving them, disinformation in the interest of maintaining custody or of ridding the father from her life, hypersensitivity to sexual abuse because of her own history, and misinterpretation of normal child sexual behaviors or normal divorce-related child behaviors of withdrawal and anxiety.

Even when armed with these perspectives, the mediator is placed in a very delicate position of having to assess the veracity of these allegations while maintaining balance between the couple and protecting the interests of the child, all at the same time. If the mediator feels that there are enough questions raised that suggest reasonable suspicion of abuse, she should stop the session and inform the parents that the allegations will have to be reported to Child Protective Services. If the investigation concludes that there is insufficient evidence to prosecute, the mediation can proceed. Unfortunately, insufficient evidence does not mean that abuse did not in fact occur. This puts the mediator in the difficult position of having to act as if it did not occur while being careful to ensure that the child will be protected by the parenting plan the couple comes up with. The issue is even more difficult with very young children (the modal age group involved in such allegations), since there are no guaranteed ways to monitor future incidents, due to the unreliability of their reporting.

Strategic interventions in this situation include informing both parents of the ambiguity about the abuse, the inability of the legal system to give much satisfaction, and the resulting emotional risks to the child and to the alleged perpetrator when he is alone with the child in the future. Often the worried parent will request supervised visitation of the alleged perpetrator, even if no criminal charges were filed. If the requesting parent is insistent, the mediator can explain to that parent (in individual caucus, if appropriate) how the court would have a difficult time supporting such a request absent evidence showing that abuse took place. Or the mediator could explain to the alleged perpetrating parent the benefits to him of being supervised for a while (similar to the strategy used for substance abusers) so that the mother would not have further reason to make such allegations and could build up some trust in him.

It is also useful to give a lecturette on the consequences of sexual molestation on children's development: "I have no way of knowing whether or not anything happened to Rebecca. However, *if* she was molested, or is molested in the future, what we know would happen to her is the following: she will be at high risk for emotional problems and self-esteem problems; she will find it difficult to trust anyone in close relationships; she may someday turn with rage on the abusing parent and maybe even file a civil lawsuit against that parent for big money." The mediator can elaborate with whatever current data she may have available on the effects of sexual abuse on children. The intent is to appeal to the parents' rational self, insert some guilt, and hope for the best. Meanwhile, the mediator must continue to facilitate a parenting plan that has built-in protections for the child, just in case.

It is clear that regardless of whether the abuse actually occurred or not, everyone is affected by such allegations for a long time thereafter. If the abuse did not occur, a cloud of suspicion forever hangs over the head of the alleged perpetrator, who often will never be fully trusted again. Anxiety hangs over the head of the accuser, who may always worry whenever the child is with the other parent. And stress and confusion are increased for the child, who may have to endure multiple examinations, both physical and psychological, and feel the continuing anxiety of both her parents.

Domestic Violence

In an early study of children of divorce, Wallerstein and Kelly (1980) reported that of their upper-middle-class, Marin County, California, research sample of 60 families and 131 children of divorce, one-quarter of the couples regularly exhibited violence during the last part of the marriage and in the course of their divorce. Moreover, 57 percent of the children personally witnessed one parent hit the other. A more recent and significantly larger sample from the California statewide study found that in a full 65 percent of families, one or both parents made allegations of domestic violence during the mediation session (Depner et al., 1992). While these are cases under California's mandatory mediation law, the incidence of reported domestic violence at large has increased to epidemic proportions.

It was earlier believed that there was little connection between spousal abuse and child abuse—that one spouse might abuse the other spouse, with the child never being abused or even affected. However, more recent data strongly suggest otherwise. A review of studies looking at the overlap of spousal abuse and child abuse occurring in the same home reveal estimates from 40 to 60 percent overlap (Pagelow, 1990). Some studies report even higher statistics. Bowker, Arbitell, and McFerron (1988), for example, report that 70 percent of abusive husbands also abused their children. And one interesting study that used two control groups—one of couples who were nonviolent but in conflict and another of satisfactorily married couples—found that almost 82 percent of the abusive men who as children observed violence between their parents were also physically abused by one or both parents (Rosenbaum & O'Leary, 1981).

But domestic violence does not always simply refer to the classic chronic wife-batterer. Johnston and Campbell's exploratory research (see Johnston, 1992; Johnston & Campbell, 1988, 1993) suggested that there is a variety of domestic violence scenarios that need to be unbundled. In two different studies of high-conflict divorcing parents (eighty parents in one study and sixty in the other), they differentiated five basic types of domestic violence:

1. *Ongoing or episodic male battering* (10 percent of the sample in the first study and 18 percent in the second). This is the classic male chronic battering syndrome described by Walker (1984), characterized at separation by stalking, terrorizing, and threats of suicide and homicide.

2. *Male-controlling interactive violence* (19 percent/20 percent). This pattern is initiated by either the man or the woman and is interactional with mutual abuse, with the man's overriding physical dominance overpowering the woman, but with restraint.

3. *Female-initiated violence* (13 percent/15 percent). The woman initiates the violence with explosive outbursts, throws and destroys objects, scratches, bites, and kicks, and the man attempts to resist by passive defense.

4. *Separation-engendered and postdivorce trauma* (17 percent/25 percent). This pattern has uncharacteristic acts of violence only at time of traumatic separation—physical aggression is absent during the marriage.

5. *Psychotic and paranoid reactions* (6 percent/5 percent). A mentally disturbed or drug-influenced spouse flips out with paranoid delusions about conspiracies and with violent behavior.

It is important to note that in Johnston and Campbell's samples, the first four types were represented with approximately similar frequencies, and the fifth type had a much lower frequency of occurrence, clearly dispelling the myth that all domestic violence is the same. These researchers note that it is important to differentiate among the various types of domestic violence when helping parents develop postdivorce plans for the sharing of their children, since parent-child relationships are likely to vary and children of different ages and gender are likely to be affected differently by the different patterns of violence.

There are also consistent research findings that children who observe domestic violence between their parents, even when not abused themselves, are more symptomatic, showing more behavioral and emotional problems and reduced social competencies than children who experience nonviolent interparental discord and significantly more than children from nonconflictual families (see Jaffe, Wolfe, & Wilson, 1990; Johnston, 1994).

The implications of these data suggest that mediators, as well as judges and other divorce professionals, must do a careful assessment for the presence of domestic violence and for the type of domestic violence being alleged. The more chronic and severe the violence, the more caution is warranted. The more acute and situational the violence, the more that the mediator can deal with it as a crisis event, one that is not predictive of future violence.

The question of whether any case involving domestic violence should ever be mediated has been a major controversy. Critics of mediation have raised concerns regarding power balance, fairness, safety, coercion, and intimidation, among others. Supporters point out that mediation is better than litigation, provided that safety precautions such as screening, separate waiting areas, separate arrival and leaving times, individual caucuses, presence of support persons, and safe terminations are used, and trained and skilled mediators who are knowledgeable about domestic violence conduct the sessions. Regional, national, and international organizations, conferences, and commissions have debated the issues and generated guidelines for mediators dealing with domestic violence cases (see Newmark, Harrell, & Salem, 1995). Two major international organizations dealing with family mediation, the Association of Family and Conciliation Courts (public sector) and the Academy of Family Mediators (private sector), have each published a special issue of their respective journals, *Family and Conciliation Courts Review, 33* (10), January 1995, and *Mediation Quarterly, 7* (4), Summer 1990, on the topic of domestic violence, dealing with both sides of this debate. Both organizations have also developed protocols for mediating in cases involving domestic violence.

Because of the immediately serious nature of overt spousal violence or violence to children, courts will more readily act to deny custody to or restrict visitations of the allegedly violent parent. Unlike allegations of substance abuse, acts of violence are more easily documented, and therefore detriment to a child is easier to prove.

As with allegations of substance abuse and sexual misconduct, allegations of violence by one spouse about the other can also be strategically motivated. If careful screening of these allegations does not reveal a substantive basis and through the early phases of the mediation process such allegations do not persist, the mediator can usually assume that they were not significant or perhaps not even valid. However, such assumptions must *always* be made with a certain degree of caution, as it is not uncommon for spouses and children who have been threatened to minimize the dangers of potential future violence. The mediator who remains cautious and sensitive to the discussion of such issues will usually be able to sense when real intimidation is being experienced. In such situations, individual sessions with the parties involved usually provide enough of a sense of safety to uncover any real dangers. If all the safeguards of careful screening and vigilant monitoring throughout the sessions are put in place, many cases that have involved some form (usually the more acute forms) of domestic violence can be successfully mediated.

In cases of persistent and serious allegations of spousal violence or violence to the children, the mediator has few options. It is not possible to facilitate constructive mediation in the face of real evidence or threats of physical, emotional, or sexual violence. And when the allegations of violence specifically regard the children, it is the moral and ethical duty of the mediator to facilitate bringing the matter to the attention of the appropriate authorities. In states with child abuse reporting laws, the law requires that any person who has a reasonable suspicion of the occurrence of physical or sexual abuse or neglect of a child report the matter (anonymously) to the children's protective services and/or to the sheriff's or police department for investigation. Penalties can be incurred for not reporting the matter.

The mediator can confront the issue with both parents or with each spouse separately if there is a chance of violence erupting as a direct result of the confrontation. She can simply tell the alleging parent that an accusation of violence is a matter for the courts to deal with and is not appropriate for mediation. She should refer the parent to the appropriate authorities and then send the case back to the court or to the attorneys involved. If, after the investigation, the allegations prove to be unsubstantiated, the case may be returned for mediation, assuming that sufficient interspousal trust remains for mediation efforts to be feasible.

Parental Alienation

In high-conflict divorces, a phenomenon described in the literature as *parental alienation syndrome* (PAL) (Gardner, 1987, 1989) characterizes children who at some point in the divorcing process adamantly refuse to be with one of their parents. The tenacity of this refusal is quite astounding, especially in light of the apparent absence of any obvious stressor, which is typical of these cases. Gardner described the dynamics of this condition as a function of the psychopathology of the preferred parent, who is unable to tolerate separation from the child, programs the child, through overt and covert manipulation, to refuse to want to be with the other parent, and uses the child to meet his or her own emotional needs. The preferred parent is regarded as psychologically disturbed, and the nonpreferred parent is seen as the healthier parent.

Other writers have posed alternate theories to account for PAL. Lund (1995) suggests that there are a number of other reasons that children might resist contact with the other parent, including developmentally normal separation problems, deficits in the noncustodial parent's skills, oppositional behavior, high-conflict divorce, serious problems that are not necessarily abuse, and actual child abuse. She suggests that such behaviors may give the appearance of PAL but do not fit the dynamics presented by Gardner. Johnston and Campbell (1988) described these children as aligned with the parent whom the child experienced as more empathic and understanding of the child's specific developmental needs and found that the preferred parent was not necessarily overtly or covertly manipulative of the child. Garrity and Baris (1994) suggested that the preferred parent lacks empathy, is inflexible, and has little or no insight into the effects of his or her behavior.

In testing these various hypotheses, Lampel (1996) conducted two studies involving forty-four children who were aligned with one parent in a divorce. She found that parents of aligned children were more rigid, naively defended, and less emotionally expressive than parents of nonaligned children. Also, aligned children preferred the more emotive, problem-solving, and extroverted of the two parents.

In an expansion of the PAL concept that encompasses normal development and nonconflictual divorces, Kelly (1993b) suggested a continuum. At one end (at point 1) are children with *equal attachment* to both parents; then (at point 2) come children with an *affinity* for one parent (which often shifts over time even in intact families). Both of these characterize normal children in intact families. The second pattern may exist because a child may have a better match of personality or temperament with one of the parents or may have shared interests. Next (at point 3) are children who *align* with one parent. This comes out of marital separation dynamics, as an attempt to help a parent who feels victimized by the divorce (for example, Dad is being left by Mom and feels hurt and angry and talks a lot with the twelve-year-old daughter, who begins to berate Mom for ruining Dad's life). Aligned children will enjoy time with the nonpreferred parent once they are there but overtly struggle against going with that parent. At the far end (at point 4) are the children who are truly *alienated* and refuse to have any contact with the other parent.

The task for the mediator is first to assess where on this continuum the child lies. Children who are at points 1 through 3 on the continuum will usually adapt to a parenting plan that has them regularly spending time with the nonpreferred parent. It is important that both parents (and their attorneys) work toward this goal; otherwise there may be a tendency for the child to force the larger system to give up the plan, creating a situation where the child refuses to visit the other parent and is reinforced for it by complicity of the adults. For children who are truly alienated, a much more intensive therapeutic approach needs to be in effect (see Johnston and Campbell, 1988, and Johnston and Roseby, 1997, for the most comprehensive model of this). Regular efforts at mediation that do not include a very intensive therapeutic regimen will almost always fail. The ultimate dilemma for mediators, attorneys, judges, and evaluators is, of course, when a case involves parental alienation within a move-away situation. The complexity of such cases is compounded exponentially, presenting a formidable challenge for the divorce professionals.

Converting Court-Ordered Evaluation into Mediation

On occasion, family therapists and mediators are requested by courts to conduct evaluations of family situations in which divorced or divorcing spouses are having disputes over custody or visitation. Such requests regularly come from courts in states where there are neither mandatory mediation laws nor informal mediation services. Even in California, a judge may override the mandatory mediation law and make such a request if, in his or her discretion, a particular case seems inappropriate for mediation. The judge may order a written report of the evaluation with recommendations for a workable custody and/or visitation plan.

The therapist or mediator receiving such a request has several choices. She may choose to follow through strictly as requested. Or she may attempt mediation and, if it is unsuccessful, then make recommendations to the court as requested. Or with the judge's permission, she may decide to function exclusively as a mediator, with full confidentiality, and, if unsuccessful, refer the case to an evaluator who will then make recommendations as originally requested.

The particular approach chosen depends on several factors, the most important of which may be the mediator's opinion of whether the case can be successfully mediated. Judges will sometimes conclude that a particular case is not suitable for mediation on the basis of superficial or erroneous factors. These may include strategically motivated spousal assertions or allegations, spousal concerns that have little to do with the best interests of the children, or a high degree of hostility expressed between the spouses within the adversarial context. Other factors include the mediator's relationship with the judge and the attorneys, their receptivity to mediation, and considerations of time and finances.

In assessing which approach to take, the mediator should first consider the details of the case within its adversarial context. If the case seems amenable to mediation, the mediator should then consult with the attorneys. If both attorneys are supportive (or can be persuaded to be supportive) of mediation, the mediator has a solid base from which to approach the judge. If one attorney is supportive and the other is resistant, the mediator may need to be more convincing with the judge. If both attorneys resist mediation, the mediator may not be able to use mediation unless she can persuade the judge to override the attorneys. The mediator, though, needs to be fully aware of the effects of resistant attorneys on their client's cooperation in these circumstances. Any efforts she can make to include the attorneys, to inform them about mediation, and to elicit their support will aid the mediation efforts.

If mediation is acceptable to the judge, the mediator needs to understand clearly what the conditions will be. The judge may agree to mediation only if the mediator submits a written report with recommendations in the event that mediation is unsuccessful. Or the judge may agree to allow mediation to proceed with complete and exclusive confidentiality, such that no recommendations would be made if it were unsuccessful. Clarifying mutual expectations with the judge ahead of time can prevent later misunderstandings.

Although it is easiest to do so at the outset, the mediator can attempt to convert an evaluation into mediation at any point along the way. If confidentiality is to be maintained, this should of course be clarified and formalized at the outset. However, if recommendations are intended as part of the process, the mediator can at any point urge the couple to reconsider their options for resolving the dispute. Assuming that mediation is feasible for the case, the mediator can educate the couple about the benefits of mediation (see Chapter One) and can use the strategies for eliciting cooperation (see Chapter Ten). Once consent—implicit or explicit—has been obtained, the mediator can proceed as usual to mediate the issues. In most cases, convincing the couple that mediation is in their best interests is a difficult task, but it is eased if they are already familiar or comfortable with the concept of mediation, if the judge and attorneys are supportive of this approach, and if the mediator feels hopeful about resolving the particular case with mediation. When successful, the mediator feels a tremendous sense of accomplishment, and the success certainly adds to the growing credibility of the mediation approach in the eyes of the court.

When direct mediation efforts are not feasible, another option for conflict resolution outside of court litigation is the use of evaluations in creative and facilitative ways. In contrast to the traditional model of custody evaluations—done in a completely adversarial context involving winners and losers, litigation, and court testimony, where the parents are silent and powerless participants in an expensive, intimidating process that often goes far beyond the parents' level of comfort—these new methods allow varying degrees of self-determination, confidentiality, reduced costs, and advisory recommendations that do not go to the court and result in reduced parental conflict. Several of the models offer feedback to the parents of evaluative data that they can use to negotiate agreements, guided by the mediation skills of the evaluator. (For more information about these emerging models, see Bordarampe, Ehrenberg, Foran, and Oksman, 1991; Mosten, 1992; and Taylor and Bing, 1994.)

ETHICS, VALUES, AND
MORALS IN MEDIATION

ANYONE WORKING in the field of child custody mediation for a significant period of time comes to appreciate the multitude of ethical and moral dilemmas in which the mediator becomes involved. Such dilemmas present even greater challenges than the process of the work itself, as mediators are forced to grapple with their own values and beliefs and continually reevaluate where they stand personally.

Quality of Parenting

Throughout this book, it has been stressed that the mediator must remain neutral and balanced at all times to be effective in facilitating an agreement between disputing spouses. It has also been stressed that the mediator must function primarily as an *advocate for the child,* not as a representative of either spouse, and that according to the most current research, what is best for most children after a divorce is a continuing and regular relationship with both parents. Although such advocacy for the regularity and continuity of children's relationships with both parents might seem to be a relatively objective, nonjudgmental, and value-free position for the mediator to assume, it is not.

One Marginal Parent

For example, while attempting to remain neutral, a mediator occasionally experiences bias against one spouse. This bias may be due to the personal style of the spouse; to his or her beliefs, attitudes, and values; or to the uncooperative stance the spouse assumes in mediation. The spouse may

enter mediation with a chip on the shoulder and verbally attack the mediator. He or she may be late for sessions and may challenge every procedure. This spouse may elaborate on beliefs, attitudes, and practices
regarding child rearing that are personally offensive to the mediator. While
falling short of child abuse, these practices might include the regular use of
corporal punishment and excessive strictness or, alternatively, the absence
of limit setting and a totally laissez-faire approach to raising young children. In contrast, the other spouse may be a relatively open, loving, generous, compromising, cooperative person whose beliefs and practices of
child rearing are congruent with those of the mediator.

Several factors make this a difficult situation. For one thing, the mediator generally does not have time to work through these feelings of bias
by getting to know other, more positive facets of the spouse who seems
offensive. And within the context of mediation, it is usually not feasible
to spend the extra time that would be needed to become better acquainted
with this spouse, not least because the mediator would have to do the
same for the other spouse.

A second contributory factor is that to carry out the mediational goal
of optimizing the children's access to both parents, the mediator must be
supportive of both parents' importance to and involvement with the children. This means, however, that the mediator must not only overlook the
offensive aspects of one spouse but also be supportive of that spouse.
Of course, to the degree that the mediator does support this spouse, he may
end up alienating the more cooperative spouse. A cooperative spouse
may well interpret the mediator's equal support of the less cooperative
spouse as evidence of the mediator's bias. That spouse may feel that the
mediator is condoning uncooperative behavior and poor-quality parenting and is ignoring behavior that may appear to that spouse to be detrimental to the children. However, if the mediator questions, lectures to, or
expresses a judgmental attitude toward the uncooperative spouse, the bias
becomes overt, and the mediator may well forfeit neutrality and further
exacerbate the uncooperative spouse's resistant behavior.

In attempting to support the best interests of the child, the mediator
typically tries to implement a plan that allows the child a regular and continuous relationship with both parents. Generally, the mediator must assume that short of blatant child abuse or parental behavior that is clearly
antithetical to the child's welfare, *both parents are adequate caregivers for
their child* and both have important individual contributions to make to
the rearing of their child. Not only do these assumptions generally follow
from the research regarding the needs of most children of divorce, but
they are congruent with the mediator's need to maintain balance and neu-

trality, to cut through the various strategies of spouses and children, and to equalize parental negotiating power.

Unfortunately, these assumptions lead the mediator to deemphasize or perhaps even completely ignore *quality of parenting*. They suggest that *minimal parental competence* is adequate to support the child's best interests. Hence a parent who manifests minimal parental competence may be given the same consideration in the development of a mediated coparenting plan as a highly competent parent. Although there is, no doubt, a continuum between a mediator's personal bias and his professional conviction about parental incompetence, a spouse who falls at the latter end of this continuum clearly poses certain dilemmas for the mediator.

Consider the following case. Jeremiah and Rebecca have been divorced for two years and have three children, Nathan, age nine; Katie, eleven; and Jordan, twelve. Nathan and Katie have been living with their mother, and Jordan has been living with his father. Jeremiah files a petition to modify Rebecca's sole custody of Nathan and Katie to joint legal and joint physical custody. In mediation, Rebecca reports that Jeremiah has never known how to be a father, that he is completely self-centered, and that he has no conception of the needs of his children. Furthermore, he has deprived Jordan continually, and Nathan and Katie during visitations, of food, clothing, and, on several occasions, even shelter ("accidentally" locking the children out of the house). His refrigerator is frequently empty or sparsely stocked with food, and he has not bought shoes or pants for Jordan in over a year. Moreover, he is seriously in arrears on child support payments and reports to Rebecca that he does not have enough money to catch up but is working on it—although he recently purchased for himself a new sports car, a small boat, and a new wardrobe. He is home infrequently and very often leaves the children home alone or with a young teenage baby-sitter. When angry at the children, he spanks them harshly and sends them to their room without dinner. About twice a year, he takes all the children to a movie, but otherwise he has instructed them to entertain themselves, since he does not have enough money "to squander on frivolous things." Jeremiah rationalizes his overall parental incompetence by saying, "Children will learn to survive best if they go without."

Rebecca, in contrast, has consistently sacrificed for the children and has held the family together through the twelve years of the marriage and the two years postdivorce. She has lived on a meager budget yet has managed to take the children to special events, spend lots of time with them, and nurture them emotionally and materially as best she could.

In separate interviews with the mediator, the children basically confirmed this imbalance in parental competence. However, all of them said that they would agree to whatever their parents worked out because they just wanted to stop the arguing. Moreover, they all said that their father would make them feel guilty if they did not spend enough time with him, and because they felt sorry for his being all alone, they wanted to keep him company.

Throughout the negotiations, Jeremiah insists on an equal sharing arrangement, Rebecca agrees to respect the wishes of the children, and the children want their parents to decide. Given this setup, it is likely that Jeremiah's proposal will prevail.

At this point, the mediator confronts a large dilemma. Should she suspend her professional concern about the imbalance of parental competence and act as if there were a genuine equality of competence—that is, assume that a questionable or minimal level of parental competence is sufficient to protect the children's best interests? Can she rest assured that having any two parents who agree on a coparenting plan is really better for children than having one competent and involved parent and one marginally competent and peripheral parent who do not agree to a coparenting plan? Or should the mediator strategically try to influence the decisions about the coparenting arrangements so that a disproportionate amount of the children's time would be spent in their mother's care? This tactic might seriously risk the mediation efforts if Jeremiah were to continue insisting on a strictly equal arrangement. Or should the mediator simply abandon neutrality altogether and directly confront Jeremiah with the fact that his parenting skills are inadequate and his proposal is simply not in the best interests of the children? Or should the mediator refuse to participate in the decision-making process and inform the couple that because she does not believe that it is best for the children to spend more time with Jeremiah, she is sending their case back to court for a child custody study?

While it is possible that having more time with the children could increase Jeremiah's sense of responsibility, the risks to the children of such minimal caregiving make the mediator's choice of action difficult.

Two Marginal Parents

Even more difficult is the case in which both parents are only marginally competent or clearly incapable of providing constructive care for their children. Consider the following case. Dean and Glenda had been separated for six months, and their six-year-old daughter, Eileen, had been living with her father and seeing her mother every other weekend. Glenda, who also had a three-year-old daughter from another relationship while she was married to Dean, petitioned for custody of Eileen. In mediation, Glenda, a sarcastic and hostile woman who carried the intense anger at her own parents into her spousal and parental relationships, said that Dean was always working and was never home. "He never learned to be no father, just like my ol' man. May the Lord burn him in hell, and my ol' lady too, while he's at it!" Glenda explained that she sought custody of Eileen after finding out that Dean was never with Eileen but was leaving her with his fiancée, Ginger. She added that Ginger "spanks, whips, and is severely strict with Eileen. She refuses to let Eileen talk or even make a sound at the dinner table, because, she says, 'Eileen spits food when she talks, and I don't want to clean it up.' Eileen also told me that she has to eat at the kitchen table while Dean and Ginger eat in the living room so they can watch TV. And Eileen is not allowed to watch TV because 'it's bad for kids.'" When the mediator asked Dean if all this was accurate, he said, "Yeah. Ginger is real religious and knows what's right, and besides, as Ginger says, it's been ten generations that kids should be seen and not heard."

On hearing this, Glenda launched a tirade about Ginger for not caring about Eileen. With a gush of anger, she accused Dean of neglecting Eileen and then, in a rambling fashion, expounded on her own deep need for Eileen. At one point, she bragged about how well she could control her own anger: "Like last night at 10:30, the baby [her three-year-old child] was watching TV and spilt some milk on the carpet. I got furious, but I just got up and started running as fast as I could down the block. I ran three and a half blocks to get away; otherwise I would have smashed her head in. I had the good judgment to leave. She was asleep when I got home—instead of dead. But Dean, he don't even care about Eileen."

Glenda then continued, "I need Eileen so badly to live with me because she is the only person who kept me out of an institution when I was about to crack. She's been my source of reality. She needs me and loves me—no one else does like her! I can't make it without her. I swear I'll get her—I'll take her and leave the country if I have to."

The mediator's choice of action in this case is even more limited than in the case of one inadequate parent. If the mediator does have the power to slant the negotiations, and chooses to do so, which way should he slant them—toward Eileen moving in with her angry, explosive, unpredictable mother or toward Eileen remaining under Ginger's strict, questionably adequate care and living with an essentially absent father?

However, if the mediator chooses to act as if both parents were adequate, he has to be able to tell himself that whatever plan the spouses agree to is probably in the best interests of the child. To justify this position, the mediator probably has to accept the fact that most children in the world grow up with less than optimal parenting.

Or are there some legitimate and consensually agreed-upon standards of minimally adequate parenting? Certainly our vast research in child development offers numerous guidelines for effective parenting, but how many parents actually follow such guidelines? Moreover, the history of the child-rearing literature is a history of pendulum-like alternations in styles, practices, and even "truths" about what is important for children. Clearly, our values about children and child rearing across the generations have been grounded in relativity, rather than in absolute truths.

A last and most serious option for the mediator to consider is the possibility of referring the case to court with a recommendation for temporary foster placement of the child or perhaps even for the permanent relinquishment of parental rights, which would free the child for adoption. However, this would indeed be a drastic move. For one thing, if the mediator is bound by a confidentiality agreement, he might have to breach it, which would put him in a difficult position. Second, such an action would certainly stretch the role of the mediator into questionable areas. And third, while the possibilities are perhaps somewhat better for temporary foster placement, the possibilities are very slim for permanently relinquishing the rights of biological parents who express interest in and involvement with their child. The right to parent one's child is held to be a basic right that lies at the heart of most court decisions and legislative enactments, and it is not relinquished easily in any court of law. MacGowan (1981) cites several cases in which it was held that the killing of one parent by the other disqualifies the surviving parent from obtaining custody only if the homicide constitutes neglect of the child. In more recent times, some experts cite the O. J. Simpson case as just such a case in point.

The ethical questions the mediator faces are numerous and challenging when handling a case like that of Dean and Glenda. It is difficult to leave such a case feeling comfortable, no matter what action one chooses to take.

Dealing with Questionable Agreements

Mediators not uncommonly encounter couples who for various reasons come to agreements that the mediator finds questionable, leaving the mediator with concerns about the agreement's appropriateness for the child, its durability, its fairness, and so forth. We will now explore a number of such difficult circumstances.

Unstable Parent

After a divorce, it is not uncommon for a parent to cope with the crisis by making a sudden and radical change in lifestyle and/or personality. It could involve abandoning a stable middle-class lifestyle for that of a promiscuous risk taker, or it could be a change from an emotionally distant personality to one that is open and accommodating. A spouse may turn in a new direction for spiritual guidance and begin to proselytize about the teachings of any of a variety of systems for personal growth, from religious conversions to initiation into a cult to New Age therapies.

Conway and Siegelman (1978) coined the term *snapping* in their investigation of the phenomenon of sudden, radical changes of personality and lifestyle. The term connotes a sudden qualitative and unpredictable alteration in one's functioning. Any sudden, radical change in personality or lifestyle is generally unstable, and this instability is compounded for a newly divorced spouse. A deterioration in parental behavior for at least the year following the divorce has been well documented. When a mediator deals with a parent who is experiencing the chaos of a new divorce and has also undergone a snapping experience, various dilemmas arise.

Let us consider an example. Mark and Marion had been married for fifteen years and had four children, aged nine, ten, thirteen, and fourteen. When Marion left Mark, he was extremely distraught and depressed for several months. After making several bids to reunite with Marion, Mark finally seemed to accept the pending divorce and wanted Marion to have primary custody of the children.

Several weeks before the divorce hearing, however, Mark got deeply involved with a religious cult and had a profound conversion experience similar to several he had had during the marriage. During his visitation times, he talked at length with the children about living in the community of this cult. When they expressed interest in his idea, he took them for a visit to the state where the community was established. The children became entranced with the apparently loving and free atmosphere there, and they made some friends.

In the mediation negotiations, Mark appeared rational and reasonable and spoke mesmerizingly as he described the structure of the religious community. He also seemed very cooperative until he stated calmly that although he would like to share parenting with Marion, he was moving to the religious community out of state and would like the children to join him there. Marion agreed that it would be fine for the children to spend the summers there but that they would need to spend the school year with her. Mark added calmly, "I've talked with the children, and they said that they wanted to live in the community with me." Marion was startled and said she would need to talk with the children about this decision.

At the next mediation session, the day before Mark was to move out of state, Marion came in looking dejected. She explained that she had talked with the children and wound up in a nasty argument with one of the older ones. Against her wishes, all four of the children did say that they wanted to live in the religious community. However, she suspected that Mark must have made some far-reaching promises to them to win them over to his side. The mediator met with the children and heard them express their wish to go with their father. To the mediator, the children were unsettlingly consistent with one another in expressing their intentions.

The mediator then met with Mark and Marion again and tried to support Marion in being cautious about this decision. He explained the various dynamic and strategic reasons why children might state such a preference. Moreover, because of his unsettled feelings about the course of events, he attempted to steer them toward a time-limited plan with lots of mutual time-sharing and mutual decision-making clauses built in. However, Mark countered these attempts in a calm, rational, and calculated fashion. He finally played his trump card, saying, "I would be willing to let Marion visit with the children anytime she wants, on twenty-four hours' notice, but the leader of the community and his board of legal consultants informed me that if I bring my children even for a short time, I must have sole custody of them, or I cannot live there." When asked why, Mark replied, "They apparently have had some difficult situations come up between ex-spouses over their children, and they don't want to deal with those problems anymore."

Marion looked even more distraught and dejected and said "All right! I'm tired of all this. You can have what you want. Since the children have obviously been brainwashed by you, there's nothing I can do about it. Besides, I don't have any money to go back to court to fight this." The mediator urged Marion to take her time and think it out further, but Mark kept reminding her that he was leaving the next day and needed a decision immediately. Marion was feeling rejected by her children, persuaded by their stated desire to move with their father, and rushed and intimidated by Mark. As a result, she would not heed the mediator's advice to refrain from a hasty decision and insisted on the mediator's writing up the agreement as Mark had proposed it. Both Marion and the mediator knew that the sudden change in Mark would probably not last, yet Marion felt powerless to counter Mark's well-devised plans. The mediator was placed in the position of either allowing this plan to proceed and implicitly condoning it or else asserting his professional judgment (and, perhaps, personal values) and refusing to condone such a plan being carried out. Efforts toward a compromise were repelled by Marion and blocked by Mark.

In such a circumstance, where the spouses are willing to agree to a proposal that seems questionable to the mediator but the mediator has no leverage for significantly modifying the proposal, what options does the mediator have? If the case were to go to court and the children were to persist in their expressed desires, a judge might well rule in favor of Mark's plan. Although its instability is obvious to the trained eye, it might well look to a judge like an acceptable plan developed by two concerned and involved parents. If, after hearing the mediator's concerns about the agreement and attempts to modify it, the two spouses decide to proceed anyway, should the mediator simply trust their decision? Or does the mediator's role as an advocate for the child obligate him to go one step further and take other action to preclude the development of a questionable parenting agreement? And what could be the nature of such action? What sacrifices would need to be made to carry out such action?

Any Agreement Versus No Agreement

Another issue is whether it is always better to protect children from court battles even if it means allowing them to participate in a questionable agreement. Does the acrimony generated in the adversarial court process always have a worse effect than the results of even a questionable mediated agreement? Or are there some issues, such as risks to physical and emotional safety, that should always preclude a mediated settlement on the grounds that the child will do much better in the long run by undergoing an adversarial court custody process? Under what conditions can a court-rendered decision really offer more protection for a child's well-being than what is offered by a mediated agreement?

Even assuming that most agreements reached between spouses, with or without mediators, are better for the children than most decisions rendered by the court, there are still a number of ethical issues that arise for the mediator. To achieve the compromises that permit agreements to be reached, the mediator often has to orchestrate sacrifices on the part of one spouse and/or the children. These sacrifices are based on certain values that the mediator believes to be important for children. If these values are not valid for the parties involved, the mediator may cause undue discomfort or harm to the family members.

Feasible Versus Fair

Consider a case in which a mother wants to retain sole legal and sole physical custody of her nine- and twelve-year-old children while the father makes a strong and insistent plea for joint legal and joint physical custody. Although the father is partly motivated by a *power assertion strategy,* he also sincerely wants to share half-time parenting responsibilities. The children, however, would like to reside with their mother but would agree, reluctantly, to an alternating weekly sharing schedule. The father and mother have remained in constant conflict because the father has felt dominated by the mother. By having sole custody, she has been able to control the father's access to the children. The children have tried many strategies for getting the parents to stop arguing, but the arguments have persisted, largely because the father has been in a "one-down" position since the divorce, a position he has constantly resisted.

With just a few strategies, the mediator could achieve a joint custody agreement, since with the mediator's support, the mother would compromise. Alternatively, the mediator could discourage such an agreement and risk having the case returned to court. He might choose the former solution, justified by the reasoning that if the father had a sense of sharing equal power with the mother, he would be less resistant and more cooperative with her, which in the long run would benefit the children by reducing the interparental tension. The mediator would thus have to sacrifice the short-run comfort of the children in trying to achieve increased harmony between the parents. This plan, then, would be *feasible* but not quite *fair* to the children. It requires the mediator to maintain a strong conviction that an equal-custody plan will result in reduced acrimony between the parents and that it is more important for the parents to reach any workable agreement between themselves than for the mediator to risk escalating the parental battle by yielding to the children's preferences.

In such a case, where the mediator can influence the outcome, what should the mediator choose to do? Should children be expected to make a sacrifice on the chance that it would reduce their parents' conflict? Or should the children be allowed their preference even if it results in further interparental tension?

The issue of feasible versus fair agreements comes up frequently when both spouses have positive parenting skills and good intentions but have an imbalanced spousal dynamic. Typically, the husband is dominating and aggressive and the wife is submissive and yielding. When they negotiate their proposals, their relational positions are directly represented in their agreement. The parenting plan to which they agree will be feasible for the children but not very fair to the wife. Feeling, as always, intimidated by her husband, the wife is unassertive and allows him to plow right past her own needs.

In this situation, to what extent should the mediator be protective of the wife's needs? Should he make mild, moderate, or vigorous efforts to encourage her to take a stronger stand on her own behalf, knowing full well that such action may antagonize the husband into a refusal to compromise at all? Or should he make no efforts at all and just assume that the spousal balance that exists at that time has no doubt existed for many years and is not likely to change in mediation? As marital therapists know well, tipping the balance of power in a marital relationship is almost always guaranteed to trigger a crisis. However, would not the mediator's laissez-faire attitude be encouraging the continuation of the imbalanced decision-making process? Should the mediator allow an agreement to be made that is feasible but unfair to the wife and encourage the wife to seek counseling later, in order to become stronger so that she could be more assertive in future modifications of the time-sharing plan?

Pushing for an Agreement

In the case just examined, the mediator's dilemma is how and whether to halt the development of an agreement that in the mediator's view is not desirable. In other cases, however, the dilemma is the extent to which it is legitimate to push a couple to reach an agreement. In many cases, a skillful mediator, using the strategies described in Chapter Eleven, can maneuver a couple into reaching an agreement even when it seems at first to be an impossible task.

There are several motives a mediator might have for intently effecting an agreement. First, the mediator may believe that any agreement will be better than a court-rendered decision. Second, the mediator may feel that if she just gets a couple past the impasse of the custody power struggle, they will be able to establish a new way of relating to one another that in the long run will work out better for the children. Third, the mediator may have an excessive caseload to get through and thus not have the time for more prolonged negotiations that might yield more mutually acceptable agreements. (This is not uncommonly the situation in conciliation court settings, where inadequate funding for staff results in a large backlog of cases.) Fourth, the mediator may strive to reach as many agreements as she can, as a personal test of her skill and influence as a mediator.

Regardless of the reasons for it, pushing for an agreement can have certain negative consequences. At least one and often both spouses may feel shortchanged, manipulated, or bullied by the mediator. This can cause one or both spouses to sabotage the agreement shortly after mediation ends and to resist returning to mediation for future modifications of the co-parenting plan. Moreover, it can result in a hastily made agreement that is unsatisfactory for the children. In the mediator's vigorous attempts to break an impasse, she may overlook risks to the children presented by a particular agreement.

However, pushing for an agreement can result in benefits for the children even if one or both of the parents are dissatisfied with the process. The agreement may in fact be better than any court-rendered decision, and it may help the couple establish a new way of relating to each other.

Can the mediator push too hard for compromise? Is compromise always the best solution? Might the mediator's stance of "peace at any cost" not sometimes have excessive and unwarranted consequences? Are there not some circumstances in which higher human principles of morals and values should take precedence over a forced compromise? Are there not some situations in which there is a *right* side to a dispute, a *right* resolution, a morally *correct* parental position that supersedes a compromised coparenting arrangement?

Recognizing that the mediator often has a good deal of power to influence the outcome of negotiations between parents, we must consider several broader issues regarding ethics, values, and morals.

Protecting Clients' Rights

To begin with, almost all mediation cases come out of an adversarial context in which each of the spouses is attempting to assert his or her parental rights at the expense of the other parent. Moreover, each parent is entitled to retain a legal advocate to ensure that these rights are protected to the maximum extent possible. In the context of litigation, the court is presumed to be responsible for protecting the rights and needs of the children. In the mediation context, however, it is the mediator who must protect these rights and needs, particularly when a parenting agreement reached in mediation is not likely to be closely scrutinized by a judge. But what values should the mediator advocate? To what extent should the mediator support a parent's *legal* rights if the mediator feels that doing so would compromise the children's needs? Or are his responsibilities limited exclusively to protecting the rights and needs of the children?

If a father's legal rights to regular and frequent access to his young child have clearly been violated by the mother and the child is supportive of the mother, what position should the mediator take? Suppose further that the father expresses minimal affection for the child but offers much more in the way of material things and educational opportunities than the mother can. And suppose that the mother offers much deeper affection for the child but lives in near-poverty conditions. Finally, add the facts that the child and mother are quite dependent on each other, that the child prefers to maintain the existing time-sharing arrangements, and that the father and his lawyer are pushing for an equal time-sharing arrangement.

This case presents a three-way intersection of conflicting rights and needs. With the strong support of his attorney, the father insists that his parental rights have been violated and he deserves redress in the form of an equal parenting arrangement. The child's rights to have open access to both parents presumably would also be satisfied if the father's proposal were adopted. However, the child's needs, which certainly are open to differing interpretations, might be best satisfied if he maintained his close relationship with his mother—that is, if the existing living and time-sharing arrangements were preserved. Yet could it not be argued that in the long run, the child's needs would best be met if he were emotionally closer to both parents? But what would be the consequences to the child of decreasing the special closeness with his mother in order to spend more time with his father, only to find that his father continued to be very limited in the affection that he was able to feel for the child? Does some universal justice prevail such that if both parents' rights were fully respected, the resulting balance would optimally meet the child's needs? Should the mediator not act strictly as an advocate for the child but rather as an advocate for the whole family unit? In this way, he would be concerned with the rights and needs of both parents and child. Is this role too similar to that of the judge, and does it not overlap the roles of the attorneys? Is it an inappropriate role for a mediator? Is it even possible?

The Child's Best Interests

Whether the mediator's role is as an advocate for the child alone or for the family unit, how far should this advocacy extend? If a child has deep and close relationships with grandparents or other relatives in addition to bonds with the parents, what position should the mediator take? Should she limit her concern to the nuclear family unit, or should she expand her influence to include extended family members?

If all else is equal, is a parent more important to a child than a very close grandparent? Or a close aunt or uncle? Should they be considered on an equal level with the parents if the child's emotional attachment to them seems equal? At what generation and at what degree of kinship should the mediator stop when considering the best interests of the child? Should family pets be considered part of a child's extended family? These questions become especially significant when one parent is moving away from the area where the other parent and all the child's extended family members reside.

The courts have repeatedly made it clear that parents shall be first in line for awards of custody, before grandparents, other extended family members, or any other interested persons. However, for the mediator, this simply means that *legal* custody should be assumed by one or both parents, unless there would be detriment to the child in doing so. Time-sharing arrangements, however, can be worked out in any way that would be in the child's best interests and that both parents would agree to. So the mediator may actually have considerable latitude in shaping the parenting agreements. Although it increases the complexity of negotiations, the mediator may be able to optimize a child's support network by including extended family members in the time-sharing plan. Maintaining such bonds has been shown to decrease the sense of isolation and loss for children of divorce (Schwartz & Kaslow, 1997).

Lawyers' Roles as Advocates and Counselors

Historically, in legal matters, attorneys have had two roles, that of *advocate* for their client's rights and interests and that of *counselor* for their client. Attorneys vary considerably in the respective emphases they place on these functions. Regarding lawyers who practice child custody law, the Committee on the Family of the Group for the Advancement of Psychiatry (1980, pp. 44–45) concluded:

> At one extreme are those who function primarily as counselors; at the other extreme are the inveterate litigators. In handling divorce and custody matters, some lawyers explore in detail the alternatives for reaching agreement, seeking therapy, or trying arbitration. They view their duty as one to the whole client in terms of long-range advantage, with due consideration for intra-family relationships. The aggressive lawyer, on the other hand, battles on behalf of his client to press for immediate advantages. Some clients who are not in a compromising mood seek out this sort of lawyer. Most lawyers, of course, fall somewhere between these extremes.

Research evidence in support of this observational conclusion was developed by Kressel (1985), who studied nearly one hundred lawyers in two separate investigations and generated a typology of six distinctive types of practicing divorce lawyers, which run the gamut from those with a cynical, pessimistic stance who believe that divorce lawyers can never solve clients' problems but at best give only limited relief (the "undertaker") to those with a moral stance and an active mission to help their client do right by the spouse and the children (the "moral agent"). In his larger study, using a statistical cluster analysis, these six types meaningfully divided into two major clusters: a group of twenty-two attorneys whom he labeled *advocates* and another group of twenty-four whom he called *counselors*. The *advocates* approached divorce work for the challenge it poses for achieving a victory for the client, viewed client emotions as obstacles to settlement, did not feel responsible for providing emotional support, and actively engaged in adversarial relationships with the opposing attorneys. In contrast, the *counselors* were concerned with producing a cooperative postdivorce climate and in protecting the welfare of children, viewed divorce work as an opportunity to learn about human psychology, and were supportive of mediation efforts by mental health professionals.

Given that approximately half of divorce lawyers function largely in the role of advocate, how can they facilitate achieving the best interests of the child in custody and visitation disputes when they operate only from the perspective of their own client? Is there any room for them to consider the effects of their one-sided advocacy on the larger family unit? Given what we now know about the destructive effects of parental conflict on children, how do they deal ethically with the effects of their maneuvers on the children?

MacGowan (1981) suggested that "an attorney deciding whether to accept a child custody case should consider an ethical obligation not specified in the Rules of Professional Conduct: the obligation to influence the client to act in a manner beneficial to the child" (p. 386). She cited cases in which this ethical responsibility in custody proceedings has been recognized by both trial and appellate courts. Of course, some *advocate* attorneys would claim that they always do fulfill this obligation because they believe (mistakenly or not) that their clients always are acting in the best interests of the child.

Several factors contribute to lawyers' difficulty in viewing custody contests from the family systems perspective. First, the one-sided data gathered by attorneys tend to be emotionally loaded and therefore very seductive. Second, shifting one's conceptual paradigm from an individual to a family systems perspective requires a leap that is difficult even for many trained psychotherapists (Watzlawick, Weakland, & Fisch, 1974; Haley, 1976). It is even more difficult for attorneys, who not only practice from an individually oriented perspective but may also feel bound by their code of ethics to keep it that way. However, if the mediator can get the attorneys on a case to suspend their adversarial role temporarily, they may be more receptive to considering a higher-order perspective in custody disputes—that a child's interests are almost always served best when the parents stop fighting with each other. If even one of the attorneys in a case is known to practice in the *counselor* role or, better yet, in the collaborative law model, the mediator can solicit the assistance of that attorney. A number of attorneys who have begun practicing collaborative law have indicated that they are often successful in beckoning and ultimately convincing counsel on the other side to consider approaching their case in a collaborative way (in their *counselor*, rather than *advocate*, role).

Individual Freedom Versus Family Integrity

Among the scenarios of contemporary divorces is that in which one spouse leaves the marriage explaining, "I'm leaving in order to find myself—to explore who I am, to be free, to get my act together, to do my own thing." Some of these spouses are leaving very conflicted, tension-laden, and oppressive marriages, but others are leaving marriages that may be structurally sound but are dynamically dampened.

An unfortunate but major consequence of one spouse seeking individual freedom is that family integrity is ruptured, and the lives of the children are often severely disrupted. This brings up a number of significant issues regarding individual and family values. Is it morally defensible for a spouse to leave a marriage and splinter a family solely to satisfy a personal need for freedom? Should a spouse be willing to compromise individual needs and desires in order to preserve the family unit? Is there not some higher human principle that individuals should make personal sacrifices for the sake of a more significant social unit, the family, and that the welfare and security of children are more important than the fulfillment of individual adults' perceived needs? Is such a notion just relative to culture and time, or is it a much more fundamental value?

Certainly, there are marriages that are best dissolved for the sake of both the parents and the children. For instance, when there is violence or abuse, chronic conflict, or incompatible and inflexible expectations of the marriage, one could hardly fault a spouse for leaving. However, how shall we view the actions of the spouse who leaves a relatively stable marriage to seek personal enlightenment and is unwilling even to attempt reconciliation? This action might be condoned from a psychological viewpoint, which tends to place value on the expression and gratification of individual needs. From a moral viewpoint, though, this action might be viewed as selfish and not in the best interests of the children or of the family as a whole. For example, is it fair for a mother who leaves the family to expect equal time sharing with the children whose lives she disrupted? Should a father who leaves his wife and children be given the same rights and privileges to the custody and control of the children as the mother, who chose to stay and work things out? Is it fair that the children have to accommodate to the needs of the parent and divide their time between two homes? Or would it be more fair for the parent to have to pay a price for leaving and sacrifice frequent contact with the children? These questions must be pondered with full awareness that societal values swing back and forth from generation to generation, making their answers all the more difficult.

For the mediator, the issue of individual freedom versus family integrity presents imposing dilemmas. Can the mediator afford to function purely on psychological and legal levels and ignore the moral implications of his work? If he chooses to attend to these implications, will his task of being neutral be impeded? Is it possible to be somewhat, but not completely, morally concerned? Or are these perspectives fundamentally incompatible, forcing the mediator to choose to be either wholly concerned or wholly disinterested?

Men as Caregivers

One of the central changes in society's values brought about by the feminist movement is the increased acceptability of men as primary caregivers for children. In general, men have become increasingly comfortable in expressing their gentleness, their playfulness, their nurturing capacities, and their emotional closeness to children. This emotional balance between men and women has developed concomitantly with changes in employment structures. More women now work outside the home, and household and child care responsibilities are more frequently, although certainly not always, shared between parents.

Although the notion of joint custody has been a great focus over the past two decades, the research data to date show that while there has been an increase in joint legal custody and in fathers being more actively involved in the parenting activities of their children, the joint custody trend has not appreciably resulted in more fathers with primary or even joint physical custody. This is the case in the general population of divorcing parents (Maccoby & Mnookin, 1992) and in the outcomes of mandatory mediation in California (Depner, Cannata, & Ricci, 1995).

Although society has given fathers both permission and the appropriate legal structures to function as primary caregivers, it has not yet provided them with the skills necessary for primary child care. In spite of how liberated some men may seem today, the majority of fathers have not had much experience or training in child rearing. It is still not socially condoned for boys to play with dolls, to play house, or to engage flexibly in the role playing of other domestic functions, which is a central way that children learn these adult roles. Traditional, stereotyped sex roles are still largely encouraged, and children's deviations from these roles are viewed by most adults with concern and discomfort. As Brooks-Gunn and Matthews (1979, p. 19) noted almost twenty years ago, "The stereotypes have not changed much since the early 1800s, when the poem 'What are little boys made of?' first appeared."

In our present society, when a mother divorces and takes primary custody of her children, she is shown little respect, is overburdened with responsibilities, and is offered little emotional or financial support. Moreover, her parenting skills are looked at critically, and she is freely blamed for any difficulties experienced by her children. However, when a father even participates in the day-to-day care of his child, he is praised for going beyond the call of duty. If he is divorced and chooses to function as a single parent and primary caregiver, he is commended, much support is offered by friends and family, and he is generally viewed with respect simply for being a single parent. If his children experience difficulties, understanding and support are given to him, but he is rarely blamed or criticized.

In light of the foregoing, the mediator often faces a dilemma when a father wants equal or primary caregiving responsibility for his children. This request almost always is disputed by the mother, who typically claims that the father does not offer proper care to the children. She may add that he knows very little about being a father, since he was never around much during the marriage, and that he neglects the children—doesn't bathe them properly, never washes their hair, doesn't supervise their play, doesn't feed them balanced meals, and so on. In response to these allegations, the father typically retorts defensively that he does just fine and then evades talking about the specifics.

The mediator is thus put in the position of having to consider the parenting skills of the father. However, if the mediator questions the father about his skills or suggests that he take a parenting class, the father is likely to react defensively and accuse the mediator of bias in believing the mother's story. If, however, the mediator ignores the issue, the care of the children may be compromised if the father does gain significant caregiving responsibility for the children and the mother's concerns turn out to be valid.

Under the assumption that fathers with effective caregiving skills are the exception rather than the rule, should the mediator routinely question fathers or steer couples away from agreements that allot significant caregiving time to the father? Should fathers be expected to prove their parenting competence before assuming such responsibilities? How could the mediator effect this without losing impartiality in the negotiations? Should he ignore the issue entirely and assume that some children will just receive less than adequate care—as no doubt occurs at times even with mothers—but that in time, out of necessity, the fathers will learn the necessary skills—as on the job training? Is this too great a sacrifice to expect of the children?

<hr>

○

The many issues of ethics, values, and morals raised in this chapter have no easy answers. However, it is my hope that those of us who are responsible for facilitating major decisions that affect the lives of children will ponder these questions well, for we need to raise our moral consciousness and learn how to act more effectively to create happiness, peace, and a sense of well-being for our children.

MAKING MEDIATION WORK

RECOMMENDATIONS FOR MEDIATORS, ATTORNEYS, AND JUDGES

DIVORCE CONTINUES TO TAKE its toll on our children. For most children of divorce, memories of the emotional pain, the confusion and turmoil, and the parental bitterness haunt them for years after the divorce and sometimes throughout their lives. For the luckier ones whose parents manage to make their parting relatively peaceful, the pain is less but not gone. When the parents keep their acrimony toward each other in check and maintain their relationships with their children through cooperative coparenting efforts, the children are better able to adjust to the divorce trauma and accept the new family structures that develop. By maintaining control over decisions about postdivorce child-rearing arrangements, parents are able to provide for their children the sense of security and trust that is created when children know their parents are mutually making decisions about their care and well-being.

Throughout this book, I have tried to emphasize the inadequacy of the adversarial approach for resolving parenting disputes. As an alternative to the ill-fitting legal tradition, mediation is sensible and effective, yet it cannot perform magic. As has become clear over the years, there is a certain population of disputing spouses with whom mediation is ineffective, and there are cases in which a mediated agreement breaks down in the months following its construction. Moreover, the various ethical and moral difficulties discussed in Chapter Fifteen cast confusion upon mediation practice and confront mediators with conceptual challenges in need of resolution. Clearly, there is still a great deal of work ahead in evaluating, clarifying, and expanding the mediator's role, conceptual framework, and methodology.

Future Research Questions

Much research is needed to answer the wide range of pragmatic questions that arise regarding the efficacy of mediation. These can be summed up as follows: Which mediators, with what kinds of training, working in what kinds of legal and social settings, with what kinds of extended community and professional support systems, using what kinds of methods and techniques, work best for which families, with what age children, in what kinds of family structures, with what kinds of family dynamics, to resolve what specific kinds of disputes?

In future research, perhaps we can avoid the mistakes made by psychotherapy researchers, who tried for scores of years to discover which therapy approach was the most effective by pitting one against the other. After it became apparent that all therapy approaches were effective some of the time, researchers began to develop an appreciation for the common elements among therapies and for the complexities of the specific factors that can lead to cognitive, emotional, and behavioral change. Conceptually and practically, mediation research should be easier to carry out than psychotherapy research because of the more circumscribed nature of the mediation task (reaching a workable and lasting agreement), which stands in contrast to the variable processes and goals of psychotherapy. Ongoing evaluation of the development of our approaches can help curtail the seemingly inevitable theoretical and pragmatic mythologies that tend to develop around new social intervention approaches.

Need for Proper Training and Sensitivity

The acutely sensitive, potentially volatile, and extraordinarily significant nature of family relationships in times of crisis demands the respect of intervenors. Ignorance, carelessness, or incompetence on the part of mediators can have devastating consequences for the lives of the family members involved. We must understand that parent-child bonds are precious and must be preserved and nurtured. Mediators who lack appropriate skill and training may not only be ineffective in mediation but may also do psychological and emotional harm to children. This is not something that we can tolerate. Because of the enormous responsibility one bears in conducting custody mediation, it is essential that the mediator be fully knowledgeable, trained, and competent in doing this kind of work.

Mediators who are attorneys need to be aware of the pain experienced by divorcing spouses. These couples must be dealt with sensitively and compassionately. The strategies used by children and spouses are their ways of coping with the emotional pain of the divorce. As such, they must be understood in terms of their emotional roots, as complex expressions of a stress that can be neither overlooked nor manipulated away. The strategies detailed in this book are not the same as attorneys' strategies, which are dispassionate legal tactics. Mediation work by attorneys requires that they maintain the interpersonal sensitivity and emotional understanding required of mental health professionals. Attorneys who want to develop their custody mediation skills should consider taking courses or professional workshops in child development, family dynamics, and clinical interviewing of couples, families, and children. Doing co-mediation work with an experienced custody mediator can provide an excellent opportunity for supervised training and experience.

Mediators who are mental health professionals also need to be well versed in child development and in marital and family dynamics. Moreover, they need to be thoroughly familiar with the legal practices and procedures of family law within their local areas of jurisdiction. In particular, they need to be fully aware of the various legal options locally available to couples who are making postdivorce parenting arrangements. Working together with an experienced attorney who specializes in family law is a useful way for the mental health professional to get access to legal information and advice on the pertinent legal literature.

Both therapists and lawyers who want information on specific training in family mediation can contact the following national organizations dealing with mediation:

Academy of Family Mediators, 5 Militia Drive, Lexington, MA 02173. Phone: (781) 674–2663. Fax: (781) 674–2690. E-mail: afmoffice@mediation.org. This is the association of family mediators within the private sector. Its journal is *Mediation Quarterly.*

Association of Family and Conciliation Courts, 329 West Wilson Street, Madison, WI 53703. Phone: (608) 251–4001. Fax: (608) 251–2231. E-mail: afcc@afccnet.org. This is the association of family court service professionals who are involved with court-connected mediation within the public sector. Its journal is *Family and Conciliation Courts Review.*

In addition to the trainings offered by these organizations, there are now a number of university programs offering advanced degrees in conflict resolution. Although not a comprehensive list, among the universities with such offerings at the time of this writing are the following:

California State University at Dominguez Hills, Carson, California: master's degree

Columbia University Teachers College, New York, New York: master's degree

George Mason University, Fairfax, Virginia: master's and doctoral degrees in dispute resolution

Maxwell School, Syracuse University, Syracuse, New York: master's and doctoral degrees in political science with concentrations in conflict resolution

McGregor School of Antioch University, Yellow Springs, Ohio: master of arts degree in conflict resolution

Montclair State University, Upper Montclair, New Jersey: certificate program

Nova Southeastern University, Fort Lauderdale, Florida: certificate, master's, and doctorate in dispute resolution

Royal Roads University, Victoria, British Columbia: master's degree

University of Massachusetts at Boston: certificate and master's degree

Wayne State University, Detroit, Michigan: master's degree

When spouses approach attorneys for assistance in a custody dispute, they are emotionally polarized and may appear angry, spiteful, and vindictive. To be optimally helpful, the attorney must understand and pay attention to the hurt and scared feelings that lie beneath the surface. Out of such vulnerable feelings arise the many coping strategies that spouses utilize. Attorneys who respond only to the surface requests for aggressive legal action while ignoring the emotional context in which such requests arise encourage actions that ultimately can have destructive consequences for the children.

Once attorneys begin to appreciate the complex and systemic nature of family dynamics, they will see that there are no heroes or villains in family disputes, only participants who very frequently have reciprocal roles in the family system. Even though attorneys may feel an ethical need to maintain their prescribed role as advocates for their clients, it would behoove them to learn to view the client within the family context. From this perspective, it becomes apparent that the interests of the client can best be served by reducing the destructive effects of divorce on the client's children. And this can best be accomplished by minimizing adversarial efforts and maximizing mediational efforts. Attorneys can accomplish this by repeatedly emphasizing to their clients the serious risks to their children of custody litigation and by informing them of the proven benefits of mediation. If more clients received strong, supportive, and convincing premediation preparation from their attorneys, then more would come to accept mediation as the better alternative and couples would doubtless reach lasting agreements more easily. To the degree that their attorneys are supportive and encouraging of mediation, most couples will strive to make it work. And to the degree that it works, attorneys will have more satisfied clients with children who will grow up psychologically healthy in spite of the trauma of their parents' divorce.

While judges are bound to function within the boundaries of, and serve as models for, established legal practices, they paradoxically also have wide discretionary powers in matters of family law. Hence in a given custody disputed case, they may choose from a range of judicial options, from hearing the case within the traditional adversarial context to ordering that the case be settled in mediation. When a judge is strongly supportive of mediation as the better way to resolve custody and visitation disputes, the attorneys and their clients tend to settle the dispute outside of litigation (King, 1979). Moreover, as attorneys in a community experience a local judge's strong support of mediation, they will more readily advise their clients to seriously consider mediation efforts. Because local court attitudes and decisions set a climate of expectations for attorneys regarding likely case outcomes, judges have the power to gradually influence the attitudes of disputing spouses via their attorneys. After a time, a ripple effect sets in and further shifts the consciousness and actions of divorcing parents within a community toward cooperative and self-determined settlements of their disputes.

Perhaps we can best end this book with a legendary story of Japanese dispute resolution, looking to history for an ideal for the future (Tanaka, 1976, pp. 306–307):

> This is a story about a trial during the Tokugawa period which is suggestive of the Japanese concept of adjudication. One day, so the story goes, a plasterer picked up on the road a purse containing three *ryo*. (A *ryo* is an old Japanese gold coin.) The purse also contained a piece

of paper identifying a certain carpenter as its owner. The plasterer took
the trouble of locating the carpenter to return the purse. For all his
pains the plasterer was told by the carpenter: "Since the purse elected
to slip out of my pocket, I don't want such ungrateful money. Go away
with the money." The plasterer insisted that the money belonged to
the carpenter. Thereupon a brawl started and finally they agreed to
take the case to arbitration by the Lord Ooka of Echizen. Having
heard the story from both sides, the Lord added one *ryo* to the three
ryo, split the sum into two, handed two *ryo* to each party, and an-
nounced: "My good men, this is my decision. The plasterer could have
gained three *ryo* if he had walked away as the carpenter told him to
do. By this decision, he will end up with two ryo, so he is to lose one
ryo. The carpenter could have recovered all three *ryo* if he had accepted
the plasterer's kindness with a good grace. Instead he refused to accept
the purse. By this decision, he is to lose one *ryo*. I also have to contribute one *ryo*. So each of the three is to end up with one *ryo* less.

APPENDIX A
UNIFORM STANDARDS OF PRACTICE FOR COURT-CONNECTED CHILD CUSTODY MEDIATION FOR THE STATE OF CALIFORNIA*

Commentary: Standards of practice are normally set to define expectations for participants and to provide a means of assessing the performance of the mediator and evaluating the service. Therefore, the standards of practice that follow cover the whole of mediation and include those sections specifically defined by Civil Code sections 4607.1: the best interest of the child; continuing contact with both parties; facilitating the transition of the family; and equalizing power relationships between the parties. These standards are put forth as Standards of Judicial Administration and should be periodically re-evaluated.

a) [Responsibility for mediation services] Superior court judges and court administrators are primarily responsible for ensuring that

1) legislatively mandated court mediation programs are implemented and operated at high professional standards, and (2) families are provided a forum that offers the highest levels of impartiality and competency the court system can provide.

Commentary: Mediation of child-related issues is a critical endeavor given the grave importance of the decisions made in the process. The unique problems and needs of the child whose parents are divorcing must be addressed with great skill and professionalism by the court. The ultimate success of any mediation service rests not only on the skill and professionalism of the mediator but also on the support of both the bench and the administration of the court. This support must include provisions for

---

* Source: Statewide Office of Family Court Services, Judicial Council of California, Administrative Office of the Courts, with text from Section 26 of The Standards of Judicial Administration in the 1991 California Rules of Court. Reprinted with permission.

329

adequate staffing and compensation for both mediation and support services, suitable facilities and equipment for service delivery, and the establishment of professionally realistic workloads. Mediation services should be administered and supervised by the superior court.

b) [Orientation of mediation parties] Each court should develop a pre-mediation education program based on current research and established court mediation practice.

Commentary: Orientation involves providing information in advance of mediation using a variety of educational methods that may include individual presentation by the mediator, group instruction, video presentations, intake forms, and written materials.

Orienting parties prior to mediation may have several benefits: 1) informing the parties about the court process, including mediation, thereby reducing their fears; 2) preparing the parties for sessions by giving them the opportunity to ask questions and raise concerns; 3) helping to normalize the family crisis; and 4) promoting an out-of-court settlement.

1) As part of its orientation process, each court should use a detailed intake form.

Commentary: The intake from is an important component of the mediation process. It should include the following information: names of parties and children, birth dates, addresses, phone numbers, attorneys of record, date of separation, date of upcoming hearing, issues in dispute, family violence occurrences, location of the child at the time of the sessions, and other requirements as specified in Civil Code sections 4607.2 and 4351.6. An intake form should state that the information is for mediation office personnel only and is subject to rules of confidentiality.

2) Before beginning mediation, the mediator or a court representative should explain the following to the parties: i) the types of disputed issues that are discussed in mediation; ii) who has access to the information communicated by the participants in the session; iii) the circumstances under which the mediator will make recommendations to the court; and iv) who has access to the mediation file.

Commentary: It is important that the mediator conduct an individualized orientation with the parties at the beginning of the session. Parties should be familiar with the content of discussions appropriate in mediation, e.g. the process of creating a parenting plan. The mediator should also make certain that the parties understand that an agreement is not required at any time during mediation. The court, attorneys, and the mediator all play a role in informing the parties as to the basic process of mediation and the manner in which the legal and mediation processes interact.

3) Each court should provide the parties with a written description of i) the mediation process and ii) the court's formal procedures as they apply to the matters stated in subdivision (b)(2).

4) Each court is encouraged to provide bilingual mediators to non-English-speaking parties or to inform parties and their attorneys that they should provide an interpreter. Parties with communication barriers should be informed by the court that they are responsible for providing an intermediary.

Commentary: Provisions should be made by the court or by the parties for orientation and education for parties who do not have the customary language or sensory literacy skills and for those with cultural communication needs. Because of fiscal constraints, these court services are limited. If these services cannot be provided by the court, the court should notify the parties sufficiently far in advance in order that the services may be arranged by the parties.

c) [Ethics and sensitivity to differences] The mediators should maintain high ethical standards of conduct because they are fundamental to providing the highest level of service to families. In addition, mediators should be knowledgeable about their own biases and be sensitive to individual, gender, racial, ethnic, and cultural values and differences.

1) The parties and the mediator should disclose any actual or potential conflicts of interest. This conflict should be resolved to the satisfaction of all parties before mediation begins. If there is a conflict of interest between the mediator and one or both of the parties, the parties, their attorneys, and the mediator should meet and confer in an attempt to resolve the conflict of interest. After they meet and confer, if the conflict has not been resolved satisfactorily, they should submit the matter to the judge for resolution. The court may order mediation to continue with another mediator. If all parties agree to continue mediation despite the disclosed conflict of interest, the parties should acknowledge their agreement in writing. If a conflict of interest has been established, the court should offer alternatives (such as referral to another county).

2) Even though the role of the mediator is defined as neutral in structuring and facilitating an agreement between the parties, the mediator should be mindful of the interests of the child. If the mediator's professional opinion is that a proposed agreement of the parties does not promote the best interest of the child, the mediator should inform the parties

of this opinion and its basis. If the mediator's opinion is that an agreement would be detrimental to the child, the mediator should inform the parents, unless doing so would put the child at further risk. The mediator may inform the court of a potentially detrimental agreement unless doing so is inconsistent with the court's confidentiality rules. In addition, the mediator may recommend to the court that an attorney be appointed under Civil Code section 4606 to represent the interests of the child.

3) In order to maintain a neutral stance the mediator should understand and be sensitive to differences including gender biases and ethnic and cultural diversity.

Commentary: If the mediator has questions or concerns about the cultural values and how they affect the child's best interest, the mediator should feel free to discuss these differences in the course of a session.

4) The mediator should maintain client confidentiality according to all requirements of state law and rules of court. Client confidentiality includes confidentiality in the storage and disposal of records accumulated during the mediation process.

d) [Minimum qualifications of mediators] The foundation of competency in mediation is the knowledge, training, and experience of the mediator. The minimum education and experience requirements provided by statute should be met within a reasonable time after the date of the new mediator's appointment.

Commentary: Code of Civil Procedure section 1745 provides for substituting a portion of education for required experience (minimum two years' experience in counseling) or experience for required education (master's degree). Courts for which recruitment of qualified personnel is a significant problem may find it necessary to apply the substitution provision in the law. However, in making that choice, the court should require the candidate to meet all of the qualifications listed within a reasonable period of time. No person should be appointed as a mediator who cannot realistically be expected to complete all qualification requirements within a reasonable time without substitutions.

e) [Training and continuing education]

1) The mediator should be knowledgeable and skillful in the performance of mediation. The court should provide a continuing opportunity for mediators to improve their knowledge and skills through such resources as formal education, conferences, workshops, seminars, and professional literature.

Commentary: The areas of training may include, but not be limited to, the following: mediation models, theory, and techniques; the nature of conflict and its resolution; family law, the legal process, and case law relevant to the performance of mediation; substance abuse; recent research applicable to the profession; family life cycles; divorce, family reorganization, and remarriage; child development; crisis intervention; psychopathology; interviewing skills; domestic violence, including child abuse, spousal abuse, and child neglect, and the possibility of danger in the mediation session; parent education; administration of mediation programs; sensitivity to individual, gender, racial, and cultural diversity and socioeconomic status; family systems theory; the development of parenting plans, and the role of the parenting plan in the family's transition.

2) Newly hired mediators should undergo a minimum of 40 hours of mediation training within their first six months of employment.

Commentary: Training for newly hired mediators may consist of, but need not be limited to, the following: training workshops, direct observation of mediations, training videos, the study of professional literature, co-mediation with an experienced mediator, and the observation of family law proceedings. Newly hired mediators with previous court-connected mediation experience need not participate in the additional mediation training mentioned here.

3) Persons responsible for the clinical supervision of new mediators should meet the statutory education and experience qualifications for mediators, have two years' experience in court mediation, and demonstrate competence.

4) Each court should make it possible for all family court directors, supervisors of mediators, and mediators to attend at least 16 hours of training each calendar year, including continuing education on domestic violence. In addition, mediators are required by section 1745.5 of the Code of Civil Procedure to participate in continuing education on domestic violence.

f) [Best interest of the child] The "best interest of the child" is a broad concept that involves the following principles; i) promoting social, cognitive, emotional, and physical well-being; ii) enabling optimal development as a productive member of our society; iii) minimizing exposure to danger, abuse, neglect, and family conflict; and iv) ensuring frequent and continuing contact with both parties so far as it is consistent with the above. While the mediator has a duty to the parties to be impartial, the overriding concern of the mediator should be the best interest of the child.

1) The mediator should strive to integrate the best interest of the child with the parents' circumstances, rights, and responsibilities. The mediator should use his or her best effort to assist the parents in reaching sound agreements and to help them work toward the reduction of acrimony, thereby reducing the negative effects of family conflict on the parents as well as on the child.

Commentary: Promoting understanding of the "best interest" standard for a particular child may require that the mediator do any or all of the following during or after the session: 1) assist the parties in examining the separate and individual needs of the child; 2) provide for discussion of the nature of the parent-child relationship, the child's need for stability, and the contact the child will continue to have with each parent; 3) interview the child if the mediator believes that such an interview would further the mediation process without causing unnecessary concern on the part of the child (e.g. excessive numbers of interviews by professionals from various agencies is generally not advisable); 4) consider the possibility that the child has had access to other significant family members, and when helpful for achieving agreement, include those family members in the mediation; 5) help the parties anticipate the implications of their agreement, e.g., potential travel time for children, new neighborhoods, new schools; and 6) report suspected child abuse and child neglect to the appropriate authorities. The mediation service should develop a protocol for the storage of child abuse reports, and for determining the scope of confidentiality of a child abuse report in regard to the issues reported and the documents created. Additionally, interagency coordination is helpful to describe and make explicit the procedures regarding confidentiality.

2) It is at the mediator's discretion to suspend or not perform mediation if child abuse or neglect is reasonable suspected. Mediation may resume after the designated agency performs an investigation and reports a case determination to the mediator.

Commentary: The mediator should provide community mental health referrals if appropriate, and serve as a resource to the court in managing the family's case while the family receives the needed service.

g) [Facilitating the family's transition] The mediator should assist the parties to:

1) focus on the needs of the child; 2) identify areas of stability for the child; 3) identify the strengths of the family; and 4) develop options that promote continuity in the child's relationships with each parent.

The mediator and the parents should carefully draft a comprehensive parenting plan (see subdivision (i)). A parenting plan may include but is not limited to the following: 1) designation of legal and physical custody and how this is related to parental authority and decision making; 2) a weekly schedule for the child with each parent; 3) a holiday schedule for the child with each parent; 4) a summer schedule for the child with each parent; 5) vacation time, i.e., time that the child may spend each year without regularly scheduled physical contact with the other parent; 6) provisions for protecting the child, such as supervised visitation if high-risk factors are present, (e.g., a history of substance abuse, debilitating illness, acts of domestic violence by one or both parents, child abuse, or neglect); and 7) special day arrangements, e.g., birthdays of the child, siblings, and parents.

Commentary: Additional topics often critical to meeting the needs of a particular family should be considered for inclusion in the parenting plan by the mediator and the parties. These may include the following: 1) geographic location and moves; 2) the child's age-level, developmental, and emotional needs; 3) the child's educational and day care needs and the choice and monitoring of school and after school arrangements; 4) the child's activities, such as special lessons, recreation, and athletic and social events; 5) family preferences for religious and cultural events and holidays; 6) the child's health care considerations, particularly choice of health care providers and treatment plans; 7) possible impediments to implementation of or compliance with the parenting plan and how the parties will handle differences that may arise between them; 8) special considerations regarding transportation for the child; 9) requirement for and amount of notice for the other parent regarding changes from the set routine; and 10) the child's contact with extended family members as appropriate.

h) [Equalizing the power relationship between the parties] A primary objective of mediation should be to assist both parties in effecting a mutual and self-determined agreement regarding the child. The mediator, therefore, should be vigilant about a power imbalance in the parental relationship. Power imbalances can take many forms, including gender-biased attributions regarding parental role, intimidation, and economic advantage.

1) [Balancing power requires continuing vigilance] Balancing power in mediation should be a continuing process and requires continuing mediator attention. An important means of empowering parties to reach informed decisions is through the provision of careful and detailed descriptions

of the mediation process by the court, counsel, and mediator, and through premediation education as described in subdivision (b).

2) [When to continue mediation] Mediation may proceed when in the mediator's judgment the parties are able to discuss their situation, including all the following factors: i) the free expression of all family members' needs; ii) exploration of available options; iii) reasonable alternatives discussed and freely agreed to by all; and iv) a plan for an agreement about the safety of all family members during the exchange of the children.

3) [When to terminate mediation] If the mediator is not able to meet the spirit and intent of the criteria identified in (1) and (2) above to his or her satisfaction, mediation should be terminated. The mediator should use his or her best efforts to effect a balanced discussion between the parties, but when the discussion or behavior of one or both parties makes this impossible, mediation should be terminated.

4) [Conditions for separate sessions] Separate sessions may be held if the mediator believes that the circumstances call for them. If there is a history of domestic violence and if a protective order is in effect, at the request of the party protected by the order, the parties shall meet with the mediator separately at separate times. Separate sessions may also be held at the request of one of the parties if there is an indication of domestic violence and no protective order is in effect. If the parties agree during their individual sessions to participate in a conjoint session, the mediator may agree to conjoint sessions.

5) [Understanding the plan] The mediator should provide the opportunity for each party to understand all parenting plan provisions. This understanding should also include the importance of safeguards involving parental contact.

6) [Additional information and assistance] If a party needs additional information or assistance for discussions to proceed in a fair and orderly manner or for an agreement to be reached, the mediator may postpone further mediation so that the parties may first obtain the needed information or assistance.

7) [Safety] Mediation should be practiced in a physically safe and nonthreatening environment and be suspended if it becomes unsafe for any of the participants, including the mediator.

Commentary: So that dangerous incidents may be averted, mediators should be aware of the potential for violence. A safe environment should include, at the minimum, the immediate availability of safety personnel upon call by the mediator. If the mediator determines that mediation should be suspended, he or she should inform the parties and their attorneys of the conditions under which mediation may resume. Use of an intake form as described in subdivision (b) of this document can allow for the early detection of issues of family violence.

i) [Concluding mediation] A detailed and clearly written parenting plan or agreement or, under certain circumstances, an oral agreement should be the end-product of the mediation process. This agreement should be reported to counsel for the parties prior to its being reported to the court. Should an agreement not be reached, the mediator should explain to the parties what the next steps are, including whether he or she will make a recommendation to the court and, if appropriate, how the parties may obtain temporary orders. Because children's needs change over time, the mediator should offer the opportunity for the parties to return to mediation if they are unable to renegotiate on their own.

Commentary: Under civil code section 4607(e), ". . . any agreement reached by the parties as a result of the mediation should be reported 1) to counsel for the parties by the mediator on the day set for mediation, or 2) as soon thereafter as practical but prior to its being reported to the court." This requirement is satisfied when the parties take the confirmed agreement to their attorneys. The mediated agreement must be of sufficient detail and construction so as to be legally enforceable unless the parties agree otherwise. As a mediation practice, it is important for the mediator to review the wording of the parenting plan with the parties at the conclusion of mediation.

j) [Program accountability] The court should establish a follow-up assessment such as an exit survey or a follow-up survey for parties and attorneys. In addition, each court is strongly encouraged to establish a policy in writing regarding handling of complaints from parties, attorneys, and interested persons.

Commentary: The invitation to comment should include to whom the evaluation should be written, as well as a mechanism for ensuring confidentiality if so desired by the parties.

Directors of Family Courts Services are encouraged to contact the Statewide FCS Office for assistance regarding the design and execution of this follow-up process as well as other program assessment procedures.

APPENDIX B
ACADEMY OF FAMILY MEDIATORS STANDARDS OF PRACTICE FOR FAMILY AND DIVORCE MEDIATION*

I. Preamble

Mediation is a family-centered conflict resolution process in which an impartial third party assists the participants to negotiate a consensual and informed settlement. In mediation, whether private or public, decision-making authority rests with the parties. The role of the mediator includes reducing the obstacles to communication, maximizing the exploration of alternatives, and addressing the needs of those it is agreed are involved or affected.

Mediation is based on principles of problem solving that focus on the needs and interests of the participants; fairness; privacy; self determination; and the best interest of all family members.

These standards are intended to assist and guide public, private, voluntary, and mandatory mediation. It is understood that the manner of implementation and mediator adherence to these standards may be influenced by local law or court rule.

II. Initiating the Process

A. Definition and Description of Mediation. The mediator shall define mediation and describe the differences and similarities between mediation and other procedures for dispute resolution. In defining the process, the mediator shall delineate it from therapy, counseling, custody evaluation, arbitration, and advocacy.

*Reprinted by permission of the Academy of Family Mediators.

B. Identification of Issues. The mediation shall elicit sufficient information from the participants so that they can mutually define and agree on the issues to be resolved in mediation.

C. Appropriateness of Mediation. The mediator shall help the participants evaluate the benefits, risks, and costs of mediation and the alternatives available to them.

D. Mediator's Duty of Disclosure
  1. Biases. The mediator shall disclose to the participants any biases or strong views relating to the issues to be mediated.
  2. Training and Experience. The mediator's education, training, and experience to mediate the issues should be accurately described to the participants.

III. Procedures

The mediator shall reach an understanding with the participants regarding the procedures to be followed in mediation. This includes but is not limited to the practice as to separate meetings between a participant and the mediator, confidentiality, use of legal services, the involvement of additional parties, and conditions under which mediation may be terminated.

A. Mutual Duties and Responsibilities. The mediator and the participants shall agree upon the duties and responsibilities that each is accepting in the mediation process. This may be a written or verbal agreement.

IV. Impartiality and Neutrality

A. Impartiality. The mediator is obligated to maintain impartiality toward all participants. Impartiality means freedom from favoritism or bias, either in word or action. Impartiality implies a commitment to aid all participants, as opposed to a single individual, in reaching a mutually satisfactory agreement. Impartiality means that a mediator will not play an adversarial role.

The mediator has a responsibility to maintain impartiality while raising questions for the parties to consider as to the fairness, equity, and feasibility of proposed options for settlement.

B. Neutrality. Neutrality refers to the relationship that the mediator has with the disputing parties. If the mediator feels, or any one of the participants states, that the mediator's background or personal experiences would prejudice the mediator's performance, the mediator should withdraw from mediation unless all agree to proceed.

C. Prior Relationships. A mediator's actual or perceived impartiality may be compromised by social or professional relationships with one of the participants at any point in time. The mediator shall not proceed if previous legal or counseling services have been provided to one of the participants. If such services have been provided to both participants, mediation shall not proceed unless the prior relationship has been discussed, the role of the mediator made distinct from the earlier relationship, and the participants given the opportunity to freely choose to proceed.

D. Relationship to Participants. The mediator should be aware that postmediation professional or social relationships may compromise the mediator's continued availability as a neutral third party.

E. Conflict of Interest. A mediator should disclose any circumstance to the participants that might cause a conflict of interest.

V. Costs and Fees

A. Explanation of Fees. The mediator shall explain the fees to be charged for mediation and any related costs and shall agree with the participants on how the fees will be shared and the manner of payment.

B. Reasonable Fees. When setting fees, the mediator shall ensure that they are explicit, fair, reasonable, and commensurate with the service to be performed. Unearned fees should be promptly returned to the clients.

C. Contingent Fees. It is inappropriate for a mediator to charge contingent fees or to base fees on the outcome of mediation.

D. Referrals and Commissions. No commissions, rebates, or similar forms of remuneration shall be given or received for referral of clients for mediation services.

VI. Confidentiality and Exchange of Information

A. Confidentiality. Confidentiality relates to the full and open disclosure necessary for the mediation process. A mediator shall foster the confidentiality of the process.

B. Limits of Confidentiality. The mediator shall inform the parties at the initial meeting of limitations on confidentiality, such as statutorily or judicially mandated reporting.

C. Appearing in Court. The mediator shall inform the parties of circumstances under which mediators may be compelled to testify in court.

D. Consequences of Disclosure of Facts Between Parties. The mediator shall discuss with the participants the potential consequences of their disclosure of facts to each other during the mediation process.

E. Release of Information. The mediator shall obtain the consent of the participants prior to releasing information to others. The mediator shall maintain confidentiality and render anonymous all identifying information when materials are used for research or training purposes.

F. Caucus. The mediator shall discuss policy regarding confidentiality for individual caucuses. In the event that a mediator, on consent of the participants, speaks privately with any person not represented in mediation, including children, the mediator shall define how information received will be used.

G. Storage and Disposal of Records. The mediator shall maintain confidentiality in the storage and disposal of records.

H. Full Disclosure. The mediator shall require disclosure of all relevant information in the mediation process, as would reasonably occur in the judicial discovery process.

VII. Self-Determination

A. Responsibilities of the Participants and the Mediator. The primary responsibility for the resolution of a dispute rests with the participants. The mediator's obligation is to assist the disputants in reaching an informed and voluntary settlement. At no time shall a mediator coerce a participant into agreement or make a substantive decision for any participant.

B. Responsibility to Third Parties. The mediator has a responsibility to promote the participants' consideration of the interests of children and other persons affected by the agreement. The mediator also has a duty to assist parents to examine, apart from their own desires, the separate and individual needs of such people. The participants shall be encouraged to seek outside professional consultation when appropriate or when they are otherwise unable to agree on the needs of any individual affected by the agreement.

VIII. Professional Advice

A. Independent Advice and Information. The mediator shall encourage and assist the participants to obtain independent expert information and advice when such information is needed to reach an informed agreement or to protect the rights of a participant.

B. Providing Information. A mediator shall give information only in those areas where qualified by training or experience.

C. Independent Legal Counsel. When the mediation may affect legal rights or obligations, the mediator shall advise the participants to seek independent legal counsel prior to resolving the issues and in conjunction with formalizing an agreement.

IX. Parties' Ability to Negotiate

The mediator shall ensure that each participant has had an opportunity to understand the implications and ramifications of available options. In the event a participant needs either additional information or assistance in order for the negotiations to proceed in a fair and orderly manner or for an agreement to be reached, the mediator shall refer the individual to appropriate resources.

A. Procedural Factors. The mediator has a duty to ensure balanced negotiations and should not permit manipulative or intimidating negotiation techniques.

B. Psychological Factors. The mediator shall explore whether the participants are capable of participating in informed negotiations. The mediator may postpone mediation and refer the parties to appropriate resources if necessary.

X. Concluding Mediation

A. Full Agreement. The mediator shall discuss with the participants the process for formalization and implementation of the agreement.

B. Partial Agreement. When the participants reach a partial agreement, the mediator shall discuss with them procedures available to resolve the remaining issues. The mediator shall inform the participants of their right to withdraw from mediation at any time and for any reason.

C. Termination by Participants. The mediator shall inform the participants of their right to withdraw from mediation at any time and for any reason.

D. Termination by Mediator. If the mediator believes that participants are unable or unwilling to participate meaningfully in the process or that a reasonable agreement is unlikely, the mediator may suspend or terminate mediation and should encourage the parties to seek appropriate professional help.

E. Impasse. If the participants reach a final impasse, the mediator should not prolong unproductive discussions that would result in emotional and monetary costs to the participants.

XI. Training and Education

A. Training. A mediator shall acquire substantive knowledge and procedural skill in the specialized area of practice. This may include but is not limited to family and human development, family law, divorce procedures, family finances, community resources, the mediation process, and professional ethics.

B. Continuing Education. A mediator shall participate in continuing education and be personally responsible for ongoing professional growth. A mediator is encouraged to join with other mediators and members of related professions to promote mutual professional development.

XII. Advertising

A mediator shall make only accurate statements about the mediation process, its costs and benefits, and the mediator's qualifications.

XIII. Relationship with Other Professionals

A. The Responsibility of the Mediator Toward Other Mediators/Relationship with Other Mediators. A mediator should not mediate any dispute that is being mediated by another mediator without first endeavoring to consult with the person or persons conducting the mediation.

B. Co-mediation. In those situations where more than one mediator is participating in a particular case, each mediator has a responsibility to keep the others informed of developments essential to a cooperative effort.

C. Relationships with Other Professionals. A mediator should respect the complementary relationship between mediation and legal, mental health, and other social services and should promote cooperation with other professionals.

XIV. Advancement of Mediation

A. Mediation Service. A mediator is encouraged to provide some mediation service in the community for nominal or no fee.

B. Promotion of Mediation. A mediator shall promote the advancement of mediation by encouraging and participating in research, publishing, or other forms of professional and public education.

APPENDIX C
CONFIDENTIALITY FORMS

Form Used in Private Mediation

STIPULATION TO CONFIDENTIALITY
OF MEDIATION SERVICES

IT IS HEREBY STIPULATED TO AND AGREED by and between

_____ and _____

AS FOLLOWS:

1. We are making this agreement because we have not agreed with each other on the custody and/or visitation privileges regarding our child(ren). We both would like to make decisions that are in the best interests of our child(ren), and we both feel that it would be best if we could settle these differences without a court fight.

2. To facilitate our making decisions that are in the best interests of our child(ren), we have agreed to hire a mediator, Donald T. Saposnek, Ph.D., who, as we understand it, will not make our decisions for us but will simply help us make our own decisions, together.

3. We recognize that to reach good decisions about this matter, we need to be able to talk in a frank, open, and honest atmosphere. To further the presence of this atmosphere, we agree that the mediation services of Dr. Donald T. Saposnek, his records, and all disclosures made in connection with mediation services rendered by him shall be deemed to be of a privileged and confidential nature. Each party agrees not to attempt to compel Dr. Saposnek to disclose any such information in any subsequent legal proceeding relating to custody and/or visitation issues. The confidentiality provision described herein applies to any disclosure made between either party and Dr. Saposnek, between both parties and Dr. Saposnek, or between the child(ren) of the parties and Dr. Saposnek. All such disclosures

shall be protected by *Section 1014 of the Evidence Code of the State of California*. The parties agree that to protect the interests of the minor child(ren), Dr. Saposnek shall not be required to disclose any subject matter covered by this confidentiality agreement, notwithstanding the written consent of the parties and Dr. Saposnek.

4. In the absence of such written consent, the parties agree that Dr. Saposnek shall not be required to disclose any subject matter or produce any records covered by this agreement or be compelled to testify in connection with the aforementioned custody or visitation proceedings or act in any other way to divulge the records or disclosures to third parties.

5. No change may be made in this stipulation without the written approval of Dr. Saposnek.

6. Either party or Dr. Saposnek may at any time file this stipulation in the court records of the foregoing proceeding.

7. Dr. Saposnek's fees shall be paid in advance of each mediation session. We agree that we will each pay one-half of the fee for each session, unless we explicitly agree to a different arrangement for fee payment.

Dated: _____

_____   _____
        Mother   Father

_____
Donald T. Saposnek, Ph.D.

Form Used by Court-Appointed Mediators for Mandatory Mediation

FAMILY MEDIATION SERVICE AGREEMENT
REGARDING CONFIDENTIALITY
OF MEDIATION SERVICES

IT IS HEREBY STIPULATED TO AND AGREED by and between
_____ and _____
AS FOLLOWS:

1. In entering mediation, we recognize that to reach good decisions about this matter, we need to be able to talk in a frank, open, and honest atmosphere. To further the presence of this atmosphere, we agree that the mediation services of our mediator, his/her records, and all disclosures made in connection with mediation services rendered by this mediator shall be deemed to be of a privileged and confidential nature. The confidentiality provision described herein applies to any disclosure made between either party and our mediator, between both parties and our mediator, or between the child(ren) of the parties and our mediator. All such disclosures shall be protected by *Section 1014 of the Evidence Code of the State of California.* The parties agree that to protect the interests of the minor child(ren), our mediator shall not be required to disclose any subject matter covered by this confidentiality agreement, notwithstanding the written consent of the parties and our mediator.

2. In the absence of such written consent, the parties agree that our mediator shall not be required to disclose any subject matter or produce any records covered by this agreement or be compelled to testify in connection with the aforementioned custody or visitation proceedings or act in any other way to divulge the records or disclosures to third parties.

3. No change may be made in this stipulation without the written approval of our mediator.

4. Either party or our mediator may at any time file this stipulation in the court records of the foregoing proceeding.

Dated: _____

_____   _____
Mother   Father

_____
Mediator

APPENDIX D
PREEMPTING STATEMENT CATEGORIES FOR COMMENCING CHILD CUSTODY MEDIATION

THE FOLLOWING CATEGORIES are the topics of the various preempting statements that can be used to set the context for cooperative negotiations during mediation. They are intended to disarm the strategies with which parents come to mediation and to put both parents on an equal footing regarding discussions about their children. The particular content that you use to fill in each preempt category will come from your own professional knowledge base and personal style. For the full, verbatim text of each, see Chapter Five.

1. Assumption of conflict between parents with possibility of cooperation for the children

2. Assumption that both parents love the children

3. Assumption of children's need for both parents

4. Mediator as child advocate

5. Effects of denigrating the other parent

6. Effects of children's strategies

7. Better parenting when alone with children

8. Children's different parental needs at different developmental stages

9. Resisting children's reuniting strategies

10. Individual needs of each child

11. Flexibility of parenting plan

12. Reconceptualizing "custody" as coparenting

13. Protecting children from psychological harm

14. Respecting the stages of the divorce process

15. Introducing new partners to children

16. The role of stepparents

17. Alcohol and drug abuse

18. Joint responsibility versus 50–50 percent custody

19. Domestic violence

APPENDIX E
STRATEGIES USED BY SPOUSES,
CHILDREN, AND MEDIATORS

FOR A FULL DESCRIPTION of each strategy, see the chapters in Part Three.

I. Strategies of Spouses
- A. Reuniting strategies
  1. Requesting extended mediation
  2. Pursuing sole custody
  3. Pursuing joint custody
  4. Yielding to all demands
  5. Refusing to see the children
- B. Emotionally disengaging strategies
  1. Taking or giving sole custody
  2. Labeling and invalidating the spouse
  3. Buffering
  4. Sabotaging visitations
- C. Emotional survival strategies
  1. Resisting mediation in favor of court
  2. Demanding sole custody
  3. Manipulating or invalidating the children's preferences
- D. Financial survival strategies
  1. Wanting primary physical custody
  2. Wanting shared physical custody
  3. Wanting the children most of the summer
- E. Power assertion strategies
  1. Wanting to win sole custody
  2. The 50–50 percent split
  3. The 51–49 percent split
  4. Use of clichés for justification
  5. Changing the child's last name
  6. Secret phone calls
  7. "Holier than thou" impression

F. Revenge and retaliation strategies
  1. Sole custody as revenge
  2. Point-counterpoint
  3. Joint custody as revenge
  4. Bait and switch
  5. Frustrating visitations
G. Pushing to lose strategies
  1. Martyrdom strategy
  2. Face-saving strategy
H. Appeasing new spouse strategies
  1. Sole custody for new spouse
  2. Pulling away
I. Multiple strategies

II. Children's Strategies
  A. Reuniting strategies
  B. Separation distress-reducing strategies
  C. Tension-detonating strategies
  D. Love-testing strategies
  E. Loyalty-proving strategies
  F. Fairness-seeking strategies
  G. Self-esteem–protecting strategies
  H. Parent-esteem–protecting strategies
  I. Permissive-living strategies

III. Strategies of the Mediator
  A. Cooperation-eliciting strategies
    1. Preempting
    2. Giving information and hope
    3. Complimenting
    4. Reframing
    5. Anecdote-telling
    6. Using physical metaphors
    7. Resisting a "time squeeze"
  B. Conflict-reducing strategies
    1. Reflective listening
    2. Absorbing
    3. Blocking and soothing
    4. Taking an assertive stance
    5. Leaving the room
  C. Conflict-diverting strategies
    1. Converting accusations to requests

2. Diversion problem solving
3. Sudden positive shifting
4. Deflecting
5. Sidestepping
D. Impasse-breaking strategies
1. Offering suggestions
2. Leveraging the children
3. Persuading with dramatic anecdotes
4. Leveraging with attorneys

APPENDIX F
SAMPLE MEDIATION AGREEMENTS

Sample Agreement A

1. Both parents agree to share joint legal custody of their children, Brandon and Lilia.

2. The children will share time with their parents according to the following schedule:

(a) Brandon will be with Mother on Monday and Tuesday and on Friday, Saturday, and Sunday of the first week and on Tuesday, Wednesday, and Thursday of the second week, with this pattern repeating on a biweekly basis. Brandon will be with Father on the other days.

(b) Lilia will be with Mother on Friday, Saturday, and Sunday of the first week and on Wednesday of the second week, with this pattern repeating on a biweekly basis. Lilia will be with Father on the other days.

(c) This plan will begin January 1, 1999, and will continue until March 1, 1999, at which time Mother and Father will evaluate the progress and negotiate a modification, if necessary.

3. During the transfer times within the above plan, Father will pick up the children from their maternal grandmother's house at the start of the children's time with him, and he will return the children to Mother's house at the end of the children's time with him.

4. Both children will spend alternate holidays with each parent throughout the year, with details to be arranged between the parents.

5. Both parents agree to inform each other of the location and duration of any special trips taken with the children.

6. Both parents agree to consult directly with each other rather than through either of the children, in the event of an issue arising regarding the children.

7. Both parents agree to allow both children to have totally open access by phone to either parent at any time.

8. In the event of any future dispute regarding the children that the parents are unable to resolve between themselves, both parents agree to seek mediation before legal action at the request of either parent, and the costs will be shared equally.

Dated: _____

_____   _____
            Mother   Father

_____
           Mediator

Sample Agreement B

1. Both parents agree to share joint legal custody of Lynette.

2. Lynette will share time with her parents according to the following schedule, until December 1, 1998:

(a) Lynette will be with Mother from Tuesdays at 8:00 A.M. to Saturdays at 2:00 P.M.

(b) Lynette will be with Father from Saturdays at 2:00 P.M. to Tuesdays at 8:00 A.M.

(c) Details of transfer times will be arranged between the parents.

3. Beginning December 1, 1998, Lynette will stay at Mother's house four days and four nights and at Father's house three days and three nights, with details to be arranged by mutual consent between the parents to fit with their schedules at that time.

4. By March 1999, both parents agree to have worked out their schedules so that they have reached their goal of equalizing the time that Lynette spends with each of them.

5. The sharing of time with Lynette during holidays will be arranged between the parents by mutual consent.

6. Both parents agree to minimize the number of primary caretakers that care for Lynette.

7. Both parents agree to call each other whenever there is any special concern regarding Lynette that needs sharing with the other parent.

8. During the summer before Lynette enters kindergarten, both parents will reevaluate the time-sharing plan either between themselves or together with a mediator if necessary.

9. In the event of any future dispute regarding Lynette that the parents are unable to resolve between themselves, both parents agree to seek mediation before legal action at the request of either parent, and the costs will be shared equally.

Dated: _____

_____   _____
            Mother   Father

_____
            Mediator

Sample Agreement C

1. Both parents agree that Mother shall retain sole legal custody of their children, Scott and Jason.

2. During the school year, the children will reside at Mother's house and be with Father every other weekend, from Friday after school until Sunday at 8:00 P.M. Also, the children will be with Father on alternate Saturday afternoons, from 1:00 P.M. until 5:00 P.M.

3. During the summers and holidays, Father agrees to make direct plans with the children on an event-by-event basis. Mother agrees to support the children in making every effort possible to spend a significant amount of available time with Father, and Mother agrees not to interfere with these plans, either by making counterplans or by discouraging plans already made.

4. Mother agrees to send to Father's house certain children's clothing (according to an itemized list), which will remain at Father's house after the children return to Mother's house, for the children to use during their subsequent stays at Father's house.

5. Both parents agree to place any written communications to each other that pertain to an issue of dispute between them in a sealed envelope before transferring the note to the other parent.

6. Both parents agree to ask the children about where they would like to keep any gifts they receive, and the children's desires will be respected.

7. Both parents agree to inform each other whenever either of the children has any illness or before the child is taken to see a doctor.

8. Mother agrees to sign and file a permission slip for Father to receive any information about the educational and medical status and condition of the children at any time he wishes.

9. Father agrees to issue health insurance identification cards to each of the children.

10. Mother agrees to indicate in writing that Father is designated "next of kin" on the children's school records.

11. Father agrees to have the children in bed by 10:00 P.M. on the nights that they are with him.

12. Both parents agree to refrain from bad-mouthing each other and each other's extended family members in the presence of the children.

13. Both parents agree to discuss between themselves small issues that may come up regarding the children. These discussions will take place when transferring the children. If one parent feels the need for more lengthy discussion, it will take place during a designated phone call. If the issue remains unresolved, the parents will arrange a face-to-face meeting on neutral ground, away from the children, to resolve the matter.

14. In the event of any future dispute regarding the children that the parents are unable to resolve between themselves, both parents agree to seek mediation before legal action at the request of either parent, and the cost will be shared equally.

Dated: _____

_____   _____
         Mother   Father

_____
        Mediator

Sample Agreement D

1. Both parents agree to share joint legal custody of their children, Danielle and Nathan.

2. The children will share time with their parents according to the following schedule, during the school year:

(a) Danielle's primary residence will be at Mother's house.

(b) Nathan's primary residence will be at Father's house.

(c) Both children together will spend alternate weekends with each parent.

(d) Fridays between 6:00 and 6:15 P.M., the parent who is to have both children for the weekend will pick up the second child at the other parent's house.

(e) Sundays between 8:00 and 8:15 P.M., the parent who does not have the children for the weekend will pick up the child whose primary residence is with that parent from the other parent's house.

(f) Wednesdays between 6:00 and 6:30 P.M., Father will bring Nathan to Mother's house and will pick up Danielle.

(g) Thursdays between 7:30 and 7:45 A.M., Mother will bring Nathan to Father's house. Father will be responsible for taking care of Danielle until 5:15 P.M. on Thursdays.

(h) Thursdays between 5:00 and 5:15 P.M., Mother will pick up Danielle from Father's house.

3. Time in the summers will be shared as follows:

(a) During the months of June and September, the regular school-year schedule will be followed.

(b) Both children will spend the month of July with Mother and the month of August with Father.

(c) During July and August, the children will spend the equivalent of four 24-hour periods with the parent with whom they are not staying. Details for this will be arranged between the parents by mutual consent.

4. If either child goes to summer camp (not to exceed two weeks), the time period at camp will be reduced equally from each parent's equivalent time with the child.

5. Holidays will be shared according to the following schedule:

(a) The children will be with Mother during Thanksgiving vacation from Wednesday after school until Friday evening at 6:30 P.M., at which time Father will pick them up; on Christmas Eve day until 11:00 P.M., at which time Father will pick them up; on New Year's Day; on Mother's Day; on Mother's birthday; and on Memorial Day weekend.

(b) The children will be with Father on Halloween; during Thanksgiving vacation from Friday evening at 6:30 P.M. until Sunday at 5:00 P.M.; on Easter Day; on Father's Day; on Father's birthday; on the Fourth of July; and on Labor Day weekend.

(c) Except for Father's Day, Mother's Day, and Father's and Mother's respective birthday, the foregoing holiday time-sharing schedule will alternate yearly.

(d) The children's birthdays will be celebrated with each parent on the weekend before or after the specific day of birth.

6. If either parent is unavailable to care for either child during his or her regular time with the child, both parents agree to offer to the other parent the first option to take care of the child before making other child care arrangements. It is agreed that the offered parent can decline without having to give any reason and without being under any obligation.

7. Both parents agree to negotiate with each other any occasional changes in the foregoing schedule for any unanticipated special events that may come up. It is understood that such opportunities would be for the benefit of the children.

8. Both parents agree to refrain from being under the influence of alcohol or drugs while with the children, especially while driving them in any motor vehicle. This also applies to any other individuals into whose care the children may be entrusted.

9. Both parents agree to keep both children restrained in government-approved seat belts while driving them in any motor vehicle.

10. In the event that a special school activity arises to which parents are invited, both parents agree to inform each other of the event and to discuss and decide between them which parent will attend the particular event.

11. If either parent anticipates a move out of the area, both parents agree to discuss with each other the consequences of the move well in advance. If either parent feels the need for assistance with such discussions, both parents agree to seek a mediator.

12. In the event of any future dispute regarding the children that the parents are unable to resolve between themselves, both parents agree to seek

mediation before legal action at the request of either parent. Father agrees to pay two-thirds of the costs and Mother agrees to pay one-third of the costs.

Dated: _____

_____   _____
            Mother   Father

_____
           Mediator

REFERENCES

Ahrons, C. R. (1994). *The good divorce.* New York: HarperCollins.

Ahrons, C. R., & Rodgers, R. H. (1987). *Divorced families: A multidisciplinary developmental view.* New York: Norton.

Allison, P. D., & Furstenberg, F. F., Jr. (1989). How marital dissolution affects children. *Developmental Psychology, 25,* 540–549.

Amato, P. (1994). Life-span adjustment of children to their parents' divorce. *The Future of Children: Children and Divorce, 4* (1), 143–164.

Amato, P., & Keith, B. (1991). Parental divorce and adult well being: A meta-analysis. *Journal of Marriage and the Family, 53* (1), 43–58.

Ambert, A.-M. (1992). *The effect of children on parents.* New York: Haworth Press.

Ambert, A.-M. (1997). *Parents, children, and adolescents: Interactive relationships and development in context.* New York: Haworth Press.

Amundson, J., & Fong, L. (1986). Systemic/strategic aspects and potentials in the Haynes model of divorce mediation. In J. A. Lemmon (Ed.), *Emerging roles in divorce mediation.* Mediation Quarterly, no. 12. San Francisco: Jossey-Bass.

Aries, P. (1962). *Centuries of childhood: A social history of family life.* New York: Knopf.

Aronson, E. (1994). *The social animal* (7th ed.). New York: Freeman.

Bateson, G., Jackson, D. D., Haley, J., & Weakland, J. H. (1956). Toward a theory of schizophrenia. *Behavioral Science, 1,* 251–264.

Benjamin, M. (1980). Abused as a child, abusive as a parent: Practitioners beware. In R. Volpe, M. Breton, & J. Mitton (Eds.), *The maltreatment of the school-aged child.* San Francisco: Lexington Books.

Bergman, J. S. (1985). *Fishing for barracuda: Pragmatics of brief systemic therapy.* New York: Norton.

Berner, R. T. (1992). *Parents whose parents were divorced.* New York: Haworth Press.

Bisnaire, L., Firestone, P., & Rynard, D. (1990). Factors associated with academic achievement in children following parental separation. *American Journal of Orthopsychiatry, 60,* 67–76.

Block, J., Block, J., & Gjerde, P. (1986). The personality of children prior to divorce: A prospective study. *Child Development, 57,* 827–840.

Bordarampe, J., Ehrenberg, P., Foran, S., & Oksman, A. (1991). Innovative approaches in child custody evaluations: The joint office interview and client feedback. *Family and Conciliation Courts Review, 29,* 160–171.

Bowker, L. H., Arbitell, M., & McFerron, J. R. (1988). On the relationship between wife beating and child abuse. In K. Yllo and M. Bograd (Eds.), *Feminist perspectives on wife abuse.* Newbury Park, CA: Sage.

Braver, S. L., Salem, P., Pearson, J., & De Lusé, S. R. (1996). The content of divorce education programs: Results of a survey. *Family and Conciliation Courts Review, 34,* 41–59.

Braver, S. L., Wolchik, S., Sandler, I., Fogas, B., & Zvetina, D. (1991). Frequency of visitation by divorced fathers: Differences in reports by fathers and mothers. *American Journal of Orthopsychiatry, 61,* 448–454.

Brooks-Gunn, J., & Matthews, W. S. (1979). *He and she: How children develop their sex-role identity.* Englewood Cliffs, NJ: Prentice Hall.

Brown, D. G. (1982). Divorce and family mediation: History, review, future directions. *Conciliation Courts Review, 20* (2), 1–44.

Bryant, S. (1992). Mediation for lesbian and gay families. *Mediation Quarterly, 9,* 391–395.

Buchanan, C. M., Maccoby, E. E., & Dornbusch, S. M. (1991). Caught between parents: Adolescents' experience in divorced homes. *Child Development, 62,* 1008–1029.

Budman, S. H. (Ed.). (1981). *Forms of brief therapy.* New York: Guilford Press.

Bush, R. A. B., & Folger, J. P. (1994). *The promise of mediation: Responding to conflict through empowerment and recognition.* San Francisco: Jossey-Bass.

California Statewide Office of Family Court Services. (1997, March). *Report 7: Serving families in the '90s: The perspective of direct service providers in California's Family Court Services.* San Francisco: Administrative Office of the Courts, Judicial Council of California.

Camara, K., & Resnick, G. (1988). Interparental conflict and cooperation: Factors moderating children's postdivorce adjustment. In E. M. Hetherington & J. D. Arasteh (Eds.), *Impact of divorce, single parenting, and stepparenting on children.* Hillsdale, NJ: Erlbaum.

Camara, K., & Resnick, G. (1989). Styles of conflict resolution and cooperation between divorced parents: Effects on child behavior and adjustment. *American Journal of Orthopsychiatry, 59,* 560–574.

Carter, B., & McGoldrick, M. (Eds). (1988). *The changing family life cycle: A framework for family therapy* (2nd ed.). New York: Gardner Press.

Castrey, R. T., & Castrey, B. P. (1987). Timing: a mediator's best friend. In C. W. Moore (Ed.), *Practical strategies for the phases of mediation.* Mediation Quarterly, no. 16. San Francisco: Jossey-Bass.

Ceci, S. J., & Bruck, M. (1995). *Jeopardy in the courtroom: A scientific analysis of children's testimony.* Washington, DC: American Psychological Association.

Cherlin, A. J., Furstenberg, F. F., Chase-Lansdale, L., Kiernan, K. E., Robins, P. K., Morrison, D. R., & Teitler, J. O. (1991). Longitudinal studies of effects of divorce on children in Great Britain and the United States. *Science, 252,* 1386–1389.

Chess, S., & Thomas, A. (1984). *Origins and evolution of behavior disorders: From infancy to early adulthood.* New York: Brunner/Mazel.

Chess, S., & Thomas, A. (1986). *Temperament in clinical practice.* New York: Guilford Press.

Clingempeel, W. G., & Reppucci, N. D. (1982). Joint custody after divorce: Major issues and goals for research. *Psychological Bulletin, 91,* 102–127.

Combs, G., & Freedman, J. (1990). *Symbol, story, and ceremony: Using metaphor in individual and family therapy.* New York: Norton.

Committee on the Family of the Group for the Advancement of Psychiatry. (1980). *New trends in child custody determinations.* Law and Business, Inc./Harcourt Brace Jovanovich.

Conway, F., & Siegelman, J. (1978). *Snapping: America's epidemic of sudden personality change.* New York: Delta.

Coogler, O. J. (1978). *Structured mediation in divorce settlement.* San Francisco: Lexington Books.

Copeland, A. P. (1985). Individual differences in children's reactions to divorce. *Journal of Clinical Child Psychology, 14,* 11–19.

Coysh, W. S., Johnston, J. R., Tschann, J. M., Wallerstein, J. S., & Kline, M. (1989). Parental postdivorce adjustment in joint and sole physical custody families. *Journal of Family Issues, 10* (1), 52–70.

Crum, T. (1987). *The magic of conflict.* New York: Simon & Schuster.

Cummings, E. M., & Davies, P. (1994). *Children and marital conflict: The impact of family dispute and resolution.* New York: Guilford Press.

Depner, C. E., Cannata, K. V., & Ricci, I. (1994). Client evaluations of mediation services: The impact of case characteristics and mediation service models. *Family and Conciliation Courts Review, 32,* 306–325.

Depner, C. E., Cannata, K. V., & Ricci, I. (1995). Report 4: Mediated agreements on child custody and visitation: 1991 California Family Court Services Snapshot Study. *Family and Conciliation Courts Review, 33,* 87–109.

Depner, C. E., Cannata, K. V., & Simon, M. B. (1992). Building a uniform statistical reporting system: A snapshot of California Family Court Services. *Family and Conciliation Courts Review, 30,* 185–206.

Derdeyn, A. P. (1977). Child custody contests in historical perspective. In S. Chess & A. Thomas (Eds.), *Annual Progress in Child Psychiatry and Child Development.* New York: Brunner/Mazel.

Deutsch, M. (1973). *The resolution of conflict: Constructive and destructive processes.* New Haven, CT: Yale University Press.

Di Bias, T. (1996). Some programs for children. *Family and Conciliation Courts Review, 34,* 112–129.

Dobson, T., & Miller, V. (1993). *Aikido in everyday life: Giving in to get your way.* New York: North Atlantic Books.

Donohue, W. A., Drake, L., & Roberto, A. J. (1994). Mediator issue intervention strategies: A replication and some conclusions. *Mediation Quarterly, 11,* 261–274.

Dooley, D. S. (1990). Immoral because they're bad, bad because they're wrong. *California Western Law Review, 26,* 395–424.

Duryee, M. (1989). Open mediation in the court: A systemic view. *Family and Conciliation Courts Review, 27,* 81–90.

Dworkin, J., Jacob, L., & Scott, E. (1991). The boundaries between mediation and therapy: Ethical dilemmas. *Mediation Quarterly, 9,* 107–119.

Elrod, L. D. (1993). *Child custody practice and procedure.* Deerfield, IL: Clark, Boardman, & Callaghan.

Emery, R. E. (1988). *Marriage, divorce, and children's adjustment.* Newbury Park, CA: Sage.

Erickson, M. H. (1964). The confusion technique in hypnosis. *American Journal of Clinical Hypnosis, 6,* 193–207.

Erickson, M. H., & Rossi, E. (1979). *Hypnotherapy: An exploratory casebook.* New York: Irvington.

Erickson, S., & McKnight Erickson, M. (1988). *Family mediation casebook: Theory and process.* New York: Brunner/Mazel.

Everson, M., & Boat, B. (1989). False allegations of sexual abuse by children and adolescents. *Journal of the American Academy of Child and Adolescent Psychiatry, 28,* 230–235.

Falk, P. J. (1989). Lesbian mothers: Psychosocial assumptions in family law. *American Psychologist, 44,* 941–947.

Faller, K. (1991). Possible explanations for child sexual abuse allegations in divorce. *American Journal of Orthopsychiatry, 61,* 86–91.

Felder, R. L. (1971). *Divorce: The way things are, not the way things should be.* New York: World.

Festinger, L. (1957). *A theory of cognitive dissonance.* Palo Alto, CA: Stanford University Press.

Fisch, R., Weakland, J. H., & Segal, L. (1982). *The tactics of change: Doing therapy briefly.* San Francisco: Jossey-Bass.

Folberg, J. (1991). Custody overview. In J. Folberg (Ed.), *Joint custody and shared parenting* (2nd ed.). New York: Guilford Press.

Folberg, J., & Milne, A. (Eds.). (1988). *Divorce mediation: Theory and practice.* New York: Guilford Press.

Folberg, J., & Taylor, A. (1984). *Mediation: A comprehensive guide to resolving conflicts without litigation.* San Francisco: Jossey-Bass.

Foster, H. H., & Freed, D. J. (1980). Joint custody: Legislative reform. *Trial, 16,* 22–27.

Fowler, J. G. (1995). Homosexual parents: Implications for custody cases. *Family and Conciliation Courts Review, 33,* 361–376.

Frank, J. D. (1974). Therapeutic components of psychotherapy: A 25–year progress report of research. *Journal of Nervous and Mental Disease, 159,* 325–342.

Frank, J. D. (1978). Expectation and therapeutic outcome: The placebo effect and the role induction interview. In J. D. Frank, R. Hoehn-Saric, S. D. Imber, B. L. Liberman, & A. R. Stone, *Effective Ingredients of Successful Psychotherapy.* New York: Brunner/Mazel.

Frost, A., & Pakiz, B. (1990). The effects of marital disruption on adolescents: Time as a dynamic. *American Journal of Orthopsychiatry, 60,* 544–553.

Furstenberg, F. F., Jr. (1990). Divorce and the American family. *Annual Review of Sociology, 16,* 379–403.

Furstenberg, F. F., Jr. (1994). History and current status of divorce in the United States. *The Future of Children: Children and Divorce, 4,* 29–43.

Furstenberg, F. F., Jr., & Cherlin, A. J. (1991). *Divided families: What happens to children when parents part.* Cambridge, MA: Harvard University Press.

Furstenberg, F. F., Jr., Morgan, S., & Allison, P. (1987). Paternal participation and children's well-being after marital dissolution. *American Sociological Review, 52,* 695–701.

Gadlin, H., & Ouellette, P. A. (1986). Mediation Milanese: An application of systemic family therapy to family mediation. In D. T. Saposnek (Ed.), *Applying family therapy perspectives to mediation.* Mediation Quarterly, no. 14–15. San Francisco: Jossey-Bass.

Galper-Cohen, M. (1989). *Long-distance parenting: A guide for divorced parents.* New York: Signet.

Gardner, R. A. (1987). *The parental alienation syndrome and the differentiation between fabricated and genuine child sex abuse.* Cresskill, NJ: Creative Therapeutics.

Gardner, R. A. (1989). *Family evaluation in child custody mediation, arbitration, and litigation.* Cresskill, NJ: Creative Therapeutics.

Garrity, C. B., & Baris, M. A. (1994). *Caught in the middle: Protecting the children of high-conflict divorce.* San Francisco: New Lexington Press.

Gately, D., & Schwebel, A. I. (1991). The challenge model of children's adjustment to parental divorce: Explaining favorable postdivorce outcomes in children. *Journal of Family Psychology, 5,* 60–81.

Gately, D., & Schwebel, A. I. (1992). Favorable outcomes in children after parental divorce. *Journal of Divorce and Remarriage, 18,* 57–78.

Gilligan, S. (1986). *Therapeutic trances: The cooperation principle in Ericksonian hypnotherapy.* New York: Brunner/Mazel.

Glick, P. C. (1988). The role of divorce in the changing family structure: Trends and variations. In S. A. Wolchik and P. Karoly (Eds.), *Children of divorce: Empirical perspectives on adjustment.* New York: Gardner Press.

Goffman, E. (1959). *The presentation of self in everyday life.* New York: Doubleday.

Gold, L. (1985). Reflections of the transition from therapist to mediator. In J. A. Lemmon (Ed.), *Legal and family perspectives in divorce mediation.* Mediation Quarterly, no. 9. San Francisco: Jossey-Bass.

Goldstein, J. (1991). In whose best interest? In J. Folberg (Ed.), *Joint custody and shared parenting* (2nd ed.). New York: Guilford Press.

Goldstein, J., Freud, A., & Solnit, A. J. (1973). *Beyond the best interests of the child.* New York: Free Press.

Goldstein, J., Freud, A., & Solnit, A. (1979). *Before the best interests of the child.* New York: Free Press.

Golombok, S., Spencer, A., & Rutter, M. (1983). Children in lesbian and single-parent households: Psychosexual and psychiatric appraisal. *Journal of Child Psychology and Psychiatry, 24,* 551–572.

Gonsiorek, J. C., & Weinrich, J. D. (Eds.). (1991). *Homosexuality: Research implications for public policy.* Newbury Park, CA: Sage.

Gordon, D. (1978). *Therapeutic metaphors: Helping others through the looking glass.* Cupertino, CA: META Publications.

Grebe, S. C. (Ed.) (1985). *Divorce and family mediation.* Rockville, MD: Aspen Systems Corp.

Greene, R., Mandel, J., Hotvedt, M., Gray, J., & Smith, L. (1986). Lesbian mothers and their children: A comparison with solo parent heterosexual mothers and their children. *Archives of Sexual Behavior, 15,* 167–182.

Grych, J. H., & Fincham, F. D. (1990). Marital conflict and children's adjustment: A cognitive-contextual framework. *Psychological Bulletin, 108,* 267–290.

Guidubaldi, J. (1988). Differences in children's divorce adjustment across grade level and gender: A report from the NASP–Kent State Nationwide Project. In S. A. Wolchik & P. Karoly (Eds.), *Children of divorce: Empirical perspectives on adjustment.* New York: Gardner Press.

Guidubaldi, J., & Cleminshaw, H. K. (1985). Divorce, family health, and child adjustment. *Family Relations, 34* (1), 35–41.

Guidubaldi, J., Cleminshaw, H. K., Perry, J. D., & McLaughlin, C. S. (1983). The impact of parental divorce on children: Report of the nationwide NASP study. *School Psychology Review, 12,* 300–323.

Haley, J. (1963). *Strategies of psychotherapy.* New York: Grune & Stratton.

Haley, J. (1973). *Uncommon therapy: The psychiatric techniques of Milton H. Erickson, M.D.* New York: Norton.

Haley, J. (1976). *Problem-solving therapy: New strategies for effective family therapy.* San Francisco: Jossey-Bass.

Haley, J. (1979, May). Remarks at conference on family therapy (private workshop), Berkeley, CA.

Haynes, J. M. (1981). *Divorce mediation: A practical guide for therapists and counselors.* New York: Springer.

Haynes, J. M. (1988). John Haynes segment of *The case of Willie: Three mediation approaches: Donald T. Saposnek, Florence Kaslow, John Haynes.* [Videotape]. Lexington, MA: Academy of Family Mediators.

Haynes, J. M. (1992). Mediation and therapy: An alternative view. *Mediation Quarterly, 10,* 21–34.

Haynes, J. M. (1994). *The fundamentals of family mediation.* Albany: State University of New York Press.

Haynes, J. M., & Haynes, G. L. (1989). *Mediating divorce: Casebook of strategies for successful family negotiations.* San Francisco: Jossey-Bass.

Healy, J., Jr., Malley, J., & Stewart, A. (1990). Children and their fathers after parental separation. *American Journal of Orthopsychiatry, 60,* 531–543.

Heckler, R. S. (Ed.). (1985). *Aikido and the new warrior.* Berkeley, CA: North Atlantic Books.

Hetherington, E. M. (1972). Effects of father absence on personality development in adolescent daughters. *Developmental Psychology, 7,* 313–326.

Hetherington, E. M. (1979a, May 9). Children of divorce. Talk presented at University of California, Santa Cruz.

Hetherington, E. M. (1979b). Divorce: A child's perspective. *American Psychologist, 34,* 851–858.

Hetherington, E. M. (1981). Children and divorce. In R. W. Henderson (Ed.), *Parent-child interaction: Theory, research, and prospects.* New York: Academic Press.

Hetherington, E. M. (1987). Family relations six years after divorce. In K. Pasley & M. Ihinger-Tallman (Eds.), *Remarriage and stepparenting.* New York: Guilford Press.

Hetherington, E. M. (1989). Coping with family transitions: Winners, losers, and survivors. *Child Development, 60,* 1–14.

Hetherington, E. M., Cox, M., & Cox, R. (1978). The aftermath of divorce. In

J. H. Stevens, Jr., & M. Matthews (Eds.), *Mother-child, father-child relations*. Washington, DC: National Association for the Education of Young Children.

Hetherington, E. M., Cox, M., & Cox, R. (1979). Family interaction and the social, emotional, and cognitive development of children following divorce. In V. Vaughn & T. B. Brazelton (Eds.), *The family: Setting priorities*. New York: Science and Medicine Publishing Co.

Hetherington, E. M., Cox, M., & Cox, R. (1982). Effects of divorce on parents and children. In M. E. Lamb (Ed.), *Nontraditional families: Parenting and child development*. Hillsdale, NJ: Erlbaum.

Hodges, W. F. (1986). *Interventions for children of divorce: Custody, access, and psychotherapy*. New York: John Wiley.

Hoeffer, B. (1981). Children's acquisition of sex-role behavior in lesbian mother families. *American Journal of Orthopsychiatry, 51*, 536–544.

Huntington, D. (1985, March 24–26). *Interviewing children and assessing their needs regarding custody: A psychologist's view*. Paper presented at the Family Court Services Conference, Anaheim, CA.

Hyde, L. M., Jr. (1991). Child custody and visitation. *Juvenile and Family Court Journal, 42*, 1–13.

Ilfeld, F. W., Ilfeld, H. Z., & Alexander, J. R. (1982). Does joint custody work? A first look at outcome data of relitigation. *American Journal of Psychiatry, 139*, 62–66.

Irving, H. H. (1980). *Divorce mediation: The rational alternative*. Toronto: Personal Library.

Irving H. H., & Benjamin, M. (1987). *Family mediation: Theory and practice of dispute resolution*. Toronto: Carswell.

Irving, H. H., & Benjamin, M. (1995). *Family mediation: Contemporary issues*. Thousand Oaks, CA: Sage.

Isaacs, M. B., Montalvo, B., & Abelsohn, D. (1986). *The difficult divorce: Therapy for children and families*. New York: Basic Books.

Jacob, H. (1988). *The silent revolution*. Chicago: University of Chicago Press.

Jaffe, P., Wolfe, D., & Wilson, S. (1990). Children of battered women. In *Developmental clinical psychology and psychiatry: Vol. 21*. Newbury Park, CA: Sage.

Johnston, J. R. (1992). *High-conflict and violent parents in family court: Findings on children's adjustment and proposed guidelines for the resolution of custody and visitation disputes*. Final report to the Judicial Council of the State of California, Statewide Office of Family Court Services. San Francisco: Judicial Council.

Johnston, J. R. (1994). High-conflict divorce. *The Future of Children: Children and Divorce, 4*, 165–182.

Johnston, J. R., Breunig, K., Garrity, C. B., & Baris, M. A. (1997). *Through the eyes of children: Healing stories for children of divorce.* New York: Free Press.

Johnston, J. R., & Campbell, L.E.G. (1986). Tribal warfare: The involvement of extended kin and significant others in custody and access disputes. *Conciliation Courts Review, 24,* 1–16.

Johnston, J. R., & Campbell, L.E.G. (1988). *Impasses of divorce: The dynamics and resolution of family conflict.* New York: Free Press.

Johnston, J. R., & Campbell, L.E.G. (1993). Parent-child relationships in domestic violence families disputing custody. *Family and Conciliation Courts Review, 31,* 282–298.

Johnston, J. R., Kline, M., & Tschann, J. M. (1989). Ongoing postdivorce conflict: Effects on children of joint custody and frequent access. *American Journal of Orthopsychiatry, 59,* 576–592.

Johnston, J. R., & Roseby, V. (1997). *In the name of the child: A developmental approach to understanding and helping children of conflicted and violent divorce.* New York: Free Press.

Jones, D., & McGraw, J. M. (1987). Reliable and fictitious accounts of sexual abuse in children. *Journal of Interpersonal Violence, 2,* 27–45.

Kalter, N., Kloner, A., Schreiser, S., & Okla, K. (1989). Predictors of children's postdivorce adjustment. *American Journal of Orthopsychiatry, 59,* 605–618.

Kantor, D., & Lehr, W. (1975). *Inside the family: Toward a theory of family process.* San Francisco: Jossey-Bass.

Kaslow, F. W. (1981). Divorce and divorce therapy. In A. Gurman & D. Kniskern (Eds.), *Handbook of family therapy.* New York: Brunner/Mazel.

Kaslow, F. W. (1995). The dynamics of divorce therapy. In R. H. Mikesell, D. D. Lusterman, & S. H. McDaniel (Eds.), *Integrating family therapy: Handbook of family psychology and systems theory.* Washington, DC: American Psychological Association.

Kaslow, F. W., & Schwartz, L. L. (1987). *The dynamics of divorce: A life cycle perspective.* New York: Brunner/Mazel.

Kay, H. H. (1990). Beyond no-fault: New directions for divorce reform. In S. D. Sugarman & H. H. Kay (Eds.), *Divorce reform at the crossroads.* New Haven, CT: Yale University Press.

Kelly, J. B. (1983). Mediation and psychotherapy: Distinguishing the differences. In J. A. Lemmon (Ed.), *Dimensions and practice of divorce mediation.* Mediation Quarterly, no. 1. San Francisco: Jossey-Bass.

Kelly, J. B. (1988). Long-term adjustment in children of divorce: Converging findings and implications from practice. *Journal of Family Psychology, 2,* 119–140.

Kelly, J. B. (1993a). Current research on children's postdivorce adjustment: No simple answers. *Family and Conciliation Courts Review, 31,* 29–49.

Kelly, J. B. (1993b, March). *Parental preferences, alignments, and alienation.* Paper presented at California Family Court Services Statewide Education Institute, Monterey.

Kelly, J. B. (1997, July). *Children's postdivorce adjustment: Research updates and implications for practice.* Paper presented at the fourteenth annual conference of the Academy of Family Mediators, Cape Cod, MA.

Kelly, J. B., Gigy, L., & Hausman, S. (1988). Mediated and adversarial divorce: Initial findings from a longitudinal study. In J. Folberg & A. Milne (Eds.), *Divorce mediation: Theory and practice.* New York: Guilford Press.

Kent, J. (1826). *Commentaries on American law: Vol. 2.* New York: Halsted.

King, D. B. (1979). Child custody: A legal problem? *California State Bar Journal, 54* (3), 156–161.

King, D. B. (1993). Accentuate the positive, eliminate the negative. *Family and Conciliation Courts Review, 31,* 9–28.

Kitson, G. C., & Morgan, L. A. (1990). The multiple consequences of divorce: A decade review. *Journal of Marriage and the Family, 52,* 913–924.

Kline, M., Tschann, J. M., Johnston, J. R., & Wallerstein, J. S. (1989). Children's adjustment in joint and sole physical custody families. *Developmental Psychology, 25,* 430–438.

Kressel, K. (1985). *The process of divorce: How professionals and couples negotiate settlements.* New York: Basic Books.

Kressel, K., Butler–De Freitas, F., Forlenza, S. G., & Wilcox, C. (1989). Research in contested custody mediations: An illustration of the case study method. In J. R. Kelly (Ed.), *Empirical research in divorce and family mediation.* Mediation Quarterly, no. 24. San Francisco: Jossey-Bass.

Kressel, K., Jaffe, N., Tuchman, B., Watson, C., & Deutsch, M. (1980). A typology of divorcing couples: Implications for mediation and the divorce process. *Family Process, 19,* 101–116.

Kressel, K., Pruitt, D. G., & Associates. (1989). *Mediation research: The process and effectiveness of third-party intervention.* San Francisco: Jossey-Bass.

Kruk, E. (1994). Grandparent visitation disputes: Multigenerational approaches to family mediation. *Mediation Quarterly, 12,* 37–53.

Kurdek, L. A. (1981). An integrative perspective on children's divorce adjustment. *American Psychologist, 36,* 856–866.

Kurdek, L. A., & Berg, B. (1983). Correlates of children's adjustments to their parents' divorces. In L. A. Kurdek (Ed.), *Children and divorce.* San Francisco: Jossey-Bass.

Kurdek, L. A., & Siesky, A. E. (1980). Children's perceptions of their parents' divorce. *Journal of Divorce, 3,* 339–378.

Lampel, A. (1996). Children's alignment with parents in highly conflicted custody cases. *Family and Conciliation Courts Review, 34,* 229–239.

Landau, B., Bartoletti, M., & Mesbur, R. (1997). *Family mediation handbook* (2nd ed.). Toronto: Butterworths.

Larson, J. M. (1993). Exploring reconciliation. *Mediation Quarterly, 11,* 95–106.

Lemmon, J. A. (1985). *Family mediation practice.* New York: Free Press.

Lerner, R. M., & Spanier, G. B. (Eds.). (1978). *Child influences on marital and family interaction: A life-span perspective.* New York: Academic Press.

Leve, R. (1980). *Childhood: The study of development.* New York: Random House.

Luepnitz, D. (1986). A comparison of maternal, paternal, and joint custody: Understanding the varieties of post-divorce family life. *Journal of Divorce, 9* (3), 1–12.

Lund, M. (1995). A therapist's view of parental alienation syndrome. *Family and Conciliation Courts Review, 33,* 308–316.

Lyster, M. E. (1996). *Child custody: Building parenting agreements that work* (2nd ed.). Berkeley, CA: Nolo Press.

Maccoby, E. E., Buchanan, C. M., Mnookin, R. H., & Dornbusch, A. M. (1993). Postdivorce roles of mothers and fathers in the lives of their children. *Journal of Family Psychology, 7,* 24–38.

Maccoby, E. E., & Jacklin, C. N. (1974). *The psychology of sex differences.* Palo Alto, CA: Stanford University Press.

Maccoby, E. E., & Mnookin, R. H., with Depner, C. E., & Peters, H. E. (1992). *Dividing the child: Social and legal dilemmas of custody.* Cambridge, MA: Harvard University Press.

MacGowan, E. (1981). Custody and visitation. In California–Continuing Education of the Bar, *Representing parents and children in custody proceedings.* Berkeley: Regents of the University of California.

Madanes, C. (1980). Protection, paradox, and pretending. *Family Process, 19,* 73–85.

Madanes, C. (1981). *Strategic family therapy.* San Francisco: Jossey-Bass.

Madanes, C. (1984). *Behind the one-way mirror: Advances in the practice of strategic therapy.* San Francisco: Jossey-Bass.

Marlow, L., & Sauber, S. R. (1990). *The handbook of divorce mediation.* New York: Plenum.

Martin, T., & Bumpass, L. (1989). Recent trends in marital disruption. *Demography, 26,* 37–52.

McIntyre, D. H. (1994). Gay parents and child custody: A struggle under the legal system. *Mediation Quarterly, 12,* 135–149.

McIsaac, H. (1981). Mandatory conciliation custody/visitation matters: California's bold stroke. *Conciliation Courts Review, 19,* 73–81.

McIsaac, H. (1985). Confidentiality: An exploration of issues. *Conciliation Courts Review, 23,* 61–67.

McIsaac, H. (1991). California joint custody retrospective. In J. Folberg (Ed.), *Joint custody and shared parenting* (2nd ed.). New York: Guilford Press.

McIsaac, H. (1994). Editor's notes. *Family and Conciliation Courts Review, 32,* 420–431.

McKinnon, R., & Wallerstein, J. S. (1986). Joint custody and the preschool child. *Behavioral Sciences and the Law, 4,* 169–183

Miller, B. (1979). Gay fathers and their children. *Family Coordinator, 28,* 544–552.

Milne, A. (1978). Custody of children in a divorce process: A family self-determination model. *Conciliation Courts Review, 16,* 1–10.

Milne, A., & Folberg, J. (1988). The theory and practice of divorce mediation: An overview. In J. Folberg & A. Milne (Eds.), *Divorce mediation: Theory and practice.* New York: Guilford Press.

Minuchin, S. (1974). *Families and family therapy.* Cambridge, MA: Harvard University Press.

Minuchin, S., & Fishman, H. C. (1981). *Family therapy techniques.* Cambridge, MA: Harvard University Press.

Mnookin, R. H., & Kornhauser, L. (1979). Bargaining in the shadow of the law: The case of divorce. *Yale Law Journal, 88,* 950–997.

Moore, C. W. (1986). *The mediation process: Practical strategies for resolving conflict.* San Francisco: Jossey-Bass.

Mosten, F. (1992). Confidential mini-evaluation. *Family and Conciliation Courts Review, 30,* 373–384.

Nachlis, L. (1996). Overview of move-away law and policy. *Family Law News, 19* (2), 1–4.

National Center for Health Statistics. (1985). Advance report of final divorce statistics, 1983 (DHHS Publication No. PHS 86–1120). *Monthly Vital Statistics Report, 34* (9, Suppl. 9). Hyattsville, MD: U.S. Public Health Service.

National Center for Health Statistics. (1996). Births, marriages, divorces, and deaths for July 1995. *Monthly Vital Statistics Report, 44* (7). Hyattsville, MD: U.S. Public Health Service.

Neal, J. H. (1982, March 29–April 3). *Children's understanding of their parents and their parents' divorce: A systems perspective.* Paper presented at the fifty-ninth annual meeting of the American Orthopsychiatric Association, San Francisco.

Newmark, L., Harrell, A., & Salem, P. (1995). Domestic violence and empowerment in custody and visitation cases. *Family and Conciliation Courts Review, 33,* 30–62.

Nichols, W. C., & Everett, C. A. (1986). *Systemic family therapy: An integrative approach.* New York: Guilford Press.

Norton, A. J., & Miller, L. F. (1992). *Marriage, divorce and remarriage in the 1990s.* Current Population Reports, Series P–23, No. 180. Washington, DC: U.S. Government Printing Office.

Norton, E., Weiss, W., Ricci, I., & Fielding, R. (1992). Development of uniform standards of practice for court-connected child custody mediation in California. *Family and Conciliation Courts Review, 30,* 217–228.

Oster, A. M. (1965). Custody proceedings: A study of vague and indefinite standards. *Journal of Family Law, 5,* 21–38.

Pagelow, M. D. (1990). Effects of domestic violence on children and their consequences for custody and visitation agreements. *Mediation Quarterly, 7,* 347–363.

Pearson, J. (1991). The equity of mediated divorce settlements. *Mediation Quarterly, 9,* 179–197.

Pearson, J., & Thoennes, N. (1982, June 11–16). *Divorce mediation: Strengths and weaknesses over time.* Paper presented at the International Society on Family Law Fourth World Conference, Cambridge, MA.

Pearson, J., & Thoennes, N. (1985). A preliminary portrait of client reactions to three court mediation programs. *Conciliation Courts Review, 23,* 1–14.

Pearson, J., & Thoennes, N. (1988). Divorce mediation research results. In J. Folberg & A. Milne (Eds.), *Divorce mediation: Theory and practice.* New York: Guilford Press.

Pederson, F. A., Rubenstein, J., & Yarrow, L. J. (1979). Infant development in father-absent families. *Journal of Genetic Psychology, 135,* 51–62.

Peterson, J., & Zill, N. (1986). Marital disruption, parent-child relationships, and behavior problems in children. *Journal of Marriage and the Family, 48,* 295–307.

Portes, P. R., Howell, S. C., Brown, J. H., Eichenberger, S., & Mas, C. A. (1992). Family functions and children's postdivorce adjustment. *American Journal of Orthopsychiatry, 62,* 613–617.

Preston, S. H., & McDonald, J. (1979). The incidence of divorce within cohorts of American marriages contracted since the Civil War. *Demography, 16,* 1–25.

Rheinstein, M. (1972). *Marriage stability, divorce, and the law.* Chicago: University of Chicago Press.

Ricci, I. (1980). *Mom's house, Dad's house*. New York: Macmillan.

Roman, M., & Haddad, W. (1978). *The disposable parent: The case for joint custody*. New York: Holt, Rinehart and Winston.

Rose, C. (1996). *Collaborative family law practice*. Eugene, OR: Mediation Center.

Roseby, V., & Johnston, J. R. (in press). Children of Armageddon: Common developmental threats in high-conflict divorcing families. *Child and Adolescent Psychiatric Clinics of North America*.

Rosen, R. (1977). Children of divorce: What they feel about access and other aspects of the divorce experience. *Journal of Clinical Child Psychology, 6,* 24–27.

Rosenbaum, A., & O'Leary, D. (1981). Children: The unintended victims of marital violence. *American Journal of Orthopsychiatry, 51,* 692–699.

Rossi, E. L. (Ed.). (1980). *The collected papers of Milton H. Erickson on hypnosis: Vol. 4. Innovative hypnotherapy*. New York: Irvington.

Rutter, M. (1978). Protective factors in children's responses to stress and disadvantage. In M. W. Kent and J. E. Rolf (Eds.), *Primary prevention of psychopathology: Vol. 3. Promoting social competence and coping in children*. Hanover, NH: University Press of New England.

Salem, P., Schepard, A., & Schlissel, S. W. (1996). Parent education as a distinct field of practice: The agenda for the future. *Family and Conciliation Courts Review, 43,* 9–22.

Samis, M.C.D., & Saposnek, D. T. (1986). Parent-child relationships in family mediation: A synthesis of views. In D. T. Saposnek (Ed.), *Applying family therapy perspectives to mediation*. Mediation Quarterly, no. 14–15. San Francisco: Jossey-Bass.

Sandler, I. N., Wolchik, S. A., & Braver, S. L. (1988). The stressors of children's postdivorce environments. In S. A. Wolchik & P. Karoly (Eds.), *Children of divorce: Empirical perspectives on adjustment*. New York: Gardner Press.

Saposnek, D. T. (1980). Aikido: A model for brief strategic therapy. *Family Process, 19,* 227–238.

Saposnek, D. T. (1983). Strategies in child custody mediation: A family systems approach. In J. A. Lemmon (Ed.), *Successful techniques for mediating family breakup*. Mediation Quarterly, no. 2. San Francisco: Jossey-Bass.

Saposnek, D. T. (1984). Short-term psychotherapy. In N. Endler and J. M. Hunt (Eds.), *Personality and the behavioral disorders* (2nd ed.). New York: Wiley.

Saposnek, D. T. (1985). What is fair in child custody mediation? In J. A. Lemmon (Ed.), *Making ethical decisions*. Mediation Quarterly, no. 8. San Francisco: Jossey-Bass.

Saposnek, D. T. (1986a). Aikido: A systems model for maneuvering in mediation. In D. T. Saposnek (Ed.), *Applying family therapy perspectives to mediation.* Mediation Quarterly, no. 14–15. San Francisco: Jossey-Bass.

Saposnek, D. T. (Ed.). (1986b). *Applying family therapy perspectives to mediation.* Mediation Quarterly, no. 14–15. San Francisco: Jossey-Bass.

Saposnek, D. T. (1987). Recent developments in joint custody: Definitions, issues, and recommendations. In P. A. Keller & S. R. Heyman (Eds.), *Innovations in clinical practice: A source book (Vol. 6).* Sarasota, FL: Professional Resource Exchange.

Saposnek, D. T. (1991a). A guide to decisions about joint custody: The needs of children of divorce. In J. Folberg (Ed.), *Joint custody and shared parenting* (2nd ed.). New York: Guilford Press.

Saposnek, D. T. (1991b). The value of children in mediation: A cross-cultural perspective. *Mediation Quarterly, 8,* 325–342.

Saposnek, D. T. (1992). Clarifying perspectives on mandatory mediation. *Family and Conciliation Courts Review, 30,* 490–506.

Saposnek, D. T. (1993a). The art of mediation. *Mediation Quarterly, 11,* 5–12.

Saposnek, D. T. (Ed.). (1993b). *Beyond technique: The soul of family mediation.* Mediation Quarterly, 11 (1).

Saposnek, D. T., Hamburg, J., Delano, C. D., & Michaelsen, H. (1983, April 4–8). *Child custody disputes: Outcomes of mandatory mediation, evaluations, and implications for social policy.* Paper presented at sixtieth annual conference of the American Orthopsychiatric Association, Boston.

Saposnek, D. T., Hamburg, J., Delano, C. D., & Michaelsen, H. (1984). How has mandatory mediation fared? Research findings of the first year's follow-up. *Conciliation Courts Review, 22,* 7–19.

Saposnek, D. T., & Rose, F. W. (1990). The psychology of divorce. In D. L. Crumbley & N. G. Apostolou (Eds.), *Handbook of financial planning for divorce and separation.* New York: Wiley.

Sargent, G., & Moss, B. (1986). Ericksonian approaches in family therapy and mediation. In D. T. Saposnek (Ed.), *Applying family therapy perspectives to mediation.* Mediation Quarterly, no. 14–15. San Francisco: Jossey-Bass.

Schwartz, L. L., & Kaslow, F. W. (1997). *Painful partings: Divorce and its aftermath.* New York: Wiley.

Selvini Palazzoli, M., Boscolo, L., Cecchin, G., & Prata, G. (1978). *Paradox and counterparadox.* New York: Aronson.

Selvini Palazzoli, M., Cecchin, G., Prata, G., & Boscolo, L. (1980). Hypothesizing, circularity, neutrality: Three guidelines for the conductor of the session. *Family Process, 19,* 3–12.

Shattuck, M. T. (1988). Mandatory mediation. In J. Folberg & A. Milne (Eds.), *Divorce mediation: Theory and practice.* New York: Guilford Press.

Shaw, D. S., & Emery, R. E. (1987). Parental conflict and other correlates of the adjustment of school-age children whose parents have separated. *Journal of Abnormal Child Psychology, 15,* 269–281.

Shears, L. E. (1996). Children's lawyers in California family law courts: Balancing competing policies and values regarding questions of ethics. *Family and Conciliation Courts Review, 34,* 256–302.

Shiono, P. H., & Quinn, L. S. (1984). Epidemiology of divorce. *The Future of Children: Children and Divorce, 4,* 15–28.

Slater, A., Shaw, J. A., & Duquesnel, J. (1992). Client satisfaction survey: A consumer evaluation of mediation and investigative services: Executive summary. *Family and Conciliation Courts Review, 30,* 252–259.

Sprenkle, D. (1985). *Divorce therapy.* New York: Haworth Press.

Steinman, S. B. (1984). Joint custody: What we know, what we have yet to learn, and the judicial and legislative implications. In J. Folberg (Ed.), *Joint custody and shared parenting.* Washington, DC: Bureau of National Affairs, Association of Family and Conciliation Courts.

Steinman, S. B., Zemmelman, S. E., & Knoblauch, T. M. (1985). A study of parents who sought joint custody following divorce: Who reaches agreement and sustains joint custody and who returns to court. *Journal of the American Academy of Child Psychiatry, 24,* 554–562.

Stevens, J. (1985). The founder, Ueshiba Morihei. In R. S. Heckler (Ed.), *Aikido and the new warrior.* Berkeley, CA: North Atlantic Books.

Strupp, H. H., Hadley, S. W., & Gomes-Schwarz, B. (1977). *Psychotherapy for better or worse: The problem of negative effects.* New York: Aronson.

Suseoff, S. (1985). Assessing children's best interests when a parent is gay or lesbian: Toward a rational custody standard. *UCLA Law Review, 32,* 852–903.

Tanaka, H. (1976). *The Japanese legal system.* Tokyo: University of Tokyo Press.

Taylor, A., & Bing, H. (1994). Settlement by evaluation and arbitration: A new approach for custody and visitation disputes. *Family and Conciliation Courts Review, 32,* 432–444.

Thoennes, N., & Pearson, J. (1992). Response to Bruch and McIsaac. *Family and Conciliation Courts Review, 30,* 142–143.

Thoennes, N., & Tjaden, P. G. (1990). The extent, nature and validity of sexual abuse allegations in custody/visitation disputes. *Child Abuse and Neglect, 14,* 151–163.

Thomas, A., & Chess, S. (1977). *Temperament and development.* New York: Brunner/Mazel.

Thomas, A., Chess, S., & Birch, H. G. (1968). *Temperament and behavior disorders in children.* New York: New York University Press.

Thomas, A., Chess, S., Birch, H. G., Hertzig, M. E., and Korn, S. (1963). *Behavioral individuality in early childhood*. New York: New York University Press.

Thomas, A. M., & Forehand, R. (1993). The role of paternal variables in divorced and married families: Predictability of adolescent adjustment. *American Journal of Orthopsychiatry, 63*, 126–135.

Thompson, R. A., Scalora, M. J., Limber, S. P., & Castrianno, L. (1991). Grandparent visitation rights: A psycholegal analysis. *Family and Conciliation Courts Review, 29*, 9–25.

Toffler, A. (1980). *The third wave*. New York: Morrow.

Tomm, K. (1985). Circular interviewing: A multifaceted clinical tool. In D. Campbell & R. Draper (Eds.), *Applications of systemic family therapy*. London: Grune & Stratton.

Tschann, J. M., Johnston, J. R., Kline, M., & Wallerstein, J. S. (1990). Conflict, loss, change and parent-child relationships: Predicting children's adjustment during divorce. *Journal of Divorce, 13* (4), 1–22.

Twilley, D. (1994). *Questions from Dad: A very cool way to communicate with kids*. Boston: Tuttle.

Ueshiba, K. (1969). *Aikido*. Tokyo: Honzansha.

Ueshiba, K. (1984). *The spirit of Aikido*. Tokyo: Kodansha.

Waldron, J. A., Roth, C. P., Fair, P. H., Mann, E. M., & McDermott, J. F., Jr. (1984). A therapeutic mediation model for child dispute resolution. *Mediation Quarterly, 3*, 5–20.

Walker, L. (1984). *The battered woman syndrome*. New York: Springer.

Wallerstein, J. S. (1991). The long-term effects of divorce on children: A review. *Journal of the American Academy of Child and Adolescent Psychiatry, 30*, 349–360.

Wallerstein, J. S. (1997, June 6). *The long-term impact of divorce on children: A first report from a twenty-five-year study*. Paper presented at the Second World Congress on Family Law and the Rights of Children and Youth, San Francisco.

Wallerstein, J. S., & Blakeslee, S. (1989). *Second chances: Men, women, and children a decade after divorce*. New York: Ticknor & Fields.

Wallerstein, J. S., & Kelly, J. B. (1980). *Surviving the breakup: How children and parents cope with divorce*. New York: Basic Books.

Warshak, R. A., & Santrock, J. W. (1983). The impact of divorce in father-custody and mother-custody homes: The child's perspective. In L. A. Kurdek (Ed.), *Children and divorce*. San Francisco: Jossey-Bass.

Watzlawick, P. (1976). *How real is real?* New York: Vintage Books.

Watzlawick, P. (1978). *The language of change: Elements of therapeutic communication*. New York: Basic Books.

Watzlawick, P., & Weakland, J. H. (Eds.). (1977). *The interactional view*. New York: Norton.

Watzlawick, P., Weakland, J. H., & Fisch, R. (1974). *Change: Principles of problem formation and problem resolution*. New York: Norton.

Weissman, H. N. (1994). Psychotherapeutic and psycholegal considerations: When a custodial parent seeks to move away. *American Journal of Family Therapy, 22,* 176–181.

Westbrook, A., & Ratti, O. (1974). *Aikido and the dynamic sphere: An illustrated introduction*. Tokyo: Tuttle.

Whitaker, C. (1982, May 7). Remarks during a workshop on family therapy, Watsonville, CA.

Wright, D. C. (1981). The new joint custody: What it does and how it works. *Alameda County Bar Association Bulletin, 11* (9), 5–7.

Zeig, J. (Ed.). (1980). *A teaching seminar with Milton H. Erickson*. New York: Brunner/Mazel.

Zill, N., Morrison, D. R., & Coiro, M. J. (1993). Long-term effects of parental divorce on parent-child relationships, adjustment, and achievement in young adulthood. *Journal of Family Psychology, 7,* 91–103.

THE AUTHOR

Donald T. Saposnek is a clinical child psychologist, the director of Family Mediation Service of Santa Cruz, California, and a member of the psychology faculty at the University of California at Santa Cruz. He currently divides his professional time between child custody mediation training, private practice of family therapy, and teaching.

Saposnek earned a B.A. degree in psychology from the University of California at Los Angeles (1966), an M.A. degree in psychology from the California State University at San Jose (1967), and a Ph.D. degree in clinical child and developmental psychology from The Ohio State University (1971). After completing a clinical internship at the Institute for Juvenile Research in Chicago, he spent the next several years in New Jersey at the Children's Psychiatric Center in the practice of clinical-child psychology and community consultation, as well as in university teaching and clinical research. Saposnek undertook custody mediation, in addition to his other professional activities, in 1978, four years after moving to California.

Over the past two decades, Saposnek has published extensively in the fields of child custody mediation and clinical-child psychology and has served as guest editor of two special issues of *Mediation Quarterly: Applying Family Therapy Perspectives to Mediation* (1986) and *Beyond Technique: The Soul of Family Mediation* (1993).

Saposnek has conducted trainings in custody mediation both nationally and internationally. He is on the editorial boards of the *Mediation Quarterly* and the *Family and Conciliation Courts Review,* and he is the editor of the Academy of Family Mediators' *Mediation News.* He has served on the board of directors of both the Academy of Family Mediators and the Association of Family and Conciliation Courts, California Chapter.

INDEX

DATE DUE

MAY 0 1 2000		
APR 2 3 REC'D		
JUN 1 9 REC'D		
APR 1 1 2002		
APR 0 8 REC'D		
6 2006		
MAY		
AUG 3 0 REC'D		
GAYLORD		PRINTED IN U.S.A.

KF 547 .S26 1998

Saposnek, Donald T.

Mediating child custody
 disputes